ZONES

and CANADA

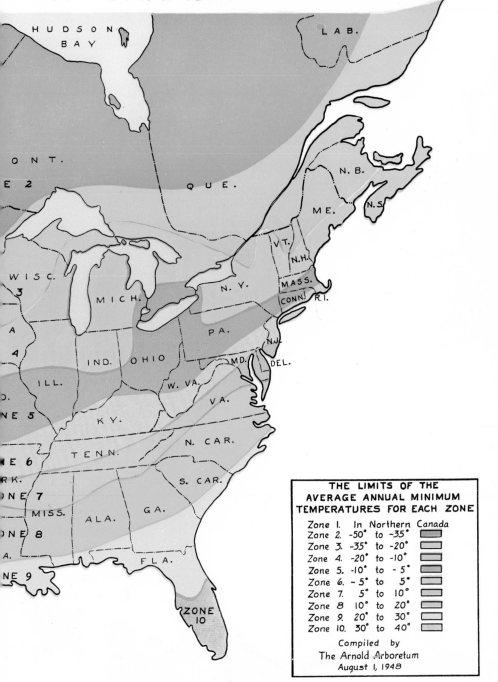

**THE LIMITS OF THE
AVERAGE ANNUAL MINIMUM
TEMPERATURES FOR EACH ZONE**

Zone 1.   In Northern Canada
Zone 2. -50° to -35°
Zone 3. -35° to -20°
Zone 4. -20° to -10°
Zone 5. -10° to - 5°
Zone 6. - 5° to   5°
Zone 7.   5° to 10°
Zone 8   10° to 20°
Zone 9. 20° to 30°
Zone 10. 30° to 40°

Compiled   by
The Arnold Arboretum
August 1, 1948

DONALD WYMAN

SHRUBS AND VINES

FOR

AMERICAN GARDENS

NEW YORK

THE MACMILLAN COMPANY

DEDICATED TO

FLORENCE DORWARD WYMAN

with deep affection and great respect, without whose

assistance this book would never have been written.

FOREWORD

GARDENING can be an enjoyable and relaxing experience, even for those who practice it professionally. The best ornamental plants should be selected which are pleasingly attractive but require a minimum amount of care. All the enjoyment is frequently taken out of gardening by people selecting the wrong plants causing maintenance drudgery. Selecting the best plant for the right place is very important for the professional plantsman as well as the amateur gardener and particularly so where space is a limiting factor.

This book was written in an effort to take some of the uncertainty out of making plant selections. Lists are given of plants noted for growing under specific conditions. The meritorious ornamental qualities of all the shrubs and vines listed are given in order to aid in personal selections by the amateur and professional gardener alike.

Approximately 1100 species and varieties of shrubs and vines are suggested as worthy of planting under certain conditions and over 1700 as of secondary interest only, certainly not needed at first by the amateur and only after careful scrutiny by the professional plantsman.

Not everyone will agree with such an arbitrary grouping and personal opinions are always exercised in the accepting or rejecting of such selections. However, this book will pave the way, I hope, for a careful study of the many shrubs and vines now being grown—some of which should not be given the space, especially in small gardens. American horticulture has advanced sufficiently so that American home owners can surround themselves with the better plants, and be able to weed out intelligently those that are less desirable. If the reader's personal likes and dislikes can be analyzed with a study of the author's suggestions, progress can be made in this direction.

Acknowledgments are due to correspondents all over the world who have assisted the author with their own personal observations over a period of many years. The splendid sketches in this book were drawn by Robert G. Williams, Superintendent of the Arnold Arboretum; the maps by Heman A. Howard of the Arboretum staff. The majority of the pictures were taken by the author or came from the extensive files of the Arnold Arboretum and from the J. Horace McFarland Company of Harrisburg, Pennsylvania. A few were contributed by Professor Ralph Curtis of Cornell University, the University of Washington Arboretum of Seattle, Washington, and Paul E. Genereux of Boston.

Particular acknowledgments are due the Arnold Arboretum of Harvard University, and those connected with it, where a majority of these plants have been growing side-by-side for years. Without the information from this excellent trial garden and the world-famous research facilities connected with it, the author's suggestions and experiences noted on the following pages would lose much of their value.

DONALD WYMAN

TABLE OF CONTENTS

INTRODUCTION

MORE varieties of plants are available for the use of American gardeners today than ever before in the history of this country. In colonial times, only a comparatively few eastern-coast plants were used in gardens together with some that had been brought over to the new country from Europe. Now, two hundred years later, thousands of plants from all over the world are available to everyone, some of the commonest being plants introduced from the most remote countries. After several centuries of intensified plant breeding, additional thousands of new plants have been introduced from Europe alone. The intense competition among modern commercial growers seems to result in a race to produce something "new," whether the new plant is better or inferior to older varieties. Since European nurseries are again clamoring for American trade, and so flooding the market with more "new" plants, it seems high time to take stock of what we have available, for any "new" ones should be critically compared with older established varieties.

The American gardener is frequently in a quandary as to which plants to select for his garden. Naturally he wants the "best," but which are in this category? The commercial nursery catalogues are overwhelming in that they offer such a tremendous number of different kinds of plants, with glowing statements about each one. Botanical reference books list many an interesting plant not even grown commercially in this country; they list still others that have died out or disappeared since they were named, and now may be represented only by dried herbarium specimens. All plants recommended in the following pages are very definitely growing in North America today, and sources for them are on record.

Woody plants are no exception. As an example, approximately 6000 different kinds of woody plants are now growing in the Arnold Arboretum at Boston, Massachusetts. Not all make good garden plants by any manner of means. Nor does this number represent all that could be grown, for many hardy varieties now actually in American gardens could be added to this collection. It does, however, give some indication as to the number of species and varieties which can be grown in a single area of this great country. There are 450 differently named lilacs, for instance, in this one collection, and it is possible to buy nearly 300 of them from commercial sources in North America. Lilacs may be very beautiful shrubs, but even after careful study it is possible to divide the varieties into only seven different groups according to the flower colors. They have no interesting fruits or autumn color. Certainly it would seem that this group of plants has been overemphasized. Even as this is being written an advertising circular was just brought to my attention claiming a new lilac variety with flowers the "biggest and best in existence!"

The American Association of Botanical Gardens and Arboretums worked on this very problem a few years ago, making a careful survey of all the lilacs in the larger collections and nurseries of this country. The result of this survey was a list of 100 varieties of *Syringa vulgaris* recommended as "the best," but even this might have been further reduced to 50 or even 25. Such cooperative surveys are excellent. There are far too few of them.

The mock-oranges belong to another group of shrubs which has been extensively hybridized. There are nearly 70 of them in the American trade today; a few years ago one nurseryman listed 29 as being grown by him. It is true that the varieties in this group may differ in size and habit of growth as well as in the size of flowers, but even 29 varieties seem far too many, since the flowers are all white, and the fruits are uninteresting, dried capsules, with no ornamental interest whatsoever.

The consensus of opinion among amateur gardeners, professional horticulturists, landscape architects and commercial growers seems to be that too many plants, especially mediocre ones, are being offered by modern nurseries. This is brought about partly by the desire to produce varieties to withstand various climatic or soil conditions, partly because it is easier to propagate certain mediocre varieties, and partly because certain mediocre varieties grow faster than do the better varieties. Commercially, these reasons are easily understandable. However, the home owner with a small garden should know and be able to obtain the best plants. He should not be satisfied to clutter up his garden with second-rate plant materials, and the more familiar he becomes with plants the more he is going to demand the better varieties. The enterprising nurseryman is the one who foresees this increasing demand for better plant materials, and prepares for it.

This book is written in an effort to bring some of the better types of shrubs and vines to the attention of plantsmen, although mention is made of some that may be decidedly second-rate. There are many plants whose landscape possibilities may be equal to but no better than a few commonly grown types. For instance, there are nearly twenty-five white-flowering lilacs in the trade today but only four single-flowered varieties and two double-flowered varieties have been selected as superior to most of those in this group.

There are plant groups, the rhododendrons for example, which contain so many species and varieties and are grown over such a wide climatic range, that no one individual can hope to examine them critically with an eye to selecting the "best." It is only by concentrated effort on the part of a nationally cooperative committee that such information can be brought together in order to be truly reliable. Because of this no rhododendrons have been included in the secondary list (pages 412–432).

Such a selection of shrubs as is made in this book can never be final nor will everyone agree with all the selections made. It can well be that certain varieties, relegated at present to the secondary list, may with time or varying climatic conditions prove superior to their near associates in the recommended list. Many plants have not been listed at all, merely because their potential landscape qualities under comparative growing conditions are not known.

It should be pointed out, however, that most of the plants, but not all, in both lists have been grown over a period of years in the Arnold Arboretum in the same soil and under the same climatic conditions. Although the Arnold Arboretum conditions may not apply to all the varied situations of soil and climate throughout the entire country, yet they may well prove indicative.

There is a distinct need for detailed information on the landscape usefulness of shrubs. Many of the best botanical references do not give all the information which is helpful to the gardener in planning a colorful and interesting garden at different seasons of the year.

Autumn color, normal height, length of time that the fruits are interesting, winter beauty and most suitable growing conditions are all items of great importance to the plantsman, and are discussed in the following pages. Pruning and transplanting are not discussed, since these subjects have been treated adequately in many texts. Spraying for control of insects and disease is not covered here for it has been treated, recently, in several excellent books. Most of what has been written on the subject up to this point may be shortly out of date, however, for the materials, and even methods used in spraying, are undergoing rapid changes.

Shrubs and vines discussed in this book are useful over practically the entire United States and Canada. Portions of the subtropical areas (especially Zone 10 on the hardiness map) are not completely covered for the simple reason that the tremendous amount of plant material possible to grow in these areas would fill a book of its own. However, much of what is listed for slightly cooler areas can be and is grown in Zone 10 so that gardeners in the subtropical United States will find much of interest in the following pages.

The information included has been collected chiefly from the records of plants growing in the Arnold Arboretum at Boston, Massachusetts. A considerable part, also, has been collected from the records at Durand-Eastman Park and Highland Park in Rochester, New York. Some of the information has been checked in the Morton Arboretum at Lisle, Illinois, and in various commercial nurseries throughout the entire United States. Admittedly not all plants are hardy in Boston but plants which can be grown here include most of those which can be grown in 75 per cent of the gardens of this country and Canada.

All plants in the recommended list of this book are actually growing in North America today, either in commercial nurseries or in arboretums, and sources for all the "rare" varieties are on file at the Arnold Arboretum. As noted before, it is wasteful of time to discuss plants, the sources for which are unknown since many may have passed completely out of existence. No such plants appear in the recommended list (pages 92–406).

There are 90 botanical gardens and arboretums in North America actively engaged in testing ornamental plant materials, together with many state and federal government experiment stations. Information accumulated from such sources is invaluable, particularly for the area in which the station is located. The great Morton Arboretum, at Lisle, Illinois; the Missouri Botanical Garden in St. Louis, Missouri; the University of Washington Arboretum in Seattle, Washington; Golden Gate Park in San Francisco, California; the David Fairchild Tropical Garden at Coconut Grove, Florida, and many others are all accumulating and distributing much information concerning ornamental plants. It is to such places that the plantsman should go for local information, and to see the plants he wants to know better. Every gardener should learn about the best plants for his individual garden in his individual area, and no better start could be made than with the lists suggested in the following pages.

In the use of scientific names in this book, the capitals of all have been dropped except in the generic name. Also, the double "ii" endings (of the Latin second declension genitive) have been reduced to a single "i." Botanists and some horticulturists do not yet agree on this proceeding, but it seems to me that scientific names are sufficiently complicated for the average gardener and that in order to get him to use them and to know them, they should be as simple as possible. Even some botanists are beginning to take this view.

I find it unnecessarily complex to have to remember that of the names of two plants, both named by one individual after the same man, one should be written *Prunus Sargentii* but the other *Malus Sargenti*. (Even the taxonomist who named both plants has missed the second "i" of the *Prunus* species on occasion, and another leading taxonomist whose books are used as standard references everywhere misspells *Malus Sargenti* in his reference books. Such mistakes are easily made, of course, but the point is that such names are often so misleading that even the trained taxonomists have difficulty in keeping them straight.)

Most gardeners are not Latin students and it seems to me that time spent in ascertaining the correctness of such names and in learning the minute inconsistencies in the spelling of such names might far better be used in learning more about the ornamental qualities of the plants in question. There will be many dissenters from this view, but the rank and file of the gardening public and others who actually use plants, far outnumber the few sticklers for academic "correctness" in Latin nomenclature. Simplicity in scientific names is consequently offered in this book (as in others recently published) as an aid to promote more uniform use of the scientific or true names of plants, rather than their common names.

HARDINESS

THE hardiness of plants is of primary importance to every gardener regardless of where his gardening interests may be. He knows that some plants will survive the winters in his garden and others will not. New plants, unknown to him, are always of interest, and naturally he would like specific hardiness notes for these, so he could tell at a glance which would survive and which would fail. To compose such a list becomes increasingly difficult as the size of the area involved increases, for hardiness is the result of several varying factors. It is essential to understand a few things about it in order to be able to make the decision as to whether or not a new plant might grow in any one particular locality.

Hardiness is closely associated with three things—temperature, rainfall, and soil, probably of importance in that order. When three variable factors such as these are tied in with one result (will it or will it not live in my garden?) it becomes very difficult to keep track of the fundamentals. The United States Department of Agriculture has studied this problem for some time, and has issued maps of the United States on which are superimposed twenty-three "climatic provinces," thirty-two "plant growth regions," and fifty "important soil regions." Such information is most valuable, but is difficult for the layman to assimilate. It would seem that a hardiness map, based on minimum temperatures alone, is sufficiently indicative on a broad basis to prove helpful, provided one understands its limitations. Such a map is used in this book, but first let us consider a few of its qualifications.

Soil, naturally, governs the use of many plants. In small gardens soil can be materially modified by fertilizers, mulches, etc., so that, if the gardener wishes to grow a particular type of plant which requires a special soil, he can frequently modify the soil to suit the plant.

Rainfall is somewhat more difficult to manipulate. If the rainfall is low, plants can be watered as long as the water supply and the willingness to do the work remain. Little can be done about an oversupply of water (rain), however, or a very dry atmosphere. Moisture-loving plants which are tried in a dry atmosphere are always going to be a problem, usually so much so that their care becomes eventually too burdensome, and the plants are discarded.

The arid areas of the southwestern United States are especially trying and only a very few plants will grow satisfactorily there without a great deal of extra care. The fact should be pointed out, however, that our large populated areas—those where gardens are most prevalent—are, for the most part, in areas where water supply is usually present in sufficient quantities to enable many plants to live, and thrive, without much additional watering. There are populated centers in the midst of drought areas such as the Great Plains, but when the number of gardens in these areas is compared with the number of gardens in northern Illinois and Ohio, or along the northern Atlantic Coast, it will be admitted that by far the greatest majority of gardeners have sufficient rainfall for growing large numbers of plants. Hence, a simplified hardiness map, of use to the greatest number of gardeners, need not necessarily include data on rainfall.

The third factor controlling hardiness is temperature which is most important to the majority of gardeners in this country. It is upon temperatures—minimum temperatures usually—that the greatest stress should be laid. We have local records to show what they are and when they can be expected. We can keep a record of them easily by the simple expedient of an outside thermometer.

Injury may occur in several ways when caused by fluctuations in temperature. It may occur with a sudden out-of-season "freeze," a sudden drop in temperature or a long period of very low temperatures. Considerable investigation has shown that very low temperature is the most important factor in killing plant tissue. Pomologists have been interested in the "sun scald" of fruit tree trunks, a killing of the living tissue usually on the southwest side (in northern orchards). A sudden drop in temperature may do this killing in one night. If a sunny, slightly warm afternoon is immediately followed by a sudden drop in temperature after sunset—possibly to 10° Fahrenheit—this may kill the living tissues of some fruit tree varieties. The temperature gradient will be steepest on the side exposed to the warm afternoon sun, hence the "sun scald" of trunks on the southwest side.

Temperature records over a long period of years in the Arnold Arboretum at Boston have yielded valuable data. There was severe winter injury during the winters of 1933–34, 1935, 1942–43, during which periods there were eight days or less when the minimum temperature went to zero or below. It is of interest to note that it was only in these three winters when plants suffered severe winter injury and in no other winters since 1933 have minimum temperatures reached zero. This does not mean that all plants suffer from a minimum temperature of zero. Far from it! There are, however, so many tender varieties of plants growing in the Arnold Arboretum that, from the evidence, when zero temperatures are reached, rather widespread damage on some of them can be expected.

There is evidence to prove that the tissues of some plants may not be injured by low temperatures, if the drop is gradual and not sudden. Just what these temperatures are, and how long they can be withstood by certain plants, can only be ascertained by careful experimentation.

Soil moisture enters the hardiness picture, also. Evergreens, particularly, give off a certain amount of water from their leaves throughout the entire winter. Deciduous plants give off some from their twigs, but not nearly as much as do the evergreens. When winter winds are high, plants give off a larger amount of water than they normally would. If the ground is frozen, as it usually is in the winter, the plant roots are unable to absorb additional soil moisture, so there comes a time, if high winds continue, when the evergreen needles or leaves give off too much water and the living tissue is injured, resulting in the characteristic browning or "burning" of the evergreen so common in late February and March.

This same injury can be caused when unseasonably warm days in late winter cause high air temperatures, but do not last sufficiently long to thaw out the ground and allow the roots to take up additional moisture. Because of this, it is important that the soil about all evergreens have plenty of water prior to the time the ground freezes in the fall. Mulching with all kinds of materials—snow included—proves helpful in keeping the ground from freezing for the longest possible time. Burlap screens and protection with evergreen boughs also prove helpful in reducing water loss due to high winds or unseasonable, warm sunshine while the ground is still frozen. The same principles hold for all areas of the country where the ground freezes in the winter or where winter droughts are pronounced.

Lack of winter hardiness is, of course, evident only after the damage has been done. The plant may die completely. A few of the more vigorous branches may be killed, indicating that those branches may have made late growth with insufficient time in the fall to properly harden or mature. Then there are the many cases of flower buds being killed. Azaleas, rhododendrons, forsythias and many of the fruit trees all suffer in this respect. Flower buds are more susceptible to cold than leaf buds. In northern gardens we often see forsythia blossoms appearing on a plant only below the former snow line when such flower buds have been protected from low temperatures by the snow cover.

In recent years, the flowering dogwood has suffered injury frequently in the North. Sometimes the cold is of sufficient intensity to kill the flower buds completely, at other times only the two outside flower bracts are injured and the so-called "flower" appears as a peculiar freak with only two white bracts developed and sometimes even these are deformed.

The hardiness map offered on the inside book covers is based solely on average annual minimum temperatures. Most of the data was taken and summarized by the United States Weather Bureau over a forty-year period, hence the map is based on sound fact. The United States and Canada are arbitrarily divided into ten zones, nine of which are in the United States. These zones are based on five-, ten- or fifteen-degree differences in the average annual minimum temperatures. Slight variations were made on the map as taken from the Weather Bureau records, in accord with known variations in plant performance on the Eastern Seaboard. My map was first published in "Hedges, Screens and Windbreaks" (Whittlesey House) in 1938. Since that time a few additional corrections have been made and incorporated in it and additional information on temperatures in Canada has been supplied by the Meteorological Division, Department of Transport of the Canadian Government.

On a small-scale map such as this, it is impossible to show all the minute climatic variations within the limits of each zone. Taking the Grand Canyon as one example, it appears in the Hardiness Map in one zone; yet there are at least four climatic zones each with a different flora in this one canyon, due to variations in altitude alone. Plants grow in the bottom of the Canyon that also thrive on the Mexican deserts, yet on the North Rim (5700 feet above the Canyon floor) plants are found which are native in southern Canada.

One other example is worthy of mention, for it represents work that is being done in several states. The Department of Floriculture and Ornamental Horticulture at Cornell University was especially interested in the hardiness limitations of ornamental woody plants in New York state. Surveys were made over a period of several years by various members of the Department (I was one) and a critical examination of all this material resulted in a hardiness map for the state (opposite page), showing minute variations not at all possible in the map of the United States and Canada on the inside covers. Two of the zones were divided (zones 3 and 4) as a result of the study. Pertinent notes were made about each zone, especially the reactions of certain ornamental plants commonly grown throughout the area. Such state maps are highly useful and show very important local variations in hardiness zones which prove most helpful to local gardeners.

Consequently, many local variations in the small map (inside book covers) submitted are to be expected. In the plant lists following a plant is usually listed in the coldest zone where it will grow normally, while at the same time it can be expected to grow in many of the warmer zones. Maximum temperatures and drought conditions would prove to be the major limiting factors. The following plants, common in many gardens, are listed in the coldest zones where they will normally grow. These should prove as reliable indicators for the type of plant material which it is possible to grow in each zone.

ZONE 2
Caragana arborescens
Cornus alba sibirica
Prunus tomentosa
Rosa rugosa
Viburnum dentatum

ZONE 3
Euonymus alata
Ligustrum amurense

Lonicera tatarica
Rhus typhina
Syringa vulgaris

ZONE 4
Cornus mas
Ligustrum vulgare
Lonicera morrowi
Rosa setigera
Taxus cuspidata

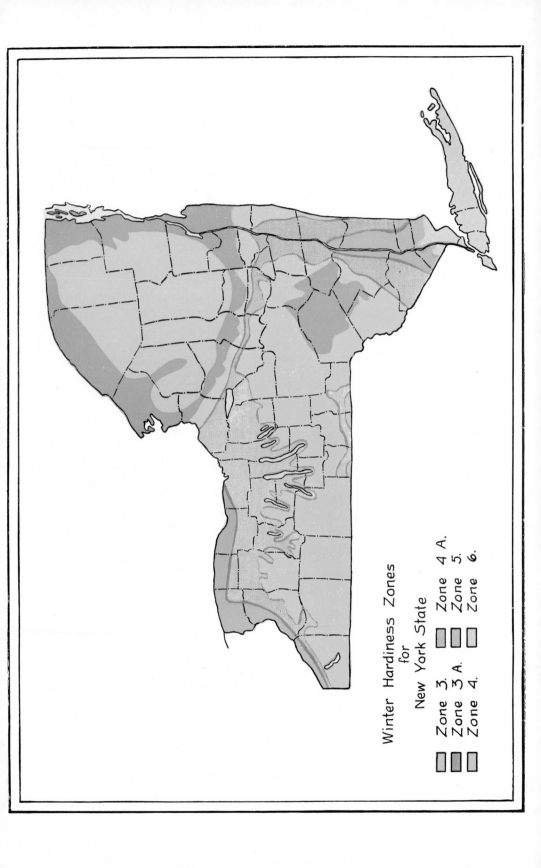

Winter Hardiness Zones
for
New York State

Zone 3.   Zone 4 A.
Zone 3 A.   Zone 5.
Zone 4.   Zone 6.

ZONE 5
Abelia grandiflora
Berberis triacanthophora
Forsythia suspensa
Pieris japonica
Weigela florida

ZONE 6
Hydrangea macrophylla
Ilex crenata
Myrica cerifera
Rhododendron fortunei
Taxus baccata

ZONE 7
Berberis darwini
Camellia japonica

Lonicera nitida
Prunus laurocerasus

ZONE 8
Campsis grandiflora
Euonymus japonica
Nerium oleander
Myrtus communis
Pittosporum tobira

ZONE 9
Ficus pumila
Hibiscus rosa-sinensis
Lonicera hildebrandiana
Sabal minor
Viburnum odoratissimum

ORDER OF BLOOM

IN order to establish a beautiful planting of flowering shrubs, one must have a knowledge of which plants bloom effectively together. The actual day on which a certain plant begins to open its flowers may vary from year to year according to the vagaries of the weather, but there are some that always bloom at the same time. This order of bloom is information which gardeners should always have available when planning new gardens and when making revisions in established gardens.

I have been keeping notes on the blooming dates of woody plants for the past fifteen years. More recently it has been interesting to check our blooming data in the Arnold Arboretum in Boston with similar data for plants grown over wide areas in the United States. After a careful study of many such records certain facts about order of bloom have become conspicuously evident and so it has been possible to note the following about this natural phenomenon.

The sequence of bloom proves a most interesting study, for it can include the bloom of wildflowers and perennials as well as trees and shrubs. The blooming period of annuals is on a somewhat different basis since the time they flower can be modified by the time they are "set out" or by the size to which they are grown in the greenhouse before they are planted outdoors. Trees, shrubs, vines, perennials and wildflowers, growing in one locality fairly unprotected from the weather, all work themselves into a definite sequence of bloom, which sequence does not vary to any appreciable extent from one year to the next. The sequence of bloom in Boston, Massachusetts, will be the same as the sequence in Augusta, Georgia, providing the same plants are normally grown out of doors in those localities.

The length of bloom, or the amount of time the plants remain ornamentally effective while in flower does vary. It varies with the kind of plant and with the season. A certain plant like *Spiraea prunifolia plena* may remain in flower for a full three weeks, and so it can be used effectively with a large number of shrubs. This particular spiraea has double flowers, and it is reasonable to expect all double-flowered shrubs to make a longer show while in flower than will plants with single flowers. Take as another example the Shadblow or Amelanchier. These have single flowers and may remain in flower a week (if the weather is cold) or may drop their flower petals only three days after they open, if the weather is unusually warm. In 1944, *Magnolia denudata* first opened its flowers in the Arnold Arboretum on May 2nd. Unseasonably warm weather occurred during the next few days so that most of the petals of this tree had fallen by May 5th. Normally the petals would have remained on the plant at least a week. This same year *Magnolia stellata* remained colorful five days longer than *M. denudata* merely because it had many more petals.

Hence, the amount of time the flowers of trees and shrubs remain in good condition varies a great deal. Length of bloom is not considered here because it is highly unpredictable, but individual gardeners who are interested in this subject could keep notes of their own observations from year to year to show just how much these periods vary in their own localities.

The specific day of the year on which a certain plant first opens its flowers varies with two things. These are important. The first is the location in which the particular plant is growing. The second is the variation of temperature in the particular year (and often in the particular location) in question.

BLOOMING DATES VARY WITH LOCATION

All plants bloom on an earlier date when grown in the South than when grown in the North. Magnolias, azaleas, lilacs and rhododendrons can be seen blooming in northern Florida at least eight weeks before they start to bloom in New England. Hence, there is a very marked difference in blooming dates due to differences in latitude.

There are also marked differences due to altitude. *Rhododendrom calendulaceum,* as an example, will bloom at the higher altitudes in the Great Smokies of Tennessee nearly at the same time it does in Maine. Certainly the differences are marked in many, many places throughout the land where flowers high up on the mountains bloom considerably later than they do in the lowlands close by.

Differences in blooming dates due to latitude alone can be graphically shown on maps in a general way so that they can be easily understood. However, variations due to differences in altitude are extremely difficult to portray except on highly complicated maps. For the purposes of this discussion, suffice it to say that differences in blooming dates due to variations in altitude do exist. In many cases they are very marked and are usually of such a local nature that they can be easily worked out and depended upon from one year to the next. However, they cannot be portrayed properly on a general map such as that on the inside book covers.

It must be admitted that even in the same locality there may be differences in time of bloom not due to altitude. Forsythia, grown next to the foundation of a warm building, will bloom days earlier than a plant of the same variety grown a hundred feet away but in an exposed situation. In New England, for instance, a very early-blooming shrub such as *Rhododendron mucronulatum* if grown in a warm, sunny location blooms sufficiently early so that its flowers may be badly nipped by late frosts, whereas, if it is grown in a shaded situation with a northern exposure, the opening of the flowers is often retarded for a sufficient number of days to escape such frost injury.

Variations in blooming dates due to latitude are easily portrayed. The march of spring from south to north is depicted by the accompanying map opposite. This is adapted from a map of the United States Department of Agriculture showing the dates of the last killing frosts over the entire United States, based on United States Weather Bureau figures assimilated over a twenty-year period (1895–1914). In adapting this map to show the advance of blooming dates and of spring in general, it is not implied that all plants are anxiously awaiting the time of the last killing frost in order to burst into bloom! However, a study of the map will show that the last killing frost in northern Florida is usually expected about March 1st, while in the vicinity of Boston, about May 1st. The difference between these two is eight weeks, the exact difference in the time of bloom of certain plants like *Cornus florida* or *Kalmia latifolia* or *Philadelphus coronarius* when grown in these two areas.

The actual blooming dates of many shrubs have been noted in widely separated areas in the United States. In general, the differences in actual bloom of specific plants in any area when compared with Boston is the same as the differences between the date of the last killing frost of that particular place and Boston. Hence this map takes on a real value. Once the sequence of bloom has been established (see page 16) and approximate blooming dates for a specific area listed (in this case Boston), then one can easily obtain an approximate estimate of when the same species will bloom in any other area of the country where they are located.

The Time *Kalmia latifolia* Blooms in Different Regions

Augusta, Georgia	mid-April
Glen St. Mary, Florida	late April
Monongahela National Forest, West Virginia	mid-May
Shenandoah Valley, Virginia	mid-May
St. Louis, Missouri	late May
Philadelphia, Pennsylvania	late May
New York, New York	early June
Columbus, Ohio	early June
Chicago, Illinois	mid-June
Rochester, New York	mid-June
Boston, Massachusetts	mid-June
Seattle, Washington	late June

Like the Hardiness Map, this map depicting the "Advance of Spring" is fallible and should be used under the same consideration as the U. S. Hardiness Map. It does, however, give an unmistakable picture of the

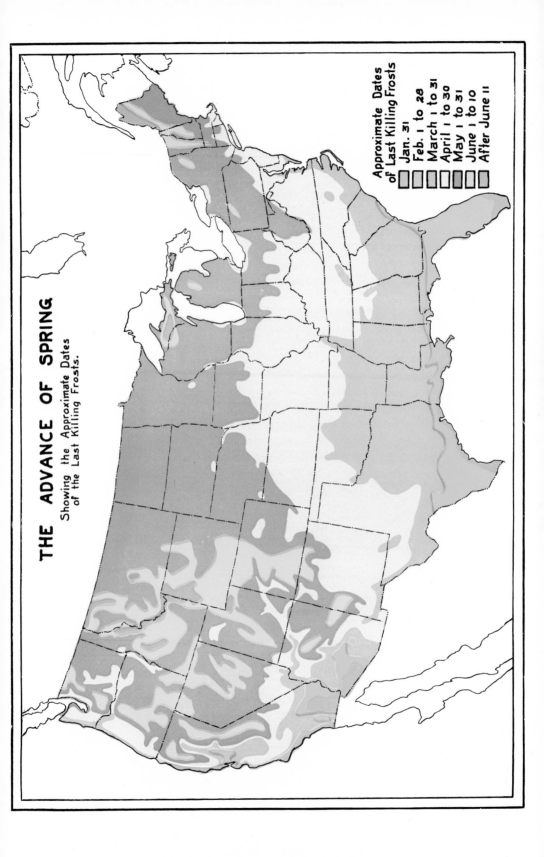

THE ADVANCE OF SPRING

Showing the Approximate Dates
of the Last Killing Frosts.

Approximate Dates
of Last Killing Frosts

Jan. 31
Feb. 1 to 28
March 1 to 31
April 1 to 30
May 1 to 31
June 1 to 10
After June 11

gradual advance of spring from south to north—and is sufficiently accurate to bear real study. Actual blooming dates of *Kalmia latifolia* for different areas are given on page 12 merely to show how well this collected information agrees with the pictorial information displayed on the map.

BLOOMING DATES VARY WITH ANNUAL WEATHER FLUCTUATIONS

The other factor causing a variance in specific blooming dates is really a series of factors which might be termed "the vagaries of the weather" or the "earliness" or "lateness" of the season. We speak of spring being "early" this year, or "late," meaning the forsythias or lilacs or azaleas or violets or narcissi are not blooming at the "normal" time. They are blooming earlier if the weather has been unseasonably mild, or later if the weather has been unseasonably cold. Every locality in the country has its own peculiarities in this respect. Take, as an example, the blooming dates of the oriental cherries planted around the Tidal Basin in Washington, D. C. Hundreds of thousands of people flock to Washington to see this beautiful sight annually. The accompanying table shows how the dates change from year to year, merely because of annual weather variations. (Blooming dates of the cherries at Washington, D. C.—data kept by Paul Russell of the Bureau of Plant Industry, U.S.D.A.)

	Yoshino Cherry (SINGLE)	Kwanzan Cherry (DOUBLE)
1930	April 1	April 22
1931	April 11	April 20
1932	April 15	April 29
1933	April 8	April 22
1934	April 15	April 29
1935	March 31	April 26
1936	April 3	April 17
1937	April 14	April 24
1938	March 23	April 14
1939	March 29	April 20
1940	April 13	April 30
1941	April 12	April 19
1942	April 6	April 19
1943	April 2	April 24
1944	April 9	April 24
1945	March 20	April 1
1946	March 22	April 7
1947	April 13	April 27

A very interesting series of figures has been kept by the Arnold Arboretum over a period of years, showing how these annual weather variations affect widely different species of plants. One year may be "early" from start to finish, another (1945) may be unusually "early" at the beginning only to be brought back to "normal" by a prolonged cold spell. It should be emphasized in this respect that in some localities in the United States, especially in Montana and parts of the South, this "catching up" process can even be depended upon annually.

Such figures merely prove what everyone knows—that actual blooming dates in one locality do vary from year to year. An unusual cold spell in the early spring followed by a warm spell may bring forsythias and lilacs into bloom at the same time. This happened in many places in 1945. Normally, forsythias are finished blooming when lilacs begin. Other variations may hold other groups in flower longer, causing a telescoping of an otherwise protracted bloom-period.

Sometimes a very cold spell in spring will greatly retard all the earlier blooming shrubs. Such was the case during the spring of 1944. Until April 28th, there were no plants showing green leaves at all, and very few plants in bloom. Then April 29, 30 and May 1st were unseasonably warm in New England with temperatures in the upper sixties and seventies. This seemed to be the spark needed for all the retarded flowers and the following ten plants are examples of many which came into full bloom suddenly for the first time that year on May 2nd.

	NORMAL BLOOMING PERIOD
Acer saccharum	early May
Prunus sargenti	late April
P. subhirtella autumnalis	late April
Forsythia species	mid-April
Prunus tomentosa	late April
P. armeniaca	late April
Lindera benzoin	mid-April
Magnolia denudata	late April
M. stellata	late April
Rhododendron mucronulatum	mid-April

It is interesting to keep a few notes on the advent of spring each year. I have noticed a particular weeping willow tree from my office window for a number of years. It has the unique habit of turning green overnight when weather conditions are just right. A few days prior to this time the buds are undoubtedly swelling, but as soon as they burst and the tiny leaf blades first appear—then the tree seems to suddenly turn green when viewed from a distance. The dates for this during the last few years are:

1940—May 1
1941—April 15
1942—April 6
1943—April 28
1944—May 1
1945—March 27
1946—March 27
1947—April 14

SOME WOODY SHRUBS LISTED IN THEIR ORDER OF BLOOM

The following plants have been listed in the order in which they bloom in the Arnold Arboretum at Boston, Massachusetts. Some common trees are included as well as perennials since these are useful in orienting the time other plants bloom. The list is made up from a long series of notes kept by the author during the past fifteen years as well as notes kept by Professor J. G. Jack of the Arboretum staff between the years of 1887 and 1893. Since 1936 additional records have been kept annually in the Arboretum so that the sequence has been checked and rechecked many times. A plant is listed only for the particular date when its bloom is first of value from a landscape point of view, although its flower buds may be conspicuous for several days prior to full bloom.

It should be stressed that some of the shrubs will remain in bloom longer than others and hence can be used effectively in gardens with

The Japanese Snowball (left) and the more tender Chinese Snowball (right) are both viburnums. They will remain effective in bloom for nearly three weeks, while certain other shrubs may drop their flowers in three days.

plants that are noted as blooming later. Still others are effective in flower bud and might be planted with varieties blooming earlier. Local studies along this line should prove of great interest to individual gardeners.

The following order of bloom is applicable in localities other than New England. If local blooming dates of a few key plants are noted and the differences checked with those given in the following sequence then all the dates can be correspondingly shifted and the sequence can be thus adapted to local climatic conditions.

Order of Bloom

(All plants in the following lists are growing in the Arnold Arboretum under practically the same soil and climatic conditions and have bloomed together in the following sequence.)

FEBRUARY

Hamamelis vernalis

MARCH

Acer saccharinum *
Corylus species
Hamamelis japonica
H. mollis
Salix * species
Snowdrop and Crocus

EARLY APRIL

Acer rubrum *
Alnus incana
A. rugosa
Cornus mas
C. officinalis
Daphne mezereum
Erica carnea
Forsythia ovata
Jasminum nudiflorum
Lonicera praeflorens
Populus species *
Prunus davidiana *
Ulmus americana *
Viburnum fragrans

MID-APRIL

Abeliophyllum distichum
Acer negundo *
Betula species *
Cercidiphyllum japonicum *
Corylopsis species
Dirca palustris
Epigaea repens
Forsythia europaea
F. intermedia varieties
F. suspensa sieboldi
F. viridissima

Lindera benzoin
Lonicera fragrantissima
L. standishi
Pieris japonica
Rhododendron dauricum
R. mucronulatum
Shepherdia argentea

LATE APRIL

Acer circinatum
A. diabolicum purpurascens
A. platanoides *
Amelanchier canadensis
A. laevis *
A. spicata
Buxus microphylla
Chamaedaphne calyculata
Euptelea polyandra *
Lonicera altmanni pilosiuscula
L. tenuipes
Magnolia denudata *
M. kobus *
M. kobus borealis *
M. salicifolia *
M. stellata
Malus baccata mandshurica *
Myrica gale
Pieris floribunda
Poncirus trifoliata
Prunus armeniaca *
P. canescens *
P. cerasifera *
P. concinna *
P. cyclamina *
P. dasycarpa *
P. domestica *
P. incisa * and varieties
P. juddi *
P. mandshurica *

* = Trees

P. nipponica *
P. sargenti *
P. subhirtella * and varieties
P. tomentosa
P. triloba
P. yedoensis *
Spiraea prunifolia
Vinca minor and varieties

EARLY MAY

Acer campestre *
A. saccharum *
Amelanchier grandiflora
A. humilis
A. sanguinea
A. stolonifera
Andromeda glaucophylla
A. polifolia
Berberis dictyophylla
Carpinus caroliniana *
Chaenomeles japonica and varieties
C. lagenaria and varieties
Crataegus arnoldiana *
Cytisus decumbens
C. elongatus
C. beani
Dandelion
Enkianthus perulatus
Exochorda giraldi
Ledum groenlandicum
Lonicera canadensis
L. coerulea
L. purpusi
L. saccata
Magnolia soulangeana and varieties *
Mahonia species
Malus adstringens and varieties *
M. arnoldiana *
M. astracanica *
M. atrosanguinea *
M. baccata *
M. brevipes *
M. floribunda *
M. halliana and varieties *
M. hupehensis *
M. micromalus *
M. prunifolia and varieties *
M. pumila niedzwetzkyana *

M. purpurea and varieties *
M. robusta and varieties *
M. scheideckeri *
M. soulardi *
M. spectabilis and varieties *
M. sylvestris *
M. zumi and varieties *
Myrica pensylvanica
Narcissus
Nemopanthus mucronatus
Orixa japonica
Osmaronia cerasiformis
Pachysandra terminalis
Phlox subulata
Primula elatior superba
P. polyantha
Prinsepia sinensis
Prunus alleghaniensis *
P. americana *
P. avium *
P. blireiana and varieties *
P. glandulosa and varieties
P. hortulana *
P. incana *
P. instititia *
P. japonica nakai
P. maritima
P. padus and varieties *
P. pensylvanica *
P. persica and varieties *
P. pumila susquehanae
P. serrulata and varieties *
(Many double-flowered forms start-
ing to bloom and continuing for two
weeks at least, depending on the
variety, some being slightly earlier
than others.)
P. sieboldi *
Pyrus communis and varieties *
Rhododendron mucronatum
R. venustum
Rhus aromatica
Ribes alpinum
R. aureum
R. gordonianum
R. odoratum
Spiraea arguta
S. thunbergi

* = Trees

Syringa hyacinthiflora and varieties
S. oblata dilatata
Tulips
Viburnum alnifolium
V. buddleifolium
V. burejaeticum
Violets
Xanthorhiza simplicissima
Zanthoxylum americanum *

MID-MAY

Acer palmatum
Aesculus arguta *
A. bushi *
A. carnea *
A. glabra *
A. hippocastanum *
A. neglecta *
Akebia quinata
A. trifoliata
Alyssum gemonense
A. saxatile
Amelanchier amabilis
Amelasorbus jacki *
Aristolochia manshuriensis
Berberis dielsiana
B. julianae
B. koreana
B. stenophylla
B. thunbergi and varieties
B. vernae
B. vulgaris
Calycanthus floridus
Caragana arborescens
C. frutex
C. sophoraefolia
Cercis canadensis *
C. chinensis
Cornus florida *
Cydonia oblonga
Cytisus praecox
C. purgans
C. purpureus
C. scoparius
Daphne altaica
D. caucasica
D. cneorum
Deutzia grandiflora

Davidia involucrata *
Elaeagnus multiflora
E. umbellata
Enkianthus campanulatus
Euonymus alata
E. latifolia
Exochorda korolkowi
E. macrantha
E. racemosa
Fothergilla species
Halesia caroliniana *
H. monticola *
Iberis tenoreana
Kerria japonica
Leitneria floridana
Lonicera alpigena
L. bella
L. chrysantha
L. muendeniensis
L. muscaviensis
L. syringantha
L. syringantha wolfi
L. thibetica
L. xylosteum
Magnolia fraseri *
M. liliflora nigra
Malus bracteata *
M. glaucescens *
M. ioensis *
M. sargenti
M. sieboldi and varieties °
Papaver orientale
Paulownia tomentosa *
Prinsepia uniflora
Prunus cerasus *
P. maacki *
P. virginiana *
Quercus species *
Rhododendron albrechti
R. canadense
R. carolinianum
R. fraseri
R. luteum
R. obtusum amoenum
R. obtusum arnoldianum
R. obtusum "Hinodegiri"
R. obtusum japonicum
R. obtusum kaempferi

* = Trees

R. *racemosum*
R. *reticulatum*
R. *schlippenbachi*
R. *vaseyi*
R. *yedoense*
R. *yedoense poukhanense*
Rhodotypos scandens
Ribes sanguineum
Sambucus pubens
Sibiraea laevigata
Sorbus aucuparia *
Spiraea cinerea
S. *gemmata*
S. *hypericifolia*
S. *inflexa*
S. *media*
S. *mollifolia*
S. *oxyodon*
S. *pikoviensis*
S. *prunifolia plena*
S. *pubescens*
Syringa vulgaris and varieties
(With over 300 varieties, it is impossible to list them here as early, medium and late, although some might be so listed.)
Vaccinium angustifolium laevifolium
Viburnum bitchiuense
V. *burkwoodi*
V. *carlesi*
V. *juddi*
V. *lantana*
Weigela "Conquerant"
W. "Fleur de Mai"
W. "Floreal"
W. *florida venusta*
W. "Gracieux"

LATE MAY

Acer ginnala
Aronia arbutifolia
A. *melanocarpa*
A. *prunifolia*
Asimina triloba *
Berberis amurensis
B. *circumserrata*
B. *gagnepaini*
B. *verruculosa*

Berchemia racemosa
Buttercup
Caragana maximowicziana
Celastrus flagellaris
C. *orbiculata*
C. *scandens*
Cornus alternifolia *
C. *controversa* *
C. *stolonifera*
Coronilla emeroides
Cotoneaster adpressa
C. *apiculata*
C. *divaricata*
C. *foveolata*
C. *nitens*
C. *racemiflora*
Crataegus crus-galli *
C. *oxyacantha* *
C. *oxyacantha pauli* *
C. *pruinosa* *
C. *punctata* *
C. *succulenta* *
Daphne giraldi
Daylilies
Deutzia candelabrum
D. *gracilis*
D. *kalmiaeflora*
D. *lemoinei* and varieties
D. *rosea* and varieties
Dipelta floribunda
Enkianthus deflexus
E. *subsessilis*
Fendlera wrighti
Fontanesia fortunei
Gaylussacia baccata
Genista pilosa
Iberis sempervirens
Juglans sieboldiana *
Laburnum species
Leucothoe racemosa
Lonicera amoena
L. *korolkowi*
L. *maacki*
L. *maximowiczi sachalinensis*
L. *morrowi*
L. *tatarica* and varieties
Magnolia cordata *
M. *soulangeana lennei* *

* = Trees

M. tripetala *
M. virginiana
M. watsoni *
Malus angustifolia *
M. coronaria *
M. coronaria charlottae *
M. ioensis plena *
M. toringoides *
Neillia sinensis
Paeonia suffruticosa
Petteria ramentacea
Philadelphus hirsutus
P. schrenki jacki
Photinia villosa
Physocarpus amurensis
P. monogynus
Potentilla fruticosa and varieties
Prunus laurocerasus schipkaensis
P. serotina *
Rhamnus cathartica
Rhododendron atlanticum
R. catawbiense "Boule de Neige"
R. catawbiense "Charles Dickens"
R. catawbiense "Mont Blanc"
R. fortunei "Duke of York"
R. gandavense hybrids
R. japonicum
R. molle hybrids
R. "Mont Blanc"
R. nudiflorum
R. roseum
R. smirnowi
Robinia elliotti
R. fertilis
R. kelseyi
R. slavini
Rosa ecae
R. hugonis
R. primula
R. xanthina
Rubus deliciosus
Schisandra chinensis
Smilax rotundifolia
Spiraea blumei
S. cantoniensis
S. multiflora
S. nipponica
S. nipponica rotundifolia

* = Trees

S. trilobata
S. vanhouttei
Staphylea colchica
S. trifolia
Symplocus paniculata
Syringa chinensis
S. julianae
S. meyeri
S. microphylla
S. persica
S. pinetorum
S. potanini
S. pubescens
S. velutina
S. wolfi
S. yunnanensis
Tamarix parviflora
Thymus serpyllum
Vaccinium corymbosum
Viburnum lentago
V. macrocephalum sterile
V. opulus roseum
V. rafinesquianum
V. rhytidophyllum
V. rufidulum
V. sieboldi
V. tomentosum
V. tomentosum sterile
V. trilobum
V. wrighti
Weigela "Dame Blanche"
W. "Lavallei"
Wisteria species and varieties

EARLY JUNE
Abelia engleriana
Actinidia arguta
Buddleia alternifolia
Ceanothus ovatus
Chionanthus retusus
C. virginicus
Cladrastis lutea *
Cornus alba
C. kousa
C. rugosa
Cotinus coggygria
Daphne pontica

Decaisnea fargesi
Elaeagnus angustifolia
Euonymus atropurpurea
E. bungeana
Genista hispanica
G. tinctoria
Halimodendron halodendron
Helianthemum nummularium
Hydrangea petiolaris
H. xanthoneura wilsoni
Idesia polycarpa
Ilex opaca *
Indigofera amblyantha
Jamesia americana
Kolkwitzia amabilis
Leucothoe catesbaei
Lonicera ruprechtiana
Magnolia sieboldi *
Periploca graeca
P. sepium
Phellodendron amurense *
Philadelphus "Banniere"
P. caucasicus
P. "Cole's Glorious"
P. "Conquete"
P. coronarius
P. "Coupe d'Argent"
P. floridus
P. laxus
P. magdalenae
P. "Manteau de Hermine"
P. maximus
P. nepalensis
P. pekinensis
P. "Rosace"
P. tomentosus
Physocarpus intermedius
P. opulifolius
Rhamnus davurica
R. frangula
Rhododendron arbutifolium
R. calendulaceum
R. catawbiense and varieties
R. ferrugineum
R. laetevirens
R. minus
R. "Mrs. C. S. Sargent"

R. "Purpureum Grandiflorum"
Rhus potanini
Robinia hartwigi *
R. hispida
R. pseudoacacia *
Rosa acicularis
R. arnoldiana
R. bella
R. blanda
R. foetida bicolor
R. harisoni
R. l'heritierana
R. roxburghi
R. rubrifolia
R. rugosa and varieties
R. spinosissima and varieties
R. willmottiae
Sassafras albidum *
Sophora viciifolia
Spiraea blanda
S. chamaedryfolia
S. henryi
S. trichocarpa
S. wilsoni
Staphylea pinnata
Styrax americana
S. japonica
S. obassia *
Syringa henryi and varieties
S. josikaea and varieties
S. komarowi
S. prestoniae and varieties
S. reflexa
S. sweginzowi
S. tomentella
S. villosa
Vaccinium stamineum
Viburnum cassinoides
V. dentatum
V. dilatatum and varieties
V. hupehense
V. lobophyllum
V. opulus
V. prunifolium
V. sargenti
Weigela florida
W. "Gratissima"

* = Trees

MID-JUNE

Amorpha fruticosa
A. glabra
Castanea pumila
Catalpa speciosa *
Ceanothus americanus
Cornus amomum
C. bretschneideri
C. coreana
C. racemosa
Cotinus americanus
Cotoneaster dielsiana
C. horizontalis
C. multiflora
Crataegus phaenopyrum *
Deutzia "Contraste"
D. "Magicien"
D. magnifica
Diospyros virginiana *
Euonymus europaea
E. fortunei vegeta
Gymnocladus dioicus *
Hydrangea bretschneideri
Ilex glabra
I. verticillata
Indigofera decora
I. kirilowi
I. potanini
Kalmia angustifolia
K. latifolia
Ligustrum amurense
L. ibolium
L. ibota
L. obtusifolium
L. obtusifolium regelianum
L. ovalifolium
L. vulgare
Liriodendron tulipifera *
Lonicera browni
L. iberica
L. japonica halliana
L. periclymenum
Lyonia ligustrina
L. mariana
Philadelphus "Albatre"
P. "Argentine"
P. "Atlas"
P. "Avalanche"

P. "Bouquet Blanc"
P. "Boule d'Argent"
P. cymosus
P. "Girandole"
P. "Glacier"
P. grandiflorus
P. "Innocence"
P. inodorus
P. lemoinei and varieties
P. microphyllus
P. monstrosus
P. "Mont Blanc"
P. "Norma"
P. "Pavillon Blanc"
P. pubescens
P. purpurascens
P. splendens
P. zeyheri
Pyracantha coccinea lalandi
Rhododendron "Album Elegans"
R. "Album Grandiflorum"
R. arborescens
Robinia viscosa
Rosa alba
R. arvensis
R. canina
R. centifolia
R. damascena
R. davidi
R. eglanteria
R. gallica
R. helenae
R. jacksoni
R. micrantha
R. moyesi
R. multiflora
R. multiflora cathayensis
R. virginiana
R. webbiana
Rubus alleghaniensis
Sambucus nigra
Spiraea veitchi
S. watsoniana
Stephanandra incisa
Symphoricarpos albus laevigatus
Syringa amurensis
S. amurensis japonica
S. pekinensis

* = Trees

Tilia platyphyllos *
Viburnum acerifolium
V. molle
V. pubescens
Weigela "Congo"
W. "Eve Rathke"
Zenobia pulverulenta

LATE JUNE

Acanthopanax sieboldianus
Actinidia polygama
Ailanthus altissima *
Ceanothus pallidus roseus
Cornus macrophylla
Cotoneaster salicifolia
Deutzia myriantha
D. scabra plena
D. staminea
Diervilla sessilifolia
Dorycnium hirsutum
Genista anglica
Ilex crenata
Indigofera incarnata alba
Itea virginica
Lavandula officinalis
Lonicera henryi
Philadelphus "Belle Etoile"
P. burkwoodi
P. "Enchantment"
P. virginalis and varieties
Rhododendron maximum
Rhus typhina
Rosa multibracteata
Sambucus canadensis
Schizophragma hydrangeoides
Sorbaria sorbifolia
Spiraea billiardi
S. bumalda and varieties
S. douglasi
S. japonica
S. latifolia
S. margaritae
S. menziesi
S. pyramidata
S. tomentosa
S. virginiana
Stephanandra tanakae
Tripterygium regeli

* = Trees

EARLY JULY

Buddleia japonica
Callicarpa dichotoma
C. japonica
Cytisus nigricans
Holodiscus discolor
Hydrangea arborescens
H. arborescens grandiflora
Hypericum kalmianum
H. patulum henryi
Lycium species
Maackia amurensis *
Marsdenia erecta
Rhododendron viscosum
Rhus glabra
Rosa setigera
Rubus odoratus
Spiraea salicifolia
Stewartia koreana *
S. pseudo-camellia *
Tilia euchlora *
T. petiolaris *
T. tomentosa *
Viburnum setigerum aurantiacum

MID-JULY

Aesculus parviflora
Albizzia julibrissin rosea *
Amorpha brachycarpa
A. canescens
Ampelopsis aconitifolia
A. cordata
Berberis aggregata
Campsis radicans
Clematis jackmani
Diervilla lonicera
Hydrangea cinerea
H. paniculata praecox
H. quercifolia
H. radiata
H. serrata
Hypericum arnoldianum
H. densiflorum
H. frondosum
Koelreuteria paniculata *
Ligustrum quihoui
Lonicera heckrotti
L. sempervirens

Rosa wichuraiana
Securinega suffruticosa
Stewartia ovata *
Symphoricarpos chenaulti
S. orbiculatus
Tamarix odessana
T. pentandra
Yucca filamentosa

LATE JULY

Acanthopanax senticosus
Abelia schumanni
Ampelopsis brevipedunculata
Aralia spinosa
Buddleia albiflora
Calluna vulgaris and varieties
Cephalanthus occidentalis
Clethra acuminata
C. alnifolia
C. barbinervis
Hypericum prolificum
Kalopanax pictus *
Lespedeza bicolor
Nandina domestica
Oxydendrum arboreum *
Sorbaria arborea

AUGUST

Abelia grandiflora
Aralia chinensis

A. elata
Buddleia davidi varieties
Caryopteris incana
Clematis virginiana
C. vitalba
Clerodendron trichotomum
Hibiscus syriacus varieties
Hydrangea macrophylla
H. paniculata
H. paniculata grandiflora
Hypericum dawsonianum
Lagerstroemia indica
Lespedeza cyrtobotrya
Polygonum auberti
Rhus copallina
Sophora japonica *
Vitex agnus-castus
V. negundo incisa

SEPTEMBER

Baccharis halimifolia
Clematis paniculata
Elsholtzia stauntoni
Franklinia alatamaha

OCTOBER

Hamamelis virginiana
Lespedeza japonica

* = Trees

ORNAMENTAL FRUITS

SECOND in importance to the flowers are the fruits of shrubs. Indeed some even surpass the flowers in ornamental value as do the fruits of the barberries and cotoneasters. The most conspicuous, of course, are the red and the yellow fruits, and some of the whites also stand out, especially if they are borne before the leaves fall and thus properly set off with a green background. The blue fruits are less noticeable, but some, like those of the Beautyberry (*Symplocos paniculata*) are remarkably beautiful when fully mature. Black fruits are least attractive of all, yet there are those people who like the Jetbead or one of the various black-fruited viburnums to such an extent that they give plants of this kind a prominent place in the garden.

Just like the sequence of blooming periods, so there is a sequence of fruiting. It starts late in spring in the Arnold Arboretum with such plants as the Fragrant Honeysuckle and some of its close relatives displaying dark red fruits in the latter part of May. During the remainder of spring, throughout summer and fall and even through winter there is a never-ceasing parade of bright-colored fruits appearing on the different types of shrubs. Some shrubs, like the lilacs, deutzias, forsythias, spireas, and mock-oranges have dried capsules which are not in the least ornamental, and therefore should not be planted in borders where fall-fruiting shrubs would prove better.

The length of time that the fruits remain colorful is important. In most cases, it is considerably longer than the time flowers are effective. It varies of course, with the season, the amount of rainfall, the type of soil, but in the following lists the sequence has been plotted in the Arnold Arboretum for many outstanding fruiting shrubs. Not all are recorded, and just because a plant is not listed does not mean that it has inferior fruit. However, the sequence is certainly important, and the length of time the fruit has proved colorful is indicative of what it may be in other years in other locations.

Some of the factors affecting the amount of the fruit on plants should be understood in order that lack of fruit production some years may be prevented, if possible. Common things like good soil and plenty of rainfall, resulting in plenty of fruit production, are easily understood. Conversely, poor soil and dry weather result in very poor or "dried up" fruits that are not nearly up to normal standards. There are some other impor-

Omei Rose (*R. omeiensis*) with bright red fruits and conspicuously colored prickles in the fall.

tant factors governing fruit production, and it would be well to take a glance at a few of them.

ALTERNATE BEARING

As every commercial fruit producer knows, "alternate bearing" is one of the most difficult processes of nature which man has to combat in his urge to produce more and more fruits each and every year. Apples, peaches, plums, pears and many other commercially produced fruits are examples which have been carefully studied by pomologists for many years. The same general principles underly the producing of fruits on many ornamental plants. Alternate bearing is the result of a series of chemical processes in orchard plants which result in the production of bumper crops one year and small crops the next. Various methods of pruning, thinning and fertilization have been suggested to check this somewhat, but the fact remains that the plants themselves tend to bear large crops only every other year.

This same tendency is noticeable in some groups of ornamentals. Lilacs, for example, tend to flower profusely only in alternate years. This marked tendency can be alleviated somewhat by cutting off the withered flower clusters to prevent the formation of seed, a good standard practice also on rhododendrons, laurel, azaleas, weigela and in fact any other shrubs the fruits of which are not ornamental.

There are some ornamentals, however, which bear so many flowers each year that this tendency, even if present, is not marked. Forsythias, viburnums (occasionally) and rose species are examples. Shrubs grown expressly for their ornamental fruits, like the cotoneasters, are frequently susceptible to alternate bearing, and when this is the case there is not much that the plantsman can do to alleviate it without a great deal of pruning and fertilizing and even then this may not help the situation.

INCLEMENT WEATHER

The fertilization necessary for the production of fruits is carried out in several different ways. For instance, there are the perfect flowers of the crabapples, the pollen borne on the stamens of one flower can fertilize the pistil of the same flower. Then there are plants like the apricots, the pistils of the flowers on one plant apparently needing pollen produced by the stamens of another plant of different parentage in order to "set" proper fruit. There are many plants like the hollies with sexes separate, that is, with the staminate flowers being borne on one plant and the pistillate flowers on another so that both of these plants must be present to insure fruiting.

Then the means by which the pollen is spread from one plant to the flowers of another plant varies. With some plants, hollies as a possible example, this may be the wind, but with many plants multitudinous insects feed on the pollen and nectar of the flowers and do the greater part of the fertilization. Bees are outstanding in this respect, but there are other insects which are important pollen carriers. For instance, the Five Leaf Akebia (*Akebia quinata*) has small purplish flowers in the very early spring. Some clusters of the small flowers are entirely staminate, others are pistillate, and still others have both staminate and pistillate flowers together. Even when these flowers are borne together on the same cluster there is no fertilization by wind or by most of the common insects. One particular type of insect must be present in that locality in order to insure proper fertilization. It is possible to produce fruits by hand pollination, of course.

Weather plays a most important part in the pollination of most plants, and we notice the result of favorable (or unfavorable) weather conditions months after that fertilization period has come and gone. Take, as an example, the peculiar conditions necessary for holly which has its sexes separate. Both wind or air circulation and the presence of many insects are necessary. If the weather is rainy during the time the pollen is ripe, there may be little opportunity for either wind pollinization or insect flight. On the other hand, if the weather is very cold during the time the pollen of a certain plant is ripe, then insect activity is at a low ebb and a plant like the viburnum, for instance, would have to depend solely on wind pollinization. If the weather is very cold and rainy with little wind during the time of ripe pollen formation, then all these conditions combine to make fertilization of many kinds of shrubs extremely difficult.

The commercial orchardist knows these things because he has studied them in relation to his fruit production for years. He finds it necessary to interplant certain varieties of fruits producing just the right type of pollen for his main crop. He puts hives of bees in his orchards to aid in the general pollen carrying, and he manipulates the hives so that they will be at maximum activity when the flowers are mature.

A year ago there were reports all over the East that the Black Alder or Winterberry (*Ilex verticillata*) had not been so fruitful for many years. The plants in most areas were covered with fruits until well after Christmas. There is no doubt that this was caused by ideal conditions during the time when pollen was ripe the previous June, a surmise fully substantiated by a study of the weather reports for that period.

There is little we can do about modifying the weather on a large scale, but if we have a few plants in our garden on which we want good fruits each year, we could study their optimum needs during the time when pollen is ripe, and endeavor to aid pollen carriers in every way.

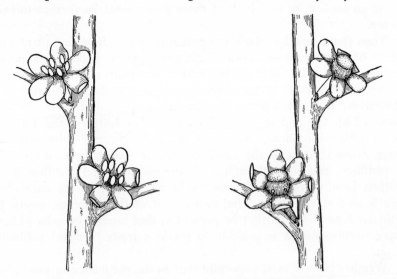

Flowers of *Ilex verticillata*. LEFT: staminate: RIGHT: pistillate.

SEXES SEPARATE

As has been mentioned, some groups of plants are dioecious, that is, they bear staminate flowers on one plant and pistillate flowers on the other. Of course, the staminate plants will never bear fruits, but neither will the pistillate plants (there are a few exceptions to this) unless the right pollen-

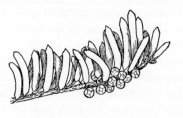

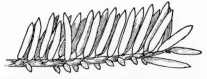

The yews are among those plants with pistillate flowers on one plant and staminate flowers on another. The flowers are open only a very short time in late spring when the determination of the sexes is easy. However, the staminate flower buds of the yew (upper sketch) are rounded and the pistillate flower buds (lower sketch) are more conical. Both can be identified with a little practice on the underside of the branches of large plants, for many months prior to blooming. Practice in the identification of these types when not in flower is well worth the effort especially when buying or selling plants of fruiting age.

bearing plant is within a reasonable distance. Just what the "reasonable distance" is we do not know, for many things enter into an understanding of this problem, and few studies have been made concerning the type of pollen carriers required. Certainly, the closer the sexes are together, the more reasonable it is to expect the pistillate plant to produce a good supply of fruit.

Genera with Flowers Dioecious

(with female or pistillate flowers on one plant, and staminate or male flowers on another plant)

Acer—many species	*Cotinus*	*Morus*	*Salix*
Actinidia	*Diospyros*	*Myrica*	*Schisandra*
Ailanthus	*Ginkgo*	*Nemopanthus*	*Securinega*
Aucuba	*Helwingia*	*Orixa*	*Shepherdia*
Baccharis	*Hippophae*	*Phellodendron*	*Skimmia*
Celastrus	*Ilex*	*Populus*	*Smilax*
Cephalotaxus	*Juniperus*	*Rhus*	*Taxus*
Chionanthus	*Lindera*	*Ribes*	*Vitis*
Comptonia	*Maclura*	*Ruscus*	*Zanthoxylum*

Some of these, namely the yews, hollies, bittersweets, and bayberries, are important for their ornamental fruits, and their fruiting habits are little understood by a great proportion of the general public. Even some nurserymen are not familiar with the facts, for if they were, such plants would be grown in the nursery so that their sexes could be determined before they are sold, either by propagating asexually from plants of known sex, or, if they must be grown from seed, to allow them to grow in the nursery until they bloom, at which time their sexes could be determined and the plants could be segregated accordingly.

There are two general groups: the one in which the sexes are definitely separated, with all the staminate flowers on one plant and all the pistillate flowers on another; and the second, in which a few of both types of flowers occur on an occasional plant. It may be that most of these genera are in the second group but it is safe to say that positive proof of this is not yet

Black Alder or Winterberry (*Ilex verticillata*) one of the hollies with sexes separate, hence only pistillate plants bear fruits.

known for some of the genera. *Celastrus, Actinidia* and *Taxus* species do have some plants with both types of flowers, and so are termed polygamodioecious. There is a great deal of discussion among plantsmen as to whether there are similar plants of *Ilex opaca* for, as some point out, certain specimens a mile or more from any other plant of the same species are known to fruit well—a good proof, say some, that the plant has both types of flowers!

But the problem is not quite so simple. Pistillate plants of the Chinese

Holly (*Ilex cornuta*), for instance, are known to produce good fruits even though no pollen is available. Then too, it has been proved that pollen from one species of holly can fertilize the pistils of flowers of another species. Hence, it is conceivable that an "isolated" plant of one species can be fertilized with pollen from numerous nearby plants of another species in the same genus. Obviously, much more should be known about each individual species, and its specific pollen requirements, before we can be too specific concerning ways to overcome non-fruiting in this large group of ornamental plants. Two examples might be cited, however, in order to aid in overcoming this difficult plant-growing problem.

Take, as an example, the common Bittersweet (*Celastrus scandens*). A home owner wants a fruiting plant to twine about the rainspout on his house. How should he be certain that such a plant will produce fruits? First, either he should buy a plant known to be pistillate, guaranteed that by the nurseryman, or dig one from the wild on which he has actually seen fruits or pistillate flowers. If his home is situated in the country near hedge rows or wooded areas where a number of the vines are present, chances are that insects or wind will insure fruiting.

If he is not living in such an area, he should obtain a small staminate plant also and place in the same hole at transplanting time. He might do well to keep the latter trimmed to a minimum so that it would not outgrow the pistillate plant. Or he could try his hand at grafting a branch of the staminate form to the pistillate plant. If this did not prove feasible he might try to obtain one of the polygamo-dioecious plants, but these are extremely hard to find in nurseries. (One of the Oriental bittersweets which grows in the Arnold Arboretum was distributed to the trade a few years ago but its fruiting qualities are not everything that could be hoped for.) If it is impossible to follow any of the above methods, the home owner could obtain cut branches from the staminate form of either *C. scandens* or *C. orbiculata,* place the bases of these branches in small jars of water and tie in the pistillate vine during flowering time. I have done this with great success. It is very simple if you have access to a supply of staminate-flowering branches and care to go to this trouble just at the right time each year.

The second example in this group worthy of citing is the Yew. Sexes are separate in all yews, but their striking beauty is greatly enhanced if they produce the bright red fleshy fruits in fall, which show off so well against the exquisite dark green of the foliage. Here again the nurseryman should help by growing sexes separately. If staminate plants are already in the near vicinity, or your neighbor has yews which fruit heavily every year (thus proving that staminate plants are nearby) the chances are that it is only necessary to obtain true pistillate plants. If there are no fruits on any plants nearby, then plants of both sexes should be purchased, possibly in the ratio of one staminate to every five pistillate plants.

FRUIT COLOR

Fruit color, too, can be modified by soil conditions and the amount of rainfall as well as by temperature when the fruit is in process of ripening. Although it is not yet possible to make the red fruit of a certain plant blue, nevertheless, nature often prevents the fruits on a plant from turning red as soon as they might, and in some cases from turning as good a red as they normally might. For instance, fruit on a plant of *Viburnum*

Siebold Viburnum—one of the best of the viburnums for
red summer fruit.

opulus growing in rich well-drained soil will not color as early as fruit on a plant of the same species growing in poor dry soil. The plant often colors best which has received a good application of fertilizer high in nitrogen, and possibly phosphorous also. Bright, sunny days will tend to aid the fruit in coloring well and quickly, if the sunshine comes at just the right time, whereas a long rainy or cloudy spell may keep the fruit from coloring normally.

Unseasonable frosts play their part also. Some fruits require a good frost in order to bring out their bright colors while other plants have fruits which turn brown, and even drop, with the advent of the first hard frost.

Some fruits color very quickly and may ripen very quickly as is evidenced by the speed with which they are eaten by birds or animals. A few years ago I wanted to photograph a particularly heavily fruited *Chionanthus virginicus.* The fruits of this plant are about the size of small grapes and borne in grapelike clusters. I watched the plant for nearly a week for I wanted to photograph it when the color was at its best. Going home past this shrub one night, I noted that it was a normal dark blue and made a mental note to be there bright and early the next morning. I was there at seven o'clock, but during this fourteen-hour period the fruits from that twelve-foot shrub had almost entirely disappeared, having been eaten by one of the numerous flocks of birds.

I would like to make a strong plea for some of the very few yellow fruiting shrubs which I think should be grown considerably more than they are. They are no better than their red-fruited relatives but they lend a lively note when grown with the red-fruiting forms. Some of the white-fruiting shrubs, too, are certainly worthwhile and in order to bring some of these to mind as possible accent points in your garden, the more outstanding are listed on pages 38–39.

LENGTH OF TIME FRUITS REMAIN EFFECTIVE

Red Fruits	Jan.	Feb.	March	April	May	June	July	Aug.	Sept.	Oct.	Nov.	Dec.
Acer ginnala								—				
A. spicatum								—				
Amelanchier grandiflora							—	—				
Arctostaphylos uva-ursi								—				
Arbutus unedo									—	—		
Ardisia crispa	—	—							—	—	—	—
Aronia arbutifolia										—	—	
Aucuba japonica	—	—									—	
Berberis circumserrata									—	—		
B. concinna									—	—		
B. gilgiana									—	—		
B. koreana	—	—							—	—	—	—
B. mentorensis									—	—		
B. potanini									—	—		
B. thunbergi	—	—	—	—	—	—	—	—	—	—	—	—
Ceanothus ovatus							—					
Cornus mas								—	—			
C. officinalis								—	—			
Cotoneaster dammeri									—	—	—	
C. divaricata									—	—		
C. francheti									—	—		
C. frigida									—	—	—	
C. harroviana									—	—		
C. henryana									—	—		
C. horizontalis									—	—		
C. microphylla	—	—							—	—	—	—
C. pannosa									—	—	—	
C. racemiflora							—	—	—			
C. salicifolia floccosa										—	—	
C. simonsi									—	—		
Cudrania tricuspidata									—	—		
Danae racemosa									—	—		
Daphne giraldi						—	—					
D. mezereum						—						
Elaeagnus multiflora						—	—					
Euonymus ala'a										—	—	
E. americana									—	—		
E. bungeana semi-persistens										—	—	
E. europaea aldenhamensis									—	—	—	
E. fortunei vegeta										—	—	
E. japonica									—	—		
E. kiautschovica									—	—		
E. latifolia										—	—	
E. nana									—	—		
E. sanguinea										—	—	

Red Fruits

	Jan.	Feb.	March	April	May	June	July	Aug.	Sept.	Oct.	Nov.	Dec.
E. yedoensis										——	——	
Gaultheria procumbens										——	——	
Heteromeles arbutifolia				——	——							
Hippophae rhamnoides										——	——	
Ilex cassine										——	——	
I. cornuta	——									——	——	
I. decidua										——	——	
I. laevigata								——	——			
I. pedunculosa								——	——			
I. pernyi								——	——			
I. verticillata								——	——			
I. yunnanensis								——	——			
Leycesteria formosa									——			
Lindera benzoin									——			
Lonicera alpigena nana									——			
L. amoena arnoldiana							——	——				
L. bella varieties								——				
L. deflexicalyx								——				
L. fragrantissima					——							
L. gracilipes						——						
L. korolkowi							——					
L. maacki									——	——		
L. morrowi							——	——				
L. saccata						——						
L. spinosa alberti								——				
L. syringantha							——					
L. tatarica						——	——					
L. tatsienensis								——				
L. thibetica						——						
Magnolia liliflora nigra									——			
M. stellata									——			
M. virginiana									——			
M. wilsoni								——	——			
Malus sargenti									——	——		
Mitchella repens									——	——		
Nandina domestica	——	——								——	——	——
Pernettya mucronata	——	——								——	——	
Phillyrea decora										——	——	
Photinia serrulata										——	——	
P. villosa										——	——	
Prinsepia sinensis								——				
Prunus glandulosa								——				
P. japonica nakai								——				
P. tomentosa							——					
Pyracantha atalantioides	——	——								——	——	
P. coccinea										——	——	

35

Red Fruits

	Jan.	Feb.	March	April	May	June	July	Aug.	Sept.	Oct.	Nov.	Dec.
P. crenulata rogersiana										—	—	
Pyracantha "Oxford"										—	—	
Rhus species	—	—								—	—	—
Ribes alpinum								—				
Robinia kelseyi								—				
Rosa alba incarnata	—	—								—	—	—
R. amblyotis								—	—			
R. canina	—	—								—	—	—
R. carolina								—	—			
R. coriifolia forebeli									—	—		
R. damascena									—	—		
R. eglanteria									—	—		
R. foetida									—	—		
R. gallica									—	—		
R. helenae	—	—							—	—		
R. hugonis									—	—		
R. l'heritierana									—	—		
R. moschata nastarana									—	—		
R. moyesi									—	—		
R. multiflora	—	—							—	—	—	—
R. omeiensis									—	—		
R. palustris								—	—			
R. pendulina								—	—			
R. primula								—				
R. roxburghi								—				
R. rubrifolia									—	—		
R. rugosa								—	—			
R. setigera	—	—								—	—	—
R. virginiana	—	—							—	—	—	—
R. webbiana										—	—	
R. wichuraiana	—	—								—	—	—
Rubus odoratus								—				
Sambucus canadensis aurea								—				
S. canadensis rubra								—				
S. pubens							—					
S. racemosa							—	—				
Sarcococca ruscifolia										—	—	
Shepherdia canadensis							—	—				
Skimmia japonica										—	—	—
S. reevesiana										—	—	—
Symphoricarpos chenaulti										—	—	
S. orbiculatus										—	—	
Taxus species										—	—	
Viburnum dilatatum	—	—								—	—	—
V. japonicum										—	—	
V. opulus	—	—								—	—	—

36

Red Fruits	Jan.	Feb.	March	April	May	June	July	Aug.	Sept.	Oct.	Nov.	Dec.
V. suspensum										—	—	
V. tomentosum mariesi								—				
V. trilobum								—	—	—	—	—

Blue Fruits

	Jan.	Feb.	March	April	May	June	July	Aug.	Sept.	Oct.	Nov.	Dec.
Berberis gagnepaini									—	—		
B. julianae									—	—		
B. triacanthophora									—	—		
B. verruculosa									—	—		
Chionanthus virginicus									—			
Clerodendron trichotomum									—	—		
Coprosma petriei									—	—		
Cornus amomum								—	—			
Fatsia japonica	—	—	—									—
Gaultheria veitchiana								—	—			
Gaylussacia brachycera								—	—			
Juniperus communis									—	—	—	
J. horizontalis									—	—	—	
Ligustrum obtusifolium	—	—									—	—
Mahonia aquifolium							—					
M. beali							—					
Sambucus coerulea								—	—			
Symplocos paniculata										—	—	
Vaccinium angustifolium laevifolium								—	—			
V. arboreum									—	—		
V. corymbosum								—	—			
V. pallidum								—	—			
Viburnum davidi									—	—	—	
V. dentatum									—	—		
V. rufidulum									—	—		

Black Fruits

	Jan.	Feb.	March	April	May	June	July	Aug.	Sept.	Oct.	Nov.	Dec.
Aronia melanocarpa									—	—	—	—
Berberis stenophylla									—	—	—	
Cornus paucinervis									—	—		
Cotoneaster foveolata									—	—	—	
C. lucida										—	—	
Eurya japonica										—	—	
Ilex crenata									—	—	—	—
I. glabra	—	—							—	—	—	—
Ligustrum amurense	—	—	—	—						—	—	—
L. henryi										—	—	—
L. ibolium	—	—								—	—	—
L. lucidum	—	—	—							—	—	—
L. ovalifolium										—	—	—
L. quihou·										—	—	

37

Black Fruits

	Jan.	Feb.	March	April	May	June	July	Aug.	Sept.	Oct.	Nov.	Dec.
L. sinense	—								———	———	———	———
L. vicaryi									———			
L. vulgare	—								———	———		
Mahonia repens							—					
Myrtus communis									———			
Osmanthus fortunei									———			
O. ilicifolius									———			
Prunus besseyi								———				
Raphiolepis umbellata	———								———			
Rhamnus davurica								———				
Ribes odoratum							—					
R. sanguineum								—				
Severinia buxifolia									—			
Siphonosmanthus delavayi								———				
Suaeda fruticosa										—		
Viburnum acerifolium									———			
V. lentago									———			
V. nudum									———			
V. prunifolium									———			
V. tinus								—				

Purple Fruits

	Jan.	Feb.	March	April	May	June	July	Aug.	Sept.	Oct.	Nov.	Dec.
Aronia prunifolia										———	———	———
Berberis beaniana									———	———		
B. candidula									———	———		
B. darwini									———	———		
Callicarpa japonica									———			
Cotinus coggygria purpureus						—						
Ficus carica								—				
Lonicera gynochlamydea									———	———		
Myrica californica	———	———							———	———		
Prunus cistena								—				
P. laurocerasus							—					
P. lusitanica							—					
P. maritima								—				
Rubus deliciosus								—				

White Fruits

	Jan.	Feb.	March	April	May	June	July	Aug.	Sept.	Oct.	Nov.	Dec.
Baccharis halimifolia										———	———	
Cornus alba sibirica							—					
C. racemosa								———				
C. stolonifera						—						
Gaultheria miqueliana									———			
Lonicera quinqueolaris									———	———		
Nandina domestica alba	———									———	———	———
Pachysandra terminalis										———		

38

	Jan.	Feb.	March	April	May	June	July	Aug.	Sept.	Oct.	Nov.	Dec.

White Fruits

Phoradendron flavescens
Prunus tomentosa leucocarpa
Symphoricarpos albus laevigatus
S. orbiculatus leucocarpus

Yellow Fruits

Cornus mas flava
Daphne mezereum alba
Elaeagnus angustifolia
Lonicera morrowi xanthocarpa
L. tatarica lutea
Poncirus trifoliata
Prunus maritima flava
Punica granatum
Stachyrus praecox
Viburnum dilatatum xanthocarpum
V. sargenti flavum
V. opulus xanthocarpum

Gray Fruits

Cotinus coggygria
Myrica cerifera
M. pensylvanica

Miscellaneous Fruits

Arctostaphylos manzanita
  (orange-brown)
A. stanfordiana (red-brown)
Clematis species (feathery)
Cornus hessei (bluish white)
Elaeagnus pungens (brown to red)
E. umbellata (silvery to red)
Fallugia paradoxa (feathery)
Kolkwitzia amabilis (brown)
Paliurus spina-christi
  (brownish yellow)
Viburnum setigerum aurantiacum
  (orange)
V. cassinoides (ripening green, red,
  black, often all colors in same
  berry cluster)
V. henryi
V. lantana
V. odoratissimum
V. rhytidophyllum roseum

39

FOLIAGE COLORS

ALTHOUGH the leaves of most woody plants are green, at least during the growing season, some plants have leaves which are differently colored. Such plants would be those with variegated foliage; those with permanently red or yellow foliage; or those with colored foliage for a short time in spring or fall. These groups of plants with more or less pronounced variations in foliage color, are the materials from which the knowing gardener can fashion colorfully-interesting gardens to be enjoyed every season of the year.

Leaves are green because they contain a complex material called chlorophyll. This is essential to the growth of all plants, except the saprophytes and a few parasites, for it is through the action of the chlorophyll that the plant can manufacture the food it requires from crude chemicals in the presence of light and heat. Chlorophyll is a highly complex chemical material being continually manufactured in the leaf and at the same time being continually destroyed. Ordinarily the rate of its breakdown about equals the rate of its manufacture.

There are two general groups of coloring pigments in the leaf with the chlorophyll. These are the carotins (yellow-coloring pigments) and anthocyanin or the red-coloring pigment, both usually omnipresent but masked by chlorophyll. In some plants this delicate balance is upset, and the yellows appear in various so-called "yellow-leaved" varieties. The red leaves of some of the Japanese maples afford an example of red-colored foliage. As the season progresses and more and more chlorophyll is manufactured, some of the plants that have colored foliage earlier in spring are capable of manufacturing sufficient chlorophyll to completely mask what was a good colored leaf. Schwedler's variety of the Norway Maple is an example of this. In the very early spring it is most conspicuous for its brilliantly red leaves, but as summer comes, the color gradually fades into a dull, reddish green which lasts until the advent of autumn coloration.

It is probable that variations in soil have some effect on leaf color. For instance, a heavy application of a nitrogenous fertilizer will make the leaves of many plants a good dark green. Plenty of moisture will also help. Soil acidity is another factor for, with a low pH, the leaves of some plants, like those of the Pin Oak, will become deficient in iron and become yellowish, a condition quickly eliminated by feeding the tree soluble ferrous sulphate salts. Consequently, there may be several reasons—physiological, physical and genetic—why the leaves of certain plants are not green at all times. Let us consider the interesting groups of plants with colored foliage, and if possible, make some new friends among them so that we can make our gardens more attractive by using them properly.

Good evergreens like the Japanese Andromeda (*Pieris japonica*) have lustrous green leaves throughout the entire year.

SPRING AND SUMMER COLOR

Some horticultural varieties of woody plants present brilliantly colored foliage in the early spring, and may have been given varietal names because of these characteristics. However, after a few weeks the foliage color gradually fades and by the end of June the leaves become a normal green. Such is the case with the common *Physocarpus opulifolius luteus*. On the other hand, some of the woody plants keep their foliage colors throughout the entire growing season, and such plants should be carefully noted. *Lonicera korolkovi* is one example, and *Berberis thunbergi atropurpurea* is another.

Because of their vari-colored foliage, some forms are actually deficient in chlorophyll and hence are sickly in growth and appearance, never developing into the good robust specimens we like to have in our gardens. These color forms should be used infrequently and only on special occasions where considerable thought has been given to their peculiar qualifications. Very few have been recommended in the following lists, although hundreds of species have variegated-leaved varieties.

Color notes have been made from observing the following varieties throughout the growing season in the Arnold Arboretum. In recording these observations, it has been found that many plants bearing the varietal names of *lutea* or *aurescens*, etc., actually do not deserve such names, since the foliage-color changes are so slight as to have no distinctive or ornamental value whatsoever. Sometimes only young plants will show variations in the foliage color and as they grow older, the foliage reverts to normal green. Such forms are not listed here.

I. Deciduous Shrubs Showing the First Foliage Colors in the Spring

The various colors of the new foliage of trees and shrubs are just as beautiful as are those of autumn foliage, only less vivid. Little attention is paid these early colors, possibly because they do not last very long, or because so much that is interesting happens in early spring that our attention is being called a hundred places at once. However, careful observation of early spring colors will repay the effort.

The following species and varieties show color by late April in the vicinity of Boston, Massachusetts, and most plants in this list gradually turn a normal green about June 1st, after which little variation in color can be noted. Only the first spring-foliage colors are reported here, for there are hundreds of trees and shrubs (the oaks, for example) the foliage of which does not appear until mid-May. Added to foliage colors are the hundreds of flower colors, the two combining to make early spring a galaxy of beauty.

The Norway Maple, for instance, is at first a clear yellow, because the yellow flowers appear before the leaves. As the flowers gradually fade, the green leaves appear and the general appearance of the tree changes completely from yellow to green. Such color changes are seen everywhere in spring. The following list should prove helpful to all who wish to anticipate the first foliage colors of early spring.

Abelia biflora	*Euonymus europaea*
Acanthopanax sieboldianus	*E. maacki*
Acer campestre	*E. sachalinensis*
A. palmatum and varieties	*E. sanguinea*
Amelanchier species	*Lonicera bella* and varieties
Artemesia sacrorum	*L. chrysantha*
Berberis gilgiana	*L. notha*
B. koreana	*L. ruprechtiana*
B. ottawensis	*L. tatarica* and varieties
B. thunbergi	*L. xylosteum*
Chaenomeles species and varieties	*Paeonia suffruticosa*
Cotoneaster divaricata	*Prinsepia* species
C. foevolata	*Ribes*—many species
C. lucida	*Rosa cinnamomea*
Deutzia glabrata	*Spiraea lucida*

II. Some Deciduous Shrubs with Leaves Variegated or Colored Throughout the Greater Part of the Growing Season

In the following list are some plants which have colored foliage (some color other than a medium or neutral green which makes the plant stand out from the surrounding background) throughout the growing season or a part of it. Plants appearing under a certain color heading have foliage of that color from the time the leaves first appear until the fall, unless another notation or date is indicated. "Normal by early July" means that the leaves of a particular plant turned a normal green in, or slightly before, early July. If no notes appear, the leaves remain colored throughout the season. Certain allowances must be made, however, for the color of the young foliage is considerably more brilliant than that of mature foliage. Thus in *Berberis thunbergi atropurpurea,* the leaves first appear as a vivid scarlet and gradually fade to red. Some plants listed as "blue-green" may border on "gray-green" or "purple-green."

It may be well to cite two examples of plants with colored foliage to show how widely this color can vary depending on soil nutrients. *Kerria japonica picta* normally has leaves with a light green leaf margin until July, after which time the leaf margin turns white. If a strong application of a nitrogenous fertilizer is given in June, the pale green margin may turn a deeper green and remain so throughout the season. On the other hand, if the plant is grown in very poor soil, the margin may first appear white and remain white throughout the season.

The second example is that of a golden-tipped form of *Tsuga canadensis* growing in Pennsylvania. It was noted by a keen-eyed nurseryman, and transplanted to his nearby nursery where the needles retained their conspicuously golden tips. Then it was taken to "Far Country" or Hemlock Arboretum, the estate of Mr. Charles F. Jenkins, in Germantown, Philadelphia, Pennsylvania. Mr. Jenkins gave it every care including good soil, with plenty of nitrogenous matter. The tips turned a normal green and the tree could not be distinguished from any other specimen of *Tsuga canadensis.* A soil examination was made and the results show that the differences in the soils between Germantown and the original habitat of the tree may have been responsible for this change in color.

With these examples in mind, it can be readily understood that plants may react differently under different conditions. The following notes taken in the Arnold Arboretum show the foliage colors and their changes during one growing season.

LIGHT GREEN

*Acanthopanax sieboldianus
Acer japonicum

A. japonicum aconitifolium*—reddish bronze, late July–late October
Ribes cereum

* Foliage turns a normal green by late June.

GRAY TO GRAY–GREEN

Amorpha canescens
Andromeda glaucophylla
A. polifolia
Artemesia species
Berberis dictyophylla
Elaeagnus angustifolia–gray
E. pungens–gray
E. umbellata
Hippophae rhamnoides
Holodiscus discolor ariaefolius–gray
Lavandula officinalis–gray
Lonicera korolkowi–blue-green

L. microphylla–blue-green
*L. praeflorens
Rosa fedtschenkoana–normal by middle
    of August
R. rubrifolia–blue-green
* R. rubrosa "Carmenetta"
Salix tristis–gray
Salvia officinalis
Shepherdia argentea
Sibiraea laevigata
Vitex agnus-castus
Zenobia pulverulenta

YELLOW TO YELLOW–GREEN

Acer japonicum aureum–normal by late
    July
Cornus alba rosenthali–turning pur-
    plish red early September
Hypericum dawsonianum–yellow-
    green
Lespedeza kiusiana–yellow-green
Ligustrum vicaryi
Lonicera japonica aureo-reticulata–yel-
    low leaves spotted green
Philadelphus coronarius aureus–yellow-
    green; greenish by middle August;
    green by early September
Physocarpus opulifolius luteus–brilliant
    yellow late April; yellow-green early
    June–early July (not outstanding);
    normal by late July
Pleioblastus distichus–foliage with

leaves of varying stripes of green
    from yellow to dark green
Ptelea trifoliata aurea–young foliage
    yellow; mature foliage yellowish
    green; not outstanding
Pterostyrax corymbosa–yellow-green
Stephanandra incisa–leaves vary from
    yellow-green to dark green
Syringa vulgaris aucubaefolia–varie-
    gated yellow
Viburnum opulus aureum–golden yel-
    low late April; yellow-green early
    June–early September
V. sargenti flavum–young leaves yel-
    low-green
* Weigela praecox variegata–varie-
    gated, dark green center, light green
    edge

RED TO REDDISH PURPLE

Acer palmatum atropurpureum
A. palmatum atropurpureum "Oshi
    Beni"–normal by late June
A. palmatum crispum–normal by mid-
    dle of August
A. palmatum hessei
A. palmatum ornatum–eventually turn-
    ing bronze-green
A. palmatum sanguineum–turning from
    a deep red to a bronze
A. palmatum versicolor–middle May–
    early June normal by late June with
    some foliage a "yellowish pink"

Berberis thunbergi atropurpurea
B. vulgaris atropurpurea–deep purple
    late April; reddish purple late May–
    late July; almost normal by middle
    August
*Prunus cistena
P. glandulosa rosea–red leaves streaked
    with some green
Weigela florida foliis-purpuriis–pur-
    plish green
W. maximowiczi–50 per cent of leaves
    red or reddish, remainder green

* Foliage turns a normal green by late June.

BRONZE

Acer palmatum—deep bronze early May; light bronze late May; green with slight reddish tinge middle June

*A. palmatum dissectum—bronze-green
*Viburnum opulus nanum—bronze to bronze-green

PURPLE

Corylus maxima purpurea—mixed light and dark bronze by middle June, old foliage normal by late July

Cotinus coggygria purpurea—normal by late July

GREEN WITH WHITE MARGIN

Acanthopanax sieboldianus variegatus—some green in leaves but mostly white and yellow early July; leaves pale yellow, blotched with green, middle August—middle September
Buxus sempervirens albo-marginata
Cornus alba argenteo-marginata
C. alba gouchaulti—margins blotched

white late June—blotched pink and white late July—middle September
Euonymus fortunei gracilis
E. fortunei "Silver Queen"
Kerria japonica picta—light green margin until late June; white margin late July—late October

GREEN WITH YELLOW MARGIN

Cornus alba spaethi—leaf margin blotched
C. mas elegantissima—early June—early September, leaves look sickly

Ligustrum ovalifolium aureo-marginatum
Weigela florida variegata—margin yellow green

GREEN WITH RED OR PINK MARGIN

Acer palmatum roseo-marginatum

VARIEGATED

Berberis thunbergi argenteo-variegata —25 per cent of leaves variegated white and pink
Lonicera tatarica fenzli—light and dark green variegated mottled late May—middle June, inconspicuous thereafter
40 Japanese Maple clons—various

shades of red and green, not listed here because of similarity or questionable names, mostly showing various shades of red but a normal green by late July
Many plants have variegated leaved varieties—too numerous to list here.

III. A Few Evergreens with Foliage Other Than Green During Spring and Summer

LIGHT GREEN

Chamaecyparis thyoides hoveyi—very light green, normal by late July
Taxus baccata variegata—young foliage

yellow-green, leaves with light green center and yellow margin; older leaves normal green

* Foliage turns a normal green by late June.

GRAY GREEN

Chamaecyparis pisifera squarrosa—
   gray-green to blue-green

Lavandula officinalis
Picea mariana doumeti

YELLOW

Chamaecyparis obtusa aurea
C. obtusa "gracilis aurea"
Taxus cuspidata aurescens

Thuja occidentalis ellwangeriana
T. orientalis decussata

YELLOW–GREEN

*Chamaecyparis pisifera aurea—*normal
   by early July
*C. pisifera "filifera aurea"—*normal by
   early July
*C. pisifera "lutescens nana"—*normal by
   early July
C. pisifera "nana aurea"
C. pisifera plumosa
C. pisifera "plumosa aureo-compacta"
C. pisifera "plumosa argentea"
C. pisifera "plumosa flavescens"
Juniperus chinensis aurea
*J. chinensis "Pfitzeriana aurea"—*normal
   by early July

J. chinensis "plumosa aurea"
*J. communis "aurea spica"—*normal by
   early July
*J. communis "depressa aurea"—*normal
   by early July
*Taxus baccata aurea—*normal by early
   July
*T. canadensis aurea—*young foliage tips
   yellowish green
Thuja occidentalis "robusta lutea"
T. occidentalis "Waxen"
*T. orientalis conspicua—*young foliage
   yellowish green

BLUE–GREEN

Abies fraseri prostrata
Chamaecyparis pisifera minima
C. obtusa ericoides
C. pisifera "squarrosa intermedia"
C. pisifera "squarrosa nana"
C. pisifera "squarrosa pygmaea"
C. thyoides glauca
Juniperus chinensis oblonga

J. chinensis reevesi
J. chinensis sylvestris
J. communis
J. glaucescens
J. recurva
J. squamata
J. squamata meyeri

VARIEGATED

Buxus sempervirens argenteo—variegata
B. sempervirens aureo-variegata
Daphne odora marginata
Elaeagnus pungens aurea
Euonymus japonicus (several varieties)
E. fortunei "Silver Queen"
Ligustrum (many species with varie-
   gated varieties)

Pieris japonica variegata
Pittosporum tobira variegata
Taxus baccata "fastigiata aurea"
Viburnum tinus variegatum
Vinca minor argenteo-variegata

AUTUMN COLOR

    The eastern United States is fortunately located in one of the few re-
gions of the world where brilliant autumn coloration of foliage prevails.

There is only one small region of autumn coloration in the southern hemisphere, and that in South America. In the northern hemisphere, there is a large section of eastern Asia, including central and northern Japan and a small part of southwestern Europe where brilliant fall coloration can be observed. In North America, the region characterized by brilliant autumn foliage extends from the Gulf of St. Lawrence to Florida and westward to

Fothergilla monticola—one of the very best of our native ornamental shrubs, of considerable interest in spring and brilliantly colorful in fall foliage.

the Great Plains, areas which have extensive deciduous forests and considerable rainfall. Here the general climatic conditions are often just what is needed to produce that lovely phenomenon of nature—the autumn coloration of deciduous foliage.

In North America the most brilliant displays of autumn color are of course in southeastern Canada, the northeastern United States and in certain other areas at higher altitudes. The farther south one goes, the less brilliant is the display, particularly in low areas along the seacoast. In the higher altitudes of the South, such as the Blue Ridge Mountains, the color is usually just as brilliant as in northeastern United States. Many places in western North America are likewise fortunate, with vivid autumn color, especially in the higher altitudes. Autumn color is excellent in the vicinity of Denver, Colorado, and east of the Cascade Mountains but less vivid in the vicinity of Seattle, Portland and San Francisco.

It is chiefly in areas of predominantly deciduous forests that autumn-color displays are best, and these areas occur chiefly in two general regions in the world. Plants growing in deciduous forests in tropical regions usually drop their leaves towards the end of the dry season. Since these leaves usually dry up before they fall (because of lack of water), they do not develop brilliant colors but usually turn brown and then fall off. In the case of plants growing in deciduous forests in temperate regions—especially in areas with ample rainfall equally distributed throughout the year—the leaves fall at the approach of cold weather, and because the plants have been well supplied with water, leaves of many trees change color before they fall. This gorgeous phenomenon in the woods and forests is what attracts our attention at this particular time each year.

In some years, the autumn color is much more pronounced than in others. There are always plants, the foliage of which turns yellow in the fall, but it is the brilliant reds and gorgeous scarlets which, in combination with the yellows, make autumn color of outstanding beauty. It is chiefly the reds and scarlets which are intensified by the right climatic conditions.

Why Leaves Are Yellow

A certain stage is reached where there is little if any chlorophyll manufactured. Most of the chlorophyll already made eventually is destroyed. This is the reason why leaves are yellow, for the two yellow pigments usually present, carotin and xanthophyll, are continually masked by the chlorophyll. When most of the chlorophyll is destroyed, these pigments become apparent. These same coloring materials are present in large quantities in egg yolk, carrots and in some yellow flowers.

When green plants are taken into dark places, such as a cellar, the leaves often turn yellow. Also, young shoots grown in the cellar are usually yellow. This is because chlorophyll is manufactured only in the presence of light. When light is absent, plants are unable to manufacture new chlorophyll and the yellow pigments become predominant as soon as the previously manufactured chlorophyll has been destroyed.

The gradual cessation of chlorophyll manufacture and the final breakdown of that previously made, completes the first stage in autumn coloration, and so certain plants become yellow. There are other plants—some magnolias for instance—the leaves of which do not turn yellow, but change from green directly to brown. For some reason, the breakdown of chlorophyll does not start soon enough or is not complete enough to result in the appearance of the yellow pigments. The yellow color appears in the foliage of many other plants regardless of the weather conditions. There is an interesting high degree of individuality in certain species. Red Maple, for instance, usually turns a good red in fall, but certain individuals may color yellow. The same can be said of sugar maples and several other plants. This is an interesting physiological problem worthy of considerable investigation.

Why Leaves Are Red

The gorgeous beauty of most autumn color combinations results from the brilliant reds and scarlets, together with the yellows. The sassafras, some of the maples, oaks, sumacs, sourwood, tupelo and other plants are particularly outstanding for their brilliant red autumn color, and the brilliance of their color apparently varies from year to year. The red in their leaves is

Virginia Rose (*Rosa virginiana*) with colorful flowers in June and bright orange and red foliage color in the fall. Incidentally this hedge can be cut to the ground with a mowing machine cutter-bar if it grows too tall, and will quickly recover in one season.

caused by a third pigment called anthocyanin, which results from the accumulation of sugars and tannins in the leaf. In some of the maples valued for their sugar production, it is probably the sugars which cause this red color. The oaks, however, probably owe their high autumn coloration to the presence of tannins.

Two factors are necessary in the production of red autumn color. The first is light. There must be warm, bright, sunny days in the fall, during which time the leaves naturally manufacture a great deal of sugar. Secondly, such days must be followed by cool nights, during which the temperature is below 45 degrees F. Plant physiologists have shown definitely that, under such conditions, there is little or no translocation of sugars and other materials from the leaf to other parts of the plant. In other words, when cool nights occur, following warm, bright, sunny days, sugars and other materials are "trapped" in the leaves. The accumulation of these products results in the manufacture of the red anthocyanin pigment.

The combination of these factors is well understood when one observes a certain tree that may be red only on that side exposed to the sun. Other leaves not directly in the sun's rays may be green or yellow. Leaves exposed to the sun have been able to manufacture more sugars which, when accumulated and "trapped" in the leaves by cold night temperatures, may result in the red color. It is interesting to note that trees and shrubs growing in swamps and other low places are often among the first to color in the fall, simply because it is in such places that cold air first settles on still nights.

With these points in mind, it can be seen easily why there is so much divergence of opinion about autumn color. When plants are located where they receive full sunlight, especially in late afternoons during early fall, they should be expected to show pronounced color if weather conditions have been favorable. On the other hand, if a plant grows in shade where it receives no direct sunlight, it cannot be expected to have marked red autumn color.

One species in the Arnold Arboretum annually demonstrates this point. There is a splendid plant of *Fothergilla monticola* exposed to full sunlight in the lowest spot in the Arboretum. In years when the climatic conditions have favored the formation of autumn color, this particular plant of *Fothergilla monticola* is a gorgeous red and yellow—on the western side. On the eastern side, where the foliage is shaded from the late afternoon sun, it is merely yellowish. Fortunately all plants do not show such great variation in autumn color when one side is compared with another, but it is a fact, that the western side usually has the deepest colored foliage when there has been plenty of sunshine. This point should be kept in mind in planting. Locations and plants should be selected that will show to best advantage during the period of autumn color.

Dull Autumn Coloration

A warm, cloudy fall, sometimes with much rain, will restrict the formation of bright colors. With insufficient sunlight, the sugar production is greatly reduced, and with warm nights, what little sugar has been manufactured in the leaves can be readily transported to the trunk and roots where it has no effect on the color of the foliage.

Some leaves of many evergreens change color in autumn. Certain junipers and arborvitaes are listed in the following groups. Some pine needles may turn yellow, but usually such color lasts only for a short time, the needles quickly turning brown. This is particularly true of those evergreen leaves which are normally shed each year, and although the autumn color may not be conspicuous in many evergreen plants, nevertheless it is evident on close examination.

All leaves eventually turn brown. This is not an autumn color, but merely the result of the death or decay of plant tissue. Sometimes, leaves turn brown while remaining on the tree, as in the American beech and some oaks. In other cases, like the sugar maple and spicebush, leaves drop while still brightly colored and turn brown afterwards.

Autumn color is, then, a physiological phenomenon which is very complex. There are plants the leaves of which will always turn yellow regardless of current climatic conditions, but many plants with red fall foliage will be striking in appearance only when warm, sunshiny days prevail, followed by nights with temperatures below 45 degrees F. The sugar formation in the leaf, the amount of sunshine received by the plants, and the temperature of the air are three variable factors which, to a large degree, control autumn coloration.

Shrubs Showing the First Autumn Color

Some species, a number of which are listed below, can be expected to change color earlier than the majority of other plants. It should be noted that the season, the situation in which a plant is growing, the amount of rainfall and its seasonal distribution, all combine to determine the actual dates on which fall color first is evident and that these dates vary from year to year. The following species are always the first to start the color procession, often before September 1st in the vicinity of Boston, Massachusetts.

Abeliophyllum distichum—yellow-green
Acanthopanax sessiliflorus—yellow-green
Aronia species and varieties—red and yellow
Berberis amurensis—deep red
B. bretschneideri—bright red
B. dasystachya—red
B. francisci-ferdinandi—bronze-green
B. purdomi—deep, reddish purple
B. thunbergi—yellow and red
B. thunbergi maximowiczi—bronze
Callicarpa dichotoma—yellow-green with little purple
Cornus alba—reddish purple
C. amomum—bronze-red
Dirca palustris—yellow-green
Euonymus alata—red
E. bungeana—some yellow and others red
E. europaea—reddish
E. sachalinensis—red

E. sanguinea—deep bronze
Hydrangea bretschneideri—yellow and brown
Lindera benzoin—yellow
Parthenocissus quinquefolia—red
Physocarpus bracteatus—brown with a little red
Prinsepia sinensis—bright yellow
Ribes aureum—red
R. odoratum aurantiacum—deep red
R. odoratum praecox—bright red
Rosa carolina—dark red
R. roxburghi and varieties—bronze
R. setigera—bronze-red
Securinega suffraticosa—yellow
Spiraea alba—yellow
S. salicifolia—bronze
Vaccinium angustifolium laevifolium—bronze-green and red
V. canadense—bronze-green and red
V. corymbosum—red
V. oldhami—deep red

Shrubs and Vines with Vivid Autumn Color

The following plants are listed according to their most conspicuous autumn color. As has been explained above, these may change from year to year, depending on climatic conditions. For instance, some years *Cladrastis lutea* will be yellow, other years the same trees will be purplish. The degree of color may also depend on soil conditions, it being a well-known fact that pin oaks, for instance, which have received heavy applications of nitrogenous fertilizers, will have a much deeper red color than those grown on poor soils without such fertilizers. With these qualifications in mind, the following lists are offered. Plants with an asterisk (*) usually show the best autumn color.

RED

*Acer ginnala
A. japonicum
A. palmatum
Aronia arbutifolia
A. melanocarpa
A. prunifolia
*Berberis, many species
*Cornus alba
C. mas
C. stolonifera
*Cotinus americanus
*C. coggygria
Cotoneaster divaricata
*Crataegus phaenopyrum
*Enkianthus campanulatus
*E. perulatus
*Euonymus alata
E. atropurpurea
E. europaea
E. obovata
*E. sachalinensis
E. sanguinea
*Fothergilla species—red and yellow
Franklinia alatamaha—red and yellow
Nemopanthus mucronatus
*Parthenocissus quinquefolia

*P. tricuspidata
Photinia villosa
Rhododendron calendulaceum
R. schlippenbachi
*R. vaseyi
*Rhus aromatica
*R. copallina—shining red
*R. glabra
*R. radicans—red and yellow
*R. typhina
R. verniciflua
Ribes aureum
R. hirtellum
R. odoratum
*Rosa rugosa—red and yellow
R. setigera
*R. virginiana—red and yellow
*Spiraea prunifolia—glossy red
Syringa oblata dilatata
*Vaccinium species
*Viburnum dentatum
*V. lantana—deep red
*V. prunifolium
*V. tomentosum—velvety, dull red
V. rafinesquianum affine

REDDISH TO REDDISH PURPLE

Abelia grandiflora
Berberis darwini
B. potanini
B. verruculosa
Cornus amomum
C. racemosa

Cotoneaster apiculata
C. horizontalis
Forsythia viridissima
*Gaultheria procumbens
*Gaylussacia brachycera
Ilex decidua

*Juniperus horizontalis plumosa
Leiophyllum buxifolium
*Leucothoe catesbaei
Ligustrum obtusifolium regelianum
*Mahonia aquifolium
*M. repens
Myrica pensylvanica—bronze
*Nandina domestica
*Pachistima canbyi
Physocarpus monogynus
Prunus alleghaniensis davisi
P. canescens
P. cyclamina
P. maritima

Rhododendron obtusum kaempferi
R. roseum
R. yedoense poukhanense
Rubus hispidus
Symphoricarpos chenaulti
*Thuja occidentalis ericoides—purple
T. plicata—bronze
*Viburnum acerifolium
V. carlesi
*V. dilatatum
*V. lentago
V. molle
V. rufidulum
Vitis coignetiae

YELLOW

Actinidia arguta
*Amelanchier species—yellow to red
Berchemia scandens
Callicarpa japonica
*Celastrus species
*Clethra acuminata
*C. alnifolia
Dirca palustris
*Hamamelis mollis

*H. vernalis
*H. virginiana
Hypericum species
Kerria japonica
*Lindera benzoin
Magnolia stellata—golden brown
Physocarpus opulifolius
Poncirus trifoliata
Prinsepia sinensis

NO AUTUMN COLOR

Akebia quinata
Baccharis halimifolia
Clematis, many species
Daphne mezereum
Elaeagnus angustifolia
Euonymus bungeana semipersistens
Hibiscus syriacus
Ligustrum vulgare

Lonicera fragrantissima
L. syringantha
L. thibetica
Lycium halimifolium
Polygonum auberti
Potentilla species
Vitex negundo

Deciduous Shrubs and Vines with Leaves Green Late in the Fall

Both the broad-leaved and narrow-leaved evergreens keep their green leaves in winter. However, the omnipresent question of latitude, and even altitude, enter the picture, for a plant which is an "evergreen" in the South may be decidedly deciduous in the North. Abelia grandiflora is just such a shrub. In the South it is evergreen, in New England it loses its leaves in winter. On the other hand, deciduous shrubs usually lose their leaves gradually in the fall. Only a few are like the Phellodendron species which hold their leaves intact until the first hard frost. The day after that occurs (usually a night temperature of 25 degrees F. is necessary) all the leaves quickly drop off the tree as soon as the sun strikes it. Some other plants which react similarly are *Celastrus flagellaris, Campsis* species and *Parthenocissus tricuspidata.*

There are some truly deciduous shrubs which hold their leaves late in fall and these should be noted in every garden for they aid the evergreens in holding off the dreary appearance of the leafless shrubs of winter. In northeastern United States some of the deciduous shrubs which hold their leaves longer than other plants (often until December) are:

Akebia quinata	*L. purpusi*
Baccharis halimifolia	*L. standishi*
Ceanothus americanus	*L. thibetica*
C. pallidus	*Lycium chinense*
Coronilla emerus	*Philadelphus splendens*
Cotoneaster glabrata	*Prinsepia* species
C. salicifolia	*Rhamnus frangula*
Cytisus albus	*R. leptophylla*
C. nigricans	*R. utilis*
C. purpureus	*Rosa longicuspis erecta*
C. sessilifolius	*R. luciae*
C. supinus	*R. serratipetala*
Dipelta floribunda	*R. watsonianae*
Euonymus bungeanus semipersistens	*Smilax hispida*
E. europaeus	*Sophora vicifolia*
E. fortunei vegeta	*Syringa vulgaris*
E. sanguinea	*Teucrium chamaedrys*
Fontanesia fortunei	*Viburnum buddleifolium*
Ilex decidua	*V. bitchuense*
Laburnum alpinum	*V. dentatum*
Ligustrum sinense	*V. erosum*
L. vulgare	*V. macrocephalum*
Lonicera affinis pubescens	*V. opulus nanum*
L. alseuosmoides	*V. rhytidophylloides*
L. fragrantissima	*V. sieboldi*
L. henryi	*V. veitchi*
L. japonica halliana	*Xanthorhiza simplicissima*
L. maacki podocarpa	*Zenobia pulverulenta*

WINTER FOLIAGE

The evergreens comprise a large group of serviceable plants, useful in the garden the entire year, particularly in winter because of their green foliage. Not all so-called evergreens remain a deep green in winter, however, especially in the North. Some of the varieties with colored foliage during the spring and summer turn a dirty brown in winter, as do some of the arborvitaes. Such plants should not be used in northern gardens if the main objective is to provide green winter foliage.

There are many trees and shrubs—well over 1500 different varieties—which can be considered evergreen in the South exclusive of sub-tropical areas. The farther North these plants are used, the fewer will be evergreen or remain in good condition through the winter. The first list includes some which have kept their foliage green on several occasions throughout New England's vigorous winters. The second and longer list includes some of the evergreen shrubs grown in North American gardens at the present time. This is not a complete list but includes many good plants which might be used within their limits of hardiness.

Japanese Yew (*Taxus cuspidata*) with brilliant red berries and excellent dark green foliage all winter, one of the best of the evergreens for northern planting.

Evergreens with the Best Green Winter Foliage in the North

Arctosaphylos uva-ursi
Buxus microphylla koreana
Chamaecyparis obtusa
C. pisifera

C. pisifera squarrosa
Chamaedaphne calyculata (bronze red)
Daphne cneorum
Euonymus fortunei colorata

E. fortunei minima
E. fortunei "Silver Queen" variegated foliage
Ilex crenata convexa
I. glabra
I. opaca
I. pedunculosa
I. rugosa
I. sugeroki
I. yunnanensis
Juniperus chinensis varieties
J. communis
J. communis hibernica
J. horizontalis varieties
J. procumbens
J. sabina tamaricifolia
J. squamata meyeri

J. virginiana varieties
Kalmia carolina
K. latifolia
Pachistima canbyi (dark reddish purple)
Pachysandra terminalis
Picea species
Pieris floribunda
P. japonica
Pinus species
Rhododendrons—many species
Taxus baccata repandens
T. cuspidata varieties
Thymus species
Tsuga species
Vinca species

Evergreen Shrubs

Many plants are "evergreen" in the deep South, but the farther North they are used the fewer the leaves which remain on them over winter. All in the following list can be used as evergreens within their hardiness limits in the South. Those marked with an asterisk (*) can be considered evergreen in the North.

Abelia grandiflora
A. floribunda
A. schumanni
Agave americana
Arbutus unedo
Ardisia crispa
Aucuba japonica
*Berberis gagnepaini
*B. julianae
*B. triacanthophora
*B. verruculosa
Buddleia asiatica
B. "Eva Dudley"
B. farquhari
B. officinalis
Buxus species and varieties
*Buxus microphylla koreana
*Chamaecyparis species
Callistemon lanceolatus
C. rigidus
Camellia japonica
C. sasanqua
Cotoneaster francheti
C. salicifolia floccosa

*Daphne cneorum
D. odora
Elaeagnus pungens
*Epigaea repens
Euonymus japonica
*E. fortunei varieties
E. kiautschovica
Fatsia japonica
Feijoa sellowiana
Gardenia jasminoides
*Gaultheria procumbens
*Gaylussacia brachycera
Hedera species
*Hedera helix
Hibiscus rosa-sinensis
Hypericum species
Ilex cassine
I. cornuta
*I. crenata
*I. glabra
*I. pedunculosa
I. pernyi
*I. yunnanensis
Jasminum species

Juniperus species
Kalmia latifolia
Lantana sellowiana
Laurus nobilis
Leucothoe species
Leucothoe catesbaei
Ligustrum amurense
L. coriaceum
L. japonicum
L. lucidum
L. nepalense
L. ovalifolium
L. quihoui
L. sinense
Lonicera etrusca
L. fragrantissima
L. japonica halliana
L. nitida
L. pileata
Loropetalum chinense
Magnolia virginiana
Mahonia aquifolium
Michelia fuscata
Myrica cerifera
M. carolinensis
Myrtus communis
Nandina domestica
Nerium oleander
Osmanthus americanus
Osmanthus fortunei
O. fragrans
Pachistima canbyi
Pachysandra terminalis
Pernettya mucronata
Picea species

Pieris floribunda
P. japonica
Pinus species
Pittosporum tobira
Plumbago capensis
Prunus laurocerasus
P. lusitanica
Pyracantha species
Raphiolepis umbellata
Rhododendron, many species evergreen
    in South
Rhododendron catawbiense
R. carolinianum
R. fortunei
R. laetevirens
R. maximum
R. obtusum
R. smirnowi
Rosa wichuraiana
Ruscus aculeatus
Salvia greggi
Santolina chamaecyparissus
Sarcocca hookeriana
Skimmia japonica
Taxus species
Teucrium chamaedrys
Thuja species
Tsuga species
Vaccinium vitis-idaea minus
Viburnum odoratissimum
V. suspensum
V. tinus
Vinca major
Vinca minor
Zenobia pulverulenta

SHRUBS FOR VARIOUS PURPOSES

IN planning a garden, one is frequently at a loss to think of more than two or three plants for a specific situation. The more difficult the growing conditions, or the more specific the requirements for the plants to fill the situation, the more difficult it becomes to think of a suitable number from which to make proper selections. The hasty gardener often feels that the path of least resistance is to select a few shrubs at random, and "try" them in the special situation. This may result successfully but it might save later disappointment if selections could be made from suggested lists of plants known to endure such specific conditions. Lists prove helpful to the experienced gardener as well as the amateur, since it is much easier to make an intelligent selection from a list of plants known to meet certain requirements, than to select unknown plants, more or less at random, without detailed information concerning their individual qualifications.

SUGGESTED LISTS

The following plants are grouped in various suggested lists. The careful gardener realizes that there are situations where it is difficult to force any plants to grow and that the first step in planting such garden spots is to try to overcome the conditions rather than select plants in the hope that they may succeed.

After considering the plants suggested in the following lists, the gardener will be much better prepared to make proper selections and to gauge the possibilities for success of other plants he may wish to add to the list as a result of his own experiences.

Shrubs for Shade

Very few shrubs require shaded conditions in which to grow, but some will withstand it. The deeper the shade, the more difficult to grow. Most plants will not flower and fruit nearly as well in shade as in full sunlight, and the deeper the shade the fewer the flowers produced. Included in the following list are those plants which actually require shaded conditions in order to grow well, together with others that will withstand shaded growing conditions better than most other plants.

Abelia grandiflora	*Alnus* species
Acanthopanax sieboldianus	*Amelanchier* species
Acer spicatum	*Andromeda polifolia*

Azaleas and rhododendrons all withstand shady conditions.

Ardisia crispa
Aronia species
Arundinaria japonica
Aucuba species
Berberis julianae
B. thunbergi
B. triacanthophora
B. verruculosa
Buxus species
Camellia japonica
Celastrus species
Cercis chinensis
Chamaecyparis species
Chimonanthus praecox
Chionanthus virginicus
Clethra alnifolia
Colutea species
Comptonia peregrina
Cornus alba
C. amomum
C. mas
C. racemosa
C. stolonifera varieties

Corylopsis species
Corylus species
Cotoneaster salicifolia floccosa
Daphne mezereum
Diervilla sessilifolia
Epigaea repens
Euonymus americana
E. fortunei and varieties
E. obovata
Fatsia japonica
Fothergilla species
Gaultheria procumbens
G. shallon
Gaylussacia brachycera
Hamamelis species
Hydrangea petiolaris
H. quercifolia
Hypericum calycinum
H. frondosum
H. prolificum
Ilex species
Illicium floridanum
Kalmia species

Laurus nobilis
Leiophyllum buxifolium
Leucothoe species
Ligustrum species
Lindera benzoin
Lonicera species
Lycium halimifolium
Lyonia mariana
Magnolia virginiana
Mahonia species
Michelia fuscata
Mitchella repens
Myrica species
Nandina domestica
Osmanthus species
Pachistima canbyi
Pachysandra terminalis
Parthenocissus quinquefolia
Philadelphus coronarius
Philesia magellanica
Photinia species
Pieris species
Pittisporum tobira
Potentilla fruticosa
Pyracantha species
Raphiolepis umbellata
Rhamnus species
Rhododendron species and varieties
Rhodotypos scandens

Rubus odoratus
Ruscus aculeatus
Sabal minor
Sambucus coerulea
S. pubens
Sarcococca ruscifolia
Severinia buxifolia
Skimmia japonica
Stachyurus praecox
Stephanandra incisa
Styrax species
Symphoricarpos species
Taxus species
Thuja species
Tsuga species
Vaccinium species
Viburnum acerifolium
V. alnifolium
V. cassinoides
V. dentatum
V. lentago
V. prunifolium
V. sieboldi
V. suspensum
V. tinus
Vinca minor
Xanthorhiza simplicissima
Zamia integrifolia
Zenobia pulverulenta

Shrubs for Moist to Wet Soils

It is usually advisable to drain wet spots, particularly those where water stands for any length of time. The following plants can withstand wet soil conditions better than most.

Alnus species
Amelanchier species
Andromeda species
Aronia arbutifolia
Calluna vulgaris
Calycanthus floridus
Cephalanthus occidentalis
Chamaedaphne calyculata
Clethra alnifolia
Comptonia peregrina
Cornus alba
C. amomum
C. sanguinea
C. stolonifera

Dirca palustris
Gaultheria veitchiana
Gaylussacia brachycera
Hippophae rhamnoides
Hypericum densiflorum
Ilex cassine
I. glabra
I. laevigata
I. verticillata
Itea virginica
Kalmia angustifolia
K. latifolia
Kalmiopsis leachiana
Ledum groenlandicum

Leiophyllum buxifolium
Leucothoe catesbaei
Lindera benzoin
Loiseleuria procumbens
Lyonia mariana
Magnolia virginiana
Myrica species
Polygonum vaccinifolium
Rhododendron arborescens
R. calendulaceum
R. canadense
R. nudiflorum
R. vaseyi
R. viscosum
Rosa palustris
Rubus odoratus
Sabal minor
Salix caprea

S. discolor
S. purpurea
S. repens
Sambucus canadensis varieties
S. pubens
Spiraea menziesi
S. salicifolia
S. tomentosa
Taxus canadensis
Thuja occidentalis varieties
Vaccinium species
Viburnum alnifolium
V. cassinoides
V. dentatum
V. opulus
V. trilobum
Zamia integrifolia
Zenobia pulverulenta

Shrubs for Dry and Sandy Soils

Very few shrubs require dry soil conditions. A greater variety of plants can be forced into growth if leaf mold or peat moss is mixed with a dry soil to increase its water-retaining properties. Mulches placed about the plants also aid in this respect. The following plants can withstand dry soil conditions better than most.

Acanthopanax species
Acer ginnala
Amorpha species
Arctostaphylos uva-ursi
Artemisia species
Atriplex species
Baccharis halimifolia
Berberis mentorensis
B. thunbergi
Buddleia alternifolia
Callistemon lanceolatus
Caragana species
Ceanothus americanus
C. thyrsiflorus
Chaenomeles lagenaria
Colutea species
Comptonia peregrina
Cornus racemosa
Cotinus coggygria
Cytisus species
Diervilla sessilifolia
Elaeagnus angustifolia
Epigaea repens

Euonymus japonica
Garrya species
Gaylussacia baccata
Genista species
Hamamelis virginiana
Hebe species
Heteromeles arbutifolia
Hypericum calycinum
H. prolificum
Indigofera species
Juniperus communis
J. conferta
J. horizontalis
J. virginiana varieties
Kolkwitzia amabilis
Lavandula species
Lespedeza bicolor
Leucothoe racemosa
Ligustrum species
Lycium species
Myrica species
Myrtus communis
Nerium oleander

Bearberry (*Arctostaphylus uva-ursi*) growing naturally on the sand dunes of Long Island, actually requires dry sandy soils.

Physocarpus species
Pittosporum species
Potentilla species
Prunus besseyi
P. maritima
Punica granatum
Raphiolepis umbellata
Rhamnus species
Rhus species
Ribes alpinum
Robinia hispida
Rosa caroliniana
R. rugosa
R. setigera
R. spinosissima

R. virginiana
Rosmarinus officinalis
Ruscus aculeatus
Salix tristis
Salvia greggi
Santolina chamaecyparissus
Shepherdia canadensis
Sophora secundiflora
S. viciifolia
Spartium junceum
Tamarix species
Vaccinium pallidum
Viburnum lentago
Vitex agnus-castus
Yucca species

Shrubs for Acid Soils

Many shrubs are tolerant of the acid soils which cover large areas of the country. Some, like those in the following list, *require* acid soil in order to grow well. It is useless to plant such shrubs in an alkaline soil unless precautions are taken to make it acid (see page 247). The following groups of plants normally grow well only in acid soils.

LEFT: The Carolina rhododendron (*R. carolinianum*).
RIGHT: The Korean rhododendron (*R. mucronulatum*).
Two serviceable shrubs for use in acid soils and partial shade.

Amelanchier species	*Juniperus communis* and varieties
Andromeda polifolia	*Kalmia* species
Arbutus unedo	*Kalmiopsis leachiana*
Calluna species	*Ledum groenlandicum*
Clethra species	*Leiophyllum buxifolium*
Cyrilla racemiflora	*Leucothoe* species
Cytisus species	*Loiseleuria procumbens*
Daboecia species	*Lyonia ligustrina*
Empetrum species	*Magnolia virginiana*
Enkianthus species	*Myrica* species, usually
Epigaea species	*Quercus ilicifolia*
Erica species	*Rhododendron* species
Eucryphia glutinosa	*Vaccinium* species
Fothergilla gardeni	*Viburnum alnifolium*
Gaultheria procumbens	*V. nudum*
Ilex species	*Xanthorhiza simplicissima*
Illicium floridanum	*Zenobia pulverulenta*
Itea virginica	

Shrubs and Vines for Seashore Planting

Many plants can be grown in gardens near the seashore, especially if the soil is good. As the soil becomes more sandy, and exposure more pronounced, fewer and fewer plants are able to withstand such conditions, year in and year out, without some injury. The following plants are well adapted for use in seashore gardens, in fact some withstand salt water spray. For really trying seashore conditions, this list of plants should be considered first before any other selections are made.

Ampelopsis quinquefolia
Arctostaphylos uva-ursi
Aronia arbutifolia
Atriplex species
Baccharis halimifolia
Calluna vulgaris
Carissa grandiflora
Celastrus species
Chamaecyparis pisifera
Clematis paniculata
Clethra acuminata
C. alnifolia
Comptonia peregrina
Cornus stolonifera
Cotoneaster species
Cytisus species
Elaeagnus species
Empetrum nigrum
Euonymus japonica
Halimodendron halodendron
Hibiscus syriacus
Hippophae rhamnoides
Hydrangea macrophylla
H. petiolaris
Ilex glabra
I. opaca
Juniperus communis
J. communis depressa
J. conferta
J. horizontalis
J. horizontalis plumosa
Lavandula species
Ligustrum amurense
L. ovalifolium
Lonicera japonica halliana
L. morrowi
L. tatarica
Lycium species

Myrica pensylvanica
Nerium oleander
Pinus mugo mughus
Pittosporum tobira
Potentilla species
Prunus maritima
Rhamnus species
Rhus species
Raphiolepis umbellata
Rosa blanda
R. eglanteria
R. multiflora
R. nitida
R. rugosa
R. spinosissima
R. virginiana
R. wichuraiana
Ruscus aculeatus
Salix humilis
S. repens
Sambucus canadensis
Schizophragma hydrangeoides
Severinia buxifolia
Shepherdia canadensis
Smilax species
Spiraea species
Suaeda fruticosa—brackish places
Syringa vulgaris
Tamarix species
Taxus cuspidata
Ulex europaeus
Vaccinium corymbosum
V. vitis-idaea minus
Viburnum cassinoides
V. dentatum
V. tinus
Wisteria sinensis
Yucca species

The Hardiest Shrubs

(Plants for gardens in the coldest areas of the United States and Canada)

ZONE 1
Diapensia lapponica
Salix uva-ursi

ZONE 2
Acer ginnala
A. spicatum
Alnus species
Amorpha canescens
Andromeda polifolia
Arctostaphylos uva-ursi
Artemisia frigida
A. stelleriana
Caragana arborescens
C. maximowicziana
Comptonia peregrina
Cornus alba sibirica
C. stolonifera
Elaeagnus angustifolia
Empetrum nigrum
Epigaea repens
Euonymus nana
Genista tinctoria
Halimodendron halodendron
Juniperus communis
J. horizontalis
J. virginiana tripartita
Kalmia angustifolia
Ledum groenlandicum
Loiseleuria procumbens
Lonicera maacki
Myrica pensylvanica
Physocarpus opulifolius
Picea abies varieties
Pinus mugo mughus
Potentilla fruticosa
Prunus cistena
P. japonica nakai
P. skinneri "Baton Rouge"
P. tenella
P. tomentosa
Rhamnus davurica
R. frangula
Rhus glabra
Ribes alpinum
Rosa amblyotis

R. rubrifolia
R. rugosa
Salix alba chermesina
S. lucida
S. tristis
Shepherdia canadensis
Symphoricarpos orbiculatus
Syringa henryi "Lutece"
S. josikaea
S. prestoniae varieties
S. villosa
Tamarix pentandra
Taxus canadensis
Thuja occidentalis
Vaccinium angustifolium laevifolium
Vaccinium vitis-idaea minus
Viburnum dentatum
Viburnum lentago
Viburnum trilobum

ZONE 3
Aralia elata
Caragana microphylla
Chamaecyparis obtusa
C. pisifera
Chrysothamnus graveolens
Clethra alnifolia
Corylus species
Cotoneaster racemiflora
Daphne giraldi
Elaeagnus umbellata
Erica tetralix
Euonymus alata
E. europaea aldenhamensis
Gaultheria procumbens
Hippophae rhamnoides
Ilex glabra
I. verticillata
Ligustrum amurense
L. obtusifolium
Lonicera spinosa alberti
L. tatarica
Mitchella repens
Pinus strobus varieties
Prunus besseyi
P. maritima

Rhus aromatica
R. typhina
Rosa canina
R. virginiana
Rubus odoratus
Sambucus canadensis varieties
Symphoricarpos albus laevigatus
Syringa josiflexa "Guinevere"
S. oblata dilatata

S. vulgaris
Vaccinium corymbosum
V. pallidum
Viburnum acerifolium
V. alnifolium
V. cassinoides
V. lantana
V. opulus
V. prunifolium

Shrubs and Vines Withstanding City Conditions

The city gardener must combat many trying conditions. Poor soil, insufficient light, insufficient water, excessive smoke and gas fumes in the air are only a few of the disadvantages. The more intense these become, the fewer the plants which can be grown. Evergreens, in particular, are difficult subjects for city gardening because of dust and soot which encrust the leaves and restrict the normal entrance of oxygen into the leaf. Serious damage also occurs from gases given off by automobiles, especially carbon monoxide. The following plants might well be considered first for city gardens, since they have been selected by plantsmen as among the best for withstanding city conditions.

Acanthopanax sieboldianus
Acer ginnala
Actinidia arguta
Aesculus parviflora
Amelanchier laevis
Amorpha fruticosa
Ampelopsis species
Aralia species
Aristolachia durior
Aronia arbutifolia
Berberis thunbergi
Campsis radicans
Caragana arborescens
Celastrus species
Chaenomeles japonica
Chionanthus virginica
Clematis paniculata
Cornus alba
C. amomum
C. mas
C. paniculata
C. sanguinea
C. stolonifera
Crataegus phaenopyrum
Deutzia scabra

Elaeagnus angustifolia
E. umbellata
Euonymus species
Fatsia japonica
Forsythia species
Hamamelis species
Hedera helix
Hibiscus syriacus
H. rosa-sinensis
Hippophae rhamnoides
Hydrangea species
Hypericum aureum
Ilex crenata
I. glabra
Juniperus chinensis pfitzeriana
Kerria japonica
Lagerstroemia indica
Leucothoe catesbaei
Ligustrum species
Lindera benzoin
Lonicera species
Lycium species
Mahonia aquifolium
Magnolia stellata
Malus species

Japanese Holly (*Ilex crenata*) is used in city gardens over a wide area. Evergreen Candytuft is here used as a facing. The dark evergreen leaves of both plants look very well against a red brick or white marble background.

Myrica pensylvanica
Pachysandra terminalis
Parthenocissus quinquefolia
Parthenocissus tricuspidata
Philadelphus coronarius
Physocarpus opulifolius
Pieris species
Pittisporum tobira
Polygonum species
Potentilla fruticosa
Prunus subhirtella
Pyracantha coccinea lalandi
Rhamnus species
Rhododendron obtusum amoenum
Rhodotypos scandens
Rhus species
Ribes alpinum
R. odoratum
Rosa multiflora
R. rugosa
R. wichuraiana

Sambucus canadensis
Sorbaria species
Spiraea bumalda
S. vanhouttei
Symphoricarpos species
Syringa amurensis japonica
S. prestoniae
S. vulgaris
Taxus baccata
T. cuspidata
Vaccinium corymbosum
Viburnum dentatum
V. lantana
V. lentago
V. macrocephalum sterile
V. opulus
V. tomentosum sterile
Vinca minor
Wisteria sinensis
Xanthorhiza simplicissima
Yucca filamentosa

Shrubs and Vines for Bank Planting

The chief objective in bank planting is to select shrubs or vines which will prevent soil erosion, usually accomplished by procumbent habit of growth, or vigorous growth, and especially by rapid underground elonga-

Sargent Juniper (*Juniperus chinensis sargenti*) does very well for covering a bank or a spot of dry, poor soil.

tion of roots or stolons. The following plants have all been used for this purpose under varying conditions. Soil, soil moisture, and the steepness of the bank in question, all govern the type of plant selected for a specific bank.

SHRUBS
Berberis thunbergi
Ceanothus americanus
Clethra alnifolia
Comptonia peregrina
Cornus alba
C. amomum
C. stolonifera
Cotoneaster horizontalis
Cytisus scoparius
Diervilla sessilifolia
Forsythia "Arnold Dwarf"
F. suspensa sieboldi

Hypericum buckleyi
H. calycinum
Indigofera kirilowi
Jasminum nudiflorum
Juniperus chinensis sargenti
J. horizontalis and varieties
Leucothoe catesbaei
Lycium halimifolium
Myrica species
Pachysandra terminalis
Physocarpus opulifolius
Rhus aromatica
R. copallina

Robinia hispida
R. kelseyi
Rosa "Max Graf"
R. multiflora
R. nitida
R. rugosa repens
R. setigera
R. virginiana
Salix tristis
Spiraea billiardi
S. salicifolia
Symphoricarpos species
Vaccinium angustifolium laevifolium
V. pallidum
Viburnum dentatum
V. lentago
V. trilobum
Vinca minor
Xanthorrhiza simplicissima

VINES

Akebia species
Arctostaphylos uva-ursi
Bignonia capreolata
Celastrus species
Clematis paniculata
C. vitalba
C. viticella
Euonymus fortunei vegeta
Hedera helix
Lonicera henryi
L. japonica halliana
Menispermum canadense
Parthenocissus henryana
P. quinquefolia
Pueraria thunbergiana
Rosa wichuraiana
Vitis species

Shrubs and Vines with Thorny Stems

(Chiefly of value as barrier plants)

Acanthopanax species
Aralia species
Berberis species
Carissa grandiflora
Celastrus flagellaris
Chaenomeles species
Elaeagnus species
Halimodendron halodendron
Hippophae rhamnoides
Lycium species

Paliurus spina-christi
Poncirus trifoliata
Prinsepia sinensis
Pyracantha species
Rhamnus cathartica
Robinia species
Rosa species
Severinia buxifolia
Smilax rotundifolia
Sophora viciifolia

Shrubs (and Trees) Used in Clipped Hedges

Almost any tree or shrub can be maintained in a hedge planting, providing the pruning is done frequently enough to keep the plants in hedge form. Some plants are more amenable to clipping in this fashion than others, and those in the following list are definitely among them. Shrubs frequently make better hedges than trees merely because they require less clipping. A few points are reviewed here to make hedge growing easy for those who have not done it before.

In the first place, since there are so many kinds of plant materials available for the purpose, it would behoove the gardener to decide just why he wants a hedge. Is a beautiful border-planting, or a definitely thorny barrier-planting, more to his purpose? How high will the hedge be allowed to grow and how wide? These are very important points to decide before the plant material is selected, since the proper material makes easier clipping later, and the proper situation can be selected more intelligently.

The exact location is important, for it is necessary to allow sufficient space for future growth in width as well as height. A hedge should always be wider at the base than at the top, to allow the lower branches plenty of

Part of the hedge demonstration plot at the Arnold Arboretum containing 115 different kinds of hedges.

light and air to develop properly. Privet and barberry hedges are so vigorous that they frequently are clipped in straight lines, but many another type of hedge plant can be grown if it is kept wider at the base than at the top.

Spacing is important. Many a hedge is started with plants only 18″ apart, but this depends on their size at the time of purchase. Evergreens might be spaced 3′ apart, or even wider, if a double row of plants is to be used. Pruning or clipping is best done just before the plants have completed their full growth in late spring, or in very early summer as far as the evergreens are concerned. If the plants have not reached the height and width at which they are to be permanently maintained, only a snipping of end shoots is necessary to make them more dense; but if the hedge is near its mature height, then it should be cut back heavily to within an inch or less of the previous year's growth. Every few years it may become necessary to cut back into the previous year's growth to keep the plants from becoming too large for the desired purpose. If deciduous hedges do become too large, they can be cut to within 6″ of the ground and started over again, since most of the deciduous hedge-plant materials can be treated in this manner and still be expected to recover satisfactorily. The best time to do this is in the very early spring before the leaf buds have opened. Such treatment will not prove successful if done too late in the growing season.

Evergreens do not respond to such vigorous treatment. It is essential that they be kept in good condition with branches close to the ground. Once

HEDGE SHAPES, GOOD AND BAD

The two hedge shapes on the left are good because the lower branches receive air and light, with the top narrower than the base. The hedge shape on the far right is bad because the lower branches are shaded by the top branches and may easily die, thus forming an undesirable open base that is practically impossible to change. The third hedge form from the left is poor for the same reason, although it must be admitted that many plants vigorous growing like the barberries and the privets, will form excellent hedges if clipped in this manner.

they are clipped too heavily or too narrow and lose some of their lower branches it is practically impossible to force them into properly shaped plants again.

Plants used in making hedges have been divided into the following twelve general groups for which each is suited. Some trees have been included in this list for, with continual shearing, they will remain shrublike in size and habit.

Plants used in hedge making have been divided into the following groups for which purposes they are best suited:

1. **Evergreen:** Plants in this group keep their leaves most of the winter in those regions where they are normally used.
2. **Dense:** Plants in this group grow dense foliage with a minimum amount of care. These naturally make the best hedges.
3. **Thorny:** Either stems or leaves thorny, making good barrier hedges.
4. **Low:** Can be grown as very low hedges with a minimum amount of clipping.
5. **Flowering:** Because of profuse flowers, these plants can be grown as informal flowering hedges, with trimming once a year (or even once every other year).
6. **Colored Fruits:** Trimming removes the majority of the flowers and fruits, yet the plants in this group have so many bright colored fruits

that, with the right trimming, some fruits will remain to give color and interest.

7. **For Poor Growing Conditions:** Some hedges must be planted where growing conditions are difficult and plants in this group may succeed where others would fail.

8. **Narrow, Columnar and Upright:** Naturally growing this way, not all make good hedges for the terminal growth is so strong that often it is difficult to force lateral branches at the ground level.

9. **For Trying Situations in the Midwest:** A special group found to be best suited to the extreme heat, cold and drought conditions of the Midwest.

10. **Windbreaks and Screens:** A special group of tall-growing vigorous plants, many of which are not suited for low, clipped hedges but which will grow rapidly into a windbreak or screen and can be kept clipped or unclipped.

11. **For the Coldest Parts of the United States and southern Canada:** These plants should be used in the coldest parts of the country where most of the other plants listed may be injured by the extreme cold.

12. **For Southern Gardens:** The farther south one goes, more kinds of plants can be used. Many not listed in this group will do very well in the South. Most of those in this group are not reliably hardy north of Philadelphia. (*Tsuga caroliniana* is an exception.)

Abelia grandiflora 5, 12
Abies concolor * 1, 2
Acanthopanax sieboldianus 2, 3, 7
Acer campestre 2
A. ginnala 2, 10
A. platanoides * 10
A. platanoides columnare * 8, 10
A. platanoides schwedleri * 10
A. rubrum columnare * 8, 10, 11
A. sacharum monumentale * 8, 10, 11
Aronia arbutifolia 6
Baccharis halimifolia 2, 7
Berberis buxifolia 1, 2, 3
B. buxifolia nana 1, 2, 3, 4
B. circumserrata 2, 3, 6
B. darwini 1, 13
B. gilgiana 2, 3, 6
B. julianae 1, 2, 3
B. koreana 2, 3, 6
B. mentorensis 2, 3, 6
B. stenophylla 1, 2, 3, 12
B. thunbergi 2, 3, 6, 7
B. thunbergi erecta 2, 3, 4, 6, 7, 8

B. thunbergi minor 2, 3, 4, 6, 7
B. triacanthophora 1, 3
B. verruculosa 1, 2, 3
Betula populifolia * 2
Buxus microphylla japonica 1, 2, 4
B. microphylla koreana 1, 2, 4
B. sempervirens and varieties 1, 2
B. sempervirens suffruticosa 1, 2, 4
Caragana arborescens 7, 9, 10, 11
Carpinus betulus * 2, 8, 10
Chaenomeles japonica 2, 3, 4, 5
C. lagenaria 2, 3, 5, 7
Chamaecyparis pisifera * and varieties 1, 2
Cornus alba 6, 11
C. mas 2, 6
C. racemosa 2, 6, 7
Cotoneaster lucida 4, 6
Crataegus crus-galli * 2, 3
C. oxyacantha * 2, 3
C. phaenopyrum * 2, 3, 6
Cryptomeria japonica lobbi * 1, 2, 8, 12
Cupressus sempervirens * 1, 2, 8, 12

* = Trees

Elaeagnus argentea 11
E. *angustifolia* 3, 7, 9
Euonymus alata 6
E. *alata compacta* 2, 4, 6
E. *fortunei radicans* 1, 4
E. *fortunei vegeta* 1, 4, 6
E. *japonica* 1, 2, 12
Fagus grandifolia * 2, 10
F. *sylvatica fastigiata* * 2, 8, 10
Feijoa sellowiana 1, 6, 12
Fraxinus pennsylvanica lanceolata * 11
Gleditsia triacanthos * 3
Hibiscus rosa-sinensis 1, 5, 12
H. *syriacus* 5
Hippophae rhamnoides 3, 6, 7
Hydrangea arborescens grandiflora 5
H. *macrophylla* 5, 12
Hypericum species 4, 5
Ilex aquifolium * 1, 3, 6, 12
I. *cornuta* 1, 3, 6, 12
I. *crenata* and varieties 1, 2, 12
I. *vomitoria* 2, 6, 12
Juniperus chinensis * and varieties
   1, 2, 6
J. *scopulorum* * and varieties
   1, 2, 6, 8, 10
J. *virginiana* * and varieties 1, 2, 6, 8,
   10, 11
Lagerstroemia indica 5, 12
Ligustrum amurense 2, 4, 5, 6, 7
L. *japonicum* 1, 2, 4, 6, 7, 12
L. *lucidum* 1, 2, 4, 6, 12
L. *obtusifolium regelianum* 2, 4, 5, 6
L. *ovalifolium* 2, 4, 5, 6, 7, 12
Lonicera fragrantissima 2, 6
L. *maacki* 2, 6
L. *maacki podocarpa* 2, 6, 10
L. *nitida* 2, 4, 12
L. *tatarica* 2, 5, 6, 7, 9
Maclura pomifera 2, 3, 7, 9, 10
Mahonia aquifolium 1, 3, 5, 6
Michelia fuscata 1, 6, 12
Morus alba * 10, 12
Myrica cerifera 1, 6, 12
Myrtus communis 1, 2, 5, 12
Nandina domestica 1, 5, 6, 12
Nerium oleander 1, 5, 12
Osmanthus ilicifolius 1, 5, 12

   * = Trees

Pernettya mucronata 1, 2, 4, 12
Philadelphus coronarius 5, 7
P. *lemoinei* "Avalanche" 2, 5
P. *lemoinei erectus* 2, 5, 6
Physocarpus intermedius parvifolius
   2, 9
P. *opulifolius* and varieties 7, 11
P. *opulifolius nanus* 2, 4, 7, 11
Picea abies * 1, 2, 10
P. *glauca* * 1, 2, 9, 10, 11
P. *glauca conica* 1, 2, 4
P. *omorika* * 1, 2, 10
P. *orientalis* * 1, 2
P. *pungens* and varieties * 1, 2, 9, 11
Pinus nigra * 1
P. *resinosa* * 1, 10, 11
P. *strobus* * 1, 2, 10
Pittosporum tobira 1, 2, 12
Plumbago capensis 1, 12
Poncirus trifoliata 3, 7, 12
Populus alba * 7, 9, 10, 11
P. *alba pyramidalis* * 7, 8, 9, 11
P. *berolinensis* * 10, 11
P. *laurifolia* * 10
P. *nigra italica* * 7, 8, 9, 10, 11
P. *simoni* * 7, 9, 10, 11
P. *tremuloides* * 10, 11
Prinsepia sinensis 2, 3, 11
Prunus laurocerasus and varieties 1, 2,
   10, 12
P. *lusitanica* 12
Pseudotsuga taxifolia * 1, 2, 9, 10
Pyracantha coccinea lalandi
   2, 3, 5, 6, 12
Quercus ilex * 1, 2, 10, 12
Q. *imbricaria* * 2, 10
Q. *macrocarpa* * 11
Q. *palustris* * 10
Q. *phellos* * 2, 10
Q. *robur fastigiata* * 8, 10
Q. *virginiana* * 1, 2, 10, 12
Raphiolepsis umbellata 1, 12
Rhamnus frangula 2, 6, 10, 11
Rhododendron obtusum amoenum
   1, 4, 5
Ribes alpinum (staminate form) 2, 4,
   9, 11
Rosa multiflora 2, 3, 5, 6

There is no hedge which surpasses the Japanese Yew, in usefulness and beauty the entire year.

R. rugosa 2, 3, 5, 6, 11
R. setigera 3, 5, 6
R. virginiana 3, 5, 6, 11
Salix alba * 11
Severinea buxifolia 1, 12
Spiraea arguta 5
S. prunifolia plena 5
S. thunbergi 5
S. vanhouttei 2, 5
Syringa chinensis 5
S. josikaea 2, 5, 10, 11
S. persica 5, 9
S. villosa 2, 5, 10, 11
S. vulgaris 5, 9, 10, 11
Tamarix odessana 5, 12
T. parviflora 5, 12
T. pentandra 5, 12
Taxus baccata and varieties 1, 2, 6, 12
T. baccata erecta 1, 2, 6, 8, 12
T. baccata fastigiata 1, 2, 6, 8, 12
T. baccata repandens 1, 2, 4, 6

T. canadensis stricta 1, 4, 6
T. cuspidata 1, 2, 4, 6, 8
T. cuspidata nana 1, 2, 4, 6
T. media hicksi 1, 2, 4, 6, 8
Thuja occidentalis * 1, 2, 8, 10
T. occidentalis "douglasi pyramidalis" 1, 2, 8, 10
T. occidentalis "Little Gem" 1, 2, 4
T. occidentalis robusta 1, 2, 10
T. orientalis * and varieties 1, 2, 10, 12
Tilia cordata * 10
Tsuga canadensis * 1, 2, 10
T. caroliniana * 1, 2, 10, 12
Ulmus pumila * 2, 7, 9, 10, 11
Viburnum dentatum 6
V. lantana 2, 6
V. lentago 2, 6, 11
V. opulus nanum 2, 4
V. prunifolium 1, 2, 6, 10
V. tinus 1, 12

* = Trees

Shrubs for Screens and Windbreaks

Best plants for this purpose are the evergreen trees like pines and hemlocks. Less expensive and faster-growing screens can be made from the following shrubs but, to be effective, these plants must be placed fairly close together, often in a double row. Such deciduous screens can be used temporarily until slower-growing evergreen trees have sufficient time to become serviceable, then deciduous plants can be removed.

Acer ginnala
Buxus sempervirens
Caragana arborescens
Cornus mas
Elaeagnus angustifolia *Rum. olive*
Euonymus bungeana sempersistens
E. europaea
E. yedoensis
Hamamelis vernalis
Kolkwitzia amabilis
Lagerstroemia indica
Laurus nobilis
Ligustrum species
Lonicera bella
L. maacki podocarpa
L. tatarica
Magnolia stellata
Philadelphus coronarius
P. grandiflorus
P. monstrosus
P. pubescens
Photinia species

Physocarpus opulifolius
Prinsepia sinensis
Prunus laurocerasus
Rhamnus frangula
Spiraea veitchi
Symplocos paniculata
Syringa amurensis japonica
S. henryi
S. josikaea
S. prestoniae
S. villosa
S. vulgaris
Thuja occidentalis
T. orientalis
Vaccinium arboreum
Viburnum dentatum
V. lantana
V. lentago
V. prunifolium
V. rufidulum
V. sieboldi

Plants Useful as Ground Covers

Typical ground covers are low, dense and rapid in growth. Some do better in shade than others. There are certain conditions, especially under such trees as the Norway Maple and the Beech where it is practically impossible to force any ground cover to grow because the feeding roots of these trees are close to the surface of the soil, and quickly take most of the nourishment and moisture from it. When such situations are encountered it may save time and expense to refrain from planting ground covers. Let such areas of ground remain bare or cover them with pebbles or paving stones.

Akebia quinata
Ampelopsis arborea
Arctostaphylos uva-ursi
Aronia melanocarpa
Calluna vulgaris

Celastrus species
Chaenomeles japonica alpina
Cornus stolonifera
Cotoneaster dammeri
C. horizontalis

Canby Pachistima (*Pachistima canbyi*) a native of western North America makes a dense evergreen ground cover, with a bronze autumn color.

Cytisus purpureus
Daphne mezereum
Diervilla sessilifolia
Euonymus fortunei
E. fortunei carrieri
E. fortunei colorata
E. fortunei minima
E. fortunei "Silver Queen"
E. obovata
Forsythia "Arnold Dwarf"
Gaultheria procumbens
Gaylussacia brachycera
Hedera helix
Hydrangea petiolaris
Hypericum buckleyi
H. calycinum
Indigofera kirilowi
Jasminum species
Juniperus chinensis sargenti
J. horizontalis
J. sabina tamariscifolia
Kalmia angustifolia

Leiophyllum species
Lonicera henryi
L. japonica halliana
Lycium halimifolium
Mahonia repens
Menispermum canadense
Mitchella repens
Muehlenbeckia complexa
Myrica pensylvanica
Pachistima canbyi
Pachysandra terminalis
Parthenocissus henryana
P. quinquefolia
Phlox subulata
Polygonum vaccinifolium
Pueraria thunbergiana
Rhus aromatica
Rosa "Max Graf"
R. wichuraiana
Salix tristis
Sasa pumila
S. variegata

S. veitchi

Symphoricarpos orbiculatus

Teucrium chamaedrys

Thymus species

Vaccinium angustifolium laevifolium

Vinca major

V. minor

Xanthorrhiza simplicissima

Shrubs of Different Heights

A quick reference is frequently needed to locate a shrub—any shrub—which will grow just so high and fill an important place in the garden. Most shrubs can be restrained at lower heights than they normally grow by continual pruning, but the following lists should prove helpful when plants are to be quickly located which grow normally at certain heights without such pruning.

DWARF SHRUBS THREE FEET OR LESS

Andromeda polifolia

Ardisia crispa

Aronia melanocarpa

Artemisia frigida

A. stelleriana

Berberis buxifolia nana

B. candidula

B. concinna

Bruckenthalia spiculifolia

Buxus microphylla compacta

B. sempervirens suffruticosa

Calluna vulgaris

Ceanothus americanus

C. ovatus

Chaenomeles japonica

Cotoneaster dammeri

C. horizontalis

C. microphylla

Cytisus albus

C. beani

C. kewensis

C. nigricans

C. purgans

C. purpureus

Daboecia cantabrica

Danae racemosa

Daphne cneorum

D. giraldi

Empetrum nigrum

Erica species

Euonymus nana

Forsythia "Arnold Dwarf"

Fothergilla gardeni

Fuchsia magellanica

Gaultheria miqueliana

G. procumbens

G. veitchiana

Gaylussacia brachycera

Genista cinerea

G. hispanica

G. pilosa

G. tinctoria

Hydrangea arborescens grandiflora

Hypericum frondosum

H. kalmianum

H. moserianum

H. patulum henryi

H. prolificum

Ilex crenata helleri

I. crenata "Kingsville"

Indigofera potanini

Juniperus chinensis sargenti

J. conferta

J. horizontalis

Kalmia angustifolia

Kalmiopsis leachiana

Lavandula officinalis

Ledum groenlandicum

Leiophyllum buxifolium

Loiseleuria procumbens

Lonicera alpigena nana

Mahonia aquifolium

M. repens

Moltkia petraea

Neviusia alabamensis

Pachistima canbyi

Pernettya mucronata

Philesia magellanica

Phoradendron flavescens

Picea abies varieties

Pinus mugho pumilio

Rhododendron **atlanticum**
R. *canadense*
R. *obtusum*
R. *racemosum*
Rhus aromatica
Robinia hispida
Rosa carolina
R. *chinensis minima*
R. *pendulina*
R. *spinosissima*
R. *wichuraiana*
Ruscus aculeatus
Sabal minor
Salix repens
S. *tristis*
Salvia greggi
Santolina chamaecyparissus
Serenoa repens
Skimmia reevesiana
Sophora secundiflora
Spiraea albiflora
S. *bumalda* "Anthony Waterer"
S. *cantoniensis*
S. *decumbens*
S. *superba*
S. *tomentosa*
Suaeda fruticosa
Symphoricarpus chenaulti
S. *orbiculatus*
Teucrium chamaedrys
Thuja occidentalis globosa
T. *occidentalis* "Little Gem"
Vaccinium angustifolium laevifolium
V. *pallidum*
Viburnum opulus nanum
Xanthorhiza simplicissima
Zamia integrifolia

SHRUBS 4–5 FEET
Abelia "Edward Goucher"
A. *grandiflora*
A. *schumanni*
Abeliophyllum distichum
Amorpha canescens
Artemisia abrotanum
A. *absinthium*
Atriplex species

Berberis triacanthophora
B. *verruculosa*
Buxus microphylla
Callicarpa japonica
Caragana maximowicziana
Caryopteris clandonensis
Ceratostigma willmottianum
Chamaecyparis obtusa
Chrysothamnus graveolens
Comptonia peregrina
Cytisus hybrids
Daphne odora
Deutzia gracilis
Diervilla sessilifolia
Elsholtzia stauntoni
Erica mediterranea
Fallugia paradoxa
Forsythia suspensa sieboldi
Gardenia jasminoides
Gaultheria shallon
Hebe buxifolia
Juniperus virginiana tripartita
Kerria japonica
Leucothoe keiskei
Lonicera pileata
L. *saccata*
L. *spinosa alberti*
L. *thibetica*
Paeonia suffruticosa
Philadelphus lemoinei
P. **purpureo-maculatus** "Sirene"
P. *virginalis*
Physocarpus intermedius parvifolius
Potentilla fruticosa
Prunus glandulosa
P. *japonica nakai*
P. *tenella alba*
Rosa amblyotis
R. *arnoldiana*
R. *gallica*
Skimmia japonica
Sophora secundiflora
Spiraea arguta
S. *japonica atrosanguinea*
S. *margaritae*
S. *salicifolia*
S. *thunbergi*
Symphoricarpos orbiculatus

Taxus canadensis
Viburnum carlesi
Weigela "Bristol Ruby"
W. maximowiczi

SHRUBS 6–9 FEET

Abelia floribunda
Acanthopanax sieboldianus
Arctostaphylos stanfordiana
Aronia arbutifolia
Artemisia tridentata
Berberis beaniana
B. circumserrata
B. gagnepaini
B. gilgiana
B. julianae
B. koreana
B. mentorensis
B. potanini
B. stenophylla
B. thunbergi
Calycanthus floridus
Caragana microphylla
Carpenteria californica
Ceanothus delilianus
Chaenomeles lagenaria
Chimonanthus praecox
Choisya ternata
Cistus albidus
C. cyprius
C. laurifolius
Clethra alnifolia
Cornus alba sibirica
C. amomum
C. paucinervis
C. stolonifera
Corylopsis spicata
Cotoneaster divaricata
C. foeolata
C. harroviana
C. lucida
C. pannosa
C. racemiflora soongorica
Cytisus dallimorei
C. multiflorus
C. praecox
C. scoparius
Deutzia candelabrum

D. grandiflora
D. hybrida "Contraste"
D. lemoinei
D. magnifica
D. parviflora
D. rosea eximea
D. scabra candidissima
Disanthus cercidifolius
Elaeagnus multiflora
Enkianthus perulatus
Euonymus alata
E. americana
E. kiautschovica
Fatshedera lizei
Fendlera rupicola
Forsythia intermedia spectabilis
F. ovata
F. viridissima koreana
Fothergilla major
Franklinia alatamaha
Garrya elliptica
G. wrighti
Halimodendron halodendron
Hebe traversi
Heteromeles arbutifolia
Hydrangea quercifolia
H. sargentiana
Hypericum hookerianum
Ilex laevigata
I. verticillata
Illicium floridanum
Indigofera amblyantha
Juniperus squamata meyeri
Lespedeza bicolor
L. japonica
Leucothoe catesbaei
Leycesteria formosa
Ligustrum obtusifolium
L. quihoui
Loiseleuria procumbens
Lonicera amoena arnoldiana
L. bella varieties
L. deflexicalyx
L. fragrantissima
L. gracilipes
L. gynochlamydea
L. morrowi
L. nitida

L. quinquelocularis
L. syringantha
L. tatarica
L. tatsienensis
Lyonia mariana
Magnolia liliflora nigra
Malus sargenti
Myrica pensylvanica
Myrtus communis
Nandina domestica
Olearia haasti
Philadelphus "Coles Glorious"
P. coronarius
P. cymosus
P. floridus
P. grandiflorus
P. incanus
P. inodorus
P. laxus
P. pubescens
P. schrenki jacki
P. splendens
Phillyrea decora
Physocarpus opulifolius
Pieris floribunda
P. japonica
P. taiwanensis
Pinus mugho mughus
P. strobus nana
Prunus besseyi
P. cistena
P. maritima
P. skinneri "Baton Rouge"
P. tomentosa
Pyracantha coccinea
Raphiolepis umbellata
Rhodotypos scandens
Ribes alpinum
R. odoratum
Robinia kelseyi
Rosa alba incarnata
R. canina
R. centifolia
R. coriifolia froebeli
R. damascena
R. eglanteria
R. foetida
R. harisoni
R. hugonis

R. moyesi
R. palustris
R. primula
R. roxburghi
R. rubrifolia
R. rugosa
R. virginiana
R. webbiana
R. xanthina
Rosmarinus officinalis
Rubus deliciosus
R. odoratus
Salix purpurea
Sarcococca ruscifolia
Severinia buxifolia
Shepherdia canadensis
Siphonosmanthus delavayi
Sophora viciifolia
Sorbaria aitchisoni
Spiraea billiardi
S. brachybotrys
S. canescens
S. nipponica rotundifolia
S. prunifolia plena
S. vanhouttei
S. wilsoni
Stephanandra incisa
Symphoricarpos albus
Syringa josiflexa "Guinevere"
S. laciniata
S. microphylla
S. persica
S. prestoniae varieties
S. sweginzowi
S. villosa
Tamarix odessana
Tripetaleia paniculata
Viburnum acerifolium
V. burkwoodi
V. cassinoides
V. dilatatum
V. fragrans
V. henryi
V. japonicum
V. rhytidophyllum roseum
V. suspensum
V. tomentosum mariesi
Vitex agnus-castus
Weigela florida alba

W. praecox
W. "Richesse"
Zenobia pulverulenta

SHRUBS 10–15 FEET
Acacia farnesiana
Aesculus parviflora
A. splendens
Arctostaphylos manzanita
Aronia prunifolia
Aucuba japonica
Baccharis halimifolia
Berberis darwini
Buddleia alternifolia
B. davidi
Cassia corymbosa
Colutea arborescens
Cornus racemosa
Corylopsis griffithi
Cotoneaster francheti
C. henryana
C. salicifolia floccosa
C. simonsi
Cycas revoluta
Elaeagnus pungens
E. umbellata
Eucryphia glutinosa
Fatsia japonica
Hamamelis vernalis
Holodiscus discolor ariaefolius
Hydrangea macrophylla hortensia
Ilex yunnanensis
Jasminum nudiflorum
J. mesnyi
Juniperus chinensis pfitzeriana
J. sabina
Kolkwitzia amabilis
Lespedeza cyrtobotrya
Leucothoe racemosa
Ligustrum amurense
L. henryi
L. ibolium
L. japonicum
L. ovalifolium
L. sinense
L. vicaryi
L. vulgare
Lindera benzoin
Lonicera korolkowi

L. ledebouri
L. maacki
Loropetalum chinense
Mahonia beali
Michelia fuscata
Osmanthus fortunei
Philadelphus monstrosus
P. purpurascens
Pieris formosa
Pittisporum tobira
Pinus densiflora umbraculifera
Prinsepia sinensis
Prunus triloba multiplex
Punica granatum
Pyracantha crenulata rogersiana
P. "Oxford"
Ribes sanguineum
Rosa chinensis minima
R. l'heritierana
R. multiflora
R. omeiensis
Sambucus canadensis
S. pubens
S. racemosa
Spartium junceum
Spiraea veitchi
Stachyurus praecox
Styrax wilsoni
Syringa henryi "Lutece"
S. josikaea
S. oblata dilatata
Tamarix parviflora
T. pentandra
Vaccinium corymbosum
V. ovatum
Viburnum alnifolium
V. lantana
V. macrocephalum sterile
V. nudum
V. odoratissimum
V. opulus
V. prunifolium
V. sargenti flavum
V. setigerum aurantiacum
V. tinus
V. trilobum
Vitex negundo incisa
Weigela "Conquerant"
W. "Dame Blanche"

W. "Esperance"
W. "Gracieux"
W. "Gratissima"
W. "Lavallei"
W. "Seduction"

TREES AND SHRUBS 15 FEET OR MORE
Acer campestre
A. circinatum
A. ginnala
A. palmatum
A. spicatum
Alnus species
Amelanchier grandiflora
Aralia elata
Arbutus unedo
Buxus sempervirens
Callistemon lanceolatus
Camellia japonica
Caragana arborescens
Carissa grandiflora
Ceanothus thyrsiflorus
Cephalanthus occidentalis
Cercis chinensis
Chamaecyparis obtusa
C. pisifera
Chilopsis linearis
Chionanthus virginicus
Clerodendron trichotomum
Clethra acuminata
C. barbinervis
Cornus mas
C. officinalis
Corylopsis glabrescens
Corylus species and varieties
Cotinus americanus
C. coggygria
Cotoneaster frigida
Cudrania tricuspidata
Cyrilla racemiflora
Eleagnus angustifolia
Enkianthus campanulatus
E. deflexus
Euonymus bungeana
E. europaea
E. japonica
E. latifolia
E. sanguinea
E. yedoensis

Eurya japonica
Exochorda giraldi wilsoni
Feijoa sellowiana
Ficus carica
Franklinia alatamaha
Hamamelis mollis
H. virginiana
Hibiscus rosa-sinensis
H. syriacus
Hippophae rhamnoides
Hydrangea paniculata grandiflora
Ilex cassine
I. cornuta
I. crenata
I. decidua
I. glabra
I. pedunculosa
I. pernyi
Jasminum officinale
Juniperus chinensis pyramidalis
J. communis
Kalmia latifolia
Lagerstroemia indica
Laurus nobilis
Ligustrum lucidum
Magnolia stellata
M. virginiana
M. wilsoni
Myrica californica
M. cerifera
Nerium oleander
Nothopanax davidi
Osmanthus ilicifolius
Paliurus spina-christi
Photinia serrulata
P. villosa
Pinus strobus varieties
Prunus laurocerasus
P. lusitanica
Poncirus trifoliata
Pyracantha atlantioides
Rhamnus davurica
R. frangula
Rhus chinensis
R. copallina
R. glabra
R. typhina
Rosa helenae
R. odorata

R. setigera
Salix alba chermesina
S. caprea
S. lucida
Sambucus coerulea
Sorbaria arborea
Stewartia malacodendron
S. ovata grandiflora
S. pseudo-camellia
Styrax japonica
Symplocos paniculata
Syringa amurensis japonica
S. chinensis
S. vulgaris

Taxus baccata
T. cuspidata
T. media
Thuja occidentalis
T. orientalis
Tsuga canadensis
Vaccinium arboreum
Viburnum dentatum
V. lentago
V. rufidulum
V. sieboldi
Weigela japonica sinica
Xanthoceras sorbifolium

Shrubs and Vines with Fragrant Flowers

Abelia grandiflora
Actinidia chinensis
A. polygama
Artemisia species
Calycanthus floridus
Carissa grandiflora
Carpenteria californica
Ceanothus americanus
Cephalanthus occidentalis
Chilopsis linearis
Chimonanthus praecox
Chionanthus virginicus
Choisya ternata
Clematis paniculata
C. vitalba
Clethra alnifolia
Daphne species
Deutzia gracilis
Elaeagnus species
Epigaea repens
Fothergilla species
Gardenia jasminoides
Genista hispida
Halimodendron halodendron
Hamamelis mollis
H. vernalis
Jasminum officinale
Kalmia latifolia
Lavandula officinalis
Lonicera—many species
Magnolia stellata
M. virginiana
Mandevilla suaveolens

Osmanthus ilicifolius
Philadelphus "Cole's Glorius"
P. coronarius
P. cymosus "Perle Blanche"
P. cymosus "Conquete"
P. lemoinei "Avalanche"
P. lemoinei erectus
P. virginalis "Virginal"
Pittosporum tobira
Raphiolepis umbellata
Rhododendron—many species
Ribes aureum
R. odoratum
Rosa—most species
Rubus odoratus
Skimmia japonica
Siphonosmanthus delavayi
Sophora secundiflora
Spartium junceum
Styrax japonica
Symplocos paniculata
Syringa vulgaris
Trachelospermum species
Ulex europaeus
Viburnum burkwoodi
V. carlesi
V. fragrans
V. japonicum
V. odoratissimum
V. suspensum
Vitex agnus-castus
Wisteria sinensis

Shrubs with Fragrant Leaves

Artemisia species

Buxus species, especially *B. semper-virens suffruticosa*

Calycanthus species

Choisya ternata

Comptonia peregrina

Hypericum calycinum

Laurus nobilis

Lavandula officinalis

Lindera benzoin

Gaultheria procumbens

Juniperus species

Myrica species

Myrtus communis

Orixa japonica

Perowskia atriplicifolia

Rhus aromatica

R. canadensis

R. trilobata

Rosa eglanteria

Santolina chamaecyparissus

Teucrium chamaedrys

Viburnum sieboldi

Vitex agnus-castus

Woody Plants with Interesting Bark in Winter

The color and general characteristics of a tree's bark come with old age, and mature trees are valued specifically for these characteristics. However, shrubs with colored twigs frequently can be forced to grow brighter-colored twigs for winter display if a few simple maintenance items are practiced.

Cornus alba, the Tatarian dogwood, is known to have red one-year twigs. The color will not be pronounced on an old plant which has been growing in poor soil for some length of time, and the one-year growth may be only two or three inches in length. This is not conducive to a colorful display. If the same plant is heavily pruned in the early spring, possibly even cut to the ground, then it will send out vigorous young shoots which will color nicely by winter. Applying a nitrogenous fertilizer will also help in the production of colorful bark. In fact, any practice which aids the rapid vegetative growth of the shoots will aid in the coloration of the bark of the twigs.

Varieties can be selected which are known to be vividly colored. The best of all the shrubby dogwoods for colored winter twigs is *Cornus alba sibirica,* the Siberian dogwood with twigs a brilliant red, and when this plant is forced into vigorous growth during the growing season, there is not a woody plant with bark more prominently colored in winter.

Sunshine plays an important part in the coloration of some twigs, just as it does in promoting more intensive color in the fall foliage. Some of the blueberries, for instance, may have green to greenish one-year twigs when grown in shade, but in sunshine their one-year twigs turn a bright red. This is especially true of such plants as *Cornus alba sibirica* and *Salix alba chermesina,* both of which can produce twigs of brilliant color. The older these plants become, the less brilliant this color, merely because the one-year twigs become smaller and more dispersed throughout the plant. When the plant is young, or when it has been pruned heavily, the one-year shoots are confined to a smaller space, and make a much more brilliant display.

The following list of shrubs and trees have colored bark or colored

Autumn Elaeagnus (*Elaeagnus umbellata*) not only has gray twigs, but gray foliage and interesting silvery red fruits as well.

twigs in winter, certainly a sufficient number to make possible an interesting selection for any winter garden. Of course, there are other plants of interest for their bark characteristics in winter, but the ones listed are some of the more important.

GRAY TWIGS

Acanthopanax sieboldianus   *L. tatarica*
Buddleia alternifolia   *Neillia sinensis*
Clethra alnifolia   *Prinsepia* species
Cornus racemosa   *Viburnum opulus* ‧
Elaeagnus umbellata   *V. sargenti*
Ilex decidua   *V. trilobum*
Lonicera morrowi

RED TWIGS OR BARK

Acer palmatum
Cornus alba
C. alba sibirica
C. amomum
C. stolonifera
Gaylussacia baccata
Leucothoe racemosa
Pinus sylvestris * (bark of upper branches and trunk red)
Rosa acicularis

R. canina
R. coriifolia cinerea
R. multiflora
R. omeiensis (colored prickles)
R. setigera
R. virginiana
Salix alba chermesina
Vaccinium corymbosum
Viburnum opulus nanum

GREEN TWIGS

Cytisus species
Jasminum nudiflorum
Kerria japonica

Poncirus trifoliata
Rosa wichuraiana
Smilax species

YELLOW TWIGS

Cornus stolonifera flaviramea
Kerria japonica aureo-vittata

Salix alba tristis *
S. alba vitellina *

GRAY TRUNK AND BRANCHES

Acer rubrum *
A. saccharinum *
Amelanchier species
Celtis * species
Cladrastis lutea *
Crataegus * many species
Euonymus sachalinensis
E. maacki

Fagus * species
Magnolia * species
Quercus borealis *
Q. velutina *
Sorbus * species
Ulmus carpinifolia *
U. hollandica superba *
U. laciniata nikkoensis *

WHITE TRUNK AND BRANCHES

Betula coerulea *
B. maximowicziana *
B. papyrifera * (best)
B. pendula *

B. platyphylla japonica *
B. populifolia *
B. utilis *

BARK OF TRUNK OR OLDER BRANCHES EXFOLIATING

(Either shredding off in long strips or flaking off in regular or irregular patches.)

*Acer griseum
*Betula species
*Carya ovata
Clethra acuminata
Cornus officinalis
Deutzia glabrata
Euonymus sanguinea
Hypericum arnoldianum
Kolkwitzia amabilis
Lonicera ferdinandi

L. iberica
*Parrotia persica
Physocarpus species
*Pinus bungeana
*Platanus acerifolia
*P. occidentalis
Rosa roxburghi
* Stewartia koreana
Stewartia pseudo-camellia
*Ulmus parvifolia

    * Trees.

Shrubs and Vines Blooming on the Current Year's Wood

The best time for pruning shrubs depends on whether they bloom on wood made the previous year, or on the current year's growth. Most shrubs are in the first category, and so when pruning is necessary, it might best be done immediately after they are through flowering in spring. The following plants are among those blooming on the current year's growth and so, when pruning is necessary, it should be done in early spring before the leaf buds open.

Franklinia alatamaha, another native American tree or shrub, blooming in September on the current year's growth. Hence, where pruning is necessary, it should be done in early spring.

Abelia "Edward Goucher"
A. *grandiflora*
A. *schumanni*
Aesculus parviflora
Amorpha species
Ampelopsis species
Aralia elata
Artemisia species
Baccharis halimifolia
Buddleia species except *alternifolia*
Callicarpa species
Calluna vulgaris
Campsis species
Caryopteris clandonensis
Ceanothus species

Celastrus species
Cephalanthus occidentalis
Clematis jackmani (See full discussion
  on page 376.)
C. jouiniana
C. lanuginosa
C. orientalis
C. paniculata
C. texensis
C. viorna
C. vitalba
C. viticella
C. virginiana
Clerodendron trichotomum
Clethra acuminata

The Fleece Vine (*Polygonum auberti*) can be cut to the ground in the very early spring and still be expected to produce flowers by fall.

C. alnifolia
C. barbinervis
C. tomentosa
Colutea species
Cytisus elongatus
C. nigricans
C. supinus
Diervilla sessilifolia
Dorycnium hirsutum
Elsholtzia stauntoni
Fatsia japonica
Franklinia alatamaha
Garrya species
Hamamelis virginiana
Hibiscus syriacus
Holodiscus discolor
Hydrangea—shrubby types
Hypericum arnoldianum
H. dawsonianum
H. densiflorum
H. frondosum
H. kalmianum
H. patulum henryi
H. prolificum

Indigofera incarnata
I. kirilowi
Lagerstroemia indica
Lespedeza bicolor
L. cyrtobotrya
L. japonica
L. maximowiczi
L. thunbergi
Lonicera heckrotti
L. sempervirens
Lycium species
Marsdenia erecta
Nandina domestica
Oxydendrum arboreum
Polygonum auberti
Periploca species
Potentilla species
Rhamnus frangula
Rosa wichuraiana
Rubus odoratus
Salvia greggi
Sambucus canadensis
Securinega suffruticosa
Smilax species

Pinkshell Azalea (*Rhododendron vaseyi*) one of the very few azaleas graced with beautiful spring flowers as well as an outstanding fall foliage color.

Sorbaria species
Sphaeralcea remota
Spirea alba
S. albiflora
S. bumalda
S. corymbosa
S. foxi
S. japonica
S. latifolia
S. margaritae
S. notha
S. pachystachys
S. pyramidata
S. revirescens

S. salicifolia
S. superba
S. tomentosa
S. watsoniana
Stephanandra tanakae
Symphoricarpos species
Tamarix odessana
T. pentandra
Thymus species
Tripetaleia paniculata
Vitex agnus-castus
V. negundo
Vitis species

A Suggested List of the Better Ornamental Shrubs and Vines for Specimen Planting—of Interest During at Least Two Seasons of the Year

It is at once apparent that all evergreens might well be included in this list as well as plants with colorful foliage during spring, summer and fall; plants of value for their form or habit of growth; and those deciduous plants of interest for colorful bark or fruit in the winter. Additions to the following list could be made from these general groups. Numbers after the plant names refer to the reasons for which they are valued at different seasons:

1. Flowers
2. Fruit
3. Summer foliage
4. Autumn coloration
5. General form
6. Winter twig or bark
7. Winter foliage

Abelia grandiflora 1, 3
Acer palmatum varieties 3, 4, 5
Akebia quinata 1, 3, 5
Amelanchier grandiflora 1, 4, 6
Arbutus unedo 1, 2, 7
Ardisia crispa 2, 7
Aucuba japonica 2, 7
Berberis species 1, 2, 4, and some 7
Camellia japonica varieties 1, 7
Clematis paniculata 1, 2
C. texensis 1, 2
C. vitalba 1, 2
Carissa grandiflora 1, 2, 7
Celastrus species 2, 4
Chionanthus virginicus 1, 2, 4
Choisya ternata 1, 7
Cornus alba sibirica 1, 4, 6
C. mas 1, 2, 4, 5
Cotinus coggygria purpureus 2, 4
Cotoneaster dammeri 2, 7
C. horizontalis 1, 2, 5, 7
C. microphylla 1, 2, 7
C. salicifolia floccosa 2, 7
Cytisus praecox 1, 6
C. scoparius 1, 6
Daphne species 1, 2
Enkianthus species 1, 4
Euonymus alata compacta 4, 5
E. fortunei vegeta 2, 3, 5, 7
E. japonica 2, 3, 7
Fothergilla species 1, 4
Gaultheria species 1, 2, 3, 7
Hamamelis species 1, 4
Hydrangea petiolaris 1, 3, 5, 6
Ilex cassine 2, 3, 7
I. cornuta 2, 3, 7
I. crenata 2, 3, 7
I. yunnanensis 2, 3, 7
Kalmia latifolia 1, 3, 7
Kolkwitzia amabilis 1, 2, 6
Leucothoe catesbaei 1, 3, 4, 7

Ligustrum henryi 1, 2, 3, 7
L. japonicum 1, 2, 3, 7
L. lucidum 1, 2, 3, 7
L. obtusifolium regelianum 1, 2, 3, 5
Lonicera amoena arnoldiana 1, 2, 5
L. bella 1, 2
L. fragrantissima 1, 2, 3, 7
L. japonica halliana 1, 3, 4, 7
L. korolkowi floribunda 1, 2, 3
L. maacki 1, 2
L. tatarica 1, 2
Magnolia stellata 1, 2, 3, 4
M. virginiana 1, 2, 3
Mahonia species 1, 2, 3, 4, 7
Malus sargenti 1, 2, 5
Nandina domestica 1, 2, 3
Pernettya mucronata 2, 3, 7
Philadelphus floridus 1, 5
P. grandiflorus 1, 5
P. laxus 1, 5
P. lemoinei "Avalanche" 1, 5
P. splendens 1, 5
Pieris species 1, 3, 5, 7
Prinsepia sinensis 1, 2, 5
Prunus laurocerasus 1, 7
P. tomentosa 1, 2
Punica granatum 1, 2
Rhododendron carolinianum 1, 7
R. catawbiense 1, 7
R. fortunei 1, 7
R. schlippenbachi 1, 4
R. vaseyi 1, 4
Rosa helenae 1, 2, 5
R. multiflora 1, 2, 5
R. roxburghi 1, 5, 7
R. rugosa 1, 2, 4
Skimmia japonica 1, 2, 3
S. reevsiana 1, 2, 3, 5
Spiraea prunifolia plena 1, 4
Taxus baccata 2, 3, 5, 7
T. cuspidata 2, 3, 5, 7

T. media 2, 3, 5, 7
Vaccinium corymbosum 1, 2, 4, 6
Viburnum cassinoides 1, 2, 4
V. dilatatum 1, 2, 4
V. japonicum 1, 2, 3, 7
V. lentago 1, 2, 3, 4
V. odoratissimum 1, 2, 3, 7
V. opulus 1, 2, 3, 4

V. prunifolium 1, 2, 3, 4, 5
V. rufidulum 1, 2, 3, 4
V. sargenti flavum 1, 2, 3, 4
V. sieboldi 1, 2, 3, 4, 5
V. suspensum 1, 2, 3, 7
V. tinus 1, 2, 3, 7
V. tomentosum mariesi 1, 2, 3, 4, 5
V. trilobum 1, 2, 3, 4

THE following plants have been selected because of their superior land-scape qualities. It is not intended that this be a record of botanical descriptions. Far from it! Rather it is a grouping of the chief characters of these plants with special reference to their landscape usefulness. Both Latin and common names are given, height, zone of hardiness referring to the map on the inside covers, origin or habitat and the approximate time of introduction. Information also is given concerning flowers, fruits, foliage, autumn color and winter-twig characters, **but only when these are ornamentally significant.** If no information is given in any one of these categories, it means that the plant in question is not valued for that particular reason in the garden.

The shrubs and vines have necessarily been chosen somewhat arbitrarily, but only after careful consideration has been given to those in the secondary list. The hardiest are growing mostly in the Arnold Arboretum where they have been under observation for years. The more tender types are among the best for the warmer areas of the United States. Both amateur and professional gardeners might do well to confine their interest to the shrubs and vines in the recommended list especially when time and space are limiting factors. All are actually growing in the United States and Canada, most of them being available from commercial sources on record in the Arnold Arboretum. When time, money and space are not limiting factors, plants might be selected from the secondary list for further trial. (See pages 412–432.)

Occasionally reference is made to the Horticultural Colour Chart of the Royal Horticultural Society. At the time of writing, this is the best color chart for comparing the colors of plants. It is made specifically for this purpose and frequently the color names are chosen accordingly. It will be noted, as an example, that the color for the flowers of the Ghent hybrid azalea "Charlemagne" is given thus: Chinese coral (614) to orange (12). These names and numbers refer directly to two of the 800 specific colors given in the chart. It is unfortunate that all colors in this book cannot be so recorded. It is hoped that, eventually, a color chart will be produced in North America to be used by American horticulturists, but until that time comes the Horticultural Colour Chart meets most contingencies.

If an "X" appears in front of the specific name, i.e. X *Abelia grandiflora*, it designates this plant as a hybrid, and seed sown from it may not yield seedlings like the parent plant. All offspring propagated from it by seed are clons (see page 408), and to obtain young plants like the parent, propagation must be by asexual means.

An asterisk (*) in front of the flowers, fruit, foliage, autumn color or twigs, means that the plant is grown particularly for this outstanding land-scape characteristic. If no asterisk appears, these characters may still be good but not meritorious.

x Abelia "Edward Goucher"   5'   Zone 5

*FLOWERS: lavender-purple, large tubular
    TIME: July–September
FOLIAGE: semi-evergreen
HYBRID ORIGIN: (*A. grandiflora x A. schumanni*) Before 1911.

Originated by the former Edward Goucher of the United States Department of Agriculture at Glenn Dale, Maryland. The flowers resemble *A. grandiflora* somewhat, but the plant is intermediate between its two parents in habit of growth.

Abelia floribunda   6'   Zone 8   Mexican Abelia

*FLOWERS: rosy red, pendulous, large
    TIME: summer
FOLIAGE: evergreen, leaves 1½" long
HABITAT: Mexico
INTRODUCED: 1841

x Abelia grandiflora   5'   Zone 5   Glossy Abelia

*FLOWERS: pink in clusters of 1–4, nearly ¾" in diameter
    TIME: August
FOLIAGE: half evergreen, glossy, leaves to 1½" long
    AUTUMN COLOR: bronze to purple
HYBRID ORIGIN: (*A. chinensis x A. uniflora*) Before 1880

The hardiest and most free flowering of the abelias, used as far north as New York City and even in Boston with some protection. Valued for its excellent foliage and small flowers that appear during a greater part of summer. A dense plant, admirably suited for hedge making.

Abelia schumanni   5'   Zone 7   Schumann Abelia

*FLOWERS: lavender-pink
    TIME: June–September
FOLIAGE: semi-evergreen, leaves about 1" long
HABITAT: western China
INTRODUCED: 1915

Abeliophyllum distichum   5'   Zone 5   Korean Abelia-leaf

*FLOWERS: white, in dense clusters
    TIME: mid-April
HABITAT: central Korea
INTRODUCED: 1924

Its dense clusters of small white flowers, borne all along the slender arching branches, come early in spring and are particularly conspicuous. Closely related

Glossy Abelia—widely grown throughout the South and as far north as New York, with flowers appearing continuously throughout the summer.

to the forsythias, the flowers are smaller and more numerous. In unusually severe winters, the flower buds are killed by low temperatures in spring in New England, but where the plant is not growing in too exposed a situation, its flowers are easily the most conspicuous of any other shrub blooming at this time of year. A good companion shrub to be used with forsythias.

Acacia farnesiana   10'   Zone 8   Opopanax

*FLOWERS: yellow, small balls, fragrant
    TIME: February and March
FOLIAGE: very small leaflets
HABITAT: southern Texas, Mexico

A popular thorny southern plant, often grown in the north as a greenhouse pot plant, for under such conditions it blooms freely all winter.

Acanthopanax sieboldianus withstands shade and city growing conditions with surprising ease.

Acanthopanax sieboldianus 9' Zone 4

HABITAT: Japan
INTRODUCED: 1859
    Probably the only member of this genus worthy of note for landscape planting. The flowers and fruit are rarely seen and even then are not particularly important. It is valued chiefly as a foliage plant. Its compound leaves with 5–7 palmately arranged leaflets remain on the plant long into the fall. It has the admirable trait of growing well in the shade and withstanding city growing conditions, one of the best shrubs for both purposes.

Acer campestre 25' Zone 4 Hedge Maple

AUTUMN COLOR: yellow
HABITAT: Europe and western Asia
INTRODUCED: early colonial times
    Commonly used in Europe in clipped hedges because of its dense growth. It does not have the vivid autumn coloration of native maples, but as a clipped hedge or screen it is ideal. Several ornamental varieties have been found and named, chiefly displaying foliage variations, but not sufficiently meritorious to warrant growing them in preference to the species. From Long Island southward, it makes a dependable screen plant requiring little attention.

Acer circinatum 25' Zone 5 Vine Maple

FLOWERS: white and purple, small drooping clusters
    TIME: late April
FRUIT: winged, red
    EFFECTIVE: summer

AUTUMN COLOR: red to orange
HABITAT: British Columbia to California

A native maple of the Pacific coast adapted for use in gardens because of its small, compact size and its ability to grow in partially shaded situations, especially under evergreens. Somewhat similar in habit to A. *palmatum*, except that its stems twist and turn in a most interesting manner, thus giving rise to its name. The wood is very tough—the Indians are supposed to have used it to make fish hooks.

Acer ginnala   20'   Zone 2   Amur Maple

FRUIT: winged, unusually red and conspicuous
    EFFECTIVE: summer
*AUTUMN COLOR: scarlet
HABITAT: central and northern China, Manchuria, Japan
INTRODUCED: about 1860

A dense shrub or small tree with comparatively small leaves about 3" long and extremely hardy. The fruits turn bright red in summer while leaves are still green, making an interesting color combination. The scarlet autumn color of the foliage is as brilliant as any of the maples. A good shrub for specimens or for screening purposes requiring practically no care.

Acer palmatum   20'   Zone 5   Japanese Maple

*FOLIAGE: green to red, leaves 5–9 lobed and up to 4" in width
    *AUTUMN COLOR: scarlet
HABITAT: Korea, Japan
INTRODUCED: 1820
VARIETIES:

atropurpureum—leaves mostly 7 lobed, deep red to almost purple, throughout the growing season. One of the best varieties for red-colored foliage.

dissectum—leaves divided almost to the base in 5–9 lobes with each lobe deeply cut—almost pinnate, green in color.

elegans—foliage green throughout most of growing season.

ornatum—leaves with extremely deeply cut lobes, deep red throughout early summer, later turning a bronze-green. The plant has a somewhat weeping habit—an excellent ornamental specimen.

"*oshiu-beni*"—leaves with 9 deeply cut lobes, red in spring but a normal green by early summer.

sanguineum—leaves usually smaller than some of the above varieties with about 7 none-too-deeply cut lobes, red throughout the growing season, though sometimes it may turn bronze by midsummer.

This is a variable species of shrub or small tree, very popular in Japan and grown to a considerable extent in this country as well. A Japanese nursery firm listed over 25 varieties a few years ago as the "best" of a large number. More recently an American nursery listed at least 15 varieties. The leaves have 5–9 lobes, some of the varieties are more deeply cut than others, with colors ranging from green to dark red. The nomenclature in the commercial nurseries both here and in Japan is pretty much confused. Some specimens have the desirable trait of holding their deep red color all summer long, others that have bright red young leaves early in the spring, disappointingly turn green in the summer. Some make poor specimens as they grow older because of poor understock on which named varieties are grafted. Then too, many nurseries adopt the questionable practice of growing from seed and "selecting" the best seedling forms, often giving accredited varietal names for clons which should be only asexually propagated. This, of course, only adds to the confusion since many of the seedling forms do not have all the traits of the varieties after which they are named.

These low shrubby maples often grow into small trees and are best used as specimen plants. They should not be jammed into the shrub border. Those with leaves variegated pink, white, yellow, etc., are not to be recommended since they are difficult to grow properly.

Acer spicatum   25′   Zone 2   Mountain Maple

FRUIT: winged, bright red
    EFFECTIVE: summer
AUTUMN COLOR: orange to scarlet
HABITAT: Labrador to Saskatchewan, Georgia and Iowa

Another extremely hardy maple, found over a wide area of North America, no better than other shrubby maples here suggested but of value for its hardiness and ability to grow in partial shade. The plant requires practically no attention.

Aesculus parviflora   8–12′   Zone 4   Bottlebrush Buckeye

*FLOWERS: white, in large pyramidal clusters
    TIME: mid-July
HABITAT: South Carolina to Alabama

This shrubby buckeye is of value for its late flowers appearing in early summer at a time when few other woody plants are in bloom. It forms a round, moundlike plant, often twice as broad as it is high, spreading by underground suckers. Its flowers appear in the typical pyramidal clusters common among the horse-chestnuts and buckeyes.

Aesculus splendens   12′   Zone 6   Flame Buckeye

*FLOWERS: bright red in pyramidal clusters 6–10″ high
    TIME: May
HABITAT: Alabama, Georgia and Mississippi

One of the most colorful of the dwarf buckeyes. However, it should be pointed out that this has no particular ornamental features except the flowers which are in evidence for a very short period only.

Alnus species   9–60′   Zone 2   Alders

FLOWERS: pendulous catkins
    TIME: early April
HABITAT: United States, Europe, Asia

Several species like A. *incana*, A. *rubra*, A. *rugosa* are used primarily for planting in wet soil where other shrubs or trees might not grow. The pendulous catkins, bearing the pollen, are of some interest in the early spring, but in general, alders need not be used where better shrubs will grow.

The name Bottlebrush Buckeye, is taken from the appearance of the flowers.

Of mounded habit this native of the lower Mississippi Valley (*Aesculus parviflora*) is perfectly hardy in parts of New England.

x Amelanchier grandiflora   25′   Zone 4   Apple Service-berry

*FLOWERS: pure white
  TIME: early May
FRUIT: red to black, berrylike, edible
  EFFECTIVE: early summer
*AUTUMN COLOR: yellow to orange
HYBRID ORIGIN: *A. canadensis x A. laevis*
ORIGINATED: 1870
    The best of the service-berries are trees. The shrubs are really not needed in gardens for they flower and fruit at times when there are many superior shrubs in flower or in fruit. Some of the native species like *A. stolonifera, A. canadensis, A. cuisicki, A. amabilis,* etc., are of value only in natural woodlands. Of the shrubby forms, *A. grandiflora* has the largest flower clusters. Amelanchiers are susceptible to attacks from scale insects, as are many other rosaceous shrubs. If the weather is very warm when the plants are in bloom, the flowers of all the service-berries may last only three days.

Amorpha canescens   4′   Zone 2   Lead-plant

FLOWERS: blue in dense clustered spikes, 3–6″ long
  TIME: July
*FOLIAGE: gray, leaves compound, leaflets to ¼″ long
HABITAT: eastern North America
    Years ago it was believed that wherever this plant was found growing wild, lead would be found also. Its conspicuous spikes of blue flowers with orange-colored anthers are very beautiful in early summer. Its chief merit is its gray foliage throughout the growing season, a predominant color that makes the plant conspicuous among others in the shrub border. It seems to do well in poor, dry soils.

Andromeda polifolia   1–2′   Zone 2   Bog Rosemary

FLOWERS: white to pinkish, in small terminal clusters
  TIME: early May
*FOLIAGE: evergreen, leaves to 1½″ long
HABITAT: northeastern United States, northern and central Europe, northern Asia.
    A low shrub with creeping rootstock, only worthwhile in gardens of the colder sections of the country, especially in moist, peaty locations.

Aralia elata   45′   Zone 3   Japanese Angelica-tree

FLOWERS: small white flowers in large pyramidal spikes
  TIME: August
FRUIT: small black berries
  EFFECTIVE: early fall
FOLIAGE: dark glossy green, compound leaves to 2½′ long
AUTUMN COLOR: reddish orange
HABITAT: northeastern Asia
INTRODUCED: 1830
    The devil's walking stick, as it is often called, is a peculiar, exotic looking plant decidedly out of place in most small gardens. It is a spindly growing shrub

or small tree, often suckering from the base, the main stems having sharp tri-
angular thorns and large compound leaves sometimes 2½' long, that are usually
clustered around the ends of the stems. The large feathery spikes of small flowers
are produced above the rather horizontal leaves so that they are conspicuous
from all sides, and are followed by small black berries which quickly fall in early
autumn.

An unusual shrub, conspicuous at all seasons, and very difficult to use
properly. It grows fairly well in almost any good soil.

Arbutus unedo   10–30'   Zone 8   Strawberry-tree
*FLOWERS: small, white
    TIME: winter
*FRUIT: strawberrylike, orange-red
    EFFECTIVE: fall
FOLIAGE: evergreen, leaves to 4" long
HABITAT: southwestern Europe
INTRODUCED: long in cultivation

An interesting shrub or tree, with small flowers turning into red strawberrylike fruits at once, which may remain on the tree for months. The dark bark
cracks open to show the bright red inner bark of the larger stems. It should not
be planted in alkaline soils.

ARCTOSTAPHYLOS

Native West Coast evergreen shrubs that are among the most beautiful of
the native plants of that area with dense clusters of drooping flowers somewhat
similar to those of the andromedas. There are many similar species in this particular genus, native to the Pacific Coast, and frequently considered so common
in the wild that they are neglected for use in gardens. Large specimens may be
too difficult to transplant from the wild, but small specimens, once established,
need little attention.

Arctostaphylos stanfordiana   6'   Zone 7   Stanford Manzanita
*FLOWERS: brilliant pink in dense panicles
    TIME: March–April
FRUIT: red-brown berries
    EFFECTIVE: fall
*FOLIAGE: lustrous evergreen, leaves to 1½" long
WINTER BARK: red
HABITAT: California

A distinctive addition to any West Coast garden where it can be grown.
It is often almost completely covered with blooms and keeps its rounded shape,
especially if grown in well-drained soil with plenty of sun.

Arctostaphylos uva-ursi   ground cover   Zone 2   Bearberry
FLOWERS: white, tinged pink, small
    TIME: May
FRUIT: bright red berry ¼" diam.
    EFFECTIVE: summer
*FOLIAGE: evergreen, leaves to 1" long
    AUTUMN COLOR: bronze

HABITAT: Europe, Asia, North America

An excellent ground cover with small leaves ½–¾″ long, especially adaptable for sandy soils. In fact it requires poor soil in which to grow. It is often used at the seashore in rocky areas where the small soil pockets may tend to dry out. In the wild, it forms dense mats which can be lifted in squares and transplanted to new locations. It is being used considerably along highways in eastern coastal regions for planting sandy banks where little else will grow. On the Pacific Coast it is equally popular and for the same reasons.

Ardisia crispa   1′   Zone 9   Coral Ardisia

FLOWERS: white, ½″ diameter
   TIME: spring
*FRUIT: bright red berries
   EFFECTIVE: fall and winter
FOLIAGE: evergreen, leathery, leaves to 3″ long
HABITAT: Malaya, China

Often grown in pots to display its fruits to better advantage. It needs considerable shade.

Aronia arbutifolia   9′   Zone 5   Red Chokeberry

FLOWERS: white or reddish, less than ½″ diameter
   TIME: late May
*FRUIT: bright red berries, less than ½″ diameter
   EFFECTIVE: fall
AUTUMN COLOR: red
HABITAT: eastern United States

A common shrub found over a wide area in the woods of eastern United States, it has ornamental value for several seasons. Its fruits are always produced in large numbers, and it is a dependable shrub in almost any soil.

Aronia melanocarpa   1½–3′   Zone 4   Black Chokeberry

FLOWERS: single, white
   TIME: late May
FRUIT: black or black-purple berries
   EFFECTIVE: fall
AUTUMN COLOR: red
HABITAT: eastern United States

A splendid shrub for naturalistic plantings especially on the edges of woodlands.

Aronia prunifolia   12′   Zone 4   Purple-fruited Chokeberry

FLOWERS: white
   TIME: late May
FRUIT: purplish black
AUTUMN COLOR: red
HABITAT: eastern United States

Not superior to *Aronia arbutifolia* but a comparable companion shrub which can be used with the other species for its purplish black fruits.

Artemisia abrotanum   4'   Zone 5   Southernwood

FOLIAGE: finely divided, aromatic
HABITAT: southern Europe
INTRODUCED: long in cultivation and often escaped
   This plant is usually grown for its finely divided and intensely aromatic foliage.

Artemisia absinthium   4'   Zone 5   Wormwood

FLOWERS: small, yellow
   TIME: summer
FOLIAGE: whitish and silky, aromatic, finely divided
HABITAT: Europe
INTRODUCED: long in cultivation and often escaped
   A common favorite in gardens for its silky, whitish foliage. In Europe it is grown for its medicinal properties as well as the fact that an "absinthe" is made from it.

Artemisia frigida   1½'   Zone 2   Fringed Sagebrush

FLOWERS: yellow, small
   TIME: late August
*FOLIAGE: silvery pubescent, aromatic, finely divided
HABITAT: western North America and Siberia
   A handsome plant for rock gardens, because of its silvery pubescent foliage.

Artemisia stelleriana   2½'   Zone 2   Beach Wormwood (Dusty Miller)

FLOWERS: yellow, small
   TIME: summer
*FOLIAGE: densely white, woolly, finely divided
HABITAT: Quebec to New Jersey, northeastern Asia

Artemisia tridentata   9'   Zone 5   Sagebrush

FOLIAGE: silvery gray, aromatic
HABITAT: western North America
   Useful, but not necessarily ornamental in situations where other good shrubs will grow. It does best in dry alkaline soils and, of course, is widely distributed in the West in areas where little else will withstand the trying soil and climatic conditions. The plant has a pungent aroma and its chief use in gardens anywhere is probably as an ever-present reminder for those who know and love the West.

Atriplex species   4'   Zone 5–7   Saltbush

   Several species, rarely grown, for they require adverse conditions such as sandy, dry soil, or planting near salt water in almost brackish conditions. Only recommended here for such conditions and providing nothing else will prove suitable. Leaves small, whitish to gray flowers and fruit not particularly ornamental.

Aucuba japonica   15'   Zone 7   Japanese Aucuba

FLOWERS: small, sexes separate, in panicles 2–5" long
    TIME: March
*FRUIT: brilliant red berries
    EFFECTIVE: winter
*FOLIAGE: evergreen, thick, glossy, leaves to 7" long
HABITAT: Japan
INTRODUCED: 1861

One of the dioecious groups of plants with staminate flowers on one plant and pistillate on another. Both sexes must be in the same vicinity to insure the production of the bright red, conspicuous fruits. Also it is important to note that this plant requires shade. In full sun the foliage tends to burn and become unsightly. It is a vigorous, spreading shrub, used in the open or as a formal "tub" plant, of chief interest for its bright-colored berries. The variegated form A. *japonica variegata* has been popularly termed the "goldust-tree."

Azalea—see **Rhododendron**, page 244

Baccharis halimifolia   12'   Zone 4   Groundsel-bush

*FRUIT: white, thistlelike heads, sexes separate
    EFFECTIVE: early fall
AUTUMN COLOR: bronze to gray-green
HABITAT: eastern United States

The numerous thistlelike heads of fruit appear only on plants with female flowers. It is one of the comparatively few plants able to withstand salt water spray, this being its chief value to gardeners.

BERBERIS

The barberries comprise a very serviceable group of dense, thorny shrubs which are well adapted to barrier plantings in many situations. At the present time there are 120 different varieties of barberries growing in the Arnold Arboretum. Since early colonial times, it has been known that certain barberries serve as host plants for the black stem rust of wheat. Especially is this true of the common barberry, *Berberis vulgaris*, which was brought over here by the earliest settlers and has become naturalized in many areas. The United States Department of Agriculture has been working on this problem for a long time and has been able to establish many facts about this dread disease. Approximately 140 different species, forms and hybrids of *Berberis* have been found to act as host plants for the black stem rust.

In the fall, this fungus forms its thick-walled over-wintering spores on the grain stems and stubble of wheat and is called "black rust" because of the spore color. In the spring, the large spores produce smaller ones that are easily carried by air currents. If these tiny spores fail to fall on certain specific host plants (the barberries are only one group) they fail to germinate and the life cycle of the rust is broken. On the other hand, if they do fall on the right plants, favorable weather produces infection and eventually other types of spores are formed in the leaves of the host plants.

These spores (some 64,000,000 of which can be produced on a single barberry bush) are the ones that infect the cereals in the northern states. In other words, this pest has five different spore forms and must spend part of its life on two different host plants—barberries on the one hand and cereals such as wheat, oats, barley and rye on the other. It is obvious that the best way to break the life cycle is to eliminate the barberries. This is just what the United States Department of Agriculture has been attempting over a long period.

Because of the extent of the eradication work which the U.S.D.A. has been conducting, I feel it advisable to recommend only those barberries which have been found to be resistant to this disease. There is a small group of barberries sufficiently rust-resistant so that the U.S.D.A. allows them to be shipped to the protected states. The list chosen, of nineteen species and varieties, is sufficiently diverse and offers a good selection of ornamental barberries. In fact, I have suggested the elimination of a few from the list which have been termed rust-resistant by the U.S.D.A., namely, *Berberis edgeworthiana, B. sanguinea,* and *B. sargentiana* since these are not sufficiently outstanding or different to warrant inclusion. With the exception of these three, all others on the suggested list for discard are susceptible to attack from the stem rust of wheat and for this reason might be eliminated from gardens.

Admittedly, not all areas in the United States are wheat-growing areas, and it might be argued that because of this, there are hidden away in this list of suggested discards a large number of ornamental gems. This is not the case. About ten or twelve have been found sufficiently outstanding in the past to be grown and offered for sale by nurseries; but when compared with those selected in the following list even these few might be forgotten. The chances are that in the years to come the restrictions on rust-carrying barberries will be tightened rather than loosened, and so it seems advisable to grow chiefly those varieties which have proved themselves rust-resistant.

Most barberries have small bright yellow flowers, borne singly or in clusters that are fairly interesting for their waxlike beauty. These are usually borne in great profusion. The leaves of the evergreen species are usually spiny and all species are protected with stout stiff thorns, sometimes branched. It is this which makes them so effective as barrier plants.

The fruits are small berries about ¼" long, bright red or bluish-black to purple, varying in size and shape with the species. They are conspicuous in fall, especially the red ones. Fruits of the evergreen types seem to fall quickly after ripening or to be eaten by birds. The same is true of some of the deciduous forms also. But the persistent and thoroughly hardy Japanese Barberry has brilliant red fruits that remain all winter long. There is nothing prettier in the spring than a Japanese Barberry displaying its new green leaves, its waxy yellow flowers and its old red fruits all at the same time. Even though this species has been more planted than almost any other in the seventy odd years since first introduced into this country by the Arnold Arboretum, it is still one of our most popular and most serviceable plants. This species is living proof that a plant can appear in almost every garden and because of its many merits, still remain tremendously popular.

The deciduous barberries usually have a brilliant red autumn color and are considered among the best in this respect. There are some very beautiful evergreen barberries too, fortunately rust-resistant, that can well be used in many gardens. Their spiny evergreen foliage is of decided winter interest. Most of those suggested in the following list have some interest each season of the year, sufficient recommendation, perhaps, to boost them from the class of merely "serviceable barrier" plants into the class of first-rate ornamentals.

Berberis beaniana   8'   Zone 6   Bean's Barberry

*FLOWERS: yellow, ¼" dia. in racemes
  TIME: mid-June
*FRUIT: purple berries
  EFFECTIVE: fall
*AUTUMN COLOR: red
WINTER TWIGS: thorny and reddish
HABITAT: western China
INTRODUCED: 1904

Berberis buxifolia nana   18"   Zone 5   Dwarf Magellan Barberry

*FOLIAGE: evergreen
WINTER TWIGS: thorny
HABITAT: Straits of Magellan
INTRODUCED: 1826
    One of the hardiest evergreen barberries, excellent for very low hedges. The flowers and fruits are rarely seen.

Berberis candidula   2'   Zone 5   Paleleaf Barberry

*FLOWERS: bright yellow, solitary, ⅜" dia.
  TIME: May
FRUIT: purplish berries
  EFFECTIVE: fall
*FOLIAGE: evergreen, leaves to 1½" long
WINTER TWIGS: thorny
HABITAT: China
INTRODUCED: 1894
    Dwarf, dense in habit, chiefly suited for rock gardens

Berberis circumserrata   6'   Zone 5   Cutleaf Barberry

FLOWERS: yellow, ¼" dia., 2–3 flowers in cluster
  TIME: late May
FRUIT: yellowish red berries
  EFFECTIVE: fall

*AUTUMN COLOR: fiery red
WINTER TWIGS: thorny
HABITAT: northwest China
INTRODUCED: 1911

Hardy and handsome, developing into a dense rounded bush. The fruits are borne singly or in small groups and do not appear as numerous as do those of *B. gilgiana* which are borne in pendulous clusters.

Berberis concinna   3′   Zone 6   Dainty Barberry

FLOWERS: bright yellow, solitary, ½″ dia.
   TIME: May
FRUIT: red berries
   EFFECTIVE: fall
FOLIAGE: half evergreen in some areas, leaves to 1½″ long
AUTUMN COLOR: red
WINTER TWIGS: thorny
HABITAT: Himalaya
INTRODUCED: 1850

Of close compact habit with under surface of leaves very white.

Berberis darwini   10′   Zone 7   Darwin Barberry

*FLOWERS: yellow, tinged with red, small, pendant racemes
   TIME: May
FRUIT: dark purple berries
   EFFECTIVE: fall
*FOLIAGE: evergreen, leaves to 1″ long
AUTUMN COLOR: purplish
WINTER TWIGS: thorny
HABITAT: Chile
INTRODUCED: 1849

A dense barberry of use only in the far South, this plant was discovered by Charles Darwin while on a voyage in the famous ship "Beagle" in 1835. The small, hollylike leaves are pleasing at all seasons. Usually it grows only 3′ high and does well if planted in moist soil in the shade.

Berberis gagnepaini   6′   Zone 5   Black Barberry

*FLOWERS: bright yellow, abundant, ½″ dia. in clusters
   TIME: late May
*FRUIT: bluish black berries
   EFFECTIVE: fall
*FOLIAGE: evergreen, leaves narrow, to 4″ long
WINTER TWIGS: thorny
HABITAT: western China
INTRODUCED: 1904

This bushy evergreen does well in New England gardens as well as those of California. It needs good soil to produce its best foliage. *Berberis chenaulti* an excellent hybrid (*B. gagnenpaini* x *B. verruculosa*, combines the good qualities of both parents and makes a splendid evergreen.

Berberis gilgiana   6'   Zone 5   Wildfire Barberry

*FLOWERS: bright yellow, ¼" dia. in pendant clusters
  TIME: May
*FRUIT: blood-red berries, in pendant clusters
  EFFECTIVE: fall
*AUTUMN COLOR: vivid red
WINTER TWIGS: thorny
HABITAT: north central China
INTRODUCED: 1910
  One of the splendid substitutes for the Common Barberry.

Berberis julianae   6'   Zone 5   Wintergreen Barberry

*FLOWERS: yellow, ⅛" dia., in clusters
  TIME: mid-May
*FRUIT: bluish black berries
  EFFECTIVE: fall
*FOLIAGE: evergreen, leaves spiny to 3" long
WINTER TWIGS: thorny
HABITAT: central China
INTRODUCED: 1900
  Very dense habit, one of the hardiest evergreen barberries and a very strong grower. A dependable asset for year-around beauty where it can be used.

Berberis koreana   6'   Zone 5   Korean Barberry

*FLOWERS: yellow, ¼" dia. in pendant clusters
  TIME: mid-May
*FRUIT: bright red berries, pendant clusters
  EFFECTIVE: fall and winter
*AUTUMN COLOR: deep red
WINTER TWIGS: thorny
HABITAT: Korea
INTRODUCED: 1905
  This Korean Barberry is rapidly proving itself in gardens and nurseries throughout the eastern United States as a perfect substitute for the somewhat taller *B. vulgaris*. The small fruit clusters have berries that are globular and bright red, and its dense growth makes it an excellent barrier plant as well as an interesting specimen.

x Berberis mentorensis   7'   Zone 5   Mentor Barberry

FLOWERS: yellow, ¼" dia.
  TIME: May
FRUIT: dull, dark red berries
  EFFECTIVE: fall
FOLIAGE: semi-evergreen, leaves spiny about 1" long
WINTER TWIGS: thorny
HYBRID ORIGIN: *B. julianae x B. thunbergi*

INTRODUCED: 1924

This barberry resulted from the hybridizing efforts of Mr. M. Horvath of Mentor, Ohio. It is semi-evergreen and shows many characteristics of both parents. Where evergreen barberries fail to survive because of winter cold, this plant might well be tried for it has withstood temperatures of −20° F. in Ohio without apparent injury. Another very important factor: it is able to survive the hot dry summer of the Midwest better than any other barberry.

Berberis potanini   8′   Zone 7   Longspine Barberry

FLOWERS: yellow, ⅓″ dia. in racemes
    TIME: May
FRUIT: red berries
    EFFECTIVE: fall
AUTUMN COLOR: purplish
WINTER TWIGS: thorny
HABITAT: western China
INTRODUCED: 1927

x Berberis stenophylla   9′   Zone 5   Rosemary Barberry

*FLOWERS: golden yellow, ⅓″ dia.
    TIME: mid-May
FRUIT: black berries
    EFFECTIVE: fall
*FOLIAGE: evergreen, leaves narrow to 1″ long
WINTER TWIGS: thorny
HYBRID ORIGIN: *B. darwini x B. empetrifolia*
INTRODUCED: 1864

South of Washington this species develops into a beautifully graceful specimen and is definitely evergreen. In New England it does not develop so well and is deciduous. E. H. Wilson was very enthusiastic in his praise of this species, saying that, where perfectly hardy, it made an admirable garden plant either as a specimen or in a hedge.

Berberis thunbergi   7′   Zone 5   Japanese Barberry

*FLOWERS: yellow, reddish outside, ⅓–½″ dia.
    TIME: mid-May
*FRUIT: bright red berries
    EFFECTIVE: fall and winter
*AUTUMN COLOR: scarlet
WINTER TWIGS: thorny
HABITAT: Japan
INTRODUCED: 1875
VARIETIES: *atropurpurea*–foliage red
    minor–4′, smaller than species in all characters
    erecta–originated about 1930, upright habit

This serviceable species was originally introduced into the United States by the Arnold Arboretum and since 1875 has become one of the most widely used hedge plants. It grows in almost any soil and is noted for its ability to withstand dry conditions. Its dense, thorny habit, its bright red fruits remaining on all winter, and its scarlet autumn-color make it an asset in any garden. In fact the only thing which might be said against it is that it has become very common. The small-leaved form, var. *minor,* often called the Box Barberry, arose as a chance seedling in the Arnold Arboretum. It is smaller in every way—height, leaves, twigs, fruit—than the species and makes an excellent low neat hedge or specimen plant.

The red-leaved form is too often grown from seed by nurserymen. Individual plants noted for their deep red color should be selected and propagated asexually, thus insuring a uniform strain.

The erect form of the Japanese Barberry, *erecta* has been listed as the True-hedge Columnberry because it grows in a rigidly upright manner. As a hedge requiring little trimming it is ideal. It is a selection from five generations of seedlings of the Japanese Barberry made by Horvath of Mentor, Ohio. Each group of seedlings were carefully scrutinized and only those with the most upright habit of growth were selected for further breeding. The result is an excellent plant.

Berberis triacanthophora   4'   Zone 5   Threespine Barberry

FLOWERS: whitish, tinged red, ¼" dia.
  TIME: May
FRUIT: blue-black berries
  EFFECTIVE: fall
*FOLIAGE: evergreen, leaves to 2" long
WINTER TWIGS: thorny
HABITAT: central China
INTRODUCED: 1907

Another of the hardy evergreen barberries, often considered the most hardy of all. It is well armed with long, slender spines. E. H. Wilson first collected and sent the plant to the Arnold Arboretum where it is able to weather most winters satisfactorily.

Berberis verruculosa   4'   Zone 5   Warty Barberry

*FLOWERS: golden yellow, ½" dia.
  TIME: late May
FRUIT: violet-black berries
  EFFECTIVE: fall
*FOLIAGE: evergreen, leathery, white underneath, leaves spiny to 1" long
AUTUMN COLOR: bronze
WINTER TWIGS: thorny
HABITAT: western China
INTRODUCED: 1904

This barberry has a neat compact habit. Its leathery evergreen foliage is interesting because the leaves are white underneath forming a pretty contrast with the lustrous green of the upper foliage.

Evergreen barberries such as this Warty Barberry (*Berberis verruculosa*) make excellent hedges.

Bruckenthalia spiculifolia   10″   Zone 5   Spike-Heath

FLOWERS: in small spikes, pale pink
    TIME: mid-June
FOLIAGE: evergreen, heathlike
HABITAT: southeastern Europe and Asia Minor
INTRODUCED: Cult. 1880
    Akin to the heathers this low evergreen shrub is suited for rock gardens be·· cause of its minute size.

Buddleia alternifolia   12′   Zone 5   Fountain Buddleia

FLOWERS: long spikes of small lilac-purple flowers
    TIME: mid-May
HABITAT: northwestern China
INTRODUCED: 1914
    This is the hardiest of all the *Buddleia* species and is well named Fountain Buddleia for its wide-spreading and arching branches certainly resemble a fountain. It grows vigorously, and in mid-spring its long arching branches are covered with the small flower clusters which make it the earliest of the buddleias to bloom. Where sufficient room is given to this plant so that it can expand in width as well as height (a spot nearly 15 feet in diameter) it makes a conspicuous and colorful show in spring well worth its space in the large garden. Its branches do not die to the ground in winter as do those of most other buddleia species and it thrives in poor but well-drained gravelly soils.

Buddleia davidi   15′   Zone 5   Orange-eye Butterfly-bush

FLOWERS: white, pink, red and purple in upright spikes
    TIME: August
HABITAT: China
INTRODUCED: about 1890
    Some of the varieties available are:
    "Charming"—flowers pink, one of the best of this color
    "Concord"—flowers at first color of the Concord grape then change to
dark red.
    "Dubonnet"—flowers dark purple
    "Fascinating"—flowers soft orchid-pink
    "Fortune"—with neat habit, flowers lilac with orange eye
    "Hartwegi"—flowers bright lavender
    "Isle de France"—flowers deep purple
    "Royal Red"—flowers reddish
    "White Bouquet"—flowers white
    The nurseries have featured many varieties of this variable species. Nor-
mally it grows 6–8′ tall with large pyramidal spikes of flowers in late summer. The
foliage, coarse in texture and open in habit of growth, is not always easy to display in the shrub border. The plants die to the ground during most winters and
in the North some soil might be thrown around the base of the plants as added
winter protection. Other species are grown, but the varieties of B. davidi seem
to be the most popular of the group. One of the reasons nurserymen like to advertise them, is because blooming plants can be obtained in one season from seed sown
in the greenhouse in early spring, thus affording salable plants in a few months
of growth. These plants might as well be avoided except by those gardeners who,
knowing the shortcomings of these varieties, like them nevertheless.

Buxus microphylla   4′   Zone 5   Littleleaf Box

*FOLIAGE: evergreen, leaves to 1″ long
HABITAT: Japan
INTRODUCED: about 1860
VARIETIES: *compacta*—one of the smallest of all box varieties, 11″ high and 26
years old. Introduced by H. J. Hohman of Kingsville, Maryland, 1940.
    japonica—larger leaves, slightly taller than species
    koreana—hardiest of all
    A compact low evergreen shrub with leaves about an inch long, not as
rapid-growing as the more common B. sempervirens. The variety B. japonica has
larger leaves and is slightly taller in growth, and B. koreana, the Korean Box,
is hardiest of all the species and varieties in this genus. In the very severe
winter of 1933–34 many box hedges and specimens around Long Island Sound
and in southern New York and Pennsylvania were killed to the ground by the
unprecedented cold, but plants of the Korean Box were not severely injured.
    The Littleleaf, Korean and Japanese Box need not replace B. sempervirens
and its many splendid varieties where these prove hardy. These Asiatic types
should be grown on the known northern limits of B. sempervirens for they will
withstand much lower temperatures. For information on culture see notes under
B. sempervirens.

Buxus sempervirens   20'   Zone 5   Common Box

*FOLIAGE: evergreen, dark lustrous green, leaves to 1¼" long
HABITAT: southern Europe, northern Africa, western Asia
INTRODUCED: during early colonial times
VARIETIES:

angustifolia—treelike in habit with leaves 1–1¼" long—the largest leaves of this species

arborescens—the typical form more or less treelike in habit

argenteo-variegata—leaves variegated with white. Normally such variegation in evergreens is not to be recommended but in this particular case it is satisfactory.

aureo-variegata—leaves variegated with yellow

bullata—a lower form with short blunt leaves that are decidedly dark green

handsworthi—a strong growing upright form with dark green leaves tending to make a wide shrub rather than a tree. Its habit of growth makes it adaptable for use in hedges. An excellent ornamental.

myrtifolia—a low variety, 4–5' tall

pendula—treelike in habit with the tips of the shoots pendulous; the entire plant has a graceful outline

rosmarinifolia—low shrub with leaves only about ¼–⅜" long, about the smallest of any *B. sempervirens* variety

suffruticosa—the true "edging box," the smallest of all varieties and one of the most popular with leaves up to ¾" long. Plants over 150 years old are no more than 3 feet high. It is very dense, compact and slow growing, making an ideal plant for edging perennial bed or garden walk. It has been known and used in European gardens for centuries. An excellent dwarf evergreen, with leaves more fragrant than other varieties and the least subject to attacks from the box leaf miner.

The Common Box has been intimately associated with gardens in North America since early colonial times when no garden in any of the southern colonies was considered complete without it. Today there are still majestic specimens that have grown continuously since those times. Many a hedge and specimen are to be seen in the famous old gardens along the James River in Virginia, at Mount Vernon on the Potomac, and in other well known gardens. More recently box has been used in plantings in Washington, D.C., especially in the famous plantings about the Lincoln Memorial.

The center of the box-growing region on the Eastern Seaboard seems to be the Chesapeake Bay region but splendid specimens are to be found throughout the entire southeastern United States. Box will grow equally well in acid or alkaline soils but responds well to mulching with peat or leaf mold, for the roots require cool, moist growing conditions.

Transplanting should always be done with a ball of earth about the roots. Plants should be protected, especially in the North, from drying winter winds or severely low temperatures, by providing a screen of evergreen boughs, burlap, or even boards about valuable plants. In building these, plenty of room should be provided for circulation of air about the plants. Shading young plants from hot sun in the heat of summer is sometimes necessary for the first year or so after transplanting, or at least until the plants become well established. It may be advisable to spray the foliage of recently transplanted specimens on a summer

This old Box has been growing on Cape Cod for a hundred years.

evening in order to keep the foliage in good condition during the first dry months of growth in a new situation. Box plants that are thoroughly watered at regular intervals seem to be more resistant to disease and insect pests and make better plants than those not so treated.

Box takes well to pruning and so makes excellent hedges but specimens should only be clipped for specific reasons. Dead twigs and debris should be removed annually from the center for fungus growth gets its initial start in such places. New methods have been found to keep the pests of box under control.

Callicarpa japonica   4½′   Zone 5   Japanese Beauty-berry

FLOWERS: pink or whitish
   TIME: early July
*FRUIT: violet to metallic-purple berries about ¾₁₆″ diameter
   EFFECTIVE: fall

AUTUMN COLOR: yellow
HABITAT: Japan
INTRODUCED: 1845

An upright shrub with fairly inconspicuous flowers but with uniquely-colored purple fruits, borne on the tips of the current year's growth, and remaining on the plant a few weeks after the leaves have fallen. Heavy pruning in early spring tends to force vigorous growth with a consequent profuse production of fruits. Other than the colorful fruits—which do not remain effective nearly as long as on some of the viburnums—this shrub has little to offer in the garden.

Callistemon lanceolatus   30'   Zone 9   Lemon Bottlebrush

*FLOWER: with bright red stamens; in spikes
TIME: February–July
FOLIAGE: evergreen, leaves 3" long
HABITAT: Australia

Rugged colorful evergreens, there are some selected strains far superior to others. Seedlings should be avoided if possible as many prove worthless ornamentals. Can be grown in dry soil, and since the foliage is fairly ineffective, the plants should be used against a foliage background for the better display of the flowers.

CALLUNA

The heathers are familiar to everyone. Particularly are they enjoyed for their diminutive size, their evergreen foliage and an Old World charm peculiar to them alone for they have often been mentioned in legend and song. Native over a wide area in Europe, they must have been brought to America by the earliest settlers and in places they have escaped cultivation and become naturalized. Although we do not see as much of them in this country as abroad (it has been noted that in the early part of the eighteenth century heathers covered one-fifth of the Netherlands alone) nevertheless the small evergreen plants with their small flowers are a familiar sight to most gardeners. They range in height from the small *Calluna vulgaris foxi* which is only a few inches tall, to the vigorous upright growing *C. calluna hammondi* which may reach two and one half feet.

Their flowers are greatly admired, and their close-growing, evergreen foliage often forms a dense mat of green over the ground. The myriads of small flowers are borne on pert, upright spikes, six to eight inches or more in length, blooming during the early part of the summer. The flower colors vary, according to the variety, from pure white through pink to deep purple and red.

The moors in Europe and the British Isles consist of many hundreds of acres of heather. The plants produce tremendous quantities of seed and so, when growing in just the right location, naturally increase rapidly. They have appeared (in Europe) chiefly on discarded areas of land or burned-over forest land, especially where the soil is of very low productivity. They have been known to cover such wide areas that it is no wonder that man, in his ever-grasping search for land, has encroached on the heaths and has devised ways of using them for his advantage. Livestock has been grazed on them, sods have been cut of them to make houses and to supply fuel, brushes and brooms have been made from them, and even medicinal extracts have been made from some of them. Consequently they have been closely associated with the lives of many people in Europe for centuries, and this is possibly one of the reasons why some of us in this country like to include them in our gardens. In fact, one of the most beautiful pictures in the room where this is being written is of a gorgeous Scottish heath, with rolling country in the background, lavender heather in the foreground completely surrounding a charming pool near a picturesque specimen of the red-barked Scotch Pine.

These plants are especially adapted for use in rock gardens, where space is limited, and for bank plantings or for naturalizing, where land is more ample. They can be used as ground covers, in and about taller-growing shrubs or in numerous other ways. However, there are certain special conditions which must be met before one can have success with them.

In the first place the soil must be acid. Secondly (believe it or not) the soil must be poor and not fertile. If the soil is fertile the plants will grow vigorously, but soon become leggy and may even die. A poor soil forces them to grow more slowly and keep their respective sizes. They will do well in soil adapted to blueberries or azaleas, mostly with a pH of about 4.5 to 6.0. There are several acidifying agents which can be added to the soil if it is not already acid enough (see page 247). The soil must be normally moist—not necessarily wet—but certainly not a soil which dries out completely during parts of the year. They must not become too leggy but should be clipped or even cut to the ground in early spring to force plenty of young succulent growth and fine bloom. Our experience has been that if this is done in summer, or even in winter, the plants may die, but it can be safely done in early spring.

In order to bloom well they should have plenty of sunshine. They will withstand shade as ground covers, but in order to yield a maximum display of flowers, they must have full sun. They are being successfully grown as far north as Bar Harbor, Maine, where moisture conditions are ideal. Sometimes in New England, we have found it necessary to cover them in winter to protect them from the brilliantly strong sunshine of the early spring months, especially if the snow cover is not adequate. Pine boughs, a light hay or straw mulch is ideal. On several occasions, the collection in the Arnold Arboretum has been almost completely killed because of failure to provide this winter protection.

In this country there are about twenty varieties of *Calluna vulgaris* available from nurseries. The chances are that the nomenclature has become slightly confused. Before the second World War, I was corresponding with a friend in Belgium who claimed he had collected sixty different varieties in his garden. I have listed only fifteen varieties, suggested none for discard, for each seems to have individuality. The most important varieties might be the tall-growing *hammondi* with white flowers; *plena* with double pink flowers; *purpurea* with purple flowers; *atrorubens* (frequently called *alporti* in the trade) with splendid crimson flowers; *aurea* with golden yellow leaves; *cuprea* also with yellow leaves that turn a splendid bronze in winter; and finally both *nana* and *foxi* which are extremely low, compact forms. The varieties *serotina* and *searlei* flower from September to November, the last of this group to bloom. One of the important assets of these plants is that cut branches, with or without flowers, quickly dry in such a lifelike form that they can be kept in dried flower arrangements for months and still be of interest.

When a group of heathers is to be planted, the individual plants should be spaced about a foot apart. Care should be taken, however, to separate more widely the vigorous forms from the slow-growing and dwarf forms, so that the strong varieties will not quickly overgrow the others. An acid peat moss mixed with the soil makes an excellent medium in which to grow them. The first year, especially during the summer, they may require a great deal of watering, but this can be gradually reduced the second growing season.

In recommending heathers, the genus *Erica* should certainly be mentioned. Plants in this genus are not quite as hardy but they have bright flowers at times when the *Calluna* species are not in bloom. One species in particular is grown in the East, *Erica carnea*, called the Spring Heath. This even survives New England's vigorous winters and its small, bright pink flowers appear in many cases immediately after the snow disappears in spring.

Other species of *Erica* are not hardy north of Zones 6 and 7, but in the Pacific Northwest some of the species are most desirable in gardens. Here the cool climate and moist atmosphere are inducive to excellent growth. *Erica darleyensis,* a hybrid from the Mediterranean area of southern Europe, is one of the most vigorous and floriferous, starting to bloom in November (in the Pacific Northwest) and continuing until early spring. Because it blooms at a time when few plants will, many gardeners like it in their gardens. Its lilac-pink flowers are not as colorful as those of some other species such as *E. cinerea*, which blooms in June and ranges in color from pure white to pink, purple and red. Other species are available from American sources, and for those who have been successful in growing the heathers, the heaths offer interesting possibilities for new trials.

Calluna vulgaris   18″   Zone 4   **Heather**

*FLOWERS: white to red according to variety, in small spikes
    TIME: summer
*FOLIAGE: evergreen, various colors, leaves minute
    AUTUMN COLOR: green to bronze
HABITAT: Europe

INTRODUCED: early colonial times
VARIETIES:

> *alba*—white flowers
> *atrorubens*—leaves grayish, flowers crimson
> *aurea*—leaves golden yellow
> *cuprea*—leaves golden yellow
> *decumbens*—with spreading partly prostrate branches
> *foxi*—dwarf, cushionlike tufts
> *hammondi*—tall, white flowers
> *hirsuta*—branchlets and leaves grayish
> *nana*—low, 5–10″ high, flowers purple
> *plena*—flowers double pink
> *purpurea*—flowers dark purple
> *searlei*—tall white flowers, late September to November
> *serotina*—flowers white, late September and November
> *variegata*—leaves variegated with white
> *erecta*—upright branches

These varieties should be considered a "selection" of the better forms but there are others. Heather, when grown properly, forms a dense carpet over the ground normally only 6–8″ high. The bright-colored flowers are highly ornamental but the foliage colors of some varieties as well as the autumn colors of a few are also intensely colorful. Because of their evergreen foliage they make ideal ground covers.

Calycanthus floridus   9′   Zone 4   Carolina Allspice

*FLOWERS: dark, reddish brown
TIME: mid-May
AUTUMN COLOR: yellowish
HABITAT: southeastern United States

This native shrub has been associated with gardens in the United States since early colonial times for it makes a dense bush with glossy foliage and grows well in almost any soil. Its dark reddish brown flowers are very fragrant and its foliage is aromatic when crushed.

Camellia japonica   45′   Zone 7   Common Camellia

*FLOWERS: conspicuous, large, white to red, single or double, 2–5″ in diameter
TIME: October–April
*FOLIAGE: evergreen, lustrous, dark, leathery, leaves to 4″ long
HABITAT: China, Japan
INTRODUCED: 1797

The popular, late-flowering camellia of the South is this species from Japan represented by several hundred varieties now being grown in this country. These range in color from pure white to a rich, deep red with all the variations in between. Flowers of some varieties are single, some are semi-double and some are very double. Popular for growing in shaded situations where other plants may not bloom well. It is interesting to note the large number of varieties which have occurred within one species. So often, as in roses for example, hybridization between several species has resulted in a large number of varieties, but here the large number of varieties has resulted chiefly from hybridization within a single species and also the raising of many bud sports.

The flower forms of these camellias differ considerably and some authors have divided the varieties into nine different groups or classes. Chief among these, however, is the single type with one row of no more than six petals with prominent yellow stamens in the center (var. "Amabilis"); the semi-double type, variously named, with mature petals around the perimeter of the flower and many small petals or modified stamens in the center ("Adolphe Audusson"); and several ramifications of the double form with petals regularly placed in a very definite arrangement ("C. M. Hovey") or with no apparent petal arrangement but still very few stamens ("Debutante"); and others very definitely double but with a center of golden stamens when fully open ("Kumasaka"). The flowers of some varieties have the general form of roses while others are suggestive of peonies. The camellia specialist is particular about his selection of just the right flower type, but for the amateur they are all beautiful and the twenty-five suggested varieties contain some of the best of all the flower types.

The camellia is widely grown from North Carolina to Florida along the Gulf Coast, and on the Pacific Coast as far north as Seattle. Even when their large waxy brilliantly-colored flowers are not evident the C. japonica makes a good evergreen shrub for its foliage alone. The varieties of this species, though they bloom at different times, come as a group after the varieties of C. sasanqua which bloom from September to October. Most varieties can be grown in normally good soil of about 6.0 pH or slightly less in the full sun, though many withstand shade very well indeed. The following popular varieties now being grown in the South and on the Pacific Coast have been selected to exemplify the wide range of color and type of flower in this most variable species. (The color notes are taken from "Camellias in America" by H. H. Hume, 1946, and refer to the English Horticultural Colour Chart.)

Red varieties:

"Adolphe Audusson"—flowers semi-double, 4" diameter, turkey red 721 to rose madder 23.

"Arajishi"—flowers double, 3–4" diameter and 1½" high, turkey red 721, blooms early for this species.

"Aunt Jetty"—flowers double, 4" diameter, 2" high, turkey red 721. The parent plant of this variety in western Florida (Tallahassee) is about 132 years old. It is not apparently injured by cold weather.

"C. M. Hovey"—flowers double, 3¼–4" diameter and flat, carmine 21, slightly variegated. This was first raised a century ago by Hovey & Co., of Cambridge, Mass., in 1847, when camellia growing in greenhouses was a popular industry in New England. This is a splendid type and might well be considered one of the best and most dependable of all.

"Gloire De Nantes"—flowers double, nearly 4" diameter by 1½" high, crimson 22/1.

"Lady Vansittart"—flowers semi-double, 4" diameter, 1¼" high, carmine rose 621. Sometimes the flowers are almost variegated, white with carmine stripes, but is a comparative newcomer to the United States having been introduced here in 1917.

"Mathotiana"—flowers double, 4" wide and 2" high; carmine 21/1 with a coloring along the edges of the petals. Flowers are shaped very much like those of a rose.

"Prince Eugene Napoleon"—flowers double, 3″ diameter, 1″ high, rather flat, crimson 22.

"Professor C. S. Sargent"—flowers double, 3–4″ diameter, 2″ high, turkey red 721. It was named after Charles Sprague Sargent, the first Director of the Arnold Arboretum, Boston, Mass. This variety is an excellent one, grows vigorously, is among the hardiest and is sometimes used as an under-stock on which other varieties are grafted.

Pink varieties:

"Debutante"—flowers double, 3″ diameter and 1¾″ high, carmine to carmine rose 621/1. This originated as a chance seedling in Magnolia Gardens on the Ashley River of South Carolina, a show garden where many excellent varieties of camellias are grown. It is free flowering, tall, compact in habit, and the flowers are of a color, size and shape desirable for use in corsages.

"Frau Minna Seidel"—flowers double, 2½″ diameter, 1¼″ high, carmine rose 621/3. This is one of the most commonly grown of all camellia varieties, often found under the name of "Pink Perfection." It is vigorous and compact in habit, a reliable sort, and one which might easily be the single selection for a small garden.

"Lady Humes Blush"—flowers double, 2¾″–3″ diameter, 1¼″ high, white, blushed pink. This is a slow grower, and though long in this country has not proved as popular as other varieties. It is a good color however and so is recommended in this small selective group.

"Magnoliaeflora"—single flowers, 3½″ wide and 1½″ high, white but blushed a very delicate light pink.

"Otome"—flowers double, 3½″ wide and 1½″ high, carmine rose 623/2 in central part of petals shading to almost white at the margins. This is another excellent type for corsages and the plant produces many fine blossoms.

"Sweeti Vera"—flowers double, 4″ diameter, 2″ high, carmine rose 621/1 and slightly lighter at the center, sometimes almost white. The flower petals are marked with red lines and dots.

White varieties:

"Alba Plena"—flowers double, 4″ diameter, often 3″ high and pure white. This is one of the oldest varieties in the United States and is still very popular. It is vigorous and compact and has been known to endure short cold spells of 10° F.

"Amabilis"—flowers single, 3″ diameter, white.

"Imura"—flowers semi-double, 4¾″ diameter, white. This originated in the Overlook Nurseries of Crichton, Alabama, from Japanese seed grown there in 1925. It is very much like a water lily in form of the flowers. Some like this variety best of all for its general habit of growth, reliability and delicate floral beauty.

"Purity"—flowers double, 3½″ diameter, 1¼″ high, white. A widely popular variety with flowers of long lasting quality and desirable for corsages. The petals are slightly wavy and almost like porcelain in texture.

Variegated varieties:

"Daikagura"—flowers double, 4″ diameter and 2″ high, carmine rose 621 with blotches of white. This early flowering variety is one of the best in its group and was introduced into this country from Japan. Unfortunately it grows slowly and tends to be slightly open in habit.

"Donckelari"—flowers semi-double, 4″ diameter, 1½″ high, turkey red 721, with some flowers having white markings. Another hardy variety, it was introduced from the Orient by that famous German naturalist Philipp Franz von Siebold, who spent several years in Japan beginning about 1823.

"Herme"—flowers double, 3½″ diameter and 1¾″ high and extremely variegated red and white. This slightly fragrant variety is known under three names: "Herme," "Souv. de Henri Guichard" and "Jordan's Pride." This might be construed as an indication of its extreme popularity.

"Kumasaka"—flowers double, 4″ diameter, 1¼″ high, carmine 21/1 or variegated with white markings. Only moderately vigorous, it is compact and upright in habit.

"Lady Clare"—flowers semi-double, 4¾″ diameter, 1¼″ high, carmine rose 621 with some variegation of darker colors in the petals. The flowers do not remain in good condition as long as do those of some other varieties.

"Sara-Sa"—flowers semi-double, 4½″ diameter, 1½″ high—a dull white with narrow broken stripes and dots of red. This is another variety that is popular on the Pacific Coast as well as in the southern United States.

Camellia sasanqua   20′   Zone 7   Sasanqua Camellia

FLOWERS: white, mostly single, 3″ in diameter
    TIME: September to December
FOLIAGE: evergreen, lustrous, leaves to 2″ long
HABITAT: Japan
INTRODUCED: 1879
VARIETIES:

"Blanchette"—flowers single, 2½″ diameter, white and tinted pink on petal margins

"Briar Rose"—flowers single, 3″ diameter, fuchsine pink 627/1 to 627/3

"Hebe"—flowers single, 3″ diameter, phlox pink 625

"Hugh Evans"—flowers single, 3″ diameter, rose madder 23/3

"Mino-no-yuki"—flowers double, 4″ diameter, white faintly scented.

"Tanya"—flowers single, 2″ diameter, rose bengal 25

Nearly 75 varieties of this species are listed in American nursery catalogues. Only a few have double flowers, most have single flowers. This species is valued because its flowers bloom just before those of *C. japonica* varieties and thus prolong the season during which these exquisite plants can be appreciated. The foliage is smaller, the shrub is more loose and open in its habit of growth. The flowers have an elusive fragrance and the colors range from pure white to deep pink.

Caragana arborescens   18′   Zone 2   Siberian Pea-tree

FLOWERS: yellow, similar to pea flowers
    TIME: mid-May
HABITAT: Siberia, Manchuria

INTRODUCED: 1752
VARIETY: *pendula* with pendulous branches and sometimes grafted high on the species.

A very hardy shrub, used a great deal as a windbreak on the plains of Manitoba, Saskatchewan and Alberta. Its upright habit, ability to withstand pruning and hardiness are its chief assets, together with its yellow pealike flowers. Otherwise it is a coarse shrub (together with other members of the genus) and usually better shrubs can be found for most gardens.

Caragana maximowicziana   4½'   Zone 2   Maximowicz Pea-tree

FLOWERS: yellow, pealike
  TIME: late May
HABITAT: western China
INTRODUCED: 1910

Of value chiefly for its densely branched and spreading habit. The specimen in the Arnold Arboretum is only about 3' high but nearly 12' in diameter. Hence it makes a sprawling mass of foliage that does have a place in certain gardens under a specific set of conditions. Other than its interesting form, it has nothing particular to recommend it.

Caragana microphylla   9'   Zone 3   Littleleaf Pea-tree

FLOWERS: yellow, pealike
  TIME: mid-May
HABITAT: Siberia, northern China
INTRODUCED: 1789

Carissa grandiflora   18'   Zone 9   Natal-Plum

*FLOWERS: white, fragrant, 2" in diameter
*FRUIT: scarlet berries, edible, 1–2" long
*FOLIAGE: evergreen, lustrous leaves 3" long
HABITAT: South Africa

Spiny, branched shrub, with lustrous leathery evergreen leaves and waxy white flowers, this plant makes an excellent sheared hedge in the warmer parts of the country, especially near the sea shore.

Carpenteria californica   8'   Zone 7–8   Evergreen Mock-orange

*FLOWERS: white in clusters, fragrant, 2–3" in diameter
  TIME: summer
FOLIAGE: evergreen, leaves to 4" long
HABITAT: California

A showy native shrub, often used as a substitute for the mock-orange in California, and often called Tree-Anemone. It is rather difficult to transplant and needs protection from cold and high winds but it is still worthy of a trial in some gardens for its summer bloom and its generally refined appearance.

x Caryopteris clandonensis   4'   Zone 5   Bluebeard

FLOWERS: bright blue in many flowered slender-stalked clusters
  TIME: late August
HYBRID ORIGIN: *C. incana* x *C. mongholica*

ORIGINATED: 1933

A late-flowering shrub of particular interest for its intense blue flower spikes, making it unusual among hardy woody plants if for nothing else than this color. One of the first clons of this species is called "Blue Mist," a fitting name. It may be killed back in severe winters and if not, a rather severe pruning in the early spring seems to keep it more compact and capable of making a better display in flower. This species can easily be treated as a perennial and planted in the perennial garden where it will give a splendid color contrast for late blooming calendulas, marigolds and zinnias.

Cassia corymbosa   10'   Zone 8   Flowery Senna

*FLOWERS: yellow, in axilliary clusters
  TIME: July to frost
HABITAT: Argentina
A free flowering plant for southern gardens.

Ceanothus americanus   3'   Zone 4   New Jersey Tea

FLOWERS: small, white, in upright oblong clusters
  TIME: mid-June
HABITAT: eastern North America
This is not a good garden plant and hard to move. It is only recommended for poor soil, where better plants will not grow. The leaves of this plant were used as a substitute for tea during the Revolutionary War. This species was the first to be cultivated and is one of the parents of many popular hybrids, which are grown on the Pacific Coast, especially in southern California where one nursery-man lists over 20 hybrid varieties. In general, the use of Ceanothus species and varieties is limited to the Pacific Coast where many recent introductions are fast becoming popular. One of the greatest areas in the world for concentration of the genus *Ceanothus* is about Santa Barbara, California. A special study of this group is being conducted by the Santa Barbara Botanic Garden.

x Ceanothus delilianus   6'   Zone 7   Delisle Ceanothus

*FLOWERS: pale to deep blue, in small terminal panicles
  TIME: April
*FOLIAGE: evergreen, leaves 1½–3" long
HYBRID ORIGIN: *C. americanus x C. coeruleus*
ORIGINATED: before 1830
Many popular hybrids valued for evergreen foliage and profuse flowers. Only used in warmer parts of Pacific Coast area:
  "Gloire de Versailles"—flowers pale blue
  "Gloire de Plantières"—flowers deep blue
  "Autumnal Blue"—flowers deep blue
  "Leon Simon"—flowers pale blue

Ceanothus ovatus   3'   Zone 4   Inland Ceanothus

FLOWERS: small white, in small clusters
  TIME: early June
*FRUIT: red capsules
  EFFECTIVE: summer

HABITAT: eastern United States

This upright shrub is superior to *C. americanus* in that it is lower and denser in habit of growth and its bright red fruits are colorful for several weeks in the summer. They are merely dry capsules but during the ripening period in mid-summer they are colorful. Used chiefly for naturalizing purposes.

Ceanothus thyrsiflorus   30'   Zone 8   Blueblossom

FLOWERS: blue, rarely white in panicles, 1–3" long
   TIME: March
FOLIAGE: evergreen, leaves to 2" long
HABITAT: Oregon to California

One of the hardiest of the evergreen *Ceanothus* species and popular on the West Coast. It is frequently infested with scale which must be guarded against. It does well in dry soils but this old fashioned popular species is being replaced in gardens by *C. griseus* which is very similar and much less susceptible to pests.

Cephalanthus occidentalis   15'   Zone 4   Buttonbush

FLOWERS: creamy white in round heads about 1" in diameter
   TIME: late July
HABITAT: eastern United States

Especially valued for its ability to grow in swampy land or on banks next to water. It does not thrive in dry soil. Its globose flowers, prominent chiefly because of many protruding pistils, make it of interest in late summer when few woody plants bloom. Unless a moist situation is available, this shrub should not be grown.

Ceratostigma willmottianum   4'   Zone 8   Willmott Blue Leadwort

*FLOWERS: bright blue, nearly 1" in diameter
   TIME: summer
HABITAT: western China
INTRODUCED: 1908

A finely-branched low shrub for poor soil but usable only in the most protected spots. Its bright blue phloxlike flowers appear continuously throughout the summer.

Cercis chinensis   40'   Zone 6   Chinese Judas-tree

*FLOWERS: rosy-purple, dense, pealike
   TIME: mid-May
AUTUMN COLOR: yellow
HABITAT: central China
INTRODUCED: before 1850

Even though this is a tree in its native habitat, it has proved more or less shrubby in this country and is better grown this way, especially in the North. Its profuse, rosy-purple pealike flowers are its chief interest to gardeners.

CHAENOMELES

This is a group of Asiatic shrubs grown chiefly for their dense, often low habit, and their bright-colored flowers, which appear before the leaves. They were very popular for hedge making in this country before the advent of the Japanese Barberry. But, with the introduction of the San Jose scale, it was found that these plants were susceptible, and because the pest was much feared, a majority of the old hedges were removed. Japanese Barberry quickly took its place as one of the most serviceable types of hedge materials available. Even now, with much better knowledge of control methods, the Japanese quinces are not used extensively in hedges for there are many other materials superior to it and free of pest troubles as well. However, this group of colorfully flowering plants is still popular and many varieties are used as specimens for early spring interest.

They have been widely grown by nurserymen in Europe for at least one hundred years, and because they hybridize readily and grow easily from seed, many varieties have originated during the years until now the nomenclature is considerably mixed. Botanists have aided somewhat in this confusion by finding it necessary to change the scientific names several times during the past few years. What used to be known as *Pyrus japonica* became *Cydonia japonica* and is now *Chaenomeles lagenaria*. In this country nurserymen have added to the confusion by growing their own stock from seed and giving their own seedlings new names. In the Arnold Arboretum, for instance, nearly fifty varieties are growing, and in comparing them recently it was found that in one color group alone (scarlet to geranium lake on the English Horticultural Colour Chart) seven varieties were identical as far as flower color was concerned.

The foliage of most varieties is a dark glossy green throughout the growing season. Some have leaves that at first are slightly bronze colored as they unfurl in spring. None have prominent autumn color except *C. sinensis*, which is not very hardy north of Washington, D. C., and is almost a small tree.

The flowers range in color from pure white (*Chaenomeles lagenaria* "Nivalis") to deep dark red, the darkest of all in the Arnold Arboretum collection being *C. lagenaria* "Umbilicata" and *C. lagenaria* "Simoni." Some varieties have single flowers, others semi-double or double. They range in size from about one inch in diameter to those of *C. lagenaria* "Kermisina semiplena" which are two inches in diameter. Some individual plants are erratic in the kind of flowers they produce, for one plant may have both single and double flowers.

Fruits are green and applelike, some turning yellow at maturity, and certainly cannot be classed as ornamental. All can be used in making jellies, since these species are, of course, closely related to the common quince, *Cydonia oblonga*, which has fruits high in pectin.

Most varieties are thorny, some of the thorns being modified branches over one inch in length, while the thorns on vigorous-growing shoots are much smaller. The plants are very dense in habit of growth, most of the *C. lagenaria* varieties having a mature height of about 6', although this can be materially reduced by intelligent pruning. The smallest and lowest of all is the little *C. japonica alpina*, which does not grow more than a foot or two in height and is literally covered with bright orange flowers in spring.

This is one group of plants which well illustrates what might be termed "over production" of ornamental varieties. Far too many have been introduced and are available in the trade today but, as with all groups of plants, there is still room for improvement. Mr. W. B. Clarke, at his nursery in San Jose, California, has done considerable work during the past few years with the hybridization of these plants and is offering many original varieties, some of which are not completely hardy in the northern states.

The quinces can be grown in any good soil and are hardy except in the severest winters when their flower buds may be killed. They require occasional renewal pruning and given this they can usually be depended upon for brilliant bloom each spring. It is of interest to note that the following species and varieties can be divided into seven different color groups according to their flowers:—orange, reddish orange, scarlet, geranium lake, carmine, turkey red and white.

Chaenomeles japonica   3′   Zone 4   Japanese Quince

*FLOWERS: single 1¼″ diameter, nasturtium red
   TIME: early May
HABITAT: Japan
INTRODUCED: about 1874
   Valued for its low habit requiring far less pruning than do varieties of *C. lagenaria*.
VARIETY: *alpina*—probably the best variety for it is the lowest, seldom over one foot high and very dense—flowers orange (12–616), single, 1¼″ diameter

Chaenomeles lagenaria   6′   Zone 4   Flowering Quince

*FLOWERS: scarlet red, varying to pink and white
   TIME: early May
FRUIT: large, green, applelike
FOLIAGE: dark green often glossy
HABITAT: China
INTRODUCED: before 1800
VARIETIES: (color according to English Horticultural Colour Chart)
Reddish orange (16–0619)
   "Apricot"—single flowers, 1⅜″ diameter
   "Double Orange"—double flowers, 1½″ diameter
   "Incendie"—double flowers, 1⅜″ diameter
Scarlet (19–620)
   "Baltzi"—single flowers, 1¾″ diameter
   "Cardinalis"—double flowers, 1½″ diameter
   "Kermesina semiplena"—semi-double flowers, 2″ diameter
Geranium lake (20–0621)
   "Phyllis Moore"—semi-double flowers, 1⅜″ diameter
   "Rosea Plena"—double flowers, 1¾″ diameter
   "Bonfire"—single flowers, 2″ diameter
   "Blood Red" (rubra grandiflora)—single flowers, 1¾″ diameter

Carmine (621)
>"Marmorata"—single flowers, 1½" diameter
>"Moerloesi"—single flowers, 1¾" diameter

Turkey red (721)
>"Simoni"—semi-double flowers, 1½" diameter
>"Umbilicata"—single flowers, 1½" diameter

White
>"Nivalis"—single flowers, 1¾" diameter

Widely planted in the gardens of many countries of the North Temperate Zone, this species varies widely and has many varieties with flowers white, pink, dark red, some single and some semi-double.

Chamaecyparis obtusa varieties   Zone 3   Hinoki Cypress

*FOLIAGE: evergreen, scalelike
HABITAT: Japan
INTRODUCED: 1861
VARIETIES:

>*compacta*—dwarf, broad, conical bush

>*filicoides*—one of the daintiest of all—the plant in Arnold Arboretum is 8' tall and only 3' in diameter, with lateral branchlets of equal length crowded along the branches making a fernlike appearance.

>*gracilis*—compact pyramidal form with the tips of the branchlets slightly pendulous

>*lycopodioides*—a dwarf shrubby form with the branchlets all in one plane

>*pygmaea*—with creeping almost prostrate branches of very slow growth. Old plants are said to be no more than 1½–2' tall. One of the smallest of the varieties of *C. obtusa*.

These are only a few of the many dwarf forms of *Chamaecyparis obtusa*, a standard tree in Japan. Unfortunately the species is frequently seen in foundation plantings and quickly grows out of scale unless severely pruned. The varieties are more slow growing and can be used with shrubs and low evergreens.

Chamaecyparis pisifera, shrubby varieties   Zone 3   Sawara False-cypress

*FOLIAGE: narrow-leaved, evergreen
HABITAT: Japan
INTRODUCED: 1861
VARIETIES:

>*filifera*—pyramidal shrub with threadlike branchlets

>*minima*—low, shrubby form, dense growth, foliage crowded on short branches

>*squarrosa*—branches frondlike with foliage soft and somewhat resembling moss from a distance

This species is a standard tree but some of the varieties are shrubby. Unfortunately the species is often used in foundation plantings as a shrub and quickly grows out of all proportion to surrounding plants. Even the Thread False Cypress (*C. pisifera filifera*) can grow tall but usually is treated as a shrub and kept within bounds by pruning. The Moss False-cypress (*C. pisifera squarrosa*) has soft foliage, gray to bluish in the growing season and slightly bronze in fall. These varieties make fairly good evergreens, but should be pruned occasionally to keep in vigorous condition. Very few of the *Chamaecyparis* grow old gracefully.

Chilopsis linearis   30′   Zone 7   Desert-willow

*FLOWERS: lilac, trumpet-shaped, resembling snapdragons, fragrant
   TIME: July until frost
FOLIAGE: leaves narrow and willowlike, to 1′ long
HABITAT: Texas and Mexico
   Willowlike in habit but with conspicuous flowers somewhat similar to those of Catalpa, in small terminal clusters.

Chimonanthus praecox   8′   Zone 7   Wintersweet

FLOWERS: yellow, striped purplish brown, very fragrant
   TIME: April
HABITAT: China
INTRODUCED: 1766
VARIETY: *praecox grandiflorus*—flowers larger and deeper yellow but less fragrant
   During mild winters this shrub appears in bloom very early. It does best with slight shade and needs little pruning.

Chionanthus virginicus   30′   Zone 4   Fringe-tree

*FLOWERS: white, in loose panicles
   TIME: early June
FRUIT: dark blue, grapelike in clusters
   EFFECTIVE: fall

The Fringe-tree (*Chionanthus virginicus*) is a close relative of the lilac and blooms just a week or so later. Although the sexes are supposed to be separate, both staminate and pistillate plants have profuse panicles of white flowers.

AUTUMN COLOR: bright yellow
HABITAT: New Jersey to Florida

The native Fringe-tree is just as ornamental if not slightly more so than its oriental relative. Its fleecy white flowers are produced in the utmost profusion. Usually the sexes are separate with the staminate flowers being larger. Closely related to the lilacs, this species also must be watched for scale infestations. Otherwise it is a splendid ornamental, especially as a specimen in the full sun. It is considered by some Europeans as the most beautiful and striking of native American shrubs. Its only draw-back, if such it might be construed to be, is the fact that it is one of the last shrubs to produce leaves in the spring. In fact they appear so late, many people think the plants are dead.

Choisya ternata   9'   Zone 7   Mexican Orange

FLOWERS: white, 1" diameter, fragrant
  TIME: late May
FOLIAGE: evergreen, aromatic, leaves to 3" long
HABITAT: Mexico

A serviceable ornamental evergreen with fragrant flowers and aromatic foliage, doing well in full sun but requiring pruning in order to force a bushy, well branched shrub.

Chrysothamnus graveolens   5'   Zone 3   Greenplume Rabbitbrush

*FLOWERS: golden yellow in heavy trusses, somewhat similar to goldenrod
  TIME: late summer
FOLIAGE: gray, aromatic, leaves to 2½" long
HABITAT: Montana to New Mexico

A native over a wide section of the western part of the United States, suitable for well-drained sunny situations in dry alkaline soil which they require in order to produce their large conspicuous trusses of golden-yellow flowers. Sometimes of interest because a small amount of rubber can be extracted from it, although not enough to be commercially important.

Cistus albidus   6'   Zone 7   Whiteleaf Rock-rose

FLOWERS: rosy lilac, petals blotched yellow, 2½" diameter
  TIME: intermittently throughout the summer
FOLIAGE: evergreen, leaves to 2" long
HABITAT: western Mediterranean region

One of the better magenta flowered species of *Cistus*. Like all members of this genus it is not easily moved and can best be transplanted into the garden from pots. Some other *Cistus* types are "Silver Pink," "Doris Hibberson," and "Sunset" with good deep pink flowers.

x Cistus cyprius   6'   Zone 7   Spotted Rock-rose

FLOWERS: white, each petal with a purple blotch, 3" diameter
  TIME: intermittently throughout the summer
FOLIAGE: evergreen, leaves to 3" long
HYBRID ORIGIN: (*C. laurifolius x C. ladaniferus*)

ORIGINATED: before 1790

A graceful, free flowering nybrid, blooming throughout the summer, and almost as hardy as *C. laurifolius*. Like other *Cistus* species it is not easily moved and is best planted into the garden from pots.

Cistus laurifolius   7'   Zone 7   Laurel Rock-rose

FLOWERS: white, yellow at base
  TIME: July
FOLIAGE: glabrous and dark, evergreen, leaves to 2½" long
HABITAT: Mediterranean region

The hardiest of the rock-roses. May grow scrawny at the base unless pruned heavily after flowering to insure sturdier plants. Not easily transplanted, best moved into the garden in pots.

x Cistus purpureus   Zone 7   Purple Rock-rose

FLOWERS: reddish purple with dark red blotch at base of each petal, 3" in diameter
  TIME: intermittently throughout summer
FOLIAGE: evergreen, leaves to 2" long
HYBRID ORIGIN: (*C. ladaniferus x C. villosus*)
ORIGINATED: before 1790

Clerodendron trichotomum   20'   Zone 6   Harlequin Glory-bower

FLOWERS: white, fragrant, 1¼" in diameter
  TIME: August
*FRUIT: blue berries, red calyx
EFFECTIVE: early fall
HABITAT: eastern China, Japan
INTRODUCED: 1880

A coarse large-leaved shrub which, if grown with a single stem, soon develops horizontal branches on which the fruits show off admirably. Flowers are slightly fragrant although not especially meritorious, but the fruit certainly is. It appears as a very bright blue berry about ¼" in diameter, conspicuously surrounded by a brilliant red star-shaped calyx which remains brilliantly colorful long after the fruit has dropped.

Clethra acuminata   18'   Zone 5   Cinnamon Clethra

FLOWERS: white, in nodding small racemes
  TIME: late July
AUTUMN COLOR: yellow to orange
*WINTER TWIGS: cinnamon-brown bark
HABITAT: southeastern United States

A native of the southern Appalachian Mountains, this plant is worth growing for its smooth, polished cinnamon-brown stems especially noticeable in the winter. Because of this it might be considered an eastern substitute for the Madrona of California. Its flowers are not as handsome as those of other *Clethra* species.

The fragrant Summersweet is a common native shrub of the eastern United States and does well in moist soils. This is the pink flowered variety.

Clethra alnifolia   9'   Zone 3   Summersweet

*FLOWERS: small, white, in narrow 4–6" spikes, very fragrant
    TIME: late July
AUTUMN COLOR: yellow to orange
HABITAT: eastern United States
VARIETY: *rosea*—flower buds pink, flowers at first pinkish

This shrub is excellent for fragrant summer bloom. It does well at the seashore and just as well inland along the coast. If the soil is too dry, it tends to get infestations of red spider which mar the foliage. Tending to grow in clumps, since it increases by underground stems, it is an excellent shrub for the border. There are places on the New England shore line where it is so profuse that it has been clipped in hedge form but this changes and mars the general effect of the plant.

Clethra barbinervis   30'   Zone 5   Japanese Clethra

FLOWERS: white, in horizontal racemes
  TIME: late July
HABITAT: Japan
INTRODUCED: 1870

This is the first of the clethras to bloom and by some is considered the most handsome. The racemes are held horizontally, and the plant is larger in every way than *C. alnifolia*, but the flowers are not so fragrant. For some reason or other, *C. barbinervis* has not been susceptible to the severe attacks of red spider often occurring on *C. alnifolia*.

Colutea arborescens   12'   Zone 5   Bladder-senna

FLOWERS: yellow to reddish in clusters, small
  TIME: May
HABITAT: southern Europe
INTRODUCED: 1570

This genus seems entirely too coarse for general landscape work. The seeds germinate readily and the plant quickly becomes a weed in the garden. Its only asset is its vigorous growth in almost any soil and hence it makes a good filler.

Comptonia peregrina   4'   Zone 2   Sweet Fern

*FOLIAGE: aromatic, fernlike
HABITAT: Nova Scotia to North Carolina, Indiana and Michigan

It is unfortunate that this excellent woody plant is so very difficult to transplant, otherwise it would be used considerably more than it is. Closely related to the *Myrica* species, its foliage is aromatic, for as one walks past it, the sweet aroma is clearly detected. Its fernlike leaves make it distinctive as a woody shrub. Peaty soil and moist locations are what it needs most. Sods, in which a major proportion of the roots are included, seem to be the best means of moving it from one place to another. It is best used in naturalistic plantings.

Coprosma petriei   3"   Zone 7   Petrie's Coprosma

FLOWERS: white or greenish, solitary, small
  TIME: spring
FRUIT: bluish purple
  EFFECTIVE: fall
FOLIAGE: evergreen, leaves about ¼" long
HABITAT: New Zealand
INTRODUCED: about 1910

A low prostrate evergreen shrub suitable only for the rock garden or some similar situation.

CORNUS

The dogwood group is a large one containing many shrubs and small trees, among which are some of the best ornamental woody plants we have at our disposal. The list of shrubby dogwoods available from nurseries in this country is, in my estimation, much too long. Some 36 species and varieties which might be omitted from commercial propagation are listed on page 416. Even the 17 species and varieties in the recommended list can be curtailed. The shrubby dogwoods are valued for their colored fruits, most of them for their bright red autumn color, and some for their bright-colored twigs during winter. The flowers are actually flat cymes or clusters of very small flowers, usually white or creamy white. They are not especially interesting yet they appear heavily massed all over the plants and give the appearance of a pleasing white blanket covering the shrubs at blooming time.

The fruits are small berries or drupes about ¼″ in diameter, usually borne in flat clusters, each drupe containing a two-celled nutlet. The fruits of *Cornus mas* and *C. officinalis* however are much larger; borne singly or in small groups they are like elongated cherries ½–¾″ long and just as fleshy. They remain on the plants from two to eight weeks, depending on the weather and the amount of bird food available at the time, for they are eaten greedily by the birds.

The autumn color of most species is a brilliant red. This varies in intensity with the season, planting situation, and exposure, but one does not have to hide the shrubby dogwoods among other plants for fear they will not be colorful in the fall.

The bright winter twigs of species like *C. alba, C. amomum* and *C. stolonifera* place these plants at the top of any list as prerequisites for the winter garden. Boldly conspicuous if given a prominent spot in a good, preferably moist soil, they are most colorful throughout the entire winter. The younger and more vigorous the twigs of these species, the brighter the winter color. Hence a vigorous renewal pruning would be in order each year to insure strong young growth from the base of the plant. When the plant becomes overgrown, it might well be cut to the ground in early spring, thus assuring many bright-colored branches the following two winters at least.

Occasionally the dogwoods are susceptible to attacks of dogwood scurfy scale. This should be known and watched for by all gardeners. It is a simple matter to spray such shrubs occasionally (while still dormant) with a miscible oil spray which affords an easy control for this pest. Other than this the dogwoods are all remarkably free from insect and disease trouble.

Cornus alba sibirica   9′   Zone 2   Siberian Dogwood

FLOWERS: yellowish white, small, in flat clusters 2″ in diameter
    TIME: late May
FRUIT: white to slightly blue berries
    EFFECTIVE: fall
AUTUMN COLOR: red
*WINTER TWIGS: bright coral-red
HABITAT: Siberia to Manchuria
INTRODUCED: 1741

OTHER VARIETIES OF *C. alba*:

argenteo-marginata—leaves bordered with white, to 5" long
gouchaulti—leaves variegated yellowish and pink, to 5" long
spaethi—leaves bordered with yellow, to 5" long

The variety *sibirica* is superior to the species because of its vivid red bark. All varieties of this species do not spread as rapidly as does *C. stolonifera,* hence they are recommended in situations where spread is undesirable. The variegated leaved forms are not as vigorous as the species. *Cornus alba sibirica* makes a splendid addition to the shrub border both because of its numerous white flower clusters and its conspicuous white fruits. For winter display there are few other deciduous plants which surpass it in colorful effectiveness.

Cornus amomum	9'	Zone 5	Silky Dogwood

FLOWERS: yellowish white, small in flat clusters 1½–2½" in diameter
    TIME: mid-June
FRUIT: blue to pale blue berries
    EFFECTIVE: summer
AUTUMN COLOR: red
WINTER TWIGS: reddish
HABITAT: eastern United States

Very similar to *C. alba sibirica* but inferior to it because the fruits are blue to pale blue—often a grayish blue and the twigs are not nearly as red. However, it is native over a wide area of the eastern United States and so should probably be included.

Cornus hessei	1½'	Zone 4	Hesse Dogwood

FLOWERS: pinkish white, small, in flat clusters
    TIME: late May
FRUIT: bluish white berries
    EFFECTIVE: late August
FOLIAGE: purplish to blackish green, leaves about 2" long
HABITAT: northeastern Asia
INTRODUCED: before 1889

Very dwarf in habit with dense leafy branches and curious dark green foliage, of value chiefly for this characteristic.

Cornus mas	24'	Zone 4	Cornelian Cherry

*FLOWERS: yellow, small, before the leaves
    TIME: early April
*FRUIT: scarlet, edible, ½–¾" long
    EFFECTIVE: August
FOLIAGE: shiny green
AUTUMN COLOR: red
HABITAT: central and southern Europe, western Asia
INTRODUCED: probably before 1800
VARIETIES:

elegantissima—leaves variegated with creamy white and tinged red, 4½" long
flava—yellow fruits
macrocarpa—fruit larger than species

One of the earliest blooming of the spring-flowering shrubs with flowers be-fore the leaves. A sturdy, vigorous plant, useful as a specimen or in the shrub border or as a hedge. Its fruits, which have been used in making preserves, are not too conspicuous for many are hidden by the foliage. The yellow fruiting form is more conspicuous in early summer but, except for color, need not be grown in preference to the species.

Cornus officinalis   30′   Zone 5   Japanese Cornel

*FLOWERS: yellow, small, before the leaves
    TIME: early April
*FRUIT: scarlet, edible, ½–¾″ long
    EFFECTIVE: August
FOLIAGE: shiny green
AUTUMN COLOR: red
*WINTER BARK: exfoliating
HABITAT: Japan and Korea
INTRODUCED: 1877

Probably much better for general landscape use than the common *C. mas* is this species because of its very interesting exfoliating bark. This character is completely hidden by the dense foliage in the summer, but during winter and early spring it is very much in evidence. Aside from this the two species are similar.

Cornus paucinervis   9′   Zone 5   Littleleaf Dogwood

FLOWERS: white, small, in clusters 2½–3½″ in diameter
    TIME: July–August
FRUIT: black berries
    EFFECTIVE: fall
FOLIAGE: nearly half evergreen, leaves to 4″ long
HABITAT: China
INTRODUCED: 1907

Cornus racemosa   15′   Zone 4   Gray Dogwood

FLOWERS: creamy white, small, in flat clusters 1½–2½″ in diameter
    TIME: mid-June
*FRUIT: white berries on red stalks
    EFFECTIVE: early summer
AUTUMN COLOR: purplish
WINTER TWIGS: gray
HABITAT: eastern United States

A much used native shrub, this plant grows vigorously and sprouts readily from the base. It withstands shearing well and because of its dense habit of growth, can be cut back harshly when necessary. Hence it can be used as a bar-rier planting and maintained easily at about 6–8′ high. It fruits earlier than many members of this genus.

Cornus stolonifera   7′   Zone 2   Red Osier Dogwood

FLOWERS: dull white, small in loose clusters 2½–3½″ in diameter
    TIME: late May

FRUIT: white berries
   EFFECTIVE: summer
AUTUMN COLOR: reddish
*WINTER TWIGS: brilliant red
HABITAT: eastern United States
VARIETIES:

> *flaviramea*—twigs brilliant yellow—Yellowtwig Dogwood
> *nitida*—twigs green—Greentwig Dogwood
> *kelseyi*—dwarf, rarely exceeding 24″ in height

This shrub and its varieties are especially valued for their highly colored winter twigs. They grow well in almost any soil but especially in moist situations. Creeping by stolons they make ideal plants for placing on banks of streams to hold the soil in place. Because these are natives they are here recommended as being superior to their European counterparts. The dwarf variety, *kelseyi*, has been used as a rather coarse ground cover. It is much branched with compact growth.

Corylopsis glabrescens   18′   Zone 5   Fragrant Winter-hazel
*FLOWERS: pale yellow, in nodding racemes, before the leaves
   TIME: mid-April
HABITAT: Japan
INTRODUCED: 1905

The hardiest of the species in this genus, this is the only species that is dependable for flowers in New England. The shrub itself, a relative of the witch-hazels, is neat, dense, somewhat flat-topped and rounded, chiefly of value for its very early flowers. *Corylopsis spicata* (Zone 6) is widely distributed but not quite as hardy.

Corylopsis griffithi   10′   Zone 7   Griffith Winter-hazel
*FLOWERS: yellow, nodding racemes, 1½–2½″ long, before the leaves
   TIME: mid-April
HABITAT: Himalayas
INTRODUCED: 1879

More ornamental than *C. glabrescens* but not nearly as hardy.

Corylus species and varieties   15–30′   Zones 3, 4   Hazels

The hazels are chiefly valued for the delicate pendulous catkins which are so prominent in early spring. Several are natives of North America and are found in thickets especially near water. Some of the European hazels are grown specifically for their nuts. Four ornamental varieties might be mentioned:

> *Corylus avellana aurea*—yellow leaves
> *Corylus avellana contorta*—twigs remarkably curled and twisted
> *Corylus avellana pendula*—with pendulous branches. If grafted high on the trunk of the species it makes an interesting plant.

One other hazel should be mentioned:

> *Corylus maxima purpurea* valued as an ornamental because of its purple leaves, about 5″ long. The purple-leaved form should be grown in full sun to produce its deepest purple. Gardeners who desire contrast in color of the foliage of their plants like to use these forms for they require practically no attention.

Cotinus americanus   30′   Zone 5   American Smoke Tree

FLOWERS: greenish
  TIME: mid-June
*AUTUMN COLOR: scarlet to orange
HABITAT: southeastern United States

The fruiting panicles are not showy but there is little to surpass it when autumn has touched the leaves a brilliant scarlet to orange. It should only be grown for its fall effect. In cases where the smaller smoke tree will suffice, this American species can be omitted.

Cotinus coggygria   15′   Zone 5   Smoke Bush

FLOWERS: greenish, sexes separate
  TIME: early June
*FRUIT: pinkish to grayish, plumose fruiting panicles
  EFFECTIVE: summer
*AUTUMN COLOR: yellow to orange
HABITAT: southern Europe to central China
INTRODUCED: 1656
VARIETY: *purpureus*—young leaves purple, fruiting panicle also with very purplish hairs.

The old-fashioned Smoke Bush is prominent because of the numerous pinkish plumose fruit panicles borne in great profusion, giving the whole plant a pink smoky appearance, later turning brown or grayish. The seeds are not numerous and some plants may be entirely staminate, thus lacking the desirable fruiting panicles. For this reason, it is of the utmost importance that this plant be propagated asexually from plants known to produce a large number of fruit panicles. If grown from seed only a small proportion may grow into desirable types. The variety *purpureus* is even more beautiful with purplish plumes and young leaves appearing purple in the spring but later remaining a purple green all summer long. The "smoky" effect of the fruit panicles of both the species and the variety lasts for weeks. The purple fruited form is now becoming increasingly difficult to locate in nurseries.

COTONEASTER

These shrubs are valued chiefly for their bright-colored berries about ¼″ or less in diameter. In form they range from almost prostrate shrubs (*C. dammeri*) to 18′ in height (*C. frigida*). Some are deciduous, some semi-evergreen and some evergreen. The flowers are only about ¼–⅛″ in diameter and either white or pink. As a group the cotoneasters are not considered showy in blossom and hence should be selected chiefly for their beauty in fruit, their habit of growth or their evergreen foliage.

Unfortunately they have their troubles, and therefore one should not be too enthusiastic and hasty in selecting them for conspicuous places in the garden without a trial to find out how they grow under local conditions. They are close relatives of *Crataegus* and certain other members of the Rose Family and as such are susceptible to infestations of fire blight, which really can mar a good collection once it has worked itself in. During hot dry weather most of them are susceptible to attacks of red spider which, in certain seasons, can cause nearly complete defoliation unless it is kept checked, as well as the lace bug.

Most are natives of the cool moist regions of northern Asia, chiefly in China, and the Himalayas, although a few occur in Europe. None is native to North America. Everything considered, there are better ornamentals of interest over a longer period of time. Especially is this true in northern gardens where several of the cotoneasters in the recommended list are not hardy. Only a few of the many already growing in this country have been selected for the recommended list, and these have been selected to demonstrate the diversity of form and habit of this variable group.

Cotoneaster bullata floribunda   6'   Zone 5   Vilmorin Cotoneaster

FLOWERS: small pinkish
  TIME: late May
*FRUIT: roundish clusters of globular scarlet berries
  EFFECTIVE: fall
HABITAT: China
INTRODUCED: 1898

One of the most brilliantly colored of the cotoneasters in fruit, standing out well in any planting during the fall. This variety is superior to the species in that there are more fruits in each cluster.

Cotoneaster dammeri   1'   Zone 5   Bearberry Cotoneaster

FLOWERS: small white
  TIME: early June
*FRUIT: bright red berries
  EFFECTIVE: fall
FOLIAGE: evergreen, leaves 1" long
HABITAT: central China
INTRODUCED: 1900

Distinct because of its prostrate long trailing habit; excellent as an evergreen ground cover and for use in the rockery.

Cotoneaster divaricata   6'   Zone 5   Spreading Cotoneaster

FLOWERS: small, pink
  TIME: late May
*FRUIT: red, thick berries
  EFFECTIVE: early fall
AUTUMN COLOR: dull red
HABITAT: central and western China
INTRODUCED: 1907

The arching spreading habit of this species is outstanding and the branches are covered with bright red fruits each fall. This species is one of the most desirable, with leaves ¾" long

Cotoneaster foveolata   9'   Zone 4   Glossy Cotoneaster

FLOWERS: small pinkish
    TIME: late May
FRUIT: black berry
    EFFECTIVE: early fall
FOLIAGE: glossy, thick leaves 1–3½" long
AUTUMN COLOR: bright scarlet to orange
HABITAT: central China
INTRODUCED: 1907

Cotoneaster francheti   10'   Zone 6   Franchet Cotoneaster

FLOWERS: small, pinkish
    TIME: mid-June
*FRUIT: orange-red berries
    EFFECTIVE: early fall
FOLIAGE: half evergreen, leaves 1½" long
AUTUMN COLOR: reddish green
HABITAT: western China
INTRODUCED: 1895

Cotoneaster frigida   18'   Zone 7   Himalayan Cotoneaster

FLOWERS: small, white
    TIME: mid-June
FRUIT: bright red berries
    EFFECTIVE: late summer and fall
FOLIAGE: bluish green, leaves 3–6" long
HABITAT: Himalayas
INTRODUCED: 1824

In England, where this species has been grown for over 100 years, this plant is considered an excellent specimen, the most robust of all the cotoneasters with fruits in large conspicuous clusters. It is the tallest growing in North America, and does very well on the Pacific Coast.

Cotoneaster harroviana   6'   Zone 7

FLOWERS: white, small
    TIME: June
FRUIT: red berries
    EFFECTIVE: fall
FOLIAGE: leathery, gray-green, evergreen, leaves about 2" long
HABITAT: western China
INTRODUCED: 1900

This has larger more leathery leaves than *C. pannosa* and does well on the Pacific Coast, especially if in a dry situation.

Cotoneaster henryana   12'   Zone 7   Henry Cotoneaster

FLOWERS: small, white
    TIME: mid-June
FRUIT: dark crimson berries
    EFFECTIVE: October

FOLIAGE: half evergreen, leaves 2–5″ long
HABITAT: central China
INTRODUCED: 1901

This has proved popular on the Pacific Coast, especially because of its graceful arching habit of growth.

Cotoneaster horizontalis   3′   Zone 4   Rock Spray

FLOWERS: small, pinkish
    TIME: mid-June
*FRUIT: bright red berries
    EFFECTIVE: early fall
FOLIAGE: semi-evergreen, leaves ½″ long
AUTUMN COLOR: reddish
HABITAT: western China
INTRODUCED: about 1880

One of the most widely grown of all the cotoneasters. Its flat, horizontal branches make it ideally suited for planting in rock gardens where these branches can rest on the ground or on a low bank where it will serve admirably as a ground cover. An excellent plant for almost any small garden.

Cotoneaster lucida   9′   Zone 4   Hedge Cotoneaster

FLOWERS: pinkish, small
    TIME: early June
FRUIT: large black berry
    EFFECTIVE: early fall
FOLIAGE: lustrous green, leaves 2″ long
HABITAT: Altai Mountains
INTRODUCED: 1840

The lustrous leaves and dense growth have been responsible for some nurserymen using it in making clipped hedges. However, it should be remembered that all cotoneasters are susceptible to fire blight and once it starts in a hedge the planting can be quickly ruined.

Cotoneaster microphylla   3′   Zone 5   Small-leaved Cotoneaster

FLOWERS: white, small
    TIME: June
FRUIT: scarlet berries (¼″ diameter)
    EFFECTIVE: fall
*FOLIAGE: evergreen, lustrous, leaves ½″ long
HABITAT: Himalayas
INTRODUCED: 1824

This species can build itself up to tangled masses of foliage and twigs 1–2′ high and up to 15′ in diameter. It has the smallest leaves of any of the cotoneasters and so is valued in rock gardens and as a foliage mat in the foreground of shrubby borders.

Cotoneaster multiflora calocarpa   8′   Zone 5

*FLOWER: small white
    TIME: mid-May

*FRUIT: light red to pink berries, ⅜" diameter
    EFFECTIVE: fall
HABITAT: China
INTRODUCED: 1900
    One of the few cotoneasters of interest in flower as well as in fruit. The flowers and fruits are profusely borne and the habit is very wide spreading. It is similar to *C. racemiflora soongorica* except that its fruits are bright red, while those of the former are more pinkish. Both are splendid, wide spreading shrubs needing plenty of room.

Cotoneaster pannosa   6'   Zone 7   Silverleaf Cotoneaster

FLOWERS: small, white
    TIME: June
FRUIT: dull red berries
    EFFECTIVE: fall
FOLIAGE: half evergreen, leaves 1" long
HABITAT: southwest China
INTRODUCED: 1888

Cotoneaster racemiflora soongorica   7½'   Zone 3   Sungari Rockspray

FLOWERS: small, white
    TIME: early June
*FRUIT: pink berries, profuse
    EFFECTIVE: fall
FOLIAGE: grayish green, leaves to 1¼" long
HABITAT: western China
INTRODUCED: 1910
    E. H. Wilson considered this cotoneaster one of the best of all—and hardiest, too. Its rounded leaves of gray-green make it unique in this group and, where it can be grown, it stands out from other plants in the shrub border.

Cotoneaster salicifolia floccosa   15'   Zone 5

FLOWERS: white, small
    TIME: late June
*FRUIT: red berries
    EFFECTIVE: late fall
*FOLIAGE: semi-evergreen in the North, nearly completely evergreen in the South, leaves to 3" long
AUTUMN COLOR: purplish red
HABITAT: western China
INTRODUCED: 1908
    Another of E. H. Wilson's introductions, this gracefully arching shrub has narrow-pointed leaves similar to those of the willow. The variety is hardier than the species and the fruits are slightly larger, hence it is recommended as a graceful, distinctive and attractive plant.

Cotoneaster simonsi   10–12'   Zone 5   Simon's Cotoneaster

FLOWERS: small, white
    TIME: mid-June

FRUIT: scarlet berries
    EFFECTIVE: October
FOLIAGE: half-evergreen occasionally, leaves to 1¼" long
HABITAT: Khasia Mountains
INTRODUCED: 1869

| Cudrania tricuspidata | 25' | Zone 7 | Silk-worm Tree |

FRUIT: red berries, edible
    EFFECTIVE: fall
WINTER TWIGS: with slender thorns
HABITAT: China, Korea, Japan
INTRODUCED: 1862

The leaves of this plant have been used for silkworm culture in China. In the South the plant is frequently used in hedges.

| Cycas revoluta | 10' | Zone 9 | Sago Cycas |

Often incorrectly called the Sago Palm, it is not a true palm but a very desirable and popular evergreen plant, native of Japan, with dark glossy fernlike foliage. It is slow in growth, sometimes taking 50 years to form a trunk 5' high, but is usually seen in Florida and the southern part of the Gulf States as a mounded fountain of fronds or leaves growing 3' long out of a stubby pineapple-like central base. It is said that very old specimens produce leaves only in alternate years, with flowers in the intervening years. This is the hardiest of the *Cycas* species now being used in the South.

| Cyrilla racemiflora | 25' | Zone 5 | American Cyrilla |

*FLOWERS: white pendulous racemes, small
    TIME: July
FOLIAGE: lustrous bright green
AUTUMN COLOR: orange to scarlet
HABITAT: Virginia to Florida, West Indies and eastern South America

An unusually distinctive flowering shrub, with its small, white summer flowers appearing in a burst of racemes from the base of the current year's growth. It is curious in flower and unlike any other woody plant in the North with its interesting arrangement of racemes. Of little merit at other times. If grown it should be planted in a soil with plenty of peat moss.

CYTISUS

Among the species of *Cytisus* are many colorful flowering plants which could be considered for planting in any garden where they might prove hardy. They are valuable assets because of their bright-colored flowers—yellow, white, purple, lemon-yellow and red; leaves which are very small and usually less than an inch long, sometimes almost missing; and green twigs that are prominently evident all winter long, giving the plants an evergreen appearance. Since all are legumes, nitrogen-bearing nodules form on their roots and thus enrich the soil.

They are not difficult to grow, most of them actually requiring poor dry sandy soil and many can be readily raised from seed. Some have been in America since earliest colonial times and have become widely distributed. Thomas Jefferson was so interested in the Scotch Broom and its landscape qualities that every time he took a trip anywhere in Virginia it is said he would take some seeds along to broadcast. There is many a place in central and southern Virginia where a naturalized planting of this species is now vigorously growing, possibly due to the singular efforts of that energetic man. This same species has escaped cultivation and become naturalized, also, on Cape Cod, Nantucket Island and in the Pacific Northwest, especially in Washington, Oregon and Vancouver, British Columbia, where it covers hundreds of acres.

Undoubtedly the name broom was given these plants in the Old World centuries ago chiefly because the vigorous, dense, stiffly upright twigs of the Scotch Broom, when cut off, trimmed and tied together at the end of a stout stick, made a good broom.

The brooms like a sunny situation and given this and well-drained soil they grow nicely. It should be noted, however, that they are rather difficult to transplant and so it is best to start with young plants, preferably pot grown. Insect and disease pests pass them by. The flowers are like those of the ordinary pea, to which they are related, and their fruits are dry uninteresting pods. They can be grown all along the Atlantic and Pacific coasts and in a very wide strip across the continent between these points, with one or two exceptions.

A glance through the recommended species will show that they vary in height from 6" to 9', that the colors of most of the species are yellow with notable exceptions. The colorful hybrids are somewhat tender and seem to be in their element in California. A few like "Dorothy Walpole" and "Lord Lambourne" are varieties originating in Europe. A large number of others have been introduced as the result of the hybridizing efforts of Mr. Sydney B. Mitchell, one time president of the California Horticultural Society. Some of his introductions like "California," "Pomona," "San Francisco," and "Stanford" are still outstanding because of their red, yellow and sometimes white flowers.

Cytisus albus   1'   Zone 5   Portuguese Broom

*FLOWERS: white or yellowish white, pealike
    TIME: late June
*WINTER TWIGS: green
HABITAT: southeastern Europe
INTRODUCED: 1806
VARIETY: *pallidus*—flowers pale yellow, pealike
    The Portuguese broom is the only low, white-flowered broom really hardy in the North.

x Cytisus beani   18"   Zone 5   Bean's Broom

*FLOWERS: deep golden yellow, pealike
    TIME: early May

*WINTER TWIGS: green
HYBRID ORIGIN: *C. ardoini x C. purgans*
ORIGINATED: 1900
    Semi-prostrate in habit and often two or three times as broad as high.

x Cytisus dallimorei   6'   Zone 6   Dallimore Broom

*FLOWERS: yellow suffused with pink, keel almost white, pealike
    TIME: mid-May
WINTER TWIGS: green
HYBRID ORIGIN: *C. multiflorus x C. scoparius* "Andreanus"
ORIGINATED: 1900

x Cytisus kewensis   6"   Zone 6   Kew Broom

*FLOWERS: pale sulfur-yellow, pealike
    TIME: mid-May
WINTER TWIGS: green
HYBRID ORIGIN: *C. ardoini x C. albus*
ORIGINATED: 1891
    Another excellent garden plant that may eventually grow into a mat 6' across, a splendid specimen for the rock garden. Flowers are slightly larger than those of *C. praecox.*

Cytisus multiflorus   9'   Zone 6   White Spanish Broom

*FLOWERS: white, pealike
    TIME: May
WINTER TWIGS: green
HABITAT: Spain and northern Africa
INTRODUCED: 1752

Cytisus nigricans   3'   Zone 5   Spike Broom

*FLOWERS: yellowish in terminal spikes, pealike
    TIME: early July
HABITAT: central and southern Europe
INTRODUCED: 1730
    An excellent plant for consistent and profuse bloom regardless of whether season is wet or dry, hot or cold. There are not many woody plants in this same category. Flowers turn black when dried, causing Linnaeus to give it the name *C. nigricans.*

x Cytisus praecox   6'   Zone 5   Warminster Broom

*FLOWERS: lemon-yellow, pealike
    TIME: mid-May
*WINTER TWIGS: green
HYBRID ORIGIN: *C. multiflorus x C. purgans*
INTRODUCED: about 1867
    The first of the brooms to flower in spring, proving perfectly hardy in New England. The pale lemon-yellow flowers are a color unique among woody shrubs. This plant is dense and actually covered with flowers each year. Makes a splen-

did color combination when planted with *Rhododendron yedoense poukhanense*. Both bloom at the same time and the flowers of the Warminster Broom can be used effectively with the pale lavender-colored flowers of the Korean Azalea.

Cytisus purgans   3'   Zone 5   Provence Broom

*FLOWERS: deep golden yellow, pealike
    TIME: mid-May
*WINTER TWIGS: green
HABITAT: southwestern Europe
INTRODUCED: 1750
    Does best in sunniest position possible, is very dense in habit with rigid upright branches.

Cytisus purpureus   18"   Zone 5   Purple Broom

*FLOWERS: purple, pealike
    TIME: mid-May
HABITAT: southern Europe
INTRODUCED: 1792
VARIETIES: *elongatus*—branches long and slender, flowers violet purple
    erectus—habit upright
    Unique among brooms because of its purple flowers, this little plant can be used satisfactorily with the yellow-flowering types. A mass of the Purple Broom in the rockery or at the front of a foundation planting is a beautiful sight when in bloom.

Cytisus scoparius   6'   Zone 5   Scotch Broom

*FLOWERS: yellow, pealike
    TIME: mid-May
*WINTER TWIGS: green
HABITAT: central and southern Europe
INTRODUCED: earliest colonial times
    The most common broom, native of Europe, and the only one native to the British Isles. It is said to have been brought to this country as early as Captain John Smith's time by one of the Virginia settlers. Well adapted to this country, it has escaped cultivation and become naturalized on Cape Cod, Nantucket Island, several places in Virginia where it is said to have been planted by Thomas Jefferson, and also in the Pacific Northwest. This bushy shrub may be killed back on the eastern Sea Coast by severe winters. The erect-growing variety, *andreanus*, is certainly an addition of merit to this group.

Cytisus hybrids   4–6'   Zone 6

English hybrids, mostly originating prior to 1934.
    "Burkwoodi"—rich deep red flowers, one of the best of the group
    "Daisy Hill"—cream-colored flowers, flushed rose
    "Dorothy Walpole"—crimson and deep rose flowers
    "Lady Moore"—flower petals primrose, wing petals bright crimson
    "Lord Lambourne"—crimson and yellow flowers tinged with rose
    "Maria Burkwood"—gold-rose and scarlet flowers

Originations of Sydney B. Mitchell of Califorina, mostly about 1934:
   "California"—vermilion, rose and cream flowers
   "Pink Beauty"—pink flowers, one of the best
   "Pomona"—red, rose and yellow flowers
   "St. Mary's"—white flowers
   "San Francisco"—rich velvety-red flowers
   "Stanford"—orange and red flowers flushed yellow and bronze
   These varieties are almost a random selection and represent a large class of hybrids now being grown in this country, most of them vigorously upright in growth, showing a great similarity, in habit at least, to *C. scoparius andreanus.*

Daboecia cantabrica   1½′   Zone 5   Irish Heath

*FLOWERS: purple, small
   TIME: summer
FOLIAGE: evergreen
HABITAT: Ireland to north Spain
INTRODUCED: 1800
VARIETIES:
   alba—flowers white
   atropurpurea—flowers rich purple
   bicolor—flowers striped white and purple
   nana—dwarf form with smaller and narrower leaves
   pallida—flowers pink
   Another of the close relatives of *Erica* and *Calluna,* it requires the same culture and is used in the same situations. Valued for its tiny bright flowers that appear continually throughout summer.

Danae racemosa   3′   Zone 7   Alexandrian Laurel

FLOWERS: white, small
   TIME: spring
FRUIT: red berry
   EFFECTIVE: fall
FOLIAGE: evergreen, leaves scalelike, apparent leaves being 4″ long and 1″ wide
HABITAT: Syria, Transcaucasia, Persia
INTRODUCED: 1739
   Rather bamboolike in habit, the "leaves" are actually flattened branches. Can be cut for indoor winter displays.

Daphne cneorum   6″   Zone 4   Rose Daphne

*FLOWERS: bright rosy pink, fragrant, small in clusters
   TIME: mid-May
FOLIAGE: evergreen making a dense mat on the ground, leaves to 1″ long
HABITAT: central and southern Europe
INTRODUCED: 1752
   Commonly grown in gardens, this beautiful low shrub is always conspicuous when in flower. Opinion has been divided as to whether it grows best in acid or alkaline soils, but it can do well in both. However, since all members of this genus are frequently difficult to "tame" and many are known to prefer a lime-

The daphnes are low shrubs with bright flowers and later, bright colored fruits, usually flowering before the leaves appear.

stone soil, this species might well be given such a soil. A cool, moist condition about the roots at all times, and some winter protection in the North, are added aids to insure good growth.

Daphne giraldi   2′   Zone 3   Giraldi Daphne

*FLOWERS: yellow, slightly fragrant, small, in clusters
    TIME: late May
*FRUIT: scarlet berries, about ¼″ long
    EFFECTIVE: July
HABITAT: northwestern China
INTRODUCED: 1910
    Mr. F. L. Skinner of Dropmore, Manitoba, says that this is one of the hardiest daphnes with him and highly recommends it for his cold area. It is probably most discerning, as are other daphnes, regarding soils in which it will grow.

Daphne mezereum   3′   Zone 4   February Daphne

*FLOWERS: lilac to rosy purple, very fragrant, before the leaves appear
    TIME: early April
*FRUIT: scarlet berries
    EFFECTIVE: June
HABITAT: Europe to the Caucasus and Altai, occasionally naturalized in northeastern states

INTRODUCED: early colonial times

A common garden shrub, nevertheless is difficult to grow in many places while in others it will do well for years and then suddenly die for no apparent reason. It makes an excellent addition to the garden if given plenty of moisture and some lime but is short lived. Most daphnes are difficult to transplant and move easiest when small. The prime ornamental feature is the small flowers, in very early spring, before the leaves appear.

Daphne odora   4–6'   Zone 7   Winter Daphne

*FLOWERS: small, rosy purple, fragrant
   TIME: March, April
FOLIAGE: evergreen, leaves to 3" long
HABITAT: Japan and China
INTRODUCED: 1771

Apparently does not require limestone soil. Once established, it is best left alone for it does not respond to pruning, fertilizing or cultivation. The most fragrant of all the daphnes.

DEUTZIA

There are approximately 70 species and varieties of deutzias growing in the United States at the present time, only 13 of which have proved themselves outstanding over a period of years. They grow well in any good soil, and although New England's winters are none too kind to them, farther south they are delightful shrubs when in full bloom. The genus was named by Thunberg after Johann van der Deutz, one of his wealthy patrons. One is impressed by the fact that eight of the better types are hybrids, all originated by one man or his associates.

Victor Lemoine, a French nurseryman (1823–1912), was very much interested in hybridizing plants and his list of meritorious accomplishments along this line is a long one. Deutzias were of special interest to him and he or his firm is accredited with naming at least 48 between the years 1896 and 1936. Not all are grown today but some of the best now available are among those originated by him or his nursery.

Most of the deutzia species are native of eastern Asia, chiefly parts of China. Dense-growing shrubs, they range in height from 3 to 8', and are easily reproduced by hard or softwood cuttings. They are grown solely for their spring flowers and have no ornamental fruits, no striking autumn color. Hence in choosing them, the important points to be considered are profuseness and size of flowers, the habit of the plant and the height to which it will grow. Most deutzias have white flowers, although some are slightly pinkish to purplish, especially on the outside of the flower.

Deutzias have few if any disease or insect troubles but, because of the very tender wood, some early spring pruning is necessary to keep plants in good condition—especially in the North where it is essential to prune annually. Since deutzias bloom at about the same time as the mock-oranges, their qualifications for garden use might be considered as competing with those of the mock-oranges. Because they lack autumn color and have no interesting fruits they are near the bottom of the list as ornamentals.

Of the thirteen selected, *Deutzia grandiflora* was chosen because it is the earliest of the group to bloom (mid-May). The two varieties of *D. scabra* were selected because they are among the last to bloom and have double flowers; *D. gracilis,* because it is the lowest growing and has a wealth of beautiful flowers. *Deutzia magnifica* also has double flowers, and the varieties "Contraste" and "Magicien" have the largest and most beautiful flowers of all. *Deutzia parviflora* has its flowers in flat panicles—unusual among the deutzias and making this plant a potential substitute for some of the spiraeas, if such a substitute is needed. *Deutzia rosea eximea* has flowers that are slightly pinkish, while *D. lemoinei, D. lemoinei erecta* and *D. candelabrum* are literally covered with flowers when in bloom and are among the best of the deutzias for this floral display.

x Deutzia candelabrum   6′   Zone 5

*FLOWERS: white in upright racemes
    TIME: late May
HYBRID ORIGIN: *D. gracilis x D. sieboldiana*
INTRODUCED: before 1907
    Similar in many respects to *Deutzia gracilis* this species has broader and denser flower panicles and is one of the best for flower display.

Deutzia gracilis   3–6′   Zone 4   Slender Deutzia

*FLOWERS: white in upright racemes
    TIME: late May
HABITAT: Japan
INTRODUCED: about 1840
    This graceful, free-flowering shrub has been widely grown because of its dense, compact habit and slender, arching branches together with its myriads of flowers in late spring.

Deutzia grandiflora   6′   Zone 5   Early Deutzia

*FLOWERS: white in upright racemes
    TIME: mid-May
HABITAT: north China
INTRODUCED: 1910
    The first of the deutzias to bloom and one with the largest flowers.

x Deutzia hybrida "Contraste"   6′

*FLOWERS: pinkish, large
    TIME: early June
HYBRID ORIGIN: *D. longifolia x D. discolor*
INTRODUCED: 1925
    Deutzia hybrida "Magicien"—similar general character to "Contraste," of similar parentage, introduced in 1927.
    Both splendid flowering specimens with large pinkish flowers.

x Deutzia lemoinei   7'   Zone 4   Lemoine Deutzia
*FLOWERS: white, in upright racemes
   TIME: late May
HYBRID ORIGIN: *D. parviflora x D. gracilis*
INTRODUCED: 1891
VARIETY: *compacta*—more dwarf and compact in habit
   One of the hardiest of the deutzias.

x Deutzia magnifica   6'   Zone 5   Showy Deutzia
*FLOWERS: white, double, in short dense panicles
   TIME: mid-June
HYBRID ORIGIN: *D. scabra x D. vilmorinae*
INTRODUCED: before 1910
VARIETY: *erecta*—flowers in more dense panicles

Deutzia parviflora   6'   Zone 4   Mongolian Deutzia
*FLOWERS: white in many-flowered clusters
   TIME: late May
HABITAT: north China
INTRODUCED: 1883
   Unlike the majority of the deutzias, this species bears its flowers in flat clusters or corymbs very much like those of some spiraeas. In fact the Mongolian Deutzia makes a better display in flower than many of the spiraeas with which it might be compared.

x Deutzia rosea eximea   6'   Zone 5
*FLOWERS: pinkish outside corolla
   TIME: late May
HYBRID ORIGIN: *D. gracilis x D. purpurascens*
INTRODUCED: 1898
   This variety of the Rose Panicled Deutzia has proved superior to the species for it has flower clusters nearly 2" in diameter.

Deutzia scabra candidissima   8'   Zone 5   Snow-flake Deutzia
*FLOWERS: white, double
   TIME: late June
HABITAT: China and Japan
INTRODUCED: after 1822
VARIETY: *scabra plena*—flowers double, rosy purple on outside of corolla
   Both varieties are among the latest deutzias to flower and, because of their many petals, remain effectively in bloom for some time. "Pride of Rochester" is similar to *D. scabra plena* but earlier to bloom.

Diapensia lapponica   4"   Zone 1   Arctic Diapensia
FLOWERS: white, small, bell-shaped
   TIME: June–July
HABITAT: Circumpolar, in North America south to alpine summits of New Hampshire and New York
   An interesting low, tufted plant, growing from the Arctic regions south to New York, adapted for the alpine garden.

Diervilla sessilifolia   4½'   Zone 4   Southern Bush-honeysuckle

FLOWERS: deep yellow, trumpet-shaped
    TIME: late June
AUTUMN COLOR: reddish
HABITAT: eastern United States

Not quite as hardy as *D. lonicera* but much more ornamental in flower. It makes a fair ground cover and spreads rapidly by underground stolons. Not of value as specimens but of some merit for holding the soil on banks and other situations where a rugged, shrubby ground cover is needed.

Disanthus cercidifolius   8'   Zone 6 or 7

FLOWERS: dark purple, ⅜" in diameter
    TIME: fall
FOLIAGE: dull greenish, leaves 2–4½" long and nearly as wide
*AUTUMN COLOR: scarlet to orange
HABITAT: mountains of central Japan
INTRODUCED: 1892

Interesting because of its brilliant scarlet-to-orange autumn color. Flowers not especially beautiful.

Elaeagnus angustifolia   20'   Zone 2   Russian Olive

FLOWERS: silvery outside, yellow inside, fragrant, small
    TIME: early June
FRUIT: yellow coated berries with silvery scales
    EFFECTIVE: early fall
*FOLIAGE: dull gray-green, leaves 1–3½" long and narrow
HABITAT: southern Europe to west and central Asia
INTRODUCED: early colonial times

Flowers and fruits are none too conspicuous, but the gray foliage is outstanding and the plant can be used for this one feature. Hardy and vigorous, it grows rather densely, and its unique crooked trunk can easily be of interest in its own right for it is covered with a brown shredding bark which is most ornamental in winter.

Elaeagnus multiflora   9'   Zone 4   Cherry Elaeagnus

FLOWERS: yellowish white, silvery and brown scales, fragrant, small
    TIME: mid-May
*FRUIT: red berries, scaly, of pleasant acid flavor, ⅝" long
    EFFECTIVE: mid-summer
FOLIAGE: dark green, silvery beneath, leaves 1½–2½" long
HABITAT: China, Japan
INTRODUCED: 1862

A vigorous shrub of interest chiefly for its red fruits, somewhat the size and shape of elongated cherries, borne in early summer before most other fruits ripen. Also of value for the contrasting foliage, dark green above and silvery beneath. Introduced by Commodore Perry from Japan.

Elaeagnus pungens   12′   Zone 7   Thorny Elaeagnus

FLOWERS: pendulous, fragrant, silvery white, small
    TIME: October
FRUIT: berries, brown at first, finally red
    EFFECTIVE: May
*FOLIAGE: evergreen, leaves 1½–4″ long
HABITAT: Japan
INTRODUCED: 1830
VARIETIES:
    aurea—leaf margin with rich yellow
    maculata—leaf with large yellow blotch in the center
    tricolor—leaf variegated with yellow and pinkish white
    variegata—leaf margin of yellowish white
    In the South this is one of the most common of evergreen shrubs. The flow-
ers, though small, have fragrance somewhat similar to that of gardenias. Vigorous
and healthy, it grows well in many difficult situations. Frequently the entire
plant seems frosted with silvery metallic scales that glitter in the sun. The variegated-leaved forms should be used with discretion.

Elaeagnus umbellata   12′   Zone 3   Autumn Elaeagnus

FLOWERS: yellowish, white, fragrant, scaly
    TIME: mid-May
FRUIT: small silvery berries mixed with brown, finally red
    EFFECTIVE: fall
HABITAT: China, Korea, Japan
INTRODUCED: 1830
    A spreading shrub, covered with silvery berries in fall and prized as well for
its young silvery foliage.

Elsholtzia stauntoni   5′   Zone 4   Staunton Elsholtzia

FLOWERS: lilac-purple, small, in loose spikes
    TIME: August and September
HABITAT: north China
INTRODUCED: 1905
    Profuse spikes of lilac-purple flowers in late summer and early fall are its
only claim to use in the garden. Except for these, other plants might well be used
in its place.

Empetrum nigrum   10″   Zone 2   Crow-berry

FLOWERS: purplish, very small, solitary
    TIME: early May
FRUIT: black, berrylike
    EFFECTIVE: fall
FOLIAGE: evergreen, leaves very small, only ¼″ long
HABITAT: northern Europe, northern Asia; in North America south to New York,
Michigan, and California
    A low evergreen shrub of value chiefly in rockeries for forming a low dense
mat of foliage.

Redvein Enkianthus (*E. campanulatus*).

Enkianthus campanulatus   30'   Zone 4   Redvein Enkianthus

*FLOWERS: yellowish or light orange, bell-shaped flowers in pendulous clusters
    TIME: mid-May
*AUTUMN COLOR: brilliant red
HABITAT: Japan
INTRODUCED: 1870
VARIETIES:
    albiflorus—flowers white
    palibini—flowers red
    An ericaceous shrub requiring the same type of cultural treatment as azaleas and rhododendrons, but differing in having small pendulous bell-shaped flowers, about ¼" in diameter and brilliant scarlet autumn color. Flowers appear just before the leaves and so are easily seen. A good acid-soil plant, not used enough in gardens.

Enkianthus deflexus   21'   Zone 5

*FLOWERS: yellowish red, ½" in diameter, bell-shaped, in clusters
    TIME: late May
*AUTUMN COLOR: scarlet
HABITAT: Himalayas, western China
INTRODUCED: 1904
    Mostly similar to *E. campanulatus* but flowers are larger and showier. A good shrub for acid-soil situations.

Enkianthus perulatus   6′   Zone 5

*FLOWERS: white, bell-shaped, in pendulous clusters
     TIME: early May
*AUTUMN COLOR: scarlet in fall
HABITAT: Japan
INTRODUCED: about 1870
     The autumn foliage of this shrub is even more conspicuous than that of
E. campanulatus. It makes a smaller, possibly neater shrub, and like other mem-
bers of this genus, requires acid soil.

Epigaea repens   ground cover   Zone 2   Trailing Arbutus

*FLOWERS: white to pink, small, very fragrant
     TIME: mid-April
FOLIAGE: evergreen, leaves to 3″ long
HABITAT: Massachusetts to Georgia, west to Ohio and Tennessee
     The flowers are very fragrant but the plant is uncommon in gardens because
it is very difficult to grow and transplant. It was supposed to have been called
"Mayflower" by the Pilgrims who named it after their ship. It can grow in either
shade or full sun and is seldom over an inch or so tall, creeping along the surface
of the soil. It does better when given some covering during winter, and grows
in very poor gravelly soil. Unless one is an expert at growing difficult plants,
this one had best be omitted from the rock garden.

ERICA

     Several species of this genus are grown in this country for their bright-
colored flowers. Their culture is very similar to that for *Calluna* (page 114).
They are ericaceous plants, usually fairly low, valued for their bright spring
or summer flowers, some species blooming in winter in warmer parts of
the country.

Erica carnea   1′   Zone 5   Spring Heath

*FLOWERS: rosy red, small, in upright racemes, 1–2″ long
     TIME: early April
FOLIAGE: evergreen, bright green, needlelike
HABITAT: central and southern Europe
INTRODUCED: 1763
VARIETIES:
     alba—flowers white
     purpurascens—flowers purple
     One of the hardier heaths valued in the North for its very early spring flow-
ers. There are many so-called "improved" varieties in the trade.

Erica ciliaris   1½′   Zone 7   Fringed Heath

*FLOWERS: rosy purple, in spikes to 5″ long
     TIME: summer
FOLIAGE: gray-evergreen, needlelike
HABITAT: western Europe from British Isles to Spain
INTRODUCED: 1773

Erica cinerea   1–2′   Zone 5   Twisted Heath

*FLOWERS: rosy purple to white, in spikes to 3″ long
    TIME: mid-June
FOLIAGE: evergreen, lustrous, needlelike
AUTUMN COLOR: bronze to orange
HABITAT: western Europe; naturalized in Massachusetts
INTRODUCED: 1750
VARIETIES:
    fulgida–flowers red
    alba–flowers white
    "Golden Gem"–compact in habit, foliage yellow to orange, bronze in winter
    The twisted heaths are sometimes difficult to grow but are worth a trial because of several color forms blooming for several weeks in early summer. They need heavy pruning immediately after flowering and will respond to an application of sand and well-rotted leaf mold as a mulch.

x Erica darleyensis   3′   Zone 6   Darley Heath

*FLOWERS: small, pale lilac-pink
    TIME: November to spring
FOLIAGE: evergreen, fine texture
HYBRID ORIGIN: *Erica carnea x E. mediterranea*
ORIGINATED: before 1894
    A vigorous-growing species that will survive in poor growing conditions where other species may fail. The poor color of its flowers is offset by its vigorous habit. Since it belongs to the winter-flowering group, it should receive little pruning. It is said that this variety can be grown in a limestone soil.

Erica mediterranea   5′   Zone 7   Mediterranean Heath

*FLOWERS: lilac-pink, small, in short racemes
    TIME: mid-April
FOLIAGE: evergreen, needlelike
HABITAT: western Europe, Ireland to Portugal and Spain
INTRODUCED: 1765
    Not as vigorous as its hybrid *E. darleyensis* but an upright habit of growth sets it apart from other spring-flowering heaths and it is recommended for this characteristic, only.

Erica tetralix   18″   Zone 3   Cross-leaf Heath

*FLOWERS: dense, rosy, small, in dense terminal clusters
    TIME: summer
FOLIAGE: evergreen, woolly, gray, needlelike
HABITAT: northern and western Europe, naturalized in Massachusetts
INTRODUCED: 1789
    An excellent species and one of the hardiest. It seems to prefer a moist, rather peaty soil.

Erica vagans   1′   Zone 5   Cornish Heath

*FLOWERS: pinkish purple, small
    TIME: summer

FOLIAGE: evergreen, dark green, needlelike
HABITAT: western Europe, from Ireland to Portugal
INTRODUCED: 1811
VARIETIES:

alba—flowers white, habit low and dense
grandiflora—flowers larger than in type
rubra—flowers more deeply colored red
Another good summer-flowering species.

Eucryphia glutinosa   15′   Zone 8

FLOWERS: white, 2–3″ diameter, one or two at the end of the branches
    TIME: summer
FOLIAGE: semi-evergreen to evergreen, leaves with 3–5 leaflets, 2″ long
AUTUMN COLOR: orange and red
HABITAT: Chile
INTRODUCED: 1859

This lovely plant is difficult to establish, requires a peaty soil devoid of lime. Good success has been obtained by planting in beds of heather where roots are protected from too much sun. An interesting South American native, worthy of a trial in southern gardens.

EUONYMUS

The Euonymus are valued chiefly for their fruit and autumn color, a few species for their evergeen foliage, and a few for their interesting habit of growth. Flowers are small and inconspicuous. They grow vigorously in a good garden soil, but are susceptible, in certain parts of the country, to serious infestations of Euonymus scale. This pest can be really serious, often making it necessary to cut the plant completely to the ground. It is important to keep this in mind when making permanent plantings of Euonymus, especially when using the vine types on brick walls. It takes a long time to grow such vines to the top of a three-story building, yet such vines frequently become so infested with scale due to the negligence of the home owner that the plants must be cut to the ground and started again.

Apparently the shrubby species are not as susceptible to scale as the evergreen vinelike types, but all must be watched carefully for first appearances of the scale. Dormant oil sprays have proved satisfactory in the past and comparatively recently a sodium salt of di-nitro-ortho cresol is apparently unusually effective as a spray material for control. One part of this material in ninety-nine parts of water has proved a most effective dormant spray in combating this particular pest.

The types of *Euonymus* selected include two very serviceable evergreen species. The *E. fortunei* group, mostly vines (page 382), sub-shrubs and ground covers, are about the hardiest evergreen vines for the North. *Euonymus japonica* varieties are shrubs much used in the South as specimens and hedges, very serviceable plants indeed. There are many varieties other than those recommended, all varying slightly either in foliage color or

The dwarf *Euonymus alata compacta* makes a perfect hedge requiring clipping only
every other year. Its fiery red autumn color is not the least of its attractions.

habit of growth. One or two of the shrubby species are of particular landscape value either because of their habit or because of the bright color of
the unfurling foliage in the early spring.

A serviceable group, easily grown almost everywhere, giving interest
and some color in the landscape but it must be remembered that the Euonymus scale is a vicious pest with which to contend and one should be continually on the watch for it.

Euonymus alata   9'   Zone 3   Winged Spindle Tree

FRUIT: scarlet, opening capsules
    EFFECTIVE: fall
*FORM: horizontal branches
*AUTUMN COLOR: scarlet
WINTER TWIGS: corky ridges
HABITAT: northeastern Asia
INTRODUCED: 1860
VARIETY:
    alata compacta—an excellent dwarf, compact variety introduced about 1926,
plants seven years old being about 4' tall
    A sturdy, easily grown plant of particular interest for its horizontal branches
and brilliant scarlet autumn color. The corky ridges on the twigs and branches are
not especially noticeable from a distance but are interesting because unique. The

compact variety (*compacta*), makes a splendid specimen and has been used in hedges requiring practically no clipping.

Euonymus americana   7'   Zone 6   Strawberry-bush or Wahoo

*FRUIT: pink to scarlet, opening capsules
 EFFECTIVE: fall
AUTUMN COLOR: red
HABITAT: eastern and southeastern United States
 Used considerably in areas where native; the fruit has peculiar, conspicuous warty growths, but this plant is not as good an ornamental as are some other *Euonymus* species.

Euonymus bungeana semi-persistens   18'   Zone 4

*FRUIT: yellowish to pinkish white, opening capsules
 EFFECTIVE: fall and winter
FOLIAGE: light green, leaves 1½–4" long
HABITAT: China and Manchuria
INTRODUCED: 1902
Euonymus bungeana variety: *pendula*—branchlets drooping gracefully
 The variety *semi-persistens* is superior to the species because the abundant fruits remain on the plant long after the leaves have fallen, thus prolonging its landscape effectiveness materially. A loose growing, vigorous shrub with light green leaves, this plant will grow into a splendid specimen or a deciduous screen in record time. One of the better large shrubs for quick growth.

Euonymus europaea aldenhamensis   21'   Zone 3   Aldenham Spindle Tree

*FRUIT: brilliant pink, opening capsules
 EFFECTIVE: fall
FOLIAGE: dark green, leaves 1½–3" long
AUTUMN COLOR: reddish
ORIGIN: chance seedling at Aldenham, England
INTRODUCED: 1922
E. EUROPAEA VARIETIES:
 europaea alba—fruit white
 europaea intermedia—bright red fruits
 europaea nana—dwarf, upright form, about 3–4' high
 The varieties *aldenhamensis* and *intermedia* are the most colorful fruiting of the varieties of this old-fashioned, popular Spindle Tree, *E. europaea,* and so should be given preference to the widely distributed European species. Of vigorous growth, all varieties retain their leaves until late in fall and so afford an excellent foliage background for the display of the colorful fruits. The plants need no attention except an occasional check for scale insects. The dwarf variety has not proved popular in nurseries, probably because the foliage is more dense than most other *Euonymus* types, therefore harbors scale more quickly and easily.

Euonymus japonica   15'   Zone 8   Evergreen Euonymus

FRUIT: pinkish to orange, opening capsules
 EFFECTIVE: fall
*FOLIAGE: lustrous evergreen foliage, leaves 1–3" long

HABITAT: southern Japan
INTRODUCED: 1804
VARIETIES:

> *alba-marginata*—leaves with a narrow white margin
> *aureo-marginata*—leaves with a yellow margin
> *fastigiata*—upright in habit
> *macrophylla*—leaves 2–3″ long
> *microphylla*—leaves 1″ or less in length

This lustrous-leaved evergreen is widely grown throughout the South where its splendid foliage is valued. Especially is it used as specimens or in hedges. The different varieties, and there are many more being grown by southern nurserymen, offer a diversity of foliage characteristics for those who desire variation.

Euonymus kiautschovica   9′   Zone 6   Spreading Euonymus

*FRUIT: pinkish to red, opening capsules
> EFFECTIVE: October–November
FOLIAGE: half evergreen in North, leaves 2–3″ long
HABITAT: eastern and central China
INTRODUCED: 1860

This plant was formerly called *E. patens*. Widely distributed in the nursery industry, it is somewhat similar to the evergreen *E. japonica* but the leaves are a lighter green and not as thick. Also it is hardier, which makes it available for some northern gardens, especially where the growing season is sufficiently long for fruiting.

Euonymus latifolia   21′   Zone 5   Broadleaf Euonymus

FRUIT: red to orange, opening capsules
> EFFECTIVE: fall
*FOLIAGE: handsome leaves, reddish underneath, leaves 3–5″ long
> AUTUMN COLOR: red
HABITAT: southern Europe
INTRODUCED: 1730

This plant has large leaves for this genus. It is vigorous and its fruits are larger than those of *E. europaeus* and more pendulous but not borne in as great profusion. This species, *E. sanguinea* and *E. sachalinensis* are the first to open their leaves in spring. Makes an excellent specimen when grown alone.

Euonymus nana   3′   Zone 2   Dwarf Euonymus

FRUIT: pink, opening capsules
> EFFECTIVE: fall
HABITAT: Caucasus to western China.
INTRODUCED: 1830

A really low shrub, often planted on rocky slopes.

Euonymus sanguinea   21′   Zone 5

FRUIT: red to orange, opening capsules
> EFFECTIVE: fall
*FOLIAGE: dark green, reddish underneath, leaves 1½–4½″ long

AUTUMN COLOR: red
HABITAT: central China
INTRODUCED: 1900

One of the best deciduous Euonymus from the standpoint of foliage. Leaves appear as early in spring as those of *E. latifolia* and at first are reddish, later becoming dark green above and reddish below. It has vigorous branches and dense foliage, and fruit which opens early but falls quickly, usually before the leaves fall. Because of this and the fact that the fruits are not borne profusely, this species should be used for its good foliage only.

Euonymus yedoensis   15′   Zone 4   Yeddo Euonymus

FRUIT: pinkish purple, opening capsules
AUTUMN COLOR: brilliant red
HABITAT: Japan and Korea
INTRODUCED: 1865

The habit of this Yeddo Euonymus is more or less flat-topped, and the leaves are as much as 5″ long.

Eurya japonica   21′   Zone 7

FRUIT: black, berrylike
   EFFECTIVE: fall
*FOLIAGE: evergreen, leaves 1½–3″ long
HABITAT: Japan and Korea
INTRODUCED: 1870

Exochorda giraldi wilsoni   15′   Zone 5   Wilson Pearl-bush

*FLOWERS: racemes of white flowers 2″ in diameter
   TIME: early May
HABITAT: central China
INTRODUCED: 1907

The most floriferous of the pearl bushes and has the largest flowers of any. Grows vigorously upright, the side branches starting to arch gracefully as the plant grows older. Its chief ornamental value is the white flowers, but they last only a short time. To obtain maximum flower production, the weaker inner branches should be pruned out occasionally. Many shrubs, more serviceable in flower, and during other seasons as well, might be used to better advantage especially in a small garden where space is a limiting factor.

Fallugia paradoxa   5′   Zone 5   Apache Plume

FLOWERS: white, 1¼″ diameter
   TIME: May
FRUIT: attractive heads of feathery purplish fruits
   EFFECTIVE: fall
HABITAT: southern Nevada and Utah to New Mexico

An interesting plant for summer and early fall display, but requires a bright sunny spot in well-drained, almost dry soil, to simulate the growing conditions in which it is found native.

Fatsia japonica   15′   Zone 7

FLOWERS: white, large branching panicles, in multiple heads or clusters, each
head 1–2″ diameter
    TIME: fall
FRUIT: light blue berries
    EFFECTIVE: winter
*FOLIAGE: evergreen, leathery, glossy, 7–9 lobed, 12″ in diameter
HABITAT: Japan
INTRODUCED: 1838

    Essentially a foliage plant with large, lobed leaves as much as a foot in di-
ameter, often used to give tropical effects. Once established it needs little attention except occasional pruning to keep it compact in habit. There are said to be
some varieties, lower in habit, which do not require this type of pruning. Does
best in shade and apparently can withstand seashore conditions. In Japan it is
the most characteristic plant of city parks and gardens and various other trying situations with poor soils.

Feijoa sellowiana   18′   Zone 8   Pineapple Guava

FLOWERS: white to purplish, 1½″ diameter
    TIME: June
*FRUIT: green-tinged red berry, 3″ long, edible
    EFFECTIVE: fall
FOLIAGE: gray, leaves to 3″ long
AUTUMN COLOR: bluish gray
HABITAT: Argentina, Paraguay, Uruguay

Fendlera rupicola   6′   Zone 5

FLOWERS: usually solitary, white or tinged rose
    TIME: May
HABITAT: Texas and New Mexico

    A deciduous shrub of considerable beauty only when grown in full sun under
conditions similar to those on the sun-drenched slopes of the mountains of Texas
and New Mexico—its native habitat. In cooler, more moist situations it does not
thrive. However, not many shrubs can be of merit where this plant does best.

Ficus carica   12–30′   Zone 6   Fig

FRUIT: large, purplish, edible
    EFFECTIVE: fall
HABITAT: western Asia
INTRODUCED: cultivated since early times

    Many varieties of *Ficus* are grown and they fruited out of doors as far north
as Long Island. Plants in tubs, taken into the greenhouse in winter, bear fruit
regularly in Boston. The fig can be grown as a tree but more often is grown as
a shrub, needing much winter protection in the North. Its large leaves make it
excellent for giving shade. In most gardens it is grown as a novelty rather than
ornamental specimen.

FORSYTHIA

Forsythias are among the most common of garden shrubs and are used a great deal in many regions, for their early spring blossoms are a great joy in many a dreary garden which has looked lifeless a greater part of the winter. Mostly native in the Orient, they were first introduced into America about one hundred years ago. Probably no other hardy garden shrub which has been introduced from the Old World can equal the forsythias in popularity and cheerful beauty, developed to its best at a season when there are few competitors.

The bright, yellow, scentless flowers are characteristic of all the species in this genus, and in the North, they appear in March or April before the leaves, thus making those plants in flower very prominent. They are easy to grow, doing well in almost any soil except those that are unusually dry; they can even withstand the tough growing conditions of the city garden. They have practically no diseases or insect pests, a valuable asset and well worth remembering. They are of value chiefly for their flowers, and in a few cases for their graceful arching—or trailing—habit of growth. Their fruits are uninteresting dry capsules and only one species (*Forsythia viridissima*) is graced with autumn color, a lovely purplish red. The leaves of all are opposite and in most cases sufficiently distinctive so that the amateur can distinguish the species apart even when they are not in flower.

Because these plants grow so vigorously they are used in plantings about public buildings where, unfortunately, they are often mutilated because of lack of intelligent care in pruning. Forsythias should be given plenty of room in which to grow and expand. They should not be crowded closely together for any reason except to make a good, dense, bank planting where the main objective is to cover the bare ground, and even here, too close crowding will result in unsightly overgrown plants. If a single bush is to be planted it should not be placed a mere two or three feet from the walk, but rather eight to ten feet, to give the plant plenty of room to expand fully at maturity.

Robert Fortune is responsible for first sending some of the forsythias from the Orient to Europe as early as 1844, and has described the manner in which he did it. In those days, the trip from the Orient to England was a long and tedious one around the Cape of Good Hope, taking approximately four or five months. It was difficult to keep seeds in a viable condition during the trip, let alone plants. If potted plants were taken, there was the problem of protecting them from salt spray and of watering them over so long a period, for fresh water on the small sailing ships of those days was very limited.

These difficulties were overcome by that early plant explorer by using one of the then new "Wardian" cases which are now more commonly known as solariums. They were made of sheets of glass sealed together so that no moisture escaped, and sufficient soil was placed in the bottom in which rooted cuttings or small plants could be grown. Just before the ship sailed the cases were well watered and then sealed; often this sufficed until the next port was reached. Sealing the cases was doubly important, not only to keep the moisture in, but to keep the salt water out, for if even a very small amount of salt water reached the plants, serious injury would result. The sealed cases had to be placed where there was plenty of light, and according to Fortune, "large vessels with poops" were always to be preferred if there was any choice.

Pruning

Forsythias are in that group of plants (see page 87) that bloom on the previous year's wood, so should be pruned *after* they have flowered. If pruned before, many flower buds might unnecessarily be removed, when pruning a week or so later would not injure the plant in any way and would save the flowers for the gardener. This group of plants is one that normally grows gracefully, with drooping or wide-arching branches, hence do not lend themselves to formal shearing. Hedges have been made of forsythias with a resulting sacrifice of flowers, but individual specimens should never be formally sheared since they are grown only for their flowers. When pruning, it is best to leave as many of the graceful side branches as possible. *Forsythia intermedia* and its varieties tend to be more or less upright in habit, while *F. suspensa* is much more drooping. *Forsythia ovata* and *F. viridissima* are between the two extremes.

Like lilacs, privets and many other shrubs, forsythias can be heavily pruned—and recover—when occasion demands. It may be that a planting has been so overgrown, or has so much dead wood, that a mere thinning out appears to be a physical impossibility. Then the plants can be cut to within about six inches of the ground, and can be expected to form new and vigorous bushes. Such a heavy pruning might be done in the early spring even before flowering, in order to give the plants plenty of time to start new growth before summer droughts set in. A heavy pruning should not be attempted in summer or even in very late spring, for hot, dry summer weather might easily cause the soil, or the remaining stubs, to dry out. If done at the right time, however, new plants should be quickly grown in two or three years time. With individual plants, a renewal pruning each year or two, in which only a few of the older branches are removed, is far better than using such drastic treatment as may be economically necessary on a large bank.

Hardiness

Although the forsythias are classed as hardy, there is a limit to their endurance, especially in some New England winters. Twigs will withstand lower temperatures than flower buds, and frequently, only those flower buds which have been covered with snow during the coldest weather are the ones that bloom. The Korean, *F. ovata,* seems to be about the hardiest and can be used in areas where the others are known to suffer. Its flowers are not as large and conspicuous as some of the other recommended varieties. *Forsythia europaea* has also proved flower-hardy in winters when others are injured, but its flowers are inferior to those of *F. ovata.*

Forms

For trailing over banks and walls there is no better form than *F. suspensa sieboldi,* a pendulous branching plant, often trailing along the ground and rooting again at the tips of the branches. This habit is frequently exploited by planting at the top of a steep bank or wall, where the long trailing stems can overhang for as much as 6' or more and make a very graceful planting. The remainder in the recommended list are upright in habit, often with gracefully arching branches, and *F. ovata* is rather wide spreading in habit, not as tall and vigorous as the others.

"Arnold Dwarf," a new low-growing form, has never flowered, but is a true dwarf which makes a dense moundlike growth, possibly making an excellent ground cover because of profuse rooting by branches. There are other forms not quite as dwarf as "Arnold Dwarf" which have flowered.

As far as flower color is concerned, many gardeners do not realize that a selection can be made in this group. *F. intermedia spectabilis* is by far the darkest in color. The palest are the Primrose Forsythia (*F. intermedia primulina*) and *F. suspensa pallida.* These are definitely different in flower color, and where this character seems desirable, these varieties might be considered. The other recommended forsythias have flowers between these two extremes. As noted previously, the flowers of *F. ovata* are neither as large nor as numerous as those of the other varieties.

The varieties producing the most flowers are *F. intermedia spectabilis* and occasionally its close, but lighter flowering, relative *F. intermedia densiflora.*

To identify the species when not in flower, the following key may prove helpful:

FORSYTHIAS

1. Leaves often deeply lobed or divided into three parts, twigs hollow but solid where leaves occur. *F. suspensa*
2. Leaves not divided into three parts.
   3. Leaves entire. *F. europaea*
   4. Leaves mostly with teeth, *i.e.,* serrate, only a few entire.
      5. Leaves broad ovate, mature branches yellowish. *F. ovata*
      6. Leaves narrow and mature branches greenish or brownish.
         7. Pith usually solid where leaves occur, leaves sometimes divided into three parts especially on vigorous growth. *F. intermedia*
         8. Pith usually in partitions—*F. viridissima*

Forsythia "Arnold Dwarf"   2'   Zone 5

HYBRID ORIGIN: *F. intermedia x F. japonica*
INTRODUCED: 1941

"Arnold Dwarf" is a low-growing forsythia which may have merit as a ground cover but in six years it has yet to produce its first flowers. It originated in the Arnold Arboretum and is proving to be a true dwarf, the original plant being only 2' tall but nearly 4' in diameter, with drooping branches that quickly strike root as soon as they touch the ground. Unless it blooms its only merit is its habit.

x Forsythia intermedia spectabilis   9'   Zone 5   Showy Border Forsythia

*FLOWERS: deep yellow
    TIME: mid-April
HYBRID ORIGIN: *F. suspensa x F. viridissima*
ORIGINATED: 1906
F. INTERMEDIA VARIETIES:
    densiflora—(1899) pale yellow flowers, more upright in habit
    primulina—(1910) very pale yellow flowers
The variety *spectabilis* is the deepest yellow of all the forsythias but the other two forms are also valued. All three varieties have an upright habit of growth which makes them splendid for specimen planting but not as good for massing as the gracefully arching *F. suspensa*.

Forsythia ovata   8'   Zone 4   Early Forsythia

*FLOWERS: yellow
    TIME: early April
HABITAT: Korea
INTRODUCED: 1917

The earliest to bloom and also the hardiest. Flowers are smaller and not as prominent as those of other species, hence to be used only where winter cold kills the flower buds of more tender species. Not nearly as floriferous as *F. intermedia spectabilis*.

Forsythia suspensa sieboldi   3-9'   Zone 5   Siebold Forsythia

*FLOWERS: bright yellow
    TIME: mid-April
HABITAT: Japan
INTRODUCED: 1833
F. SUSPENSA VARIETIES:
    fortunei—Fortune Forsythia, vigorous upright habit
    pallida—Pale Forsythia—light-yellow flowers
Siebold Forsythia is often trailing over the ground and for this reason has frequently been planted to overhang rocky walls or ledges. Also frequently used in bank planting, for branches root readily where they touch ground, and so hold the soil in place. The two other varieties are sometimes used to give flower color variation.

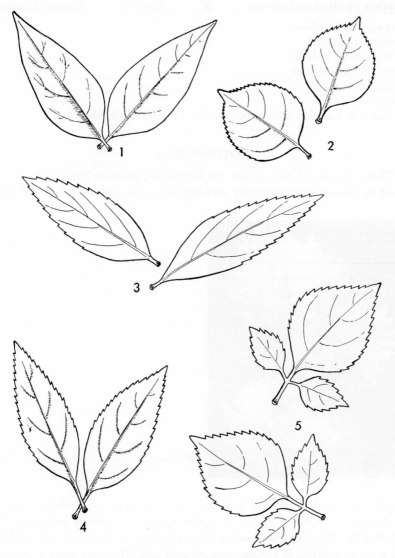

FORSYTHIA LEAVES

Here are typical leaf sketches of the common forsythias, which should prove most helpful in telling them apart when they are not in bloom.

1. *Forsythia europaea*
2. *F. ovata*
3. *F. viridissima*
4. *F. intermedia* (*viridissima x suspensa*)
5. *F. suspensa*

Forsythia viridissima koreana   9'   Zone 5   Korean Forsythia

FLOWERS: bright yellow
    TIME: mid-April
AUTUMN COLOR: reddish
WINTER TWIGS: greenish
HABITAT: Korea
INTRODUCED: 1917
    The only forsythia with autumn color. Of little merit otherwise.

FOTHERGILLA

Three species of this genus are mentioned because the plants are excellent in flower and brilliantly striking again in autumn color. All three

Fothergilla species have interesting heads
of small white flowers in mid-May.

are native to southeastern United States, and have peculiar white, thimble-like flowers in terminal heads or spikes. They are closely related to the witch-hazels, although the flowers are certainly not similar. In the fall, the foliage turns a brilliant yellow, orange and red. They are among the best of ornamental shrubs, especially because of their two full seasons of usefulness. They do well in foundation plantings and in plantings with an evergreen background. Fothergillas are not used nearly enough in modern gardens.

Fothergilla gardeni   3'   Zone 5   Dwarf Fothergilla

*FLOWERS: white in terminal spikes over 1" long
    TIME: mid-May
*AUTUMN COLOR: brilliant yellow to scarlet
HABITAT: Virginia to Georgia

Fothergilla major   9'   Zone 5   Large Fothergilla

*FLOWERS: white in terminal flower spikes often 2" long
    TIME: mid-May
*AUTUMN COLOR: brilliant yellow to scarlet
HABITAT: Georgia
    Upright and pyramidal in habit.

Fothergilla monticola   6'   Zone 5   Alabama Fothergilla

*FLOWERS: white in terminal spikes often 2" long
    TIME: mid-May
*AUTUMN COLOR: brilliant yellow to scarlet
HABITAT: North Carolina to Alabama
    More spreading in habit than *F. major*, with slightly larger flowers. Excellent in foundation plantings, especially where evergreens serve as a background.

Franklinia alatamaha   30'   Zone 5   Franklinia

*FLOWERS: white, yellow center, 3" in diameter
    TIME: September–October
*AUTUMN COLOR: red and orange
HABITAT: Georgia
    John Bartram, one of the early American plant collectors, found this in 1770 and obtained a few plants for his garden in Philadelphia. Strangely enough, since 1790 this plant has never been found in the wild, hence all plants in commerce today are descendants of those which Bartram collected. In New England, this plant is best grown as a shrub, with many stems from the base, for it tends to winterkill slightly in severe winters. Soil mounded about the base of the plants in winter helps to protect the roots.
    Farther South the plant is grown as a tree. Its large conspicuous white blossoms in late summer and early fall, followed by brilliant autumn color, when it is grown in full sun, are its chief assets.

Fuchsia magellanica   3'   Zones 5–6   Magellan Fuchsia

*FLOWERS: usually solitary, red and violet
    TIME: mid-June
FOLIAGE: bright green
HABITAT: Peru, Chile
INTRODUCED: 1800
    One of the very few shrubs from Peru which will grow in northern United States. A variable species, but varieties under the name of "Scarlet Beauty" and "Senorita" have proved hardy in Cleveland, Ohio, and even in some parts of Maine, although they are practically herbaceous. Plants may not be long-lived but specimens have been known to live at least five years and to be covered with hundreds of flowers at blooming time. A five-year-old plant growing in Cleveland was 3' high and 2½' in diameter, with 5,000 flowers. Of course it had optimum growing conditions.
    In the North these plants should be treated as novelties, to be grown in the rock garden or in a protected part of the perennial garden. They have little

ornamental value as shrubs when not in bloom. Many other fuchsias are grown in the warmer parts of southern California, most of them considered as sub-tropical.

Gardenia jasminoides   4–6′   Zones 8–9   Cape-jasmine, Gardenia

*FLOWERS: Waxy white, extremely fragrant, single and double, 3″ diameter
   TIME: May–September
*FOLIAGE: evergreen, thick, leathery, glossy, leaves to 4″ long
HABITAT: China
INTRODUCED: colonial times

This is the much prized gardenia of the florists. It is grown in the same way as are camellias, except that a few flowers only are left on each stem. The others are pinched off, in order to obtain larger flowers. At first it was thought to be a native of the Cape of Good Hope, South Africa, hence its common name. However, it was later found to be a native of China and had probably reached South Africa on one of the old sailing vessels bound from China to England. It used to be very popular but with the wider range of colors and varieties of camellias now available it has long since fallen into second place. It is difficult to transplant, needs plenty of moisture and some shade, especially during the hottest days of summer.

Garrya elliptica   8′   Zone 8   Silk-tassel

FLOWERS: greenish or yellowish tapering catkins, 2–12″ long
   TIME: December–February
FRUIT: silky berries
   EFFECTIVE: summer
FOLIAGE: evergreen, leaves to 3″ long
HABITAT: Oregon to California

Grows well on gravelly ground or rocky slopes and is of considerable interest because the catkins appear early in the year.

Garrya wrighti   6′   Zone 6   Wright Silk-tassel

FLOWERS: greenish catkins 2–3″ long
   TIME: July–August
FRUIT: silky berries
   EFFECTIVE: late summer
HABITAT: Arizona, New Mexico, Texas

The hardiest of this genus, especially suitable for planting in the Arizona–New Mexico area.

Gaultheria miqueliana   1′   Zone 5   Miquel Wintergreen

FLOWERS: white, in nodding racemes, 1–2½″ long
   TIME: May
FRUIT: white berries, sometimes pinkish, rather showy
   EFFECTIVE: fall
FOLIAGE: evergreen, leaves ½–1¼″ long
HABITAT: Japan
INTRODUCED: 1892

Gaultheria procumbens   3″   Zone 3   Checkerberry or Wintergreen
FLOWERS: white, bell-shaped, solitary
    TIME: mid-May
*FRUIT: scarlet berries
    EFFECTIVE: fall
*FOLIAGE: evergreen, lustrous bright green, often variegated
AUTUMN COLOR: bronze
HABITAT: eastern North America

Spread widely throughout the woodlands of eastern North America, it is commonly used as a ground cover in naturalistic plantings. Its waxy white flowers, aromatic foliage and red fruits are commonly used as a flavoring agent. It grows by creeping stems and quickly forms a mat over the soil if sufficiently moist and in partial shade.

Gaultheria shallon   5′   Zone 5   Salal, Shallon
*FLOWERS: white to pink, about ½″ long
    TIME: early June
FRUIT: purple, becoming black, edible
    EFFECTIVE: late summer
*FOLIAGE: evergreen, dark green, leathery, leaves to 5″ long
HABITAT: Alaska and British Columbia to southern California

Salal is native over the entire Pacific Coast region and therefore often overlooked for garden use. It should be planted far more than it is. Growing with the

Gaultheria shallon, native on the Pacific Coast, an excellent evergreen for the garden there.

Oregon Grape it makes an excellent plant in nature as well as in gardens and is to be highly recommended for placing along the borders of evergreen plantings. It may be grown in either full sun or shade. If grown on poor soil, in full sun, it becomes a low mat covering the ground; whereas in shade, with plenty of moisture, it tends to become a vigorous upright bush, requiring little pruning.

Gaultheria veitchiana   3′   Zone 7   Veitch Wintergreen

FLOWERS: white, sometimes flushed pink, bell-shaped
  TIME: May
*FRUIT: indigo blue berries, ¼″ in diameter
  EFFECTIVE: August
FOLIAGE: evergreen, lustrous, dark, leaves to 3½″ long
HABITAT: western China
INTRODUCED: 1908
  A low evergreen shrub doing well in a moist situation

Gaylussacia brachycera   18″   Zone 5   Box-Huckleberry

FLOWERS: white, or pink, small, bell-shaped
  TIME: mid-May
FRUIT: blue berry
  EFFECTIVE: August
FOLIAGE: evergreen, leaves to 1″ long
HABITAT: Pennsylvania to Virginia, Tennessee and Kentucky
  A rare native plant forming a small rounded mass of evergreen foliage suitable for display in the rock garden, resembles *Vaccinium vitis—idaea minor,* and at one time almost lost to cultivation but fortunately again introduced through the efforts of the Arnold Arboretum.

Genista cinerea   2½′   Zone 7   Ashy Woadwaxen

*FLOWERS: yellow, pealike in racemes 8″ long
  TIME: early June
FOLIAGE: sparingly leafy
HABITAT: southern Europe, northern Africa
INTRODUCED: before 1850
  A dependable species, rather low in habit, with many bright yellow flowers, and requiring poor soil.

Genista hispanica   1′   Zone 6   Spanish Gorse

*FLOWERS: bright yellow, pealike
  TIME: early June
WINTER TWIGS: green, thorny
HABITAT: Spain to northern Italy
INTRODUCED: 1759
  This shrub is covered with large green spines, which with the green twigs, gives it a decidedly evergreen appearance in winter. The flowers are brilliantly colored and almost completely cover the shrub when fully open. Like other genistas it actually requires dry soil. One of the best low plants in this group.

Genista pilosa   1'   Zone 5   Silky-leaf Woadwaxen

*FLOWERS: yellow, pealike
   TIME: late May
WINTER TWIGS: gray-green
HABITAT: Europe
INTRODUCED: 1789

A low prostrate shrub, useful for covering poor soil even under trees and shrubs where the situation is not too shaded. It requires poor sandy soil for best growth, is hard to move once it becomes well established and makes an interesting low shrub for the rock garden.

Genista tinctoria   3'   Zone 2   Dyer's Greenweed

*FLOWERS: yellow, pealike
   TIME: early June
FOLIAGE: bright green
WINTER TWIGS: green
HABITAT: Europe and western Asia, sometimes naturalized in the eastern states in this country.

The hardiest of the genistas, requiring a hot, sunny situation in poor soil, preferably sandy and dry. Like other genistas, it does not transplant easily but in the rockery its bright yellow flowers are most prominent. The double-flowered variety *plena* is more colorful than the species because of its increased number of petals.

Halimodendron halodendron   6'   Zone 2   Salt-tree

FLOWERS: pale purple, fragrant, in short clusters
   TIME: early June
FOLIAGE: silvery, leaves to 1½" long
HABITAT: Transcaucasia to Turkestan
INTRODUCED: 1779

The Salt-tree is closely related to the *Caragana* species and is only recommended here for its ability to grow in heavy limestone soil or near the seashore. The spiny branches, silver foliage and graceful appearance in flower are its chief assets. Very difficult to propagate except by grafting on *Caragana* or *Laburnum* understock; and in fertile soils, many other shrubs will be found that make better ornamentals.

Hamamelis mollis   30'   Zone 5   Chinese Witch-hazel

*FLOWERS: yellow, ribbonlike petals, fragrant
   TIME: March
*AUTUMN COLOR: yellow
HABITAT: central China
INTRODUCED: 1879

This Witch-hazel has the largest flowers (nearly 1½") of this group and is very fragrant—hence a desired specimen. It grows in a neat, rounded form and can easily be kept under control with occasional judicious pruning.

One of the first shrubs to bloom in the very early spring is the Chinese
Witch-hazel (*Hamamelis mollis*).

Hamamelis vernalis   10'   Zone 5   Vernal Witch-hazel

*FLOWERS: yellow to reddish, ribbonlike, fragrant
    TIME: February
*AUTUMN COLOR: yellow
HABITAT: central United States

This native shrub is the first of all the shrubs in the Arnold Arboretum to
bloom in the spring. Sometimes it blooms in January, sometimes in February,
occasionally even in December, depending on weather conditions. Its small, very
fragrant flowers, about ½" in diameter, have the interesting quality of opening
fully on warm sunny days, and closing or rolling their petals together on cold
days, and so remain effectively in bloom for several weeks. This species is a
vigorous-growing one and a mature plant makes an excellent, dense specimen.

Hamamelis virginiana   15'   Zone 4   Common Witch-hazel

*FLOWERS: yellow, ribbonlike petals
    TIME: early October
*AUTUMN COLOR: yellow
HABITAT: eastern and central United States

This native American shrub, common in the woods of nearly half the United
States, is the last shrub (in the North) to bear flowers in the fall. Because of this
and its bright-yellow autumn color, it is valued. Recommended for shade planting, but in full sun, grows into a splendid well-rounded specimen. Sometimes

when planted near birch trees, a peculiar insect makes small cones on the under-surface of the witch-hazel leaves. This does not seriously hurt the plant and controlling it (by eliminating the birches) is usually not practical.

Hebe buxifolia 4' Zone 7 Boxleaf Hebe

*FLOWERS: white in spikes 1" long
    TIME: July
FOLIAGE: lustrous dark evergreen, leaves ½" long
HABITAT: New Zealand
INTRODUCED: 1885

The hebes do best in a dry, almost sandy, soil and should not receive too much water. This species, in particular, will break up in the center if it grows too vigorously. The low, spreading habit and glossy foliage are its chief ornamental characteristics.

Hebe traversi 6' Zone 7 Travers Hebe

*FLOWERS: white spikes, 2" long
    TIME: July
FOLIAGE: dull dark green, evergreen, leaves to 1" long
HABITAT: New Zealand
INTRODUCED: 1868

Probably a more dependable ornamental than *H. buxifolia*, this species is vigorous and sturdy, forming a round, mounded mass of small dull green leaves. Its profuse flowers in midsummer make it a desirable plant. Many other species are grown for ornamental purposes in Zones 7–9.

Heteromeles arbutifolia 6–10' Zone 9 Christmas-berry

FLOWERS: small, white, in flat clusters
    TIME: June–July
*FRUIT: red berries, hollylike
    EFFECTIVE: winter
*FOLIAGE: evergreen, leathery, glossy green, leaves to 4" long
HABITAT: California

An excellent native shrub in certain parts of California, much used in Christmas decorations because of its profuse and brilliant scarlet fruits. Can be grown in dry soils but responds well to watering. However, it should not be unduly forced as it may become too scrawny and open at the base. A dense, compact shrub is more desirable. Occasionally susceptible to fire-blight, control can be attained with proper use of Bordeaux mixture.

Hibiscus rosa-sinensis 30' Zone 9 Chinese Hibiscus

*FLOWERS: white, pink, red, single and double as much as 6" in diameter
    TIME: summer
HABITAT: China
INTRODUCED: 1850

A fast growing shrub with glossy leaves and handsomely striking flowers adapted for growing in central and southern Florida and southern California. Several varieties are available from subtropical nurseries.

Hibiscus syriacus   15'   Zone 5   Shrub Althea

*FLOWERS: large, white to blue, single and double, 2–4" in dia.

TIME: August

HABITAT: China, India

INTRODUCED: before 1790

There are many species of *Hibiscus* grown in the tropics, but only one, *Hibiscus syriacus*, can be grown over a greater part of the United States and southern Canada. Commonly called the Shrubby Althea or the Rose of Sharon, it is of ornamental interest only because it flowers in late summer at a time when few other woody plants are in bloom. It was first brought to this country before 1790, and was listed in European nurseries for nearly two hundred years prior to that time. A native of China and India, it has no interesting ornamental fruits, nor does its foliage turn color in the fall.

In some gardens, this plant has been difficult to grow. Young plants are certainly less winter-hardy than older plants, and might well be given special winter protection for the first few years after transplanting. Larger plants, well established, seem to be able to live satisfactorily. Some gardeners erroneously believe the plant requires a dry soil. This is not true. In fact, it is one of the first plants to show the effects of lack of water in summer. Given a normal garden loam, not too moist and certainly not the driest place in the garden, it should grow satisfactorily if it will survive the winters.

Once it has started satisfactory growth, it becomes a bushy plant so dense that it has been used in hedges. It varies considerably when grown from seed for there are single- and double-flowered varieties, ranging in color from pure white, to pink, red, blue and variations with flowers as much as 4" in diameter. There are even some varieties with variegated leaves.

If the plant is let alone with little pruning, flowers may be numerous but small. On the other hand, if large blooms are wanted, the best way to obtain them is to prune the previous year's shoots back considerably, leaving only three or four buds on each shoot. This is done in early spring, before leaves start to grow, and practically ruins the general appearance of the plant for a period, but the resulting flowers are unusually large and handsome. Many of the large number of varieties grown in the trade today are superfluous. A few of the better varieties would be those in the following list:

"Admiral Dewey"—flowers double, pure white
"Amplissimus"—flowers double, pink
"Anemonaeflorus"—flowers semi-double, white with dark center
"Ardens"—flowers double, bluish purple
"Coelestis"—single flowers, violet-blue
"Duc de Brabant"—double flowers, red
"Hamabo"—single flowers, blush, carmine blotched

"Jeanne d'Arc"—double flowers, white
"Lucy"—semi-double, rose
"Monstrosus"—single flowers, white, purple center
"Pulcherrimus"—double flowers, pink and white
"Rubis"—single flowers, clear pink
"Snowdrift"—single flowers, white

Hippophae rhamnoides   30'   Zone 3   Sea-Buckthorn

FLOWERS: inconspicuous, sexes separate
    TIME: early April
*FRUIT: bright orange berries, profusely borne on pistillate plants
    EFFECTIVE: fall
FOLIAGE: leaves willowlike, grayish-green on upper surface, silver-green beneath
WINTER TWIGS: thorny
HABITAT: Europe and Asia
INTRODUCED: colonial times

Grown chiefly for its profuse, bright-orange or orange-yellow fleshy fruits about ¼" in diameter. However, sexes are separate, with pistillate flowers all on one tree and staminate flowers on another. Both must be present to insure fruiting, preferably in a ratio of one staminate plant to every six pistillate plants. The fruit is very acid, not quickly eaten by birds, and remains on the plant a long time. The English think highly of this shrub, some even saying that it should be present in every garden. For some reason we have had much difficulty in getting it established in the Arnold Arboretum but once established, it makes a splendid ornamental shrub for fall display.

Holodiscus discolor ariaefolius   12'   Zone 5   Ocean Spray

*FLOWERS: creamy white, panicles 8" long
    TIME: early July
FOLIAGE: grayish green, leaves to 4" long
HABITAT: British Columbia to California and Idaho

Not usually seen in eastern gardens, yet it has considerable merit as a summer-blooming shrub. Its conspicuous, pyramidal, flower clusters are nearly as wide as long, and borne on gracefully arching branches. Similar in general appearance to the Ural False Spirea but blooms earlier. As a background for the perennial border (especially if delphiniums are present) it can be outstanding.

Hydrangea arborescens grandiflora   3'   Zone 4   Hills-of-Snow

*FLOWERS: white, in large, rounded clusters about 6" in diameter
    TIME: early July
HABITAT: found wild in Ohio before 1900

Upright, often dense-growing, with conspicuous, large, creamy white flowers in early summer. These are borne on the ends of the stalks, often profusely, so that a bush in full bloom is a rolling mass of white. This shrub is easily grown, blooms on the current year's growth and frequently is killed back severely in the winter. It is very popular, particularly because of its easy culture.

Hydrangea macrophylla hortensia   12′   Zones 5–6   House Hydrangea

*FLOWERS: blue or pink, all flowers sterile in rounded heads, 5–10″ or more in diameter

TIME: August

FOLIAGE: bright green, lustrous, leaves to 8″ long

HABITAT: Japan

INTRODUCED: 1790

The large, rounded, flower clusters of this variety are most interesting in that they can be either pink or blue depending on the soil constituents. If growing in an alkaline soil, with plenty of lime, the flowers are pink; and in acid soils, or those to which alum or various forms of iron have been added, the flowers are blue. This is a highly variable group of popular flowering plants. In the South and on the Pacific Coast they are used out-of-doors a great deal. In the North they are not completely hardy and although used in gardens occasionally as far north as Cape Cod, they are more popular as house plants where their large shiny green leaves and prominent flowers make a conspicuous display. There are over fifty named varieties in the trade, some are selections from other countries, some the result of hybridization in America. In fact some forms are called "French Hydrangeas" merely because the hybridization was done in France.

E. H. Wilson brought back many varieties from Japan, one of them being *H. macrophylla coerulea* with perfect flowers deep blue, and sterile flowers blue or white. Usually these large-flowered hydrangeas are produced only on the end of the terminal growth from buds formed the previous year. Hence in northern areas where terminal twigs are partly killed by winter cold, few flowers will form.

Hydrangea paniculata grandiflora   25′   Zone 4   Peegee Hydrangea

*FLOWERS: white, nearly all sterile in foot-long pyramidal clusters

TIME: August

HABITAT: Japan

INTRODUCED: 1862

A large, coarse, easily grown shrub which has been much overplanted. Easily propagated from cuttings, it makes a big bush in a short period—one of the reasons it has been favored commercially. The flower panicles at first are white but gradually turn pink to purplish and frequently remain on the plant in a semi-dried form long after the leaves have fallen. *Hydrangea paniculata praecox* is similar, blooming about three weeks before the larger flowering form. Both are valued for conspicuous late summer bloom at a time when few woody plants are in flower, but they are coarse in texture and because of their conspicuous character are very hard to use properly in the garden.

Hydrangea quercifolia   6′   Zone 5   Oak-leaved Hydrangea

FLOWERS: erect panicles of small flowers, 4–8″ in height, white, turning purplish at maturity

TIME: mid-July

AUTUMN COLOR: reddish

HABITAT: Georgia, Florida to Mississippi

A handsome, dense, stoloniferous shrub with leaves somewhat the same shape as those of the Red Oak. This is truly a handsome shrub for its foliage alone, and in the North is grown solely for this, since the tops frequently die to the ground and few flowers are produced. Farther South, where it does flower, the conspicuous panicles make an important showing. This plant is somewhat difficult to use in combination with others and is better used alone.

Hydrangea sargentiana   9'   Zone 7   Sargent Hydrangea

FLOWERS: pale violet, white, in large pyramidal clusters
    TIME: late July
FOLIAGE: dull green, hairy, leaves to 10" long
HABITAT: central China
INTRODUCED: 1907

A striking shrub because of its stout, hairy branches, large leaves and large flower clusters.

HYPERICUM

The St. Johnsworts are low woody shrubs, sometimes ground covers, valued for their bright yellow flowers. Some of them, as they grow tall, will have a very interesting shiny brown exfoliating bark of considerable ornamental value in the winter. The ground covers, especially, are frequently avid growers and can quickly crowd out other low plants in the rockery if not restrained. Their fruits are dry capsules and have little autumn coloring. However, a splendid feature of this group, especially the ground covers, is the fact that they grow well in dry, sandy soil. Some of them, like *Hypericum prolificum* continue to produce flowers over many weeks in the summer and, of course, summer-flowering shrubs, especially those with bright yellow flowers, are none too numerous.

Hypericum buckleyi   Ground cover   Zone 5   Blue Ridge St. Johnswort

*FLOWERS: single, yellow, 1" in diameter
    TIME: mid-June
HABITAT: North Carolina to Georgia

A procumbent, almost creeping shrub, seldom over 10" tall, used as a mass in the rockery or as a ground cover. A single plant will quickly grow into a round mat of foliage several feet in diameter.

Hypericum calycinum   Ground cover   Zone 5   Aaronsbeard St. Johnswort

*FLOWERS: solitary, bright yellow, 3" in diameter
    TIME: late July
*FOLIAGE: evergreen or half-evergreen, leaves to 4" long
AUTUMN COLOR: purplish
HABITAT: southeastern Europe, Asia Minor
INTRODUCED: colonial times

In sandy soil this species makes an excellent ground cover. Very nearly the most beautiful of the genus, it has become naturalized in many places in the British Isles. It thrives in semi-shade, in situations where other shrubs would not do well at all and has the admirable trait of flowering continuously a greater part of the summer. Easily propagated by division.

Hypericum frondosum   3′   Zone 5   Golden St. Johnswort
*FLOWERS: single, yellow, 2″ in diameter
     TIME: mid-July
HABITAT: South Carolina to Texas
     John Bartram, the famous American botanist of Revolutionary times, is responsible for discovering this plant in Georgia, about 1776. The flowers are larger and perhaps more numerous than those of the more common *H. prolificum*.

Hypericum hookerianum   6′   Zone 7   Hooker's St. Johnswort
*FLOWERS: cup-shaped, single, yellow, 2½″ in diameter
     TIME: early August
FOLIAGE: dark, evergreen or half-evergreen, leaves to 4″ long
HABITAT: Sikkim, western China
INTRODUCED: before 1853
     Compact shrub, handsome in flower but one of the least hardy of this genus.

Hypericum kalmianum   3′   Zone 4   Kalm St. Johnswort
*FLOWERS: bright yellow, single, 1″ in diameter
     TIME: early July
HABITAT: Quebec and Ontario to Michigan and Illinois
     Another species that is handsome in flower, and among the hardiest.

x Hypericum moserianum   2′   Zone 7   Gold-flower
*FLOWERS: single yellow, 2½″ in diameter
     TIME: July
HYBRID ORIGIN: *H. patulum x H. calycinum*
ORIGINATED: about 1887
     The important feature of this species is its length of bloom, practically the entire summer. The leaves are neat and oblong in shape. Used on the Pacific Coast where it is one of the few so-called ground covers that will thrive under Eucalyptus trees.

Hypericum patulum henryi   3′   Zone 6   Henry St. Johnswort
*FLOWERS: single, yellow, 2½″ in diameter
     TIME: July
FOLIAGE: half-evergreen, leaves to 3″ long
HABITAT: China
INTRODUCED: 1898
     A variety superior to the species in every way and a delightful plant for it is one of the best of its group for garden use.

Hypericum prolificum   3′   Zone 4   Shrubby St. Johnswort
*FLOWERS: bright yellow, single, ¾″ in diameter
     TIME: late July
*WINTER TWIGS: brown, lustrous, smooth bark
HABITAT: New Jersey to Iowa and Georgia
     This plant is very shrubby and one of the hardiest of the several species in this group. The leaves are small, narrow; the plant itself is dense, mounded in habit, and covered with continuous blooms for several weeks at a time.

Iberis gibraltarica   15″   Zone 7   Gibraltar Candytuft

FLOWERS: lilac-pink, partly white, flowers small, in umbels
   TIME: mid-May
FOLIAGE: evergreen, leaves 1–2″ long
HABITAT: Spain, Morocco
INTRODUCED: 1732

An interesting, evergreen, rock-garden plant or possibly of value for the front of an evergreen foundation planting.

Iberis sempervirens   12″   Zone 5   Evergreen Candytuft

*FLOWERS: white, small in umbels
   TIME: late May
FOLIAGE: evergreen, leaves to 1½″ long, narrow

A common garden plant, especially in rockeries where its low habit, narrow evergreen leaves and profuse white flowers make it conspicuous in early spring. The leaves are not entirely evergreen in the North but it makes a sturdy, dependable plant, blooming a little later than *Alyssum saxatile*.

Iberis tenoreana   8″   Zone 5   Tenore Candytuft

*FLOWERS: small, white in umbels, sometimes pinkish
   TIME: mid-May
FOLIAGE: evergreen, leaves linear, about 1½″ long
HABITAT: Italy
INTRODUCED: 1822

This low evergreen is of chief value for its bloom that appears at the same time as the profuse yellow flowers of *Alyssum saxatile*. Hence these two low plants should be used together. The more common *Iberis sempervirens* does not flower until later, when most of the *Alyssum saxatile* flowers are gone.

ILEX

The hollies comprise a most valuable group of ornamental trees and shrubs, some evergreen and some deciduous. There are those that are native of Asia, many are native of South America, some native to Europe and, of course, some native to North America. The hollies most commonly thought of when the name is mentioned are the European Holly (*Ilex aquifolium*) and our native American Holly (*I. opaca*), both being small trees and highly valued for their ornamental red berries. Both have been cultivated for such long periods that there are nearly one hundred varieties of each, truly a bewildering number. However, it is the shrubby species with which we are here interested and many of these are most worthwhile.

A few, like *Ilex cornuta*, *I. glabra*, *I. pedunculosa* and *I. yunnanensis* have evergreen foliage which makes them more valuable as ornamentals than the deciduous types, *I. decidua* and *I. verticillata*. Those species with bright red berries are much more attractive than those with black berries, but most have a definite use in garden planting. The flowers of all species are small and inconspicuous. (See page 28.)

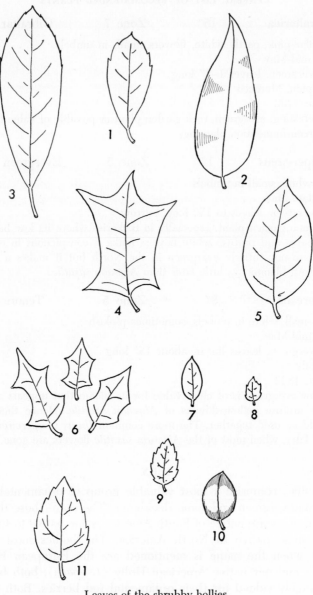

Leaves of the shrubby hollies

1. Ilex glabra
2. I. pedunculosa
3. I. cassine
4. I. cornuta
5. I. cornuta burfordi
6. I. pernyi
7. I. crenata microphylla
8. I. crenata helleri
9. I. crenata
10. I. crenata convexa
11. I. yunnanensis

Hollies belong to that group of plants with separate sexes, staminate flowers on one plant and pistillate flowers on another. Both must be present in the near vicinity to insure the fertilization of the pistillate flowers. In some regions where hollies are native, wind-blown pollen or even insect-carried pollen may be sufficient so that only the pistillate form of the species need be planted in the garden. Usually the safer method to insure fruiting is to have both sexes in the same garden. One need not always go to these extremes with the less conspicuous black-fruiting forms for it is not so important that they bear fruit, but with the red-fruiting forms it is best to do so. Planting a small staminate plant in the same hole with the pistillate plant is another method to insure good fruiting, and pains might be taken, as these plants grow older, to prune the staminate plant to a minimum number of branches. Pollen from one species of holly may fertilize the flowers of another species, but it is essential for the two to be in bloom together.

One happy exception to this general rule on fruiting seems to be found in the Chinese Holly (*I. cornuta*), for the pistillate plants of this species seem to have the ability to produce fruit (but not fertile seed) without the pollen of other hollies. Another species, *I. laevigata* is performing the same way in some of my experiments with this group of plants. Fortunately, some commercial growers are recognizing the importance of growing the holly sexes separately and it is from these sources that plants should be obtained. There is no positive way to identify the different sexes until they flower.

Hollies are propagated by cuttings and seeds, but the seeds take two years to germinate, sometimes three. The shrubby species are, for the most part, rather rugged individuals and easy of culture. A normally good garden soil is all they need in which to thrive. Two of the species, *I. glabra* and *I. verticillata,* seem to grow well in very moist soil, in fact the latter is found native in swamp lands throughout the entire eastern United States. However, both do almost as well in normally well drained soil. If grown in a dry, sandy soil, it might be advisable to mulch the plants with oak leaves or pine needles. Most hollies are comparatively free of insect and disease pests and where these troubles exist they can be eliminated by applying commonly available materials.

Only a few species are recommended here, but each one could easily make a splendid garden specimen within its limits of hardiness. Other species are being grown, especially the vigorous *I. purpurea* about which there are many good reports but the few here mentioned are certainly among the best.

Ilex cassine 36′ Zone 7 Dahoon

FLOWERS: inconspicuous, sexes separate
  TIME: May
*FRUIT: red berries, ¼″ in diameter, profusely borne
  EFFECTIVE: fall and winter

LEFT: The Chinese Holly (*Ilex cornuta*).
RIGHT: *Ilex crenata helleri* in the foreground is a dwarf form of the Japanese Holly. At the rear are the Weeping Hemlock, Arborvitae and Mugo Pine, all plants used frequently in foundation plantings.

FOLIAGE: evergreen, leaves 1½–5″ long
AUTUMN COLOR: purplish green
HABITAT: southeastern United States
 Native in wet soils in the South and valued for its heavy fruit production.

Ilex cornuta   9′   Zone 7   Chinese Holly
FLOWERS: inconspicuous, sexes separate
   TIME: early June
*FRUIT: bright red berries, ⅜″ in diameter
   EFFECTIVE: fall and winter
*FOLIAGE: evergreen, lustrous, leaves 1½–5″ long
HABITAT: eastern China
INTRODUCED: 1846
VARIETY: *burfordi*—foliage darker, habit more globose with drooping branches
 Most hollies are dioecious and both sexes must be present in the near vicinity to produce fruits, but this species is reliably reported to produce fruits without the aid of pollen. Of course there are no seeds in the fruits. This is a most desirable asset. The leaves usually have five spines, two at the base and three at the top. Some strains and hybrids of this species are hardy in southern New York State. A splendid holly, wherever it can be grown, its lustrous dark green leaves are always beautiful, and its large bright red berries are most effective. It was one of the plants discovered by Robert Fortune when he visited China.

Burford Holly—a good form of the Chinese Holly.

Ilex crenata 20′ Zone 6 Japanese Holly

FLOWERS: inconspicuous, sexes separate
 TIME: late June
FRUIT: small black berries, ¼″ in diameter
 EFFECTIVE: fall
*FOLIAGE: lustrous dark green, evergreen, leaves ½–1½″ long
HABITAT: Japan
INTRODUCED: 1864
VARIETIES:
 convexa—unusually good ornamental form, twice as broad as high
 helleri—dwarf compact form
 "Kingsville"—very dwarf compact form
 microphylla—leaves smaller than species, most hardy form

The Japanese Holly (*Ilex crenata*) withstands clipping very well and so makes excellent hedges. *Cotoneaster horizontalis* is used at the side of the steps in a charming way, and *Buxus sempervirens suffruticosa* is the dwarf edging material at the base of the bank.

In Japan this is widely used for clipping purposes, both in hedges and in unique topiary figures. Its small leaves, about ½–1½″ long, are densely borne so that it does make a splendid screen or barrier plant. The variety *convexa* is of broad-spreading habit, often being twice as broad as high, and in New England it is the best substitute for boxwood. The leaves of this variety are not much larger than those of *Buxus sempervirens*.

Ilex decidua 30′ Zone 5 Possum Haw

FLOWERS: inconspicuous, sexes separate
    TIME: late May
*FRUIT: orange to scarlet berries, ⅜″ in diameter
    EFFECTIVE: fall and winter
FOLIAGE: deciduous, lustrous
HABITAT: southeastern United States

Ilex glabra 21′ Zone 3 Inkberry

FLOWERS: inconspicuous, often solitary, sexes separate
    TIME: mid-June
FRUIT: black berries, small, ¼″ in diameter
    EFFECTIVE: fall
*FOLIAGE: evergreen, lustrous, leaves dark, 1–2″

HABITAT: eastern United States and Canada

Common over a wide area, especially in swampy areas, its evergreen foliage and willowy growth are its chief assets.

Ilex pedunculosa   30'   Zone 5   Long-stalk Holly

FLOWERS: inconspicuous, sexes separate
    TIME: mid-June
*FRUIT: bright red on slender stalks nearly 1" long, ¼" in diameter
    EFFECTIVE: early fall
*FOLIAGE: evergreen, lustrous, leaves 1–3" long
HABITAT: Japan
INTRODUCED: 1892

This is one of the hardiest of evergreen hollies and should be better known, especially in northern gardens. The fruits are often as large as those of *I. aquifolium*.

Ilex pernyi   30'   Zone 6   Perny Holly

FLOWERS: inconspicuous, sexes separate
    TIME: late May
*FRUIT: red berries in clusters, ¼" in diameter
    EFFECTIVE: late summer and early fall
*FOLIAGE: glossy, evergreen, with a few spines on each, ½–1¼" long
HABITAT: central and western China
INTRODUCED: 1900

Somewhat similar to the Chinese Holly, it has smaller leaves and when young is very definitely pyramidal in habit. Since there are none too many red-fruiting evergreens, this species is kept in the recommended list. The fruits are unusually large and borne in the axis of the leaves.

Ilex verticillata   9'   Zone 3   Black Alder, Winterberry

FLOWERS: inconspicuous, sexes separate
    TIME: mid-June
*FRUIT: bright red berries, ¼" in diameter
    EFFECTIVE: fall and winter
FOLIAGE: deciduous
AUTUMN COLOR: yellow
HABITAT: eastern North America
VARIETY: *chrysocarpa*—fruit yellow

The bright red fruits of this native species appear while the leaves are still green, making an excellent color combination. They remain on the plant long after the leaves have fallen, frequently until Christmas when they appear in all sorts of decorations throughout the east. *Ilex geniculata* is somewhat similar although its fruits are borne on delicate inch-long stalks. It does not have sufficient ornamental characteristics to warrant its use in preference to the easily obtained native species. Although the Winterberry is frequently found in swamps it can be grown in almost any good garden soil. Another closely related species, *I. laevigata*, is more difficult to locate in nurseries but in some of my recent experiments is demonstrating the admirable trait of setting fruit without pollenization.

Ilex yunnanensis   12'   Zone 7   Yunnan Holly

FLOWERS: inconspicuous, sexes separate
    TIME: early June
*FRUIT: bright red berries, produced singly; ¼" in diameter
    EFFECTIVE: early fall
*FOLIAGE: lustrous evergreen, leaves about 1" long
HABITAT: western China
INTRODUCED: 1901

There is not a wide use or demand for this species at this time because it is unfortunately extremely difficult to locate staminate plants. Once these are found or some other species is found which will easily fertilize it, *I. yunnanensis* can quickly become one of our best evergreens for fall and winter display. It is closely related to the Japanese Holly, but its red fruit and neat pyramidal habit, make it much more ornamental.

Illicium floridanum   9'   Zone 7   Florida Anise Tree

*FLOWERS: red, 2" in diameter
    TIME: July
FOLIAGE: evergreen, aromatic, leaves to 6" long
HABITAT: Florida and Louisiana

An unusual evergreen, doing best in partial shade and in slightly acid soil.

Indigofera amblyantha   6'   Zone 5   Pink Indigo

*FLOWERS: small, pale lilac-purple in 3–4" spikes
    TIME: early June
HABITAT: China
INTRODUCED: 1908

This Indigo is valued for the length of bloom of its flowers, first appearing in June and continuing for many weeks in the summer at a time when few woody plants bloom. Indigoferas are members of the Pea Family with very small flowers about ¼" long and pinnately compound leaves which do not have any particular autumn color. The fruits are dried capsules. All indigo shrubs may die back somewhat in even normal winters, and therefore some pruning is usually in order. However, the shrubs quickly recover and bloom on the current year's wood.

Indigofera kirilowi   3'   Zone 4   Kirilow Indigo

*FLOWERS: small in rose-colored spikes 5" long
    TIME: June
HABITAT: China, Korea
INTRODUCED: 1899

A low, dense shrub which makes an excellent ground cover by suckering and spreading rapidly by underground stems. It grows to a uniform height and makes a more dense ground cover than does the Yellow Root. If, in severe winters, the branches are killed, it quickly sprouts from the base again and flowers in summer on the current year's shoots.

Indigofera potanini 3' Zone 5 Potanin Indigo

*FLOWERS: small, lilac-pink, in 2–5" spikes
    TIME: June
HABITAT: northwestern China
INTRODUCED: 1925

This Indigo is valued chiefly for its length of bloom, bearing its colorful flower spikes for many weeks during early summer at a time when few woody shrubs bloom.

Juniperus chinensis pfitzeriana 10' Zone 4 Pfitzer's Juniper

FRUIT: blue berries
    EFFECTIVE: fall
*FOLIAGE: evergreen, needlelike
HABITAT: originated in Germany
INTRODUCED: 1901

This is a broad, often flat-topped, pyramidal shrub used a great deal in American plantings. The foliage of young plants has a light, feathery texture that is decidedly pleasing. Plants have been pruned so that columnar types are simulated, but its chief value is its natural habit of wide-spreading growth, not commonly seen in other junipers.

Juniperus chinensis pyramidalis 15'+ Zone 4 Pyramidal Chinese Juniper

FRUIT: blue berries
    EFFECTIVE: fall
*FOLIAGE: bluish green, evergreen, needlelike
INTRODUCED: 1907

A very dense, pyramidal form, with bluish green, juvenile foliage, often erroneously grown as *J. excelsa stricta*. It is at its best as a young plant with vigorous shoots facing the ground on all sides. As it matures, it may grow straggly and open at the base and becomes rather undesirable for this reason.

Juniperus chinensis sargenti Ground cover Zone 4 Sargent Juniper

FRUIT: blue berries
    EFFECTIVE: fall
*FOLIAGE: steel-blue, evergreen, needlelike
HABITAT: Kurile Islands
INTRODUCED: 1892

A low, prostrate, creeping shrub, found in seashore areas, its native habitat, in mats often 8–10' in diameter. It makes an excellent ground cover with foliage a different color from most other junipers used for this same purpose.

Juniperus communis 36' Zone 2 Common Juniper

FRUIT: bluish berries
    EFFECTIVE: fall
FOLIAGE: evergreen, needlelike
HABITAT: northern North America, Europe, northeastern Asia
VARIETIES:

    depressa—(Prostrate Juniper) rarely exceeding 4', low with ascending branches

The Shore Juniper (*Juniperus conferta*) does best in the dry sandy situations at the seashore.

hibernica—(Irish Juniper) dense, upright form

suecica—(Swedish Juniper) somewhat similar to above variety except that the tips of the branchlets droop more and the branches themselves are slightly more wide-spreading.

The Common Juniper of the pastures of a wide area of North America varies considerably, and several forms can be usually noted growing in the same pasture. It unfortunately takes on a brownish winter color which is not at all attractive. The dried, ripe fruit is ground and used as a stimulant.

Juniperus conferta　　　　1'　　　　Zone 5　　　　Shore Juniper

FOLIAGE: evergreen, needlelike
HABITAT: Japan
INTRODUCED: 1915

A low shrub for ground-cover planting, especially adapted for planting on sand dunes in the vicinity of the seashore where other junipers cannot be grown successfully.

Juniperus horizontalis　　　Ground cover　　　Zone 2　　　Creeping Juniper

FRUIT: blue berries
　　EFFECTIVE: fall
FOLIAGE: bluish green or steel-blue, needlelike
HABITAT: Nova Scotia to Alberta, to New Jersey, Minnesota and Montana

VARIETIES:

douglasi—a trailing form with steel blue foliage named after the Douglas Nurseries of Waukegan, Illinois. Called the Waukegan Juniper.

plumosa—foliage more feathery, a lighter green—turning purple in fall. Andorra Juniper

procumbens—very dwarf, some plants only 5″ tall but 12′ in diameter, foliage bluish green. Flat Creeping Juniper

A low creeping shrub with dark green foliage, the variety, *plumosa,* being more compact and with lighter green foliage, and *douglasi* being dark green, with *procumbens* being the lowest of all varieties. These all make good ground covers.

Juniperus sabina   10′   Zone 4   Savin Juniper

FOLIAGE: evergreen, needlelike
HABITAT: southwestern Europe to Siberia
INTRODUCED: early colonial times
VARIETY: *tamariscifolia*—low, spreading shrub with ascending branches, usually not over 2′ high, blue-green foliage

Usually the Savin Juniper is more or less upright in habit but not of particularly good foliage at maturity. However it does grow well on limestone soil.

Juniperus squamata meyeri   6′   Zone 4   Meyer's Juniper

FOLIAGE: blue evergreen, needlelike
HABITAT: China
INTRODUCED: 1914

This variety has foliage a striking blue color, differing from all other junipers in this respect. It has ascending branches but usually its growth habit is such that it is not a definite pyramid of foliage, but rather one of slightly unusual shape with the central leader slightly off center or growing off at an angle. A good ornamental only while the foliage is kept in a vigorous condition.

Juniperus virginiana tripartita   5′   Zone 2   Fountain Red-cedar

FRUIT: blue berries
    EFFECTIVE: fall
FOLIAGE: evergreen, needlelike
HABITAT: eastern and central North America

One of several forms of the serviceable Red Cedar with dark green foliage. *Juniperus virginiana globosa* is round in outline with light-green foliage as is also *J. virginiana pendula.* This last when grafted at the ground level can form a moundlike ball of foliage as broad as it is tall with all the good qualities of the native Red Cedar.

Kalmia angustifolia   3′   Zone 2   Sheep-laurel

FLOWERS: rosy red to crimson in loose clusters
    TIME: mid-June
FOLIAGE: evergreen, leaves to 2½″ long
HABITAT: northeastern North America

Of value only in acid soil where there is a large amount of moisture—even wet conditions. In other words it is to be recommended for growing in such

Mountain-laurel blooming in late spring, is an evergreen which can be used to brighten many situations.

situations where few other plants will. The foliage, if eaten in large amounts by livestock, may be poisonous, giving rise to one of its common names "Lambkill."

Kalmia latifolia   30′   Zone 4   Mountain-laurel

*FLOWERS: pink and white in large clusters
    TIME: mid-June
FOLIAGE: evergreen, leaves to 5″ long
HABITAT: eastern North America
VARIETIES:
    fuscata—flowers with a broad purple band inside of corolla
    rubra—flowers deep pink
    A very lovely native American evergreen shrub, widely planted and appreciated. It requires acid soil but given that and a mulch of pine needles or well-rotted oak leaves it will do well. This plant has been dug up and shipped by the car load from its native habitat in the mountain areas of the eastern states. It has been much used in foundation planting, in the naturalized planting of wooded areas and in planting slopes especially along highways. A leaf spot disease, sometimes serious, can be easily controlled by dusting with micronized sulfur several times during the growing season.

Kalmiopsis leachiana   1′   Zone 6

FLOWERS: rosy purple
FOLIAGE: evergreen, leaves small

HABITAT: Oregon

One of the most recently discovered natives, this diminutive evergreen has splendid possibilities in the rock garden where it is at its best if grown in clumps in a moist peaty soil and in a sunny situation.

Kerria japonica 4–6' Zone 4 Kerria

FLOWERS: yellow, nearly 1¾" in diameter
    TIME: mid-May
WINTER TWIGS: green all winter
HABITAT: central and western China
INTRODUCED: 1834
VARIETIES:

aureo-variegata—leaves edged with yellow, leaves 2" long

aureo-vittata—branches striped green and yellow—so much so that it is outstanding in winter.

pleniflora—flowers double; usually ball shaped—nearly 1½" in diameter—from whence it gets its name "Globe Flowers." The flowers remain effective on the plants much longer than do the single flowers of the species.

The Kerria has bright yellow flowers and green twigs all winter but needs quite a bit of renewal pruning. A thick-growing shrub used frequently in the foreground of shrub borders.

Kolkwitzia amabilis 10' Zone 4 Beauty-bush

*FLOWERS: pink, similar to Weigela, but profuse
    TIME: early June
*FRUIT: brown, bristly seeds
AUTUMN COLOR: reddish
WINTER TWIGS: with exfoliating bark
HABITAT: central China
INTRODUCED: 1901

A widely advertised shrub, sometimes I think it has been too much recommended. The flowers, somewhat like those of Weigela, vary in degree of pink from nearly a white to a deep pink. Occasionally the plants are grown from seed and this results in rather marked variation of flower color. It is best to propagate only asexually from selected strains.

The Beauty-bush was brought to this country by E. H. Wilson and has been growing in the Arnold Arboretum since 1901. However, early commercial attempts at distributing it proved a failure because the plant was not sufficiently well known. In 1922 one enterprising nursery decided to distribute it as "new." Large numbers were propagated and an expensive advertising campaign made the plant popular almost overnight. Its tall, upright-growing and arching branches, vigorous growth and ornamental interest in spring, summer and winter have combined to make it a serviceable shrub in the garden. It requires no special attention of any kind.

Lagerstroemia indica 21' Zone 7 Crape-myrtle

*FLOWERS: bright pink to red, up to 1½" in diameter
    TIME: August
HABITAT: China, tropical and subtropical countries

The Sweet Bay or Laurel has been used in gardens since ancient times.

INTRODUCED: 1747

Hardy as far north as Baltimore, the Crape-myrtle is grown widely through-out the South, especially for its profuse summer bloom. Its privetlike leaves are not seriously affected with pronounced pest troubles. Blooming on the current year's growth, it is thus amenable to heavy winter pruning when necessary to force compact growth. It blooms over a lengthy period and the crinkled flowers, combined with its vigorous, rounded habit, make it popular. It is difficult to transplant and should have a ball of earth about the roots whenever it is moved. Several varieties of crape-myrtle are available with white, pink, red, lavender or bluish flowers.

Laurus nobilis   30'   Zone 6   Sweet Bay, Laurel

FLOWERS: greenish white
    TIME: early June

FRUIT: dark green, finally black berries
  EFFECTIVE: fall
*FOLIAGE: evergreen, leaves to 4" long, aromatic
HABITAT: Mediterranean region
INTRODUCED: colonial times

This is the famous Laurel of ancient history and poetry, cultivated for centuries by the Greeks and Romans. Amenable to shearing, it is often kept closely clipped and grown in tubs, especially in formal plantings. The aromatic leaves are used as seasoning for various purposes, and the oil from the fruit is used in making a perfume.

Lavandula officinalis   3'   Zone 5   True Lavender

FLOWERS: very small, lavender, spikes 2" long, aromatic
  TIME: late June
FOLIAGE: semi-evergreen, aromatic, gray, leaves linear to 2" long
HABITAT: southern Europe, northern Africa
INTRODUCED: colonial times

A low shrub, usually only about a foot high, that has been cultivated since ancient times for its aromatic gray-green foliage. Its spikes of lavender flowers (there are varieties with white or even pink flowers) are numerous and deliciously aromatic. Good for the rockery or evergreen border where emphasis is placed on color variations of foliage. It is probably safe to say that the flowers of this plant are more prized for their fragrance than any other flowers except the rose. Dried flower spikes continue to give off their aromatic odor for many years. It is dense and compact in habit and prefers a sunny spot in rather light soil. One of my acquaintances had an unusually large specimen of this right by his front door step, and although his garden contained many interesting and beautiful things, it was this particular plant, so adeptly placed, that was remembered by his visitors for its fragrance seemed always to be inseparably connected with his delightful home.

Ledum groenlandicum   3'   Zone 2   Labrador Tea

FLOWERS: white, ½" diameter
  TIME: early May
FOLIAGE: evergreen, leaves oblong, to 2" long
HABITAT: Greenland to Alberta and Washington, south to Pennsylvania and Wisconsin

A small upright shrub of value only in peaty, boggy soil where few plants will grow.

Leiophyllum buxifolium   18"   Zone 5   Box Sandmyrtle

FLOWERS: small, waxy white, somewhat similar to those of blueberries
  TIME: May
FOLIAGE: lustrous, evergreen, leaves ½" long
AUTUMN COLOR: brownish green

A small evergreen of value only in acid soil, ericaceous plantings of *Erica*, *Calluna*, etc., where it adds variation. It should not be planted singly but in clumps.

Leptodermis oblonga   3'   Zone 5   Chinese Leptodermis

FLOWERS: few flowered clusters, violet-purple, ½" long
     TIME: July to September
HABITAT: northern China
INTRODUCED: 1905

An attractive, low shrub of particular interest for its lilac-colored flowers in summer. It seems to do best in full sun.

Lespedeza bicolor   9'   Zone 4   Shrub Bush-clover

*FLOWERS: rosy purple, pealike, in small clusters
     TIME: late July
HABITAT: northern China to Manchuria, and Japan
INTRODUCED: 1856

Valued solely for its late summer flowers, which are small and pealike but produced in large quantity. It does well in light sandy soils and can be cut to the ground without seriously affecting its bloom.

Lespedeza cyrtobotrya   15'   Zone 5

*FLOWERS: small, purple, pealike
     TIME: August
HABITAT: Japan, Korea
INTRODUCED: 1899

A peculiar type of bush-clover with dense racemes of rosy-purple flowers. Not as easily found in nurseries as *L. bicolor* but unique and valued for its late bloom.

Lespedeza japonica   6'   Zone 5   Japanese Bush-clover

*FLOWERS: white, pealike
     TIME: October
HABITAT: Japan
INTRODUCED: 1900

Few woody plants bloom this late in the fall and this species can be effectively used to flower after the rosy-purple *L. bicolor*

Leucothoe catesbaei   6'   Zone 4   Drooping Leucothoe

FLOWERS: white, waxy, in small racemes, similar to blueberry flowers
     TIME: early June
*FOLIAGE: evergreen to semi-evergreen, dark, leaves to 7" long
AUTUMN COLOR: bronze
HABITAT: Virginia to Georgia and Tennessee

An excellent shrub for ericaceous borders, often an even 3' high, with lustrous dark green leaves throughout the entire spring and summer, turning a delightful bronze in the fall. The small racemes of waxy-white flowers often 3" long appear along the entire underside of the gracefully arching stems. It is advisable to cut out the older canes occasionally to keep the plant in vigorous condition. It increases by underground stems, and, although it may not be ideally suited for specimen planting, it is excellent in borders or mixed in the foreground of evergreen plantings, in situations suitable for rhododendrons.

Leucothoe keiskei   4'   Zone 5   Keisk's Leucothoe

FLOWERS: white, small, similar to blueberry flowers
    TIME: late May
FOLIAGE: evergreen, leathery, leaves to 3" long
HABITAT: Japan
INTRODUCED: 1915

A graceful, slender shrub with pendulous waxy-white flowers the largest of any in this genus, nearly ⅜" in length. Probably not as vigorous a grower as *L. catesbaei;* nevertheless it has merit as a unique acid soil plant for the rockery.

Leucothoe racemosa   12'   Zone 5   Sweet Bells

FLOWERS: in racemes white or pinkish, small and waxy, similar to blueberry flowers
    TIME: late May
AUTUMN COLOR: scarlet
HABITAT: Massachusetts to Florida and Louisiana

An upright shrub with bright green leaves and waxy-white to pinkish flowers, of chief value in natural woods or in a somewhat shaded corner of the rockery, growing well in a fairly dry soil.

Leycesteria formosa   6'   Zone 7   Formosa Honeysuckle

FLOWERS: purplish to white, small
    TIME: late summer
FRUIT: red-purple berries
    EFFECTIVE: fall
HABITAT: Himalaya, southwestern China
INTRODUCED: 1824

Easily grown in any normal garden soil, this fast-growing shrub has gracefully arching branches with drooping clusters of 4" long dark purple bracts with small purplish to white flowers set in the axils of the bracts. The roots are hardy in Zone 7 but the tops are frequently killed. One method of maintenance is to prune the plant almost to the ground in the fall and the following spring vigorous 6' long shoots will be produced. These will flower profusely during the late summer.

LIGUSTRUM

Fortunately or unfortunately the privets are automatically considered hedge plants everywhere, for without a doubt there are more privet hedges in this country than any other kind. Since this is true, more species have been recommended than would otherwise be necessary. Many shrubs, and even trees, can be pruned to make excellent clipped hedges, but the privets somehow have proven their worth the country over and will probably continue to be popular hedge plants.

All the species are vigorous, quick-growing shrubs with leaves entire and opposite, flowers white and very small, in pyramidal clusters, followed by similar clusters of small berries, some blue, some shining black. In the South, there are serviceable evergreen species like *Ligustrum japonicum* and *L. lucidum,* which have been confused one with the other for many years. Both are serviceable plants and many varieties are offered by the nurserymen. Privets in general are remarkably free from insect pests, and most are free from disease pests. The one exception is the common privet of Europe, *L. vulgare.* There is a serious blight which frequently kills the plants of this species in some areas and for which there is no known cure. Where this blight is prevalent, this species had best not be grown. The European Privet is so widely distributed throughout the United States that it has become naturalized in certain areas, reason enough why it is mentioned here.

These plants are valuable because they will grow in almost any type of soil and under all kinds of conditions. In fact, *L. vulgare* and the Regel Privet are known to withstand dry soil and in places where they will not grow it would seem useless to experiment further with other woody plants.

The privets are also serviceable as screens and for growing in shady places. The Regel Privet is an excellent one to use in a foundation planting even with evergreens, for its foliage blends well with other plants used in such groups. The profusely borne flowers are conspicuous, and the fruit, more lustrous and conspicuous in some species than in others, frequently remains a greater part of the winter and affords considerable food for the birds. It should be pointed out that there are too many privets in the recommended list and each gardener and commercial grower would do well to further eliminate species and varieties. In the South it would be obviously wasted effort to grow more than four species at the most (with their varieties). In the North (north of New York) only about four species are really perfectly hardy and one of these is frequently disease infested. It is only when they are grown as fully developed plants in screens or shrub borders, that the small ornamental differences between the species are obviously noticeable.

Ligustrum amurense   15′   Zone 3   Amur Privet

FLOWERS: white, in small spikes
    TIME: mid-June
FRUIT: small black berries, dull
    EFFECTIVE: September–October
HABITAT: northern China
INTRODUCED: 1860
    Similar to the California Privet but considerably hardier and hence recommended in northern areas where the more interesting California Privet might be killed to the ground by severe winters.

Ligustrum henryi   12′   Zone 7   Henry Privet

FLOWERS: white, in small clusters
    TIME: August
FRUIT: black berries
    EFFECTIVE: fall

The evergreen Japanese Privet makes an excellent clipped hedge for year around usefulness. This and the Glossy Privet (*Ligustrum lucidum*) are almost hopelessly confused in the South, but the true *L. japonicum* is considered to make the better plant.

FOLIAGE: evergreen, leaves 2″ long, lustrous
HABITAT: central China
INTRODUCED: 1901

x Ligustrum ibolium   12′   Zone 4   Ibolium Privet

FLOWERS: white, in small spikes
  TIME: mid-June
FRUIT: black berries
  EFFECTIVE: fall and winter
HYBRID ORIGIN: *L. ovalifolium x L. obtusifolium*
ORIGINATED: about 1910
    Slightly hardier than the California Privet, but very much like it in general appearance, this is a vigorous shrub, more handsome than *L. amurense*.

Ligustrum japonicum   9–18′   Zone 7   Japanese Privet

FLOWERS: white, small clusters
  TIME: mid-July
FRUIT: black berries
  EFFECTIVE: fall
*FOLIAGE: evergreen, leaves to 4″ long
HABITAT: Japan and Korea

INTRODUCED: 1845

VARIETY: *rotundifolium*—only about 6' high, branches shorter, leaves spaced more closely together, foliage glossy.

This species is greatly confused with the following *L. lucidum*. Both have several varieties in the trade but the foliage of the true *L. japonicum* is superior and more glossy, hence it might well be selected first.

Ligustrum lucidum   30'   Zone 7   Glossy Privet

FLOWERS: white, small clusters
 TIME: August
FRUIT: blue-black berries
 EFFECTIVE: September to February
FOLIAGE: glossy, mostly evergreen, leaves to 6" long
HABITAT: China, Korea, Japan
INTRODUCED: 1794

Ligustrum obtusifolium   9'   Zone 3   Border Privet

FLOWERS: white
 TIME: mid-June
FRUIT: black to blue-black, dull berries
AUTUMN COLOR: russet to purplish
HABITAT: Japan
INTRODUCED: 1860
VARIETY: *regelianum*—Regel Privet, low variety with almost horizontal branches

Another very hardy privet. The variety, *regelianum* is very popular. It is low in habit, usually not over 4–5' tall, with horizontal branching. Since the leaves on all privets are opposite, the neat horizontal branches with regularly spaced leaves give this variety a unique appearance. It should be grown from cuttings since plants grown from seed may not have the desired form.

Ligustrum ovalifolium   15'   Zone 5   California Privet

FLOWERS: creamy white, in small clusters
 TIME: mid-June
FRUIT: black berries
 EFFECTIVE: fruits are seldom produced in North
FOLIAGE: half-evergreen, glossy
HABITAT: Japan
INTRODUCED: 1847
VARIETY: *aureo-marginatum*—leaves have a broad, yellow margin

Not as hardy as some other privets but nevertheless widely planted in the North and South as well. Its lustrous green leaves are its chief asset. In severely cold winters, like the one of 1933–34, this privet was killed to the ground in most places north of New York City. Because of this the Amur privet is recommended for areas north of New York.

Ligustrum quihoui   6'   Zone 6   Quihou Privet

FLOWERS: white, in small clusters
 TIME: mid-July

FRUIT: black berries
EFFECTIVE: September–November
HABITAT: China
INTRODUCED: 1862
One of the last privets to bloom.

Ligustrum sinense   12′   Zone 7   Chinese Privet

FLOWERS: white, in large panicles
TIME: mid-July
FRUIT: black berries
EFFECTIVE: September–January
HABITAT: China
INTRODUCED: 1852
VARIETY: *stauntoni*–lower and more spreading
Often mentioned as the most graceful and handsomest of privets when covered with its numerous large panicles of flowers. Also used a great deal in making clipped hedges, one of the oldest in the country being on the old Berkmans Nursery grounds in Augusta, Georgia, planted in the early 1860's where it has been maintained at less than 4′ tall ever since.

x **Ligustrum vicaryi**   12′   Zone 5   Vicary Golden Privet

FLOWERS: white, in small clusters
TIME: July
FRUIT: blue-black berries
EFFECTIVE: fall
*FOLIAGE: golden-yellow entire season
HYBRID ORIGIN: *L. ovalifolium aureum x L. vulgare*
ORIGINATED: before 1920
This excellent hybrid probably originated in the garden of Vicary Gibbs of Aldenham, England. It is of particular merit because of its handsome golden-yellow foliage throughout the entire growing season. For this it is superior to some privets with variegated leaf margins which may become unsightly at certain times of the year.

Ligustrum vulgare   15′   Zone 4   Common Privet

FLOWERS: white, small clusters
TIME: mid-June
*FRUIT: black, lustrous berries
EFFECTIVE: fall and winter
FOLIAGE: half-evergreen, leaves to 2½″ long
HABITAT: Europe
INTRODUCED: early colonial times
VARIETIES:
  pyramidale–of pyramidal habit, not wide-spreading like the species
  sempervirens–leaves nearly evergreen
This privet is more widely grown than any other species. In certain areas it is susceptible to a serious blight for which there is no known cure and in such areas this species had best not be grown. Its prominent pyramidal clusters of flowers later followed by shiny black berries make it a conspicuous plant wherever it is not closely clipped.

Lindera benzoin   15′   Zone 4   Spice Bush

FLOWERS: greenish yellow, dense
    TIME: mid-April
FRUIT: scarlet berries
    EFFECTIVE: early fall
*AUTUMN COLOR: yellow
HABITAT: eastern United States

Although there are several exotic spice bushes, possibly more handsome than *Lindera benzoin,* nevertheless it is this species which is widely distributed in the eastern United States and should be grown. It is a dense shrub, with small spicy-fragrant yellow flowers in the early spring before the leaves appear. The twigs and foliage when crushed are also spicy. In the fall the leaves turn a clear golden yellow and when they fall the small red berries are left on the pistillate plants. The male or staminate plants of course have no fruits. This shrub is best used in moist soils.

Loiseleuria procumbens   6″   Zone 2   Alpine Azalea

FLOWERS: pink, small
    TIME: summer
FOLIAGE: evergreen, leaves less than ¼″ long
HABITAT: Europe, northern Asia; in North America, from Alaska to Newfoundland to New Hampshire

Another low evergreen shrub for the rockery, somewhat similar to *Leiophyllum buxifolium.* It does best in a peaty soil where the summers are cool and not too hot. A cool, moist spot in the lower part of the rockery might be the best situation for it.

LONICERA

The number of *Lonicera* species and varieties being grown in this country today is not an indication of their extended usefulness in the garden. We need some of them certainly, for they can be used under many conditions and in a wide variation of soils. However, a few of the better species and varieties easily suffice. The Arnold Arboretum is growing over 150 species and varieties, while in the trade a few years ago, 109 species and varieties were offered for sale. Truly a confusing number! An examination of this large group of plants will show a marked similarity among the species as far as landscape usefulness is concerned. It has not been difficult to limit the recommended varieties to 35 (not including the vines) and even in this list there are probably some that could be eliminated also.

The honeysuckles are mostly vigorous shrubs or vines. They can be depended upon to produce a wealth of bloom annually, and the small flowers are followed by small bright-colored berries. In many cases these berries are most ornamental, and at the same time are very attractive to the birds. The season of bloom is an extended one, and fruiting occurs (in the North) from June to Thanksgiving.

These plants are not susceptible to serious disease or insect pests, al-

Honeysuckles are noted for their flowers and their fruits.
LEFT: Fruit of the Amur honeysuckle, which is the last of this genus to have colorful fruits in the fall, lasting until Thanksgiving.
RIGHT: Flowers of the native Trumpet Honeysuckle, a twining vine (page 388) with bright colored summer flowers.

though a few of the vinelike species, under certain conditions, may be troubled with infestations of plant lice, but this can be controlled by spraying.

In general, the honeysuckles have no autumn color. Their habit of growth is vigorously upright with a few exceptions, and the flowers as a rule are either pink, white or red, and in a few species orange or purple. Hence many species are similar from a landscape viewpoint. The fruits of most are red, some are black or blue, a few are yellow or white. Black or blue fruits are not nearly as ornamental and conspicuous as red fruits and so many species have been justly rejected merely because they do not have bright-colored fruits. Hardiness is, as always, one of the variable factors in such a large group as this.

The honeysuckles do best when grown in the full sun. Some will withstand partial shade, but like other sun-loving plants they will not flower and fruit as well. They will grow in many different kinds of soil. Some species seem to withstand dry soils better than others, none seem to do particularly well under wet soil conditions. The flowers are small, funnellike, with a prominent upper and lower "lip" and if white, may change yellowish as the flowers mature. The fruit is a small, fleshy berry often bright colored, somewhat under a quarter of an inch in diameter; although the fruits of *Lonicera alpigena* may be one-half inch in diameter. All honeysuckles withstand pruning, even heavy pruning, which makes them easy to move and to keep in a healthy condition.

The best for early flowering and fruiting is *L. fragrantissima*. For general all-purpose use there are *L. amoena, L. korolkowi, L. maacki, L. morrowi* and *L. tatarica*. It is likely that none of them have the dainty grace and beauty of *L. amoena arnoldiana* for even when its pale pink blossoms have gone, its delicate leaves and gracefully arching branches make it a specimen of interest throughout the year. For late fruit *L. maacki* is best. Two varieties are prominent for the best white flowers, *L. tatarica alba* and *L. tatarica parvifolia;* and for the deepest pink flowers *L. tatarica sibirica;* for the largest flowers *L. tatarica virginalis* and *L. amoena arnoldiana;* and for outstanding yellow fruit *L. tatarica lutea*. For lilac flowers and moundlike habit of growth, *L. thibetica* is very good and for semi-evergreen to evergreen foliage, *L. fragrantissima, L. nitida* and *L. pileata* are suggested. The plants with the best pink flowers might be *L. amoena arnoldiana, L. korolkowi floribunda,* and *L. tatarica pulcherrima*. *Lonicera korolkowi* is of particular value for its gray-green foliage, and so is of special value throughout the growing season.

These few selections are enough to show that the varieties of the Tatarian Honeysuckle are among the best for several reasons, and this bears emphasis because many of the *Lonicera* species should be compared with *L. tatarica* before they are recommended. The Tatarian Honeysuckle is widely distributed in this country, it is known to do well under a wide set of growing conditions, it will withstand heavy pruning and is easily propagated. Several of the best varieties are available in the trade today. Hence it would seem that unless a species is considerably superior to one of the *L. tatarica* varieties, it should not be recommended. There are no reasons for actually discarding some of the many honeysuckle species once they are established in gardens, for they may undoubtedly serve as well as others. The point is that the differences among them are not sufficiently pronounced for the nurseryman to grow and advertise large numbers of them, nor for the gardener to cultivate a desire for new ones and make room for them by discarding old ones. Rather let us admit there are many that are similar from the landscape viewpoint, and concentrate on growing only a few of the best.

Lonicera alpigena nana   3'   Zone 5   Dwarf Alps Honeysuckle

FLOWERS: deep red, not showy
   TIME: mid-May
*FRUIT: bright red, ½" long
   EFFECTIVE: late September
HABITAT: central and southern Europe

This is one of the few dwarf honeysuckles, of value for this reason only.

x **Lonicera amoena arnoldiana**   9′   Zone 5   Arnold Honeysuckle

*FLOWERS: white, flushed pink
    TIME: mid-May
FRUIT: red berries
    EFFECTIVE: summer
HYBRID ORIGIN: *L. tatarica x L. korolkowi*
ORIGINATED: 1899

A very graceful and floriferous shrub, it is meritorious for its arching habit and profuse flowers as well as its delicate foliage.

x **Lonicera bella varieties**   6′   Zone 4   Belle Honeysuckle

*FLOWERS: pinkish, fading yellowish
    TIME: late May
*FRUIT: red berries
    EFFECTIVE: late June and July
HYBRID ORIGIN: *L. morrowi x L. tatarica*
VARIETIES:
    atrorosea—flower buds pink, flowers white but tips of petals tinged pink making a very delicate color combination
    candida—flowers pure white
    rosea—flowers deep pink
    The hybrid vigor in this group is evident in their fast growth. They also have splendid foliage, good flowers and fruits, more upright in habit than *L. morrowi* but not quite as hardy as *L. tatarica*. A splendid group for specimen use or for massing in screens or borders. The early summer fruits like those of their parents are most attractive to birds.

Lonicera deflexicalyx   9′   Zone 5

FLOWERS: yellowish
    TIME: early June
FRUIT: orange to red berries
    EFFECTIVE: late July and August
HABITAT: western China, Tibet
INTRODUCED: 1904
    Flowers are profusely produced on the upper side of feathery branches.

Lonicera fragrantissima   6′   Zone 5   Winter Honeysuckle

*FLOWERS: white, fragrant
    TIME: mid-April
FRUIT: red berries
    EFFECTIVE: late May to June
*FOLIAGE: half evergreen
HABITAT: east China
INTRODUCED: 1845
    The stiff, leathery, half-evergreen leaves are one of its chief attractions. Its early, very fragrant flowers are another, coming at a time when very few other woody plants are in bloom. The fruit is produced about as early as fruit on any

woody ornamental, except possibly *Daphne mezereum,* and the birds usually eat it quickly. The plant has been used with good success as a clipped hedge, but it should be noted that since the flowers of this species are borne on the previous year's twig growth, the fruits appearing later are frequently hidden by the current year's growth. Most other honeysuckles bear their flowers and fruits on the current year's growth where they are easily conspicuous.

Lonicera gracilipes   6′   Zone 5   Spangle Honeysuckle

*FLOWERS: light pink to carmine
    TIME: early May
FRUIT: scarlet berries
    EFFECTIVE: June
HABITAT: Japan
INTRODUCED: 1870

Lonicera gynochlamydea   6′   Zone 5

FLOWERS: pink, hidden by foliage
    TIME: mid-May
*FRUIT: pale purple to white berries
    EFFECTIVE: September–October
HABITAT: western China
INTRODUCED: 1907

Lonicera korolkowi   12′   Zone 5   Blue-leaf Honeysuckle

*FLOWERS: rose, rarely white
    TIME: late May
*FRUIT: bright red to orange berries
    EFFECTIVE: July and August
*FOLIAGE: blue to gray-green
HABITAT: Turkestan
INTRODUCED: 1880

    Outstanding chiefly for its blue to gray-green foliage color, this plant and its large-flowering variety are chiefly used for color variation in the shrub border. The flowers are prominent, but the foliage color marks the plant as something different throughout the entire growing season. However, it must be admitted that this is one of the most difficult of all the honeysuckles to get established and young plants frequently die for no apparent reason. The variety *floribunda* is supposed to produce more flowers than the species but it is highly probable that the two are mixed up in the trade and in botanic gardens as well.

Lonicera ledebouri   15′   Zone 5   Ledebour Honeysuckle

*FLOWERS: orange and scarlet
    TIME: June
FRUIT: black berries
    EFFECTIVE: July and August
FOLIAGE: dark green
HABITAT: California
INTRODUCED: 1838

Lonicera korolkowi floribunda is noted for its profuse bloom, red fruits, but chiefly its gray-green foliage which is an asset in almost any landscape picture.

Lonicera maacki   15'   Zone 2   Amur Honeysuckle

*FLOWERS: white, changing yellowish, fragrant
    TIME: late May
*FRUIT: dark red berries
    EFFECTIVE: September–November
FOLIAGE: remains on plant late in the fall
HABITAT: Manchuria and Korea
INTRODUCED: 1860
VARIETY: *podocarpa*—blooms in early June, hardy in Zone 4, native of China—this variety keeps its leaves longer than the species

The Amur Honeysuckles have late flowers as honeysuckles go and are among the tallest growing of all. Added to this is the fact that they hold their leaves late in the fall, and the profuse bright red fruits are often still on the plant (with the green leaves) at Thanksgiving. This makes the vigorous growing Amur Honeysuckles among the best of the honeysuckle group for fall display.

Lonicera morrowi   6'   Zone 4   Morrow Honeysuckle

*FLOWERS: white, changing to yellow
    TIME: late May
FRUIT: dark red berries
    EFFECTIVE: June–July
HABITAT: Japan

INTRODUCED: 1875

VARIETY: *xanthocarpa*—yellow fruits, flowers white

The Morrow Honeysuckle is noted for its dense, moundlike habit of growth, sometimes being nearly twice as broad as it is high. In this respect it differs markedly from the Tatarian Honeysuckle but both species are very popular and among the most common in American gardens.

Lonicera nitida   6'   Zone 7   Box Honeysuckle

FLOWERS: creamy white, fragrant
    TIME: June
FRUIT: blue-purple berries
    EFFECTIVE: fall
FOLIAGE: evergreen in South, leaves to ½" long
HABITAT: west China
INTRODUCED: 1908

In the South this is considered a broad-leaved evergreen and is frequently used in low-clipped hedges where its small leaves make it an ideal substitute for box. It is supposed to withstand salt spray.

Lonicera pileata   4'   Zone 5   Privet Honeysuckle

FLOWERS: whitish
    TIME: early May
FRUIT: violet-purple berries
    EFFECTIVE: fall
FOLIAGE: evergreen or half evergreen, leaves to 1½" long
HABITAT: central and western China
INTRODUCED: 1900

The stiffly horizontal-branching habit of this species gives it considerable ornamental value where it is hardy—its handsome glossy-green leaves also are ornamental and it withstands some shade. The common name comes from the fact that it does resemble a small-leaved privet.

Lonicera quinquelocularis   6'   Zone 5   Mistletoe Honeysuckle

FLOWERS: yellowish
    TIME: early June
FRUIT: whitish, translucent berries
    EFFECTIVE: September–October
HABITAT: Himalaya to Afghanistan
INTRODUCED: 1840

Of interest chiefly because of its white translucent berries in which the black seeds can easily be seen, otherwise it is no better ornamentally than many of the more common species.

Lonicera saccata   4½'   Zone 5

FLOWERS: white, tinged pink
    TIME: early May
FRUIT: bright red berries
    EFFECTIVE: June
HABITAT: central and western China
INTRODUCED: 1910

Lonicera spinosa alberti   4'   Zone 3   Albert-thorn Honeysuckle
*FLOWERS: rosy pink, fragrant
    TIME: late May
FRUIT: reddish berries
    EFFECTIVE: August
FOLIAGE: bluish green
HABITAT: Turkestan
INTRODUCED: 1880

The leaves of this differ from those of the other honeysuckles by being small and bluish green. Its habit is prominent because of its pretty, arching branches.

Lonicera syringantha   6–9'   Zone 4   Lilac Honeysuckle
FLOWERS: pinkish white to rosy lilac, fragrant
    TIME: mid-May
FRUIT: red to orange berries
    EFFECTIVE: June
HABITAT: northwest China
INTRODUCED: about 1890
VARIETY: *wolfi*–flowers carmine, fragrant, branching partly prostrate

This is a charming honeysuckle when it flowers well, which unfortunately is none too often. Its moundlike habit of growth makes it adaptable for certain types of landscape use.

Lonicera tatarica   9'   Zone 3   Tatarian Honeysuckle
*FLOWERS: pink to white
    TIME: late May
*FRUIT: red berries
    EFFECTIVE: June and July
HABITAT: southern Russia
INTRODUCED: 1752
VARIETIES:

> *alba*–flowers pure white
> *angustifolia*–flowers pale pink
> *lutea*–fruit yellow, flowers pink
> *nana*–flowers pink, habit dwarf, about 3' high
> *parvifolia*–one of the best for white flowers
> *pulcherrima*–flowers deep pink to red, better than *rosea*
> *rosea*–flowers rosy pink outside–light pink inside
> *sibirica*–flowers deep pink, deepest pink of any *Lonicera*
> *virginalis*–rose-pink flower buds and flowers–with largest flowers of any
L. *tatarica* variety

The Tatarian Honeysuckle can be considered one of the best of all the hardy ornamental woody shrubs for garden planting because of its vigorous growth and tidy appearance at all times, its profuse display of bright-colored flowers and fruits every year, its ability to grow in almost any soil and its very definite lack of disease and insect pests. In making comparisons of *Lonicera* species, many have not been recommended because they could not measure up to the high standards set by *L. tatarica* and its several excellent varieties. These varieties should be recognized and grown more than they are.

Lonicera tatsienensis   7½′   Zone 5

FLOWERS: dark purple
    TIME: late May
FRUIT: red berries
    EFFECTIVE: August
HABITAT: western China
INTRODUCED: 1910
    The peculiar purple flowers and frequently lobed leaves have some orna-
mental value.

Lonicera thibetica   4′   Zone 4   Tibet Honeysuckle

FLOWERS: pale purple, very fragrant
    TIME: mid-May
FRUIT: red berries
    EFFECTIVE: June
HABITAT: western China
INTRODUCED: 1897
    Suited for planting on rocky slopes where its sprawling habit quickly enables
the plant to adapt itself well to any topography.

Loropetalum chinense   12′   Zones 7–8

FLOWERS: white, similar to those of witch-hazel
    TIME: March
FOLIAGE: evergreen, leaves to 2″ long
HABITAT: China
INTRODUCED: 1880

Lyonia mariana   6′   Zone 5   Stagger-bush

FLOWERS: small but profuse, cup shaped, ½″ long, white to pinkish
    TIME: mid-June
HABITAT: eastern and southeastern United States
    Planted in masses in acid soil or boggy situations, it quickly becomes very
handsome and so can be used where many other plants can not.

Magnolia liliflora nigra   9′   Zone 6   Purple Lily Magnolia

*FLOWERS: dark purple outside, light purple inside
    TIME: mid-May
FRUIT: red, podlike
    EFFECTIVE: early fall
HABITAT: Japan
INTRODUCED: 1861
    This magnolia has the darkest flowers of all magnolias and blooms later than
most. Actually it is a shrub and not a tree, hence should not be trained with one
central trunk for, grown in this way, it will prove unsatisfactory.

Magnolia stellata   20′   Zone 5   Star Magnolia

*FLOWERS: double, white, fragrant, over 3″ in diameter
    TIME: mid-April

The Star Magnolia is the first of the magnolias to bloom in the spring.

FRUIT: red podlike
    EFFECTIVE: early fall
*FOLIAGE: dark green
AUTUMN COLOR: bronze to yellow
HABITAT: Japan
INTRODUCED: 1862
VARIETY: *rosea*—flower buds pink, flowers fading white at maturity

The Star Magnolia is the hardiest and in many respects the most ornamental of all the magnolias. The flowers have 12–18 petals and are very fragrant, some- times nearly 4″ in diameter. The long narrow leaves are thick and dark green, turning an excellent bronze in the fall especially when grown in direct sunshine. The plant is dense, either a shrub or small tree, and is best used as a specimen plant for its branches face the ground well. In the North, near its northern limit of hardiness, it may tend to bloom too early if given a southern exposure, for late frosts frequently mar the blossoms. With a northern exposure the flower open- ing is retarded somewhat and this proves helpful during those seasons with late frosts.

Magnolia virginiana   60′   Zone 5   Sweet Bay

*FLOWERS: white, fragrant, 2–3″ diameter
    TIME: late May
FRUIT: dark red, podlike
    EFFECTIVE: early fall
*FOLIAGE: green above, white below

The fragrant Star Magnolia flowers are either white or pale pink (in the variety *rosea*) and 4″ in diameter.

HABITAT: coastal area of eastern United States

The very fragrant waxy-white flowers appearing in June and early summer, the gray bark and good foliage with leaves white on the undersurface, make this an attractive species. In the deep South this plant is a tree and nearly evergreen, but in New England it is much more shrubby and deciduous.

Magnolia wilsoni   24′   Zone 6   Wilson Magnolia

*FLOWERS: white, fragrant, 6″ diameter
    TIME: May
FRUIT: red, podlike
    EFFECTIVE: fall
HABITAT: western China

INTRODUCED: 1908

Pendulous, cup-shaped, fragrant flowers are the chief attraction of this rare magnolia. Although introduced over forty years ago, only one nursery lists it for sale. It is not superior to other magnolias but in the warmer parts of the country it might have merit for its flowers.

Mahonia aquifolium   3' rarely 6'   Zone 5   Oregon Holly-grape

*FLOWERS: bright yellow, spikes
    TIME: early May
*FRUIT: bluish black, like small grapes
    EFFECTIVE: summer
*FOLIAGE: lustrous dark green, semi-evergreen to evergreen
AUTUMN COLOR: bronze to purplish
HABITAT: British Columbia to Oregon

The Lewis and Clark Expedition into the Northwest Territory is credited with bringing this splendid native plant back to the East where it has been grown and appreciated as an ornamental ever since. There are several mahonias and many hybrids but this glossy-leaved species seems to be the most popular on the West Coast as well as along the Atlantic Seaboard. It thrives under adverse conditions and is grown very easily—possibly the most popular of the native Pacific Northwest plants now grown in the East. Its lustrous dark green, leathery leaves, pyramidal spikes of bright-yellow flowers and light blue grapelike fruits in early summer, make it effective for use in many situations, especially in evergreen foundation plantings and in partially shaded spots. It can be kept low by proper pruning. The spiny hollylike leaflets of its compound leaves are interesting, and its vigorous habit of increasing by means of underground stolons makes it effective as a ground cover of fair height.

Mahonia beali   12'   Zone 6   Leatherleaf Mahonia

*FLOWERS: lemon-yellow in pyramidal clusters, fragrant
    TIME: early May
*FRUIT: bluish black, grapelike
*FOLIAGE: evergreen, dull, dark bluish green
HABITAT: China
INTRODUCED: 1845

Incorrectly termed *Mahonia* or *Berberis japonica*, this species has bold, leathery compound leaves up to 16" in length. These are held stiffly horizontal on the shrub giving it a stiff, often unnatural appearance. It is interesting to note that this plant was one of Robert Fortune's introductions from China. A striking specimen when grown in partial shade, its spiny, lustrous leaves do not turn color markedly in the fall.

Mahonia repens   10"   Zone 5   Creeping Mahonia

*FLOWERS: small, yellow, in spikes
    TIME: early May
*FRUIT: black, grapelike
    EFFECTIVE: summer
*FOLIAGE: dull bluish green

HABITAT: British Columbia to California

The only advantage in using this species in place of *M. aquifolium* is its smaller size and its vigorously stoloniferous habit, making it a good ground cover, but its foliage is not nearly as lustrous.

Malus sargenti   6′   Zone 5   Sargent Crab-apple

*FLOWERS: pure white, single, ½″ diameter
 TIME: mid-May
FRUIT: dark red crabapples, ¼″ diameter
 EFFECTIVE: fall
HABITAT: Japan
INTRODUCED: 1892

The only crabapple small enough to be considered a shrub, this may grow twice as broad as high, is dense and moundlike and covered with pure white, fragrant blossoms in mid-May. The fruit is comparatively small for the crabapples, but colors before the leaves drop in the fall making an excellent red-green color combination. They may remain on the plant long in the fall, especially if there are not too many birds in the vicinity. Like other crabapples it is susceptible to borers and San Jose scale but can be grown wherever apples prove hardy. Since it is a native of the Orient, it is not an alternate host for the Juniper rust.

Michelia fuscata   15′   Zone 7–8   Banana-shrub

FLOWERS: yellowish white, edged maroon, 1½″ diameter
 TIME: spring
FOLIAGE: evergreen, leaves to 3″ long
HABITAT: China
INTRODUCED: 1850?

A splendid southern evergreen, the flowers giving off a bananalike fragrance.

Mitchella repens   Ground cover   Zone 3   Partridge Berry

FLOWERS: white, tinged purple, fragrant, small
 TIME: mid-May
FRUIT: red berries, ¼″ diameter
 EFFECTIVE: fall
FOLIAGE: often variegated whitish, dark green, lustrous evergreen
HABITAT: eastern North America

A dainty little creeping ground cover, seldom over a few inches high and frequently found in the woods of eastern United States, of value chiefly in rock gardens or in shaded spots in the pine woodlands where the soil is not too dry. It is this diminutive plant that adds so much to the woodland material collected for solariums. A flavoring material is made from the dried plant.

Moltkia petraea   1½′   Zone 6

FLOWERS: pinkish purple at first, becoming violet-blue, in small terminal clusters, 1–1½″ diameter
 TIME: June
FOLIAGE: semi-evergreen, grayish leaves ½–1½″ long
HABITAT: southeastern Europe

INTRODUCED: 1840

A low attractive shrub, suitable only for use in rockeries and in full sun. When not in flower it resembles the Common Lavender.

Myrica californica   36′   Zone 7   California Bayberry

*FRUIT: purple berries (sexes separate, see page 29)
    EFFECTIVE: fall and winter
FOLIAGE: lustrous evergreen, bronze colored, leaves to 4″ long
HABITAT: Washington to California

A slender, upright-growing shrub, used on the Pacific Coast for its berries and evergreen leaves. It is easily grown.

Myrica cerifera   36′   Zone 6   Wax-myrtle

*FRUIT: gray berries, small (sexes separate, see page 29)
    EFFECTIVE: fall and winter
FOLIAGE: evergreen, leaves to 3″ long
HABITAT: New Jersey to Florida and Texas

Shrub or small tree, merely the southern form of *M. pensylvanica*. Both species make good shrubs in the garden, their foliage and gray berries being their chief ornamental characteristics.

Myrica pensylvanica   9′   Zone 2   Bayberry

*FRUIT: gray berries (sexes separate, see page 29)
    EFFECTIVE: fall and winter
FOLIAGE: dull green, semi-evergreen
HABITAT: Newfoundland to western New York and Maryland chiefly along seashore

A deciduous shrub with aromatic, semi-evergreen leaves, it is noted particularly for its waxy-gray berries from which candles are frequently made. This shrub is best grown in poor sandy soil. The sexes are usually separate so that both staminate and pistillate flowering plants must be close together in order to insure the production of the very ornamental fruit which remains on the plant far into the winter. A fine ornamental, for its foliage as well as its fruits.

Myrtus communis   5′–10′   Zone 8–9   Myrtle

FLOWERS: small, creamy white, ¾″ diameter
    TIME: summer
FRUIT: blue-black berries
    EFFECTIVE: fall
*FOLIAGE: evergreen, leaves 2″ long, aromatic
HABITAT: Mediterranean Region

The true myrtle, so much written about in the literature of the ancients. It varies greatly in size, leaf color and general habit, and can be clipped to form an excellent evergreen hedge. Especially does this plant grow well in hot, dry situations in seashore gardens.

Nandina domestica   8′   Zone 7   Nandina

FLOWERS: white, in large clusters
    TIME: late July

In the South the Nandina is widely planted for its bright red berries and scarlet autumn color.

*FRUIT: bright red or purplish berries
   EFFECTIVE: fall and winter
FOLIAGE: evergreen, leaflets, 1–1½′ long
AUTUMN COLOR: bright red to scarlet
HABITAT: central China to Japan
INTRODUCED: 1804

Sometimes referred to as the Chinese Sacred Bamboo, it is actually a member of the Barberry family but its long stems are unbranched. The colorful new leaves are tinted pink to bronze as they unfold in the spring. The large clusters of flowers are not nearly as prominent as are the scarlet red berries which remain on the plant long into the winter. There is a white-fruiting clon which is well used if planted in front of a group of red-fruiting members of this species. Widely grown throughout the South and on the Pacific Coast. There is an opinion among commercial growers that the plants with the smaller leaves make the better ornamentals because they are more dense and especially because they do not drop their leaves as early as the larger-leaved types.

Nerium oleander   20'   Zone 7–8   Oleander

*FLOWERS: white, yellow to red and purple, 3" in diameter, single and double
    TIME: April throughout summer
FOLIAGE: evergreen, bamboolike
HABITAT: Mediterranean Region

A popular southern garden plant, frequently grown in tubs in the North and wintered in greenhouses. The plants are sturdy in the South, requiring little attention and available in several varietal colors, some single and some very double. They withstand hot, dry situations and should be root pruned occasionally to keep them down to size.

Neviusia alabamensis   3–6'   Zone 5   Snow-wreath

*FLOWERS: solitary, white, feathery
    TIME: mid-May
HABITAT: Alabama

Probably of chief interest only in southeastern United States where it is native. The flowers, nearly 1" in diameter, are noticeable chiefly because of conspicuous and numerous stamens. Rather unique, but not necessarily outstanding, for many other shrubs make much better year-round ornamentals.

Nothopanax davidi   18'   Zone 7   David False Panax

FLOWERS: small, greenish yellow
    TIME: summer
FRUIT: flattened black berry
    EFFECTIVE: fall
*FOLIAGE: evergreen, leathery, dark glossy green, variable in shape
HABITAT: central and western China
INTRODUCED: 1907

A handsome evergreen shrub or small tree, easily identified from other shrubs by its peculiar, variable leaves. Normally the leaves have three main longitudinal veins, but sometimes the leaf consists of two leaflets, in which case the smaller leaflet will have one longitudinal vein and the larger leaflet will have two main veins.

Olearia haasti   9'   Zone 8   New Zealand Daisy-bush

*FLOWERS: white, daisylike, fragrant
    TIME: summer
FOLIAGE: lustrous dark evergreen to grayish green, leaves to 1¼" long
HABITAT: New Zealand
INTRODUCED: 1858

The New Zealand Daisy-bush is one of the hardier and most ornamental of the shrubby composites, its leathery gray-green foliage being not the least of its attractions. The leaves are about an inch long and though the plant may grow to 9' tall, it can grow to be 15' in diameter, making a dense, rounded shrub, requiring some early spring pruning to maintain its desirable form. On well drained soil, or on a hot sunny bank it can be expected to do better than many another plant.

x **Osmanthus Fortunei**   12′   Zone 7–8   Fortune's Osmanthus

FLOWERS: small axillary clusters, very fragrant
    TIME: June
FRUIT: bluish black berries
    EFFECTIVE: fall
*FOLIAGE: evergreen, hollylike, leaves to 4″ long
HYBRID ORIGIN: *O. ilicifolius x O. fragrans*
INTRODUCED: from Japan 1856

A vigorous shrub with attractive lustrous leaves, popular in the South as well as on the Pacific Coast.

Osmanthus ilicifolius   18′   Zone 6   Holly Osmanthus

FLOWERS: yellowish green, fragrant
    TIME: July
FRUIT: bluish black berries
    EFFECTIVE: fall
*FOLIAGE: lustrous dark green, evergreen, leaves to 2½″ long and spiny
HABITAT: Japan
INTRODUCED: 1856

One of the handsomest of evergreens with lustrous green foliage, very similar to that of holly, except, of course, the leaves are opposite while those of all hollies are alternate. An excellent ornamental shrub growing well in either sun or partial shade, serving well as a specimen plant. It has been admirably used in a clipped hedge. Several species are being tried, this one being more easily available at present.

Pachistima canbyi   12″   Zone 5   Canby Pachistima

*FOLIAGE: evergreen, leaves less than 1″ long
*AUTUMN COLOR: bronze
HABITAT: eastern North America

A low evergreen with small dark green to bronze leaves, which, if given acid soil, can make a splendid ground cover, dense and of good texture. Given a little shade it will make a solid mass of fine foliage and can be featured in clumps in the rockery or in the foreground of foundation plantings.

Pachysandra terminalis   Ground cover   Zone 5   Japanese Spurge or Pachysandra

FLOWERS: small, white spikes
    TIME: early May
FRUIT: white berries
    EFFECTIVE: fall
*FOLIAGE: evergreen, dark green and lustrous
HABITAT: Japan

Japanese Spurge or Pachysandra is one of the best evergreen ground covers available, especially adapted for shaded situations.

INTRODUCED: 1882

A valued evergreen ground cover, creeping by underground stolons, that apparently grows better in partial shade than in full sun. The whorled evergreen leaves are produced on a six-inch stem and a bed of this plant is usually one uniform height throughout. The flowers and fruits are not borne profusely. One of the best ground covers especially for partial shade.

Paeonia suffruticosa   4–5′   Zone 5   Tree Peony

FLOWERS: solitary, single and double, white rose or red, 6–12″ in diameter
    TIME: late May
HABITAT: northwestern China
INTRODUCED: 1800

There are several collections of tree peonies in this country like those in the parks of Rochester, New York, with over 5000 seedlings, and at Swarthmore College in Pennsylvania, where over 200 named varieties are growing beautifully. These plants are not grown as frequently in American gardens as might be expected, for their culture is somewhat difficult. Their large single or double flowers range in size from 6″ to 12″ in diameter, and in color from white to pink to red, with some of the new hybrids having considerable yellow.

Planting is best done in the middle of October, preferably in a rich, well-drained soil. Lime should be applied occasionally, especially where the soil is acid. It is only necessary to cut out old or weak stems. The tree peony has proved popular in Chinese gardens for over fifteen centuries. It was taken to Japan by Buddhist monks in about the seventeenth century and the Japanese have developed many good varieties also.

"Reine Elizabeth"
"Carolina d'Italie" } are among the best double varieties of the species.
"Souvenir de Ducher"

However, there are some hybrid varieties made by crossing *P. suffruticosa* with *P. lutea* and other species. One of the best of these is "Souvenir de Maxine Cornu," a very double yellow, with red markings, looking almost like a large dahlia. The flowers are so large and heavy that they frequently have to be staked to prevent them from bending and becoming hidden by the foliage altogether. Other good varieties are:

"Alice Harding"	"Festival"	"Roman Gold"
"Argosy"	"Flambeau"	"Silver Sails"
"Banquet"	"La Lorraine"	"Surprise"
"Black Pirate"		

Paliurus spina-christi   18'   Zone 7   Christ Thorn

FLOWERS: greenish yellow, small
    TIME: summer
FRUIT: brownish yellow, 1" diameter
    EFFECTIVE: fall
WINTER TWIGS: very spiny
HABITAT: southern Europe to western Asia
INTRODUCED: early colonial times

An interesting plant, unusually thorny, with numerous small flowers and fruits somewhat resembling small hats. Not of outstanding ornamental value, but sometimes grown as a hedge, or because it is the plant—according to legend— from which Christ's Crown of Thorns was made.

Pernettya mucronata   1½'   Zone 6–7   Chilean Pernettya

*FRUIT: white to dark purple berries, ½" diameter
    EFFECTIVE: fall and winter
FOLIAGE: lustrous, evergreen
HABITAT: Chile to the Magellan Straits
INTRODUCED: 1828
VARIETIES:
    alba—fruit, white
    coccinea—fruit, bright red
    lilacina—fruit, lilac
    purpurea—fruit, violet-purple
    rosea—fruit, pink

A very important ornamental shrub especially valued for its colorful fruits, prominent throughout the fall and winter. This is apparently like some fruit trees, for although the flowers are perfect, two strains are needed, growing near each other, in order that proper fertilization can take place. Several plants, preferably of different varieties are even better, for if they have different colored

One of the very few South American shrubs growing in the United States in Zones 6–7, is *Pernettya mucronata.*

fruits, then it is obvious they are different strains. Single plants, by themselves, do not yield many fruits and hence have not proved popular. This native from South America has frequently been termed one of the best fruiting ornamentals we have. In full sun it will remain a neat shrub, but in shade it may tend to grow untidy and somewhat open, requiring restrained pruning.

PHILADELPHUS

The Philadelphus, or Mock-oranges as they are frequently called, are chiefly valued because of their white and often very fragrant flowers. Their foliage does not turn a vivid color in the fall, their fruits are dry capsules that are not ornamental, they have no particular character which makes them of interest in the winter when the leaves have fallen. In other words, mock-oranges are in that large group of plants which are cultivated fifty weeks of the year in order that their flowers may be appreciated for two weeks.

It must be said in their favor, however, that as a group, they are vigorous growing shrubs which usually bloom very early in life. They are dense in habit, making good screens. They withstand heavy pruning, and when given the proper care, are covered with white flowers ranging in size from ½″ to almost 2½″ in diameter. Some are low in habit, others are tall growing. In the northern United States many have been used around college buildings for they bloom at about commencement time and their white flowers and fragrance add much to the appearance of the campus grounds during commencement week. They will grow in any good soil and require a minimum amount of attention. Usually a small amount of renewal pruning every few years will suffice. They are not susceptible to any serious or unusual insect or disease pests. Because of these facts, they are widely used and greatly appreciated.

However, the fact remains that they are only predominant in the landscape for the short period during which they are in flower. There are over 108 species and varieties growing in the Arnold Arboretum, and naturally when grown in a collection of this sort, it is easy to compare their individual habits and ornamental possibilities. I do not believe that they should be considered superior to plants like the viburnums or rose species, for instance, since the latter are of interest during several seasons of the year. In the small garden, where space is very limited, the mock-oranges might be passed over altogether in preference to some more valued shrubs. However, if mock-oranges are to be grown, some points of especial interest should be considered when selections are made.

About forty species are known to be growing in the northern hemispheres and half are native to North America. Some are valued ornamentals, as, for instance, the old fashioned mock-orange of Europe, *Philadelphus coronarius*. This at one time was commonly called Syringa, a name since outmoded for it belongs to the Lilac, the generic name of which is *Syringa*. The Hairy Mock-orange of the southeastern United States, *P. pubescens*, is also valued because of its vigorous growth. It is one of the taller growing species. Then *P. laxus, P. grandiflorus* and *P. floridus* are also valued because of their moundlike habit of growth. The mock-oranges prove very confusing to identify one from the other because of the ease with which one species crosses with another. They all bloom about the same time, and this indiscriminate crossing, whether it has been done by chance or is carefully planned, has given rise to many hybrids, some of which have turned out to be the best ornamental plants of the entire group.

There are natural hybrids, of course, those that have occurred in nature, or which have occurred in botanical collections. One such would be *P. splendens,* a probable cross between two species native of the United States but widely separated until they were brought together by plant collectors.

A general discussion of *Philadelphus* would not be complete without a word about Victor Lemoine, that great French nurseryman who did so much to enrich our supply of ornamental plants. Many of the varieties of *Philadelphus* which are highly valued in the trade today originated in the nurseries of Lemoine and his successors. In fact, all the named varieties but one in the following suggested list are credited to him. Born of a long line of horticulturists in 1823, he graduated from college and learned his gardening practically. As was customary in those times, he worked for others

Philadelphus grandiflorus grows in a large mound, with branches sweeping the ground on all sides.

until he was finally able to branch out for himself. Among the places at which he worked was that of Louis Van Houtte, at Ghent, Belgium.

In 1850, Victor Lemoine established his own business at Nancy, France. Two years later the first hybrid was offered by the new firm, a double flowering Portulaca, and since that time hundreds of new plants have been offered by this one concern. In fact, Lemoine's nursery became noted as one of the leaders in the world for hybridizing and introducing new woody plants. Although he himself was responsible for originating hun-dreds of new plants, some (notably the newer varieties of *Philadelphus*) were originated by his firm after his death.

The number of different plants with which he worked is astounding. Some of the plant groups include *Gladiolus, Paeonia,* the double flowered *Begonia, Deutzia, Diervilla, Delphinium, Heuchrea, Syringa, Philadelphus* and many others. During his life he was the recipient of many honors, both in his own country and abroad. When he died in 1911, horticulture lost a man who did more than any other individual in modern times in originat-ing new varieties of ornamental woody plants.

As for the hybrid mock-oranges, the Lemoine Nursery was respon-sible for originating practically all of the better known hybrid varieties, especially the popular *P. lemoinei* and *P. virginalis.* He was responsible for first crossing the native *P. coronarius* of Europe with the intensely fragrant

"Avalanche" one of the many plants originating in the French nursery of Victor Lemoine.

but tender *P. microphyllus* of America. The resulting hybrid plants first appeared in 1844, and were the forerunners of a whole line of interesting and very fragrant hybrids, among which the widely distributed "Avalanche," "Mont Blanc" and *erectus* are only a few.

Habit

Other than the flower, the most important features of the mock-orange are their respective habits. Some, like "Virginal," the most widely advertised variety of *P. virginalis,* do not have a pleasing habit. They grow about 6–8′ tall with upright branches and frequently are very open and bare at the base. Such plants may be valued for their flowers, but after the flowers have gone, they provide sorry ornamental specimens which may well mar an otherwise beautiful garden. If grown at all, they should be at the rear of the shrub collection, with other plants in front to hide their spindly stems which so frequently are devoid of foliage near the base.

Some mock-oranges have an excellent shape. Take, as an example, the *P. lemoinei* variety "Avalanche." The branches arch in a very pleasing manner, and even after the flowers have gone this plant, with its comparatively low habit, arching branches, and small leaves has a certain effectiveness. The same can be said of *P. lemoinei erectus,* of about the same height but with rigidly upright branches, which is desirable in some formal situations.

There is another group, however, and a most important group (I think it has been overlooked), which bears branches well down to the base of the plant so that it can be used alone as a specimen. Most of these are mound-like in habit, being well clothed with branches from top to bottom and almost as broad as tall. Included in this group would be *P. floridus, P. grandiflorus, P. inodorus, P. laxus, P. monstrosus, P. splendens,* and the hybrid clon "Mont Blanc." Because of their dense, moundlike habit they have merit as specimens even after flowers have fallen and so are valued simply from the standpoint of foliage. *P. inodorus* possibly stands out from the rest slightly, for its foliage has a definite luster which makes it prominent among the others.

Height

All the mock-oranges do not grow to the same height, a factor which is frequently important when varieties are to be selected for particular situations. For instance, most of the hybrids belonging to the *P. lemoinei* group like "Avalanche," *P. erectus,* "Boule d'Argent" are under 4' in height. "Mont Blanc" is slightly taller. On the other hand, *P. pubescens* is one of the tallest growing species, reaching about 12', but *P. inodorus, P. grandiflorus* and *P. magnificus* are almost as tall when grown in good soil. Some of the species like *P. laxus, P. pekinensis* and *P. schrenki* are 6–8' tall, as is also the common European species, *P. coronarius.* The lowest growing of all is probably a variety, *P. coronarius pumilus,* which has little other than its dwarf size to recommend it since it seldom blooms.

Fragrant Flowers

The fragrance of the flowers of mock-oranges is one of the chief reasons for their popularity and in fact is responsible for the name mock-orange. Not all mock-oranges have fragrant flowers, and some, like *P. splendens* and *P. inodorus* are practically scentless. One of the most fragrant species is the little southern *P. microphyllus,* which is not particularly ornamental in flower but which has been used a great deal in hybridization work and lends to the *P. lemoinei* crosses its exquisite fragrance. All of the following clons which are at the top of the list for outstanding fragrance owe their fragrance in whole or in part to this small species which appeared at one time in their early history: "Avalanche," "Conquete," "Cole's Glorious," "Innocence," *P. lemoinei* varieties, "Perle Blanche" and "Virginal." The species which is of sufficient size and shape to be in the recommended list for fragrance is the old-fashioned *P. coronarius.* These constitute the "most fragrant" of the *Philadelphus,* and although there are certainly others, these can be considered among the best.

Double Flowers

Any plant which has double flowers is usually considered superior to those with single flowers, other things being equal, for the simple reason

LEFT: *Philadelphus* "Conquete."
RIGHT: *Philadelphus lemoinei.*
Both these are among the most fragrant of all the mock-oranges.

that the flowers with the greater number of petals make a greater display and often remain on the plant longer. This is true of double flowers in *Prunus, Malus, Kerria* and several other genera. Especially is it true among the *Philadelphus,* for since the fruits are not ornamental, the fact that the stamens are modified petals does not reduce the ornamental value by reduction of fruit production. In the crab apples, for instance, the double-flowered varieties may not have any fruits or may not have as many fruits as their single-flowered relatives, and this must be taken into consideration, since the crab apples are planted for both their flowers and their fruits. However, the varieties of mock-oranges with double flowers are very much to be desired. It must be admitted that single-flowered species like *P. grandiflorus* have beauty also because of a bright yellow center composed of numerous stamens. The varieties with double flowers are frequently pure white, with the yellow stamens being very few in number or practically nonexistent.

Varieties to be recommended for their double flowers would be "Albatre," "Argentine," "Boule d'Argent," "Girandôle," "Glacier" and "Virginal." Of these, "Glacier" might be the least interesting, its flowers being borne in spikes more or less like those of a Deutzia. "Virginal" has proved very popular being widely distributed by American nurseries. It is highly probable that these varieties are mixed up in the trade since at least four of them belong to the *P. virginalis* group. However, all have value. There is much which governs the size of the flower, *i.e.,* the soil, culture, amount of moisture, climate, etc. Some of these double-flowered varieties are highly vari-

The Big Scentless Mock-orange (*Philadelphus grandiflorus*) has single flowers that are square in outline.

able and when grown under a certain set of circumstances may have many single flowers. The plant which is growing vigorously, having plenty of good soil, moisture and sunlight, is usually the plant with the most and the largest double flowers. Because of these growth factors, it is inadvisable to select any one double flowering variety and call it "the" best.

Single Flowers

Most of this selected group of mock-oranges has single flowers. The flowers of some species and varieties are borne singly or in twos or threes while those of others are borne in clusters. Both can be effective if well distributed over the entire plant. Of special mention should be the square flowers of *P. grandiflorus*. Those species with single flowers but very well distributed over the entire plant are *P. laxus, P. grandiflorus, P. splendens,* and *P. floridus.* These have stamens of deep yellow and in sufficient number so that the center of the flower looks yellow from a short distance. There are some species which bear the flowers in spikes or racemes, such as *P. monstrosus,* and these too are prominent when well covered. Those varieties which bear the largest single flowers would be "Atlas," "Belle Etoile," "Bouquet Blanc," "Gerbe de Neige," "Norma" and "Sirene."

Two species are included in the recommended list because of the time they bloom, namely, *P. schrenki jacki* since it is the first to come into flower, and *P. incanus* because it is one of the last. These two species aid perceptibly in lengthening the bloom of the group to nearly four weeks when suitable species and varieties are chosen. The fact still remains that no single species or variety commonly holds its flowers in good condition for more than two weeks.

One other species, *P. purpurascens,* is chosen because it is supposed to have purple calyxes which form a pleasing contrast to the small white flowers that are borne in racemes. Although the flowers are not large, this particular color combination is a good one providing the true plant can be obtained.

There are other species, especially the hybrid species *P. burkwoodi* and *P. purpureo-maculatus,* which have flowers with a pale tinge of pink in the center. It has been our experience at the Arnold Arboretum, however, that this color is not sufficiently pronounced to be outstanding, sometimes it even lends a faded look to the flowers. Because of the Mexican ancestry of the *P. purpureo-maculatus* varieties they have never proved sufficiently hardy under New England conditions to be worth while. Farther south they might do better.

Little can be said regarding the long list of species and varieties, which have been suggested for discard. Some are definitely inferior to those in the selected list. A few might, if given the proper growing conditions, equal some of those in the selected list as far as fragrance and general beauty are concerned. In view of the large number selected however, the garden enthusiast will have plenty to try out first in the recommended list before he contemplates experimenting with others.

x Philadelphus "Coles Glorious"   6'   Zone 5
*FLOWERS: white, single, 2" in diameter
    TIME: early June
HYBRID ORIGIN: "Virginal" x "Rosace"
INTRODUCED: by Cole Nursery Co., Painesville, Ohio, 1940

Philadelphus coronarius   9'   Zone 4   Sweet Mock-orange
*FLOWERS: white, single, 1–1½" diameter, fragrant
    TIME: early June
AUTUMN COLOR: yellowish
HABITAT: southern Europe
INTRODUCED: early colonial times
    Very fragrant and especially good for planting in dry situations.

x **Philadelphus cymosus** varieties   6–8'   Zone 4–5

*FLOWERS: single or double, white
    TIME: early mid-June
HYBRID ORIGIN: *P. lemoinei x P. grandiflorus* or closely related forms
ORIGINATED: by Victor Lemoine or Lemoine's Nursery
    "Atlas"—flowers single, 2" dia. (1924)
    "Norma"—flowers single, 1¾" dia. (1914)
    "Perle Blanche"—flowers single, 1½" dia. (1900) one of most fragrant of all
    "Conquete"—flowers single, 2" dia. (1903) very fragrant, one of best

Philadelphus floridus   9'   Zone 5   Beadle Mock-orange

*FLOWERS: white, single, 2" diameter
    TIME: early June
HABITAT: North Carolina and Georgia
    Outstanding for its excellent habit of growth, well branched all the way to the ground, making a dense mass of foliage and so good as a specimen.

Philadelphus grandiflorus   9'   Zone 4   Big Scentless Mock-orange

*FLOWERS: white, single, 1¾" diameter
    TIME: mid-June
HABITAT: southeastern United States
    Good habit but no fragrance to the flowers.

Philadelphus incanus   9'   Zone 5   Gray Mock-orange

*FLOWERS: white, single, 1" in diameter
    TIME: late June
HABITAT: western China
INTRODUCED: 1895

Philadelphus inodorus   9'   Zone 5   Scentless Mock-orange

*FLOWERS: white, single, 2" in diameter
    TIME: mid-June
FOLIAGE: lustrous green
HABITAT: southeastern United States
    Splendid upright habit but scentless flowers.

Philadelphus laxus   6'   Zone 4   Drooping Mock-orange

*FLOWERS: white, single, 1¾" in diameter
    TIME: early June
HABITAT: Georgia
    With branches facing the ground on all sides this is one of the few members of this genus which is adapted for specimen planting.

x **Philadelphus lemoinei** varieties   4–8'   Zone 5

*FLOWERS: white, single or double
    TIME: mid-June
HYBRID ORIGIN: *P. microphyllus x P. coronarius*

Philadelphus "Boule d'Argent."

ORIGINATED: by Victor Lemoine or Lemoine's Nursery

"Avalanche"—flowers single, 1″ diameter, 4′ high (1896) splendid arching branches and one of the most fragrant

"Belle Etoile"—flowers single, 2¼″ dia., 6′ high (1925)

"Boule d'Argent"—flowers double, 2″ dia., 5′ high (1894)

erectus—flowers single, 1″ dia., 4′ high (1894) noted for its very definite compact, upright habit

"Girandole"—flowers double, 1¾″ dia., 4′ high (1916)

"Mont Blanc"—flowers single, 1¼″ dia., 4′ high (1896) one of the hardier varieties of moundlike habit. This will show little winter injury when all other varieties are badly injured

"Innocence"—flowers single, 1¾″ dia., 8′ high (1927) one of the most fragrant varieties

x Philadelphus monstrosus   10'   Zone 5

*FLOWERS: white, single, 1¼" in diameter
    TIME: mid-June
HYBRID ORIGIN: *P. gordonianus? x P. pubescens*
INTRODUCED: 1897
    The flowers of this species are much better and more equally distributed about the plant than in either *P. floridus* or *P. grandiflorus.*

Philadelphus pubescens   9'   Zone 4   Hoary Mock-orange

*FLOWERS: white, single, 1½" in diameter
    TIME: mid-June
AUTUMN COLOR: yellowish
HABITAT: southeastern United States
INTRODUCED: 1800
    This has an excellent wide-spreading habit.

Philadelphus purpurascens   12'   Zone 5   Purplecup Mock-orange

*FLOWERS: white, single, 1" in diameter, calyx violet-purple
    TIME: mid-June
HABITAT: western China
INTRODUCED: 1904
    Very fragrant—the pure white color of the flowers is effectively set off by the purple calyx.

x Philadelphus purpureo-maculatus "Sirene"   4'   Zone 5

*FLOWERS: white, single, 1¼" in diameter
    TIME: mid-June
HYBRID ORIGIN: *P. lemoinei x P. coulteri*
ORIGINATED: by Victor Lemoine about 1910
    Apparently "Sirene" is the hardiest of this hybrid species.

Philadelphus schrenki jacki   8'   Zone 5   Jack Mock-orange

*FLOWERS: white, single, 1" in diameter
    TIME: late May
HABITAT: Korea, northern China
INTRODUCED: 1905
    The first of the mock-oranges to bloom.

x Philadelphus splendens   8'   Zone 5

*FLOWERS: white, single, 1½" in diameter
    TIME: mid-June
HYBRID ORIGIN: *P. grandiflorus x P. gordonianus?*
ORIGINATED: before 1900
    Of excellent habit, it is unfortunate that this has only mediocre fragrance. It is rounded in habit with branches facing the ground all around, making it an excellent plant to use as a specimen. Its flowers are borne in groups of five with brilliant yellow stamens.

For facing the ground well on all sides, *Philadelphus splendens* can be used as a specimen plant.

x Philadelphus virginalis   5–9′   Zone 5

*FLOWERS: white, single or double, 1–2″ in diameter
    TIME: mid-June
HYBRID ORIGIN: *P. lemoinei x P. nivalis plenus?*
ORIGINATED: by Victor Lemoine or Lemoine's Nursery
VARIETIES:

    "Albatre"—flowers double, 1¼″ dia., 5′ high (1914)
    "Argentine"—flowers double, 2″ dia., 4′ high (1914)
    "Bouquet Blanc"—flowers single, 1″ dia., 6′ high (1894) of a moundlike habit, bearing its flowers evenly distributed over the whole plant.
    "Glacier"—flowers double, 1¼″ dia., 5′ high (1914)
    "Virginal"—flowers double, 2″ dia., 9′ high (1907), very fragrant, probably the most widely distributed of all the hybrid mock-oranges and one of the most fragrant. However, as a specimen shrub it fails miserably. It grows vigorously and quickly, devoid of branches at the base. After it has bloomed there is nothing about the plant that is attractive and several other mock-oranges quickly surpass it in this respect. If it is to be grown, place it at the rear of the shrub collection where lower shrubs in the foreground will hide its unsightly base. For cut sprays of flowers it is probably without peer in this group.

Philesia magellanica   3′   Zone 8   Magellan Box-lily

FLOWERS: rosy red, 2″ long
    TIME: fall

FOLIAGE: evergreen, dark green above, whitish beneath, 1½" long
HABITAT: southern Chile
INTRODUCED: 1847

A very handsome dwarf evergreen, which is valued ornamentally for its late flowers in early fall. It is one of the remarkable group of shrubs closely allied to the lilies, requiring a peaty soil and half shady, sheltered position.

Phillyrea decora   9'   Zone 6   Lanceleaf Phillyrea

FLOWERS: white, ¼" dia. in dense axillary clusters
    TIME: April
FRUIT: red and finally purplish black berries
    EFFECTIVE: fall
FOLIAGE: evergreen, lustrous, leaves bronzy green, 1½" long
HABITAT: western Asia
INTRODUCED: 1867

The best of the Phillyreas for the garden, this species makes a handsome bush with spreading branches.

Phoradendron flavescens   3'   Zone 6–7   American Mistletoe

FRUIT: white berries in clusters
    EFFECTIVE: fall
HABITAT: southern United States

This is a parasitic shrub, one of several so-called mistletoes and only mentioned here because of its popular interest, not its ornamental value. It grows as a parasite on many trees and has been "cultivated" by slitting the tender bark of willow, poplar, maple or sycamore and rubbing in the seeds some time between January and April.

Photinia serrulata   36'   Zone 7   Chinese Photinia

FLOWERS: white, small, in flat heads, 6" in diameter
    TIME: mid-May
*FRUIT: bright red berries
    EFFECTIVE: fall and early winter
*FOLIAGE: evergreen, dark lustrous green, leaves to 8" long
HABITAT: China
INTRODUCED: 1804

A very vigorous shrub, which may become too leggy unless occasionally restrained. The new foliage is a reddish bronze, a brilliant color, and considered by some to be sufficient reason to recommend it. If new growth is occasionally cut back, new shoots will be forced so that the young foliage can be evident for a considerable part of the growing season. It needs well-drained soil and not too much moisture especially during the summer. However, its lustrous evergreen leaves are really its best display.

Photinia villosa   15'   Zone 4   Oriental Photinia

FLOWERS: small white, in flat clusters
    TIME: late May
*FRUIT: bright red berries
    EFFECTIVE: fall

FOLIAGE: dark green and glabrous
*AUTUMN COLOR: red-bronze
HABITAT: Japan, Korea, China
INTRODUCED: 1865

One of the hundreds of ornamental woody plants belonging to the rose family, this Oriental species is sometimes susceptible to fire blight.

Physocarpus intermedius parvifolius   4'   Zone 4   Dwarf Illinois Ninebark

FLOWERS: small, white in clusters
    TIME: early June
FRUIT: dried pods
    EFFECTIVE: fall and winter
ORIGINATED: about 1918

This shrub is much more refined than its close relative *P. opulifolius*, with foliage very much like that of *Ribes alpinum*. A dense, upright-growing shrub, suitable for hedge making or any low-barrier planting. A reliable foliage plant, free from most insect and disease pests.

Physocarpus opulifolius   9'   Zone 2   Eastern Ninebark

FLOWERS: small, white or pinkish in clusters
    TIME: early June
FRUIT: reddish to brown dry capsules
    EFFECTIVE: fall
WINTER TWIGS: bark of older branches exfoliating
HABITAT: Quebec to Virginia, Tennessee and Michigan, occasionally escaped cultivation
VARIETY: *luteus*—foliage yellow to yellowish a greater part of the growing season

A common shrub, rather coarse in all its parts, the Eastern Ninebark has been used a great deal. It does well in almost any soil, grows vigorously and makes a big show in a short time. The flowers are small, white and in clusters, and the fruits, although dried capsules, are an attractive reddish color before they are fully mature, after which they turn brown and remain on the plant all winter. The shrub resembles a coarse spirea in all its parts and certainly cannot be considered refined by any means. It can be used in the background or as filler in the general shrub border. The yellow-leaved variety retains its foliage color a greater part of the season if grown in the full sunlight, although near the end of summer the leaves eventually turn a light green. The shredding bark is interesting on the larger plants in the winter. All in all a dependable shrub, but not sufficiently refined to feature in small plantings.

Picea abies varieties   1–12'   Zone 2   Norway Spruce

FOLIAGE: evergreen, needlelike
HABITAT: north and central Europe
INTRODUCED: early colonial times

The dwarf varieties of the Norway Spruce are in the most part low formal bushes of very definite outline. There are perhaps fifty of them. Each time a Norway Spruce develops a sport or "witches broom" on one of its branches, the discoverer thinks he has found a unique form and propagates it asexually. Perhaps it is a new form but more than likely it is identical with one of the following forms which have been cultivated for many years. These varieties are used chiefly as specimens in the rockery or in the small formal garden. They are all very slow of growth and it takes years for them to amount to sizable plants. Most of them could be classed as collectors' items—plants which eventually show differences one from the other but such minor differences that the average gardener is not interested in many of them. They are hopelessly misnamed in the trade. Only a few of the better known forms are here listed:

clanbrasiliana—a wide-spreading rounded form, seldom growing over 2½′ in height. The plant in the Arnold Arboretum was this size for years and then very quickly developed normal vigorous growing branches which have to be cut out periodically.

maxwelli—a common form, low and moundlike, growing twice as broad as it is high.

microsperma—a dense, pyramidal form. The plant in the Arnold Arboretum, over 40 years old, is 10′ high and 10′ wide at the base.

nidiformis—with light green foliage, neither globose nor pyramidal like other varieties, but growing upright with a very definitely flat top. A plant about 20 years old is 3′ tall and 5′ in diameter.

parsonsi—a pleasing, rounded form, not too regular in outline. An old plant in the Arnold Arboretum is 5′ tall and 8′ in diameter at the base.

procumbens—one of the lowest forms, almost procumbent, keeping to a uniform height of no more than 3–4′ although it may be as much as 15′ in diameter.

Pieris floribunda   6′   Zone 4   Mountain Andromeda

*FLOWERS: white, nodding pyramidal clusters to 4″ high, small, like blueberries
    TIME: late April
FOLIAGE: evergreen, leaves to 3½″ long

One of the most serviceable of all broad-leaved evergreens in the North because it seems to do well in any normal soil and has no serious pests or diseases. The erect to nodding clusters of white flowers are composed of numerous small waxy flowers similar in size and shape to those of the blueberry. The flower buds are prominently evident all winter long—somewhat of a conspicuous promise that spring-blossoming time is just around the corner.

Pieris formosa   12′   Zone 7   Himalayan Andromeda

FLOWERS: white or tinged with pink in drooping panicles to 6″ long
    TIME: April
FOLIAGE: evergreen, leaves to 6″ long
HABITAT: eastern Himalaya
INTRODUCED: 1858?

This more tender species has larger flower clusters than either *P. japonica* or *P. floribunda,* and in the warmer regions of the South and on the Pacific Coast it might well be used in preference to them.

Pieris japonica   9′   Zone 5   Japanese Andromeda

*FLOWERS: creamy white, pendulous clusters to 5″ long
    TIME: mid-April
*FOLIAGE: lustrous dark, evergreen, leaves to 3½″ long

Japanese Andromeda (*Pieris japonica*) an excellent early flowering evergreen with lustrous leaves.

HABITAT: Japan
INTRODUCED: 1870
VARIETY: *variegata*—leaves with a very thin white margin. This type of variegation is not at all objectionable

An excellent broad-leaved evergreen for the same reasons *P. floribunda* is popular. In addition, the Japanese Andromeda has a lustrous dark green foliage and flower clusters that are pendulous. A well-grown specimen of the Japanese Andromeda, covered with lustrous leaves and pendulous flower clusters, is about as beautiful an evergreen as it is possible to grow. In New England it should be grown in protected places but farther South this is unnecessary. Young foliage is usually a rich bronze in spring, later turning a normal green. This species can be grown in a shaded situation but, like many other plants, will not produce as many flowers there as in full sun.

Pieris taiwanensis   6'   Zone 7   Formosa Andromeda

*FLOWERS: pure white, similar to other *Pieris* species, clusters to 6" long
     TIME: early spring
*FOLIAGE: evergreen, glossy, leaves to 3" long
HABITAT: Formosa
INTRODUCED: 1918

A strikingly handsome broad-leaved evergreen, worthy of a trial in any garden where it might prove hardy.

Pinus densiflora umbraculifera   12′   Zone 4   Japanese Umbrella Pine
(Tanyosho Pine)

FOLIAGE: evergreen, needlelike
HABITAT: Japan
INTRODUCED: 1862

A popular Japanese pine frequently planted because of its peculiar flat-topped habit of growth.

Pinus mugo mughus   8′   Zone 2   Mugo Pine

FOLIAGE: evergreen, needlelike
HABITAT: southern Europe
INTRODUCED: 1779
VARIETIES:

compacta—dense, globe shaped, smaller than the species
pumilio—usually a prostrate shrub

These three low pines are closely related and are often difficult to tell one from the other. They are serviceable in foundation plantings and have been used as hedges but are susceptible to severe infestations of scale which can quickly become serious and do considerable damage. In areas where this pest is prevalent these low pines should be used singly and not in hedges. The present control methods are to use lime-sulfur, or a miscible oil, as dormant sprays; or nicotine sulfate with soap or DDT applied in late May or early June just after insects are hatched.

A word of caution should be given to suggest that the two dwarf varieties be purchased from nurserymen who have propagated them asexually. Some merely sow seed of *P. mugo* and select the slower growing plants as these varieties, but such plants are not true and may eventually grow 8′ tall!

Pinus strobus varieties   30′   Zone 3   White Pine

FOLIAGE: evergreen, needlelike
HABITAT: eastern North America
VARIETIES:

nana—dwarf, rounded bush
umbraculifera—bush, wider at top than bottom, shaped something like an umbrella

These low forms of the White Pine can be used as shrubs in gardens but are rarely seen, merely because other good evergreens grow faster or because the species can be grown and kept clipped to the same general shape as is natural for these varieties to assume without clipping.

Pittosporum tobira   10′   Zone 8   Japanese Pittosporum

FLOWERS: creamy white 1″ in diameter, fragrant
    TIME: May
°FOLIAGE: evergreen, leaves to 4″ long
HABITAT: China and Japan
INTRODUCED: 1804

A most serviceable evergreen hedge plant in the warmer parts of the country. Its leaves are blunt and leathery, a dark lustrous green, and its flowers remind one of the fragrance of orange blossoms. Common in the deep South but not grown as much in Pacific Coast gardens as it might be.

The Japanese Pittosporum is used either as a specimen or as a clipped hedge.

Polygonum vaccinifolium   Trailing plant   Zone 7   Rose Carpet Knotweed

*FLOWERS: rose-red in upright spikes
    TIME: August
FOLIAGE: dark green
HABITAT: Himalaya
INTRODUCED: 1845

A prostrate, or trailing, shrub prone to form carpets of foliage with upright spikes of rose-red flowers in late summer. Does best in rockeries where soil is moist.

Poncirus trifoliata   35′   Zone 5–6   Hardy-orange

FLOWERS: white, 2″ in diameter
    TIME: late April
FRUIT: yellow, like a small orange 2″ in diameter
    EFFECTIVE: fall
FOLIAGE: leathery, dark green
HABITAT: north China, Korea
INTRODUCED: 1850

Frequently used as a hedge in the South because of its dense growth and prominent spines; also because it withstands shearing well. Its small white flowers do not remain effective very long, but its leathery dark green leaves and its small, bitter-tasting oranges, are its chief ornamental characteristics. Dense growth, too, is of importance. It has proved hardy in protected places as far north as Boston, but is not dependably hardy north of Philadelphia. It prefers acid soil. A unique plant, not among the best of ornamental specimens, but nevertheless serviceable in some situations, and once established in the right place is a vigorous grower.

Potentilla fruticosa 4' Zone 2 Bush Cinquefoil

*FLOWERS: yellow, single, 1½" diameter
TIME: mid-May
HABITAT: northern hemispheres
VARIETIES:
grandiflora—flowers deep yellow, single, 1¼" diameter
veitchi—flowers white, single, 1" diameter
parvifolia—flowers deep yellow, single ½" diameter

Many varieties of this species have been found over a wide area of the northern hemispheres. The sturdy, very hardy plants, bloom in mid-May and continue throughout summer, sometimes even into September. Because of its comparatively low height, its lack of interesting fruits and autumn color, its garden effectiveness is easily supplanted by annuals or perennials. Incidentally, a large number of potentillas are herbaceous.

When comparing *P. fruticosa* varietal differences with those of the massive lilac, they do not appear very important. The three varieties selected are the best of nearly a dozen growing in the Arnold Arboretum. The extremely long blooming season is their only redeeming factor for the places where they might be used in the garden are limited.

Prinsepia sinensis 10' Zone 4 Cherry Prinsepia

FRUIT: red, cherrylike
EFFECTIVE: July
FOLIAGE: bright green
HABITAT: Manchuria
INTRODUCED: 1896

A thorny, dense shrub of merit in hedge making. The spreading, arching branches are adapted to medium or high hedges, and the stout thorns make the plant an effective barrier. This species is one of the first to show its green leaves in spring. Red fruits in summer and shredding bark in winter are added points of interest. Among other species of this genus, *P. uniflora* is lower-growing and more dense in habit with white twigs in winter.

Prunus besseyi 7' Zone 3 Western Sand Cherry

FLOWERS: white, about ½" in diameter, single
TIME: May
FRUIT: purple, black, about ½" in diameter
EFFECTIVE: fall
HABITAT: Wyoming and Manitoba south to Kansas

Cultivated for its sweet fruits. Very hardy, it has been used in fruit-breeding work and large numbers of seedlings have been grown for selecting heavily fruiting clons. It is said that as many as 16 quarts of fruit have been picked from a single three-year-old bush. However, it must be admitted that these plants do not always fruit as well in the East as they do under their native mid-western conditions.

x **Prunus cistena**   7'   Zone 2   Purpleleaf Sand Cherry

FLOWERS: single white
    TIME: May
FRUIT: blackish purple cherries
    EFFECTIVE: fall
FOLIAGE: reddish
HYBRID ORIGIN: *P. pumila x P. cerasifera atropurpurea*
ORIGINATED: before 1910 by Dr. Niles E. Hansen, formerly of South Dakota State
Experiment Station, as an ornamental with good fruits, which is valued for its
colored foliage as well.

Prunus glandulosa   4½'   Zone 4   Dwarf Flowering Almond

*FLOWERS: pink or white, single or double
    TIME: early May
FRUIT: red cherries, ½" in diameter
    EFFECTIVE: summer
HABITAT: China and Japan
INTRODUCED: 1835
VARIETIES:
    albo-plena—flowers, double, white
    rosea—flowers, pink
    sinensis—flowers, double, pink
    Low shrubs—valued for the numerous showy flowers.

Prunus japonica nakai   4½'   Zone 2   Nakai Chinese Bush Cherry

FLOWERS: pink or white
    TIME: early May
FRUIT: red cherries, ⅜" in diameter
    EFFECTIVE: summer
HABITAT: Korea
INTRODUCED: 1918

Prunus laurocerasus   18'   Zone 6–7   Cherry-laurel

FLOWERS: white in racemes, 2–5" long
    TIME: late May
FRUIT: purple to black cherries only about ½" diameter
    EFFECTIVE: late summer
*FOLIAGE: evergreen, lustrous leaves 4–6" long
HABITAT: southeastern Europe
INTRODUCED: 1576
VARIETY: *schipkaensis*—hardier than the species, hardy in Zone 5, found in 1886
    A most serviceable shrub. Vigorous, with shiny, evergreen leaves, leathery
in texture, and able to withstand heavy pruning. Often used in hedges and wind-
breaks, both sheared and unsheared. One of the most popular shrubs of the
South, used rarely north of Philadelphia. Many varieties are available but most
differ from the species only slightly. If not clipped, it is a rapid grower and the
greedy roots frequently starve plants close by.

Prunus lusitanica   6–60′   Zone 7   Portugal-laurel
FLOWERS: white, ½″ diameter, in racemes 10″ long
    TIME: May
FRUIT: purplish cherries
    EFFECTIVE: summer
*FOLIAGE: evergreen, glossy, leaves to 5″ long
HABITAT: Spain and Portugal
INTRODUCED: early colonial times
    An extremely serviceable, glossy-leaved evergreen for southern gardens which may grow into tree form or be confined as a shrub.

Prunus maritima   6′   Zone 3   Beach Plum
FLOWERS: white, single or double
    TIME: early May
FRUIT: dull purple, ½″–1″ in diameter, sometimes crimson
    EFFECTIVE: late summer
HABITAT: New England coastal area and eastern coastal area
VARIETY: *flava*—fruit yellow
    Of increasing economic importance because of its delicious fruits. Some clons have been selected by the U. S. Department of Agriculture and a few growers, especially Mr. Wilfrid Wheeler of Hatchville, Mass., and are being propagated because they bear better and larger fruit. Some of these varieties, with fruits nearly 1″ in diameter, are "Eastham," "Hancock," and "Premier." A rounded, dense bush, which can be used occasionally in the shrub border, adapted especially to seashore plantings.

x Prunus skinneri "Baton Rouge"   6′   Zone 2
FLOWERS: bright pink
    TIME: mid-May
FRUIT: green cherries
HYBRID ORIGIN: *P. tenella x P. japonica*
ORIGINATED: 1934
    Of value chiefly for its extreme hardiness and long branches covered with rosy pink flowers in mid-spring. F. L. Skinner of Dropmore, Manitoba, Canada, rates this a better ornamental in his area than either *P. japonica* or *P. nana*.

Prunus tenella alba   4½′   Zone 2   Dwarf Russian Almond
FLOWERS: white, ¾″ diameter
    TIME: May
FRUIT: red cherries almost 1″ in diameter
    EFFECTIVE: summer
HABITAT: southeastern Europe
INTRODUCED: 1683
VARIETY: *gessleriana*—flowers red, 1″ in diameter

Prunus tomentosa   9′   Zone 2   Manchu Cherry
*FLOWERS: white, slightly pinkish
    TIME: late April

*FRUIT: scarlet cherries, ½" in diameter
  EFFECTIVE: June and July
HABITAT: northwest China and Japan
INTRODUCED: 1870
VARIETY: *leucocarpa*—fruits white
    Excellent shrub, often used in flowering hedge, with its flowers appearing profusely just before the leaves. A serviceable ornamental, the bright red fruits of which are edible. It can be used as a specimen.

Prunus triloba multiplex   15'   Zone 5   Flowering Almond
*FLOWERS: double, pink, 1" in diameter
  TIME: late April
HABITAT: China
INTRODUCED: 1855
    Popular ornamental shrub with large, double, pink blossoms in early spring before the leaves. Of no other ornamental value, however.

Punica granatum   15'   Zone 7–8   Pomegranate
*FLOWERS: scarlet, over 1" in diameter
  TIME: summer
FRUIT: deep yellow, 2½" diameter
  EFFECTIVE: fall
HABITAT: southeastern Europe to Himalayas
INTRODUCED: probably early colonial times
VARIETIES:
    albescens—flowers white
    flavescens—flowers yellow
    legrellei—flowers double, striped red and yellowish white
    multiplex—flowers white, double
    nana—low form with smaller linear-lanceolate to linear leaves, smaller flowers and fruit. Zone 6
    pleniflora—flowers double, scarlet
    The Pomegranate is a popular garden shrub in parts of the deep South and the Pacific coastal area. The praises of this shrub have been handed down in the earliest songs and notes recorded by man, and thus bestows a sentimental value partly responsible for its popularity. Its flowers appear throughout summer, and are colored variously according to variety. It should be grown only in the more protected parts of very warm gardens in zones 7–8. The varieties have not proved as hardy as the species.

PYRACANTHA

    The firethorns are particularly valued for their profuse clusters of brilliant red berries, colorful all fall and far into the winter. They are frequently grown in foundation plantings or in espalier form against warm walls, to which type of growth they are ideally suited. They also are used to some extent in hedges because of dense growth and lustrous green leaves, but close clipping of course materially reduces the amount of fruit produced.

The Pomegranate is familiar in the warmer regions of the world.

Unfortunately, all the species in this genus are susceptible to fire blight, some species more so than others. One new hybrid "Oxford" is proving the most resistant to the disease and so is well worthy of a trial.

Pyracantha atalantioides   18′   Zone 6   Gibbs Firethorn

FLOWERS: small, white
　　TIME: early June
*FRUIT: scarlet or bright crimson berries, ¼″ in diameter
　　EFFECTIVE: fall and winter
FOLIAGE: lustrous green, evergreen in South, leaves to 2½″ long
HABITAT: southeastern to western China
INTRODUCED: 1907
　　Although the fruit of this species is smaller than that of *P. coccinea*, it is more desirable, possibly because it will remain in good condition on the plant a

Scarlet Firethorn noted for its masses of brilliant red berries in the fall and winter.

month or two longer, a decided advantage. It has frequently been called *P. gibbsi* in the trade, for it was at first named after the Hon. Vicary Gibbs, in whose garden in England a magnificent 20′ specimen was growing. However, further botanical investigation revealed that it had been given the name *P. atalantioides* in 1877. It is the tallest of the firethorns recommended here.

Pyracantha coccinea   6′   **Zone 6**   **Scarlet Firethorn**

FLOWERS: small white, in clusters
    TIME: mid-June
*FRUIT: bright red berries, ¼″ in diameter
    EFFECTIVE: fall and winter
FOLIAGE: deciduous in North, evergreen in South, leaves to 1½″ long
HABITAT: Italy to western Asia, naturalized in Pennsylvania and South

INTRODUCED: 1629

This species, and its variety *lalandi,* are the most popular and common of the firethorns. Fruits are borne in the greatest profusion. When it does well, perhaps no other shrub supplies as much vivid winter color as do these plants. The variety is more vigorous and possibly slightly more hardy, but both are used as wall shrubs, as foundation plants or (in the South) as specimen plants.

Pyracantha crenulata rogersiana   10′   Zone 7   Rogers Firethorn

FLOWERS: white, small in clusters
    TIME: late May
*FRUIT: orange-red berries, ¼″ in diameter
    EFFECTIVE: fall and early winter
FOLIAGE: lustrous bright green, evergreen, leaves to 1½″ long
HABITAT: western China
INTRODUCED: 1911

The Rogers Firethorn has the smallest leaves (½–1½″) and is hardier and more ornamental than the species.

x Pyracantha "Oxford"   10′   Zone 7

FLOWERS: small, white, in flat clusters
    TIME: June
*FRUIT: bright orange to red berries
    EFFECTIVE: fall
HYBRID ORIGIN: *P. angustifolia x P. crenato-serrata*
ORIGINATED: University of California, Fruit Testing Station, 1941

Similar to the parents except, that of all the firethorns, it has proved to be the most resistant to fire-blight disease.

Raphiolepsis umbellata   6′   Zone 7   Yeddo-Hawthorn

FLOWERS: white, fragrant, in dense upright panicles
    TIME: late May
FRUIT: bluish black berries, ⅜″ in dia.
    EFFECTIVE: fall and winter
*FOLIAGE: evergreen, dark green, leathery, leaves to 3″ long
HABITAT: southern Japan
INTRODUCED: before 1859

A handsome evergreen shrub, easily grown either in full sun or partial shade, and appears to be fairly drought resistant. Normally it will only grow about 4′ tall and possibly 6′ in diameter, but in a good situation it may grow several times this size.

Rhamnus davurica   30′   Zone 2   Dahurian Buckthorn

FRUIT: shiny black berries, ¼″ diameter
    EFFECTIVE: fall
*FOLIAGE: lustrous
HABITAT: North China, Manchuria, and Korea
INTRODUCED: 1817
    Vigorous shrub.

Rhamnus frangula   18'   Zone 2   Alder Buckthorn

FRUIT: berries changing from red to dark purple
   EFFECTIVE: late summer and fall
*FOLIAGE: dark lustrous green
AUTUMN COLOR: yellow
HABITAT: Europe, western Asia, North Africa
INTRODUCED: early colonial times

A vigorous shrub, widely distributed by birds, of value for its lustrous green foliage, dense habit of growth and numerous small berries about ¼" in diameter. These change color at different times so there are green, red, and black berries on the plant at the same time during late summer. The shrub is easily grown in almost any soil. The dried bark is used as a laxative.

RHODODENDRON

The genus *Rhododendron* comprises more species, varieties and hybrids than any other group of ornamental woody plants, over 2000 of them having been listed. They come from all parts of the world and many have been in cultivation for centuries. Very few individuals have seen more than a small part of them and, therefore, it is difficult to critically examine the group. Approximately 27 species occur in North America, but the real and rich storehouse for the group is the Orient. Many of our best types originally came from China, Japan or Korea, and some of them must have been cultivated in Chinese gardens for many centuries.

Horticultural literature is rich with records of how these natives from different parts of the world have been brought together eventually and crossed. John Bartram, the early American plant collector; Robert Fortune, the great English plant explorer of a hundred years ago; Engelbert Kaempfer of the Dutch East India Company, and undoubtedly many others whose business interests were chiefly in trade during those days of the old sailing vessels, along with such modern explorers as E. H. Wilson and Charles Sprague Sargent of the Arnold Arboretum and Kingdon Ward of England —these and hundreds of others have all made contributions to this Rhododendron group. Also, new hybrids and new species are continually appearing.

So, with plants contributed from all parts of the temperate regions as well as from the mountains of Lapland, Switzerland, the Himalayas and Australia, it is evident that this is a most extensive group. The plants are both evergreen and deciduous, marked with colorful and often fragrant flowers, although the fruits are uninteresting dry capsules. A number of the best are native of eastern North America and are valued features in gardens in this area. However, it is fast becoming evident that the area around Seattle, Washington, is ideal for these plants, and over 150 species have flowered there in recent years. It is highly probable that with this increased interest on the part of the gardeners in the Pacific Northwest, it will be

Azaleas bring bright colors to any garden where they are grown.

found that more azaleas and rhododendrons can be grown there than in any other part of the country.

In a large part of central North America it is difficult, if not impossible, to grow these plants. Either soil conditions are wrong, summers are too hot or winters too cold. On the eastern Atlantic Coast, only about one-third of the evergreen rhododendrons are proving hardy, and this is true in a large majority of northern gardens. In the South, except in strictly coastal or mountainous areas, many species cannot be grown, especially of the evergreen types, because of extreme summer heat. Then too, alternate freezing and thawing in mild winters, when continued for long periods, is unconducive to good growth.

Both those plants which are popularly called azaleas, and those which are considered rhododendrons, are correctly members of the genus *Rhododendron*. Actually, there are no clear-cut lines for distinguishing all azaleas from all rhododendrons. They must be separated by a combination of characters. However, true rhododendrons are evergreen except *R. mucronulatum* and *R. dauricum*, although there is an evergreen variety of the latter. The true rhododendrons have mostly ten or more stamens and the leaves are often scaly or with small dots on their undersurface. Plants popularly termed azaleas are mostly deciduous (although there are some evergreen forms of these, too) and the flowers have mostly five stamens, the leaves are

UPPER LEFT: Azalea flower "hose in hose" or actually one flower corolla superimposed on another.

UPPER RIGHT: A typical azalea flower cluster, each flower with five stamens.

LOWER: A typical cluster of rhododendron flowers, each flower with ten stamens, and the leaves large, leathery and evergreen.

never dotted with scales and frequently are hairy. These distinguishing characteristics should prove helpful in the proper use of the popular terms, azalea and rhododendron.

With centuries of experimentation as a backlog in growing these diverse plants, and at least a century of painstaking effort in crossing them, it is easily seen why this group is so diverse. It is impossible to mention all the hybrid groups and all the species but the general discussion which follows should prove of assistance for those interested in further study of this very large genus.

Soil

All azaleas and rhododendrons should be given acid soil conditions. Their roots should be kept cool and moist and surrounded with plenty of rich humus. They simply cannot be grown in dry or alkaline soil. The oft-mentioned mulches of rotted-oak leaves, peat moss or pine needles are all good and can be left on the plants as a mulch all winter. Spent hops have been used in England for many years and are being tried in the Arnold Arboretum. This mulch should do well since it is acid in reaction, but should be applied with discretion for on warm days, if applied wet as it comes from the brewery, it heats sufficiently to kill young or mature shoots. A mulch of maple leaves is not advisable for two reasons; it is not acid and the flat maple leaves tend to pack down considerably more than do oak leaves, thus excluding much needed air from the roots. Azaleas and rhododendrons are fibrous rooted with their roots usually within the upper twelve inches of soil, hence a mulch keeping the top soil cool and moist aids materially in their growth.

A soil with a pH value of from 4.5 to 6.5 is usually about right for most acid-loving plants, and simple tests and equipment have been devised for ascertaining this acidity. In making these tests it is important to have an accurate sample of the soil by digging 3–4″ before taking a sample. The surface inch of the soil might be entirely different from that at a lower level. Since azaleas and rhododendrons are shallow-rooted plants, one is interested only in the upper 12″ of soil. It is always a good plan to make several tests throughout the proposed site since one test would not tell the whole story.

If the bed of ericaceous plants is to be placed in a heavy, clay soil that is found to test strongly alkaline, one should dig out all the soil to a depth of at least 12–18″. Presupposing that the drainage is good, for all ericaceous plants as a rule like good drainage, a layer of cinders from 1–2″ thick is placed on the bottom of the bed to keep earthworms from bringing up the sub-soil. If the drainage is not good, the soil is excavated 6″ deeper, and a tile drain is laid to carry off all excess water. Then the bed is filled with rich, acid woods' soil which contains plenty of humus, and has been tested for its acidity. If woods' soil is not available, some good garden loam which is neutral or acid may be used, if such humus material as rotted-oak leaves or pine needles, acid peat moss, acid muck (usually black) or sedge peat is mixed with it. If it is impossible to use any of these materials, then a soil may be made acid by adding aluminum sulfate in the following amounts:

Acidity of soil used at start	*Aluminum sulfate per square yard*
Medium acid (pH 5.5 to 6.0)	¼ pound
Slightly acid (pH 6.5 to 7.0)	½ pound
Neutral to slightly alkaline (pH 7.0 to 8.0)	¾ pound

Care should be exercised in using aluminum sulfate, for in large amounts it may be decidedly injurious to the plants. After the aluminum sulfate has been applied to the surface of the soil, it should be carefully watered in. A week later the soil is tested for final acidity and, if satisfactory, the plants are set. Commercial fertilizers which leave an acid reaction in the soil can be used on ericaceous plants, but only when one is perfectly familiar with their resulting action on the plants concerned. Decomposing woods' loam, with a decided acid reaction, is about the best soil for ericaceous plants and if available nothing else should be considered. Certainly lime, bone meal, wood ashes and other materials containing a decided amount of calcium should be avoided at all times.

Water

It has been found best to refrain from watering an ericaceous planting with too much "hard" water containing a large amount of calcium. Of course, the plants must not be allowed to dry out just because the water available is "hard." Pure rain water is excellent. It may be expedient to collect some of this from rainspouts, if acid-loving plants are being grown in areas where other available water is calcareous.

The soil should be tested occasionally to see whether it is becoming more or less acid. If less acid, small amounts of aluminum sulfate can be sprinkled over the bed as previously mentioned.

In this same connection it is wise to keep in mind that an ericaceous bed, planted next to a stucco or brick house, may suffer some injury since splashing rain water dissolves small amounts of calcium in the wall, and this amounts up over a period of years. It may be advantageous to have the ericaceous bed in some other situation than against such a plastered wall.

Pruning and Fertilizing

All azaleas and even the rhododendrons can be pruned, but usually they need it only occasionally when they become too dense or have broken, diseased or dying branches. It is best to prune the older branches by cutting them off at the base of the plant and thus encouraging young and vigorous growth. Some of my rhododendron pruning experiments this past year have demonstrated that if pruning is done very early in the spring, many rhododendrons can be cut to within 6" of the ground and still be expected to send up shoots during the current growing season. Of course it is far better to practice annual renewal pruning, a bit at a time, but if the plant must be cut to the ground, and this is done very early, it may recover (in 75% of the cases at least) and result in a much better and more vigorous specimen at the end of several growing seasons.

When purchasing azaleas as well as rhododendrons it is wise to keep in mind the fact that many of the choice varieties are clons and so should be propagated asexually, and not by seed. Unscrupulous growers may propagate such named varieties by seed for it is easier, but the resulting plants do not have the same colored flowers as the original. With rhododendron and azalea species, propagation by seed is satisfactory, especially if the seed has been collected from isolated plants where there is little danger from cross fertilization. The prospective purchaser should know these things in advance and be certain that the desired plants have been propagated in the correct manner if it is not possible to see them in bloom before he buys.

The late Mr. C. O. Dexter of Sandwich, Massachusetts, experimented with many fertilizers for rhododendrons and azaleas until he finally found one which seemed to force his plants into remarkable productiveness. This was made of 7 pounds of Chilean nitrate of potash, 3 pounds of nitrate of potash and 20 pounds of superphosphate. He applied this at reasonable rates in early spring to all his azaleas and rhododendron specimens, and with remarkable success. Nitrogenous fertilizers, leaving an acid reaction in the soil will promote vegetative growth, but the above recommended formula might well be tried for forcing plants into profuse bloom.

A formula which has been recommended for the Puget Sound area by Herbert Ihrig who has grown hundreds of azaleas and rhododendrons in the vicinity of Seattle, Washington, is as follows:

10 lbs. sulfate of ammonia
35 lbs. superphosphate
20 lbs. sulfate of potash
20 lbs. cotton seed meal
15 lbs. aluminum sulfate

This is applied to the surface of the soil above the roots of the plants in early spring, in small amounts.

General Maintenance

General maintenance is simple, for once established in good soil with the correct mulch and water, both azaleas and rhododendrons pretty much take care of themselves. They grow naturally close together so that weeds are not a serious problem. They do not need cultivation for their roots are always near the surface. Occasionally the very tall or broken branches may have to be removed early in the spring. Also it is advisable to cut off the faded flower clusters and so prevent seed formation, for nourishment which might go into the production of seeds would be much better diverted into the formation of flower buds for the next year.

The best way to keep rhododendrons and azaleas free of insect and disease troubles is to provide good growing conditions at the time they are planted.

Occasionally, especially in the North, some winter protection may be advisable. Evergreen boughs, burlap screens or some such protective materials are arranged about the plants to prevent them from winter winds, and to prevent early spring sun from causing the leaves to give off too much water. Evergreen leaves are giving off water into the atmosphere continually. This is one of the reasons why the rhododendrons always must be transplanted with a ball of earth about the roots. Since azaleas lose their leaves in the fall, they can be transplanted either in spring or in fall when dormant, without the ball of earth about the roots. When winds cause this rate of water loss to increase—with the soil water unavailable because the ground is frozen—then too much water may be lost from living cells and the foliage will dry or show the characteristics of browning or burning commonly referred to as "winter injury." The same thing can happen from warm sunshine in the very early spring especially on those days when the ground remains frozen. The plants do not need this protection to be kept warm, but they do need protection from winter winds, and shade from late winter or early spring sun, to prevent water loss from the leaves.

Plants growing in the right soil and in the right location seldom are attacked by serious pests, except possibly the lace bug. A small insect about ⅛" long, it usually appears in late June and in summer on the underside of the leaves. It can be controlled by spraying the under surface of the foliage with nicotine sulfate or DDT.

Borers occasionally eat their way into some of the older stems and once noted, the entire branch should be cut out and burned at once. There is also a wilt which has recently appeared on the flowers of azaleas, especially prevalent in southern gardens. Pathologists in the United States Department of Agriculture have been working on the control of this disease for several years and at the moment suggest the removal and burning of all flowers killed by the disease and the replacing of soil on which the flowers have fallen. Also, to spray flowers with a diluted solution of acetic acid seems to help.

CLASSES OR GROUPS OF AZALEAS

There are several important groups of azaleas and, with proper selection, azaleas can bloom in the garden for two consecutive months. First, there are the species and their botanical hybrids. These come from all parts of the world's northern temperate regions. Those native to North America are well worth growing as ornamentals. Those from China and Japan add vivid colors to this important, stable and dependable group. It was noticed hundreds of years ago that azaleas hybridized readily, and hundreds of varieties have originated as a result of the work of many hybridizers who used the species as the parents of original crosses.

Some species have contributed color to these hybrids, other species have contributed size of flower and hardiness. Today, with possibly a thousand different azaleas being grown in this country, the relationships of one plant to another become rather confused to all but the rhododendron and azalea specialists.

It will be sufficient for the purposes of this book to mention only a few of these general hybrid groups. There are several excellent references which can be used for more careful study of this diverse and colorful clan of flowering shrubs.

The Indian Azaleas

The large-flowered azaleas, commonly grown in greenhouses in the North, are at their best outdoors in the famous gardens of the deep South. Some are strains introduced from England as early as 1830. Single- and double-flowered forms are available, ranging in color from white to rose, with many variegated forms and flowers 1½″ to 3″ in diameter. They are not derived from a single species, as the Kurume azaleas, but are the result of cross-breeding a number of different species, R. simsi, R. pulchrum, R. mucronatum and some of their varieties. All have had a strong influence on the hybrids of this group as they are grown today. Years ago this heterogenous mixture became known as the Indian azaleas, although R. indicum probably has had little to do with their ancestry and they certainly are not natives of India.

Kurume Azaleas

Ernest H. Wilson was responsible for first introducing this excellent group into American gardens in 1916. He found that all of these can be traced more or less directly to the various forms of R. obtusum. Japanese gardeners had been developing certain strains of the wild R. obtusum of Japan for over a century, when Wilson visited that country in 1914 and found over 200 named variations of this one species.

As a group, the Kurume azaleas are hardier than the Indian azaleas, with smaller flowers, smaller leaves and more dense in habit of growth. Certain of the better forms such as "Apple Blossom," "Christmas Cheer," "Salmon Beauty," and others are grown outdoors in sheltered situations as far north as Long Island. As a rule they have dense, twiggy growth and small leaves. In this group belong such azaleas as "Hinodegiri," R. obtusum amoenum and R. obtusum album, all of which are commonly grown outdoors in Philadelphia, and with protection, on Long Island. Their flowers may be single or double, depending on the variety, and are usually a delicate pink to bright scarlet, about ¾″ to 1½″ in diameter.

There are over 50 named varieties of Kurume azaleas available today in the United States, many of them grown as greenhouse pot plants. Their bright-colored flowers, dense twiggy habit of growth and quick response to clipping, make them excellent specimens regardless of whether they are grown as pot plants in the greenhouse or as specimens out-of-doors. When these varieties are well grown, and particularly if clipped properly, they are a solid mass of color when in full bloom.

The Ghent Azaleas

Three American azaleas, R. *calendulaceum* (orange), R. *viscosum* (white and fragrant), and R. *nudiflorum* (pink) were introduced into England in 1783. About fifty years later the large-flowered yellow R. *luteum* was introduced into western Europe, and soon crosses among these species began to appear. It was in Ghent, Belgium, that a greater part of the breeding was done, so it is from this Old World town that this group of azaleas takes its name. The specific name of the group is R. *gandavense*. As early as 1836, approximately 107 "Ghent" azaleas were known, and the number today is far in excess of this.

The Ghent hybrids are considerably hardier than either the Indian or the Kurume hybrids, many being hardy even in central Maine where temperatures may go as low as −20° F. The colors vary between pure yellow and pure white, to combinations of pink and scarlet having much more yellow than either the Indian or the Kurume azaleas. There are varieties with double flowers. They do not grow very well in the far South, but where they do thrive, their gorgeous flowers afford brilliant spots of color that are unsurpassed by any other hardy woody shrub.

The Mollis Azaleas

The Mollis hybrids are based on a cross between tender, yellow R. *molle*, the Chinese azalea, and the hardy, red R. *japonicum* of Japan, given the specific name R. *kosterianum*. The most famous member of this group is the much advertised "Miss Louisa Hunnewell," raised by the late Mr. T. D. Hatfield of Wellesley, Massachusetts. It should be pointed out that this strain should be asexually propagated, since the seed does not always yield the true "Miss Louisa Hunnewell." Because of the hardiness of R. *japonicum*, several of the Mollis hybrids have proved reliably hardy in New England.

The Mucronatum Azaleas

Particular mention should be made of the very valuable and popular Snow Azalea, offered in the trade under the names of A. *indica alba* or A. *ledifolia alba*, the correct name being R. *mucronatum*. The best of all the white-flowering evergreen azaleas, it is hardy as far north as Boston if well protected in the winter. The flowers are pure white, often 2″ in diameter. The plant itself sometimes grows 6′ tall, though commonly it is low, dense and compact. Occasionally forms arise with flowers tinged pink, and there is a double-flowered variety as well. A splendid plant and one which should be used wherever azaleas are grown.

Catawba hybrid rhododendrons are particularly noted for their hardiness and are among the most popular of the rhododendrons used in American gardens today.

CLASSES OR GROUPS OF RHODODENDRONS

Catawba Hybrids

These are perhaps the oldest and most common among the gardens of the Eastern United States. *Rhododendron catawbiense*, native in the southern Appalachian Mountains, was introduced into England in 1809, and shortly after was crossed with such tender species as the blood-red flowering *R. arboreum* from the Himalayas. These hybrids were backcrossed and also *R. ponticum* was used considerably. Today, some of the hardiest and most dependable clons for growing in the northeastern United States belong to this serviceable group of hybrids.

The Maximum Hybrid Rhododendrons

Rhododendron maximum is the hardiest native broad-leaved rhodo-dendron in North America, yet not among the best ornamentals because its flowers appear after the young foliage has grown considerably so that the flowers are masked somewhat by the leaves. However, its vigor, hardiness and large size of leaves are desirable assets in a rhododendron, so it has been used in hybridization. One of the hybrids resulted from crossing it with *R. cinnamomeum,* known as "Cunningham's White" after the man who made the cross in 1850. This has not proved too hardy north of New York, but its vigor is unquestioned and it has been used extensively as an understock in grafting. This group of hybrids has not proved as important ornamentally as have the Catawba hybrids.

The Griffithianum Hybrid Rhododendrons

One of the largest flowered species of the Himalayan rhododendrons is *R. griffithianum,* and because of these large flowers (single flowers being 3–7" in diameter) it has been used considerably in breeding work. The plant itself is not hardy in the northeastern United States, but it has been crossed with some of the Catawba hybrids, with *R. arboreum, R. fortunei* and several other species, and has yielded some interesting seedlings with these in turn yielding some interesting clons.

Fortune Hybrid Rhododendrons

Much has been written about the Fortune hybrid rhododendrons, and although they are not as attractive as the Griffithianum hybrids, they certainly are hardier, many of them thriving as far north as Cape Cod. *Rhododendron fortunei* is one of the hardiest of the Chinese rhododendrons, with larger flowers than those of most native American species. The late Mr. C. O. Dexter of Sandwich, Massachusetts, on Cape Cod, did considerable hybridizing in this group, some of his hybrids having flowers three to four and even five inches in diameter. It must be admitted however that the larger the individual flower in the cluster, the fewer the flowers, hence those hybrids with large individual flowers were not necessarily the most orna-mental of the hybrids. There is opportunity for more hybridizing work with this species, possibly crossing it with some of the hardier Catawba hybrids in order to produce hardy progeny.

Caucasian Hybrid Rhododendrons

This is a very small group of hybrids represented in America by a mere dozen varieties, yet these are important because of their hardiness and early bloom. They are not quite as hardy as the Catawba hybrids, but some are grown in New England with protection. In this area these varieties are the first of the broad-leaved evergreen rhododendrons to bloom, appearing a full two weeks before the flowers of most Catawba hybrids. Some of the older varieties are "Venustum," "Nobleanum" and "Boule de Neige."

Many other evergreen species have been crossed and have resulted in progeny which can grow in the milder areas of the United States. The few hybrid groups mentioned are perhaps the largest though not necessarily the most important. The possibilities of making crosses in this large group of plants is almost limitless, and if increased hardiness is one of the objectives (*i.e.*, to produce varieties hardy in the northern United States) then there are many opportunities yet waiting for some enterprising plant breeder to explore.

Meritorious Azaleas and Rhododendrons

The following azaleas and rhododendrons should not be considered "the best" by any manner of means. Others have proved just as good and still others may prove better. Groups like the "Belgian Forcing," "Rutherfordiana" "Macrantha Hybrids," "Sander Azaleas" and the recent "Glenn Dale Hybrids" (now being planted in large numbers in the National Arboretum at Washington, D. C.) all have an important place in American horticulture. However, the ones selected have all been grown successfully in this country and are among the best now being grown. They are all worthy subjects for the garden. The amateur or new professional gardener would do well to confine his first selections to this list. As he becomes more interested and more experienced in the group he may have the patience, knowledge, time, space and money to experiment with the hundreds of others which are also available. (In many cases the flowers of these species and varieties of azaleas and rhododendrons have been matched with the colors of the Horticultural Colour Chart, to which many of the color names and figures in parentheses refer.)

Rhododendron albrechti   4½'   Zone 5   Albrecht Azalea

*FLOWERS: rose bengal (25/2), 2" in diameter
    TIME: mid-May
AUTUMN COLOR: yellow
HABITAT: Japan
INTRODUCED: 1892

A very interesting azalea, not yet commonly grown, with flowers a unique red to rose color, without any of the lilac or purple-red that is common in so many of the earlier blooming species.

Rhododendron arborescens   9'   Zone 4   Sweet Azalea

*FLOWERS: white, very fragrant
    TIME: mid-June
FOLIAGE: bright green
AUTUMN COLOR: dark glossy red
HABITAT: southern Pennsylvania to Georgia, chiefly in mountains

An unusually fragrant species, blooming near the end of the azalea sequence. Even though the flowers do appear after the leaves, they are conspicuous and their delicious fragrance makes them useful in mass plantings.

Rhododendron atlanticum   1½′   Zone 6   Coast Azalea

*FLOWERS: white, flushed crimson, 1½″ diameter, very fragrant
    TIME: late May
HABITAT: Delaware to South Carolina
    One of the few azaleas that are stoloniferous, used to some extent in nat-
uralistic plantings for its very fragrant flowers.

Rhododendron calendulaceum   9′ rarely 15′   Zone 5   Flame Azalea

* FLOWERS: yellow or orange to scarlet
    TIME: early June
HABITAT: Pennsylvania to Georgia, west to Ohio and Kentucky
VARIETIES:
    croceum—flowers 2″ diameter, orange buff to cadmium orange
    aurantiacum—flowers 2⅛″ diameter, orange to scarlet
    This is the most showy of the native American species and is among the
best for northern gardens. It has the unique property of retaining its colorful
flowers in good condition in full sun for nearly two full weeks. The flowers of
many Asiatic azaleas quickly fade in direct sun and so must be used with partial
shade if they are to be enjoyed for a longer period. When large numbers of
seedlings are grown it is noticed that the flower colors vary from yellow (orange
buff 507 to cadmium orange 8) to scarlet (19). The lighter colored forms have
been given the varietal name *croceum,* and the red-colored types the varietal
name *aurantiacum.* Since very few azaleas are in flower at the time this species
blooms, this variation in color is most helpful in making an interesting display—
when planted singly and in groups in an open oak woods, there is nothing at this
time of year that is more colorful.

Rhododendron canadense   3′   Zone 2   Rhodora

*FLOWERS: rose-purple
    TIME: mid-May
FOLIAGE: dull bluish green
HABITAT: Newfoundland and Labrador to central New York and Pennsylvania
VARIETY: *albiflorum*—white flowers
    Native of New England, commonly found in moist places, it is valued for its
early flowers (before the leaves appear) especially in naturalistic plantings. Its
flowers are smaller than those of many Asiatic and American species and from
the standpoint of massive display when in bloom, it is inferior to many species.
However, when planted by itself in bog gardens or a moist part of the rockery, it
can easily earn its space for its early spring interest.

Rhododendron carolinianum   6′   Zone 5   Carolina Rhododendron

*FLOWERS: pale rosy purple
    TIME: mid-May
*FOLIAGE: evergreen, leaves brown on underside to 3″ long
HABITAT: North Carolina
VARIETY: *album*—flowers white or nearly white
    The first of the northern evergreen rhododendrons to bloom, this little species
makes a splendid showing. When grown from seed, the plants will range in flower

Catawba hybrid rhododendrons have flowers ranging in color from white through pink and red to purple, and are frequently well displayed when massed together in a bank planting.

color from pure white to a deep rose—excellent for use in any garden. Plants of this species are compact in habit, generally rounded in outline and good as individual specimens or when planted together in masses. In winter it is the first rhododendron to "roll" its leaves when temperatures reach about 15° F. and lower, a natural method of protection from severe cold but detracting somewhat from its beauty.

Rhododendron catawbiense 6′ rarely to 18′ Zone 4 Catawba Rhododendron

*FLOWERS: lilac-purple spotted olive-green
    TIME: early June
*FOLIAGE: evergreen, leaves to 5″ long
HABITAT: Virginia to Georgia
VARIETIES:
    album—flowers white, 2¼″ diameter with yellow markings
    compactum—dense, compact habit of growth
    The Catawba Rhododendron is a spreading evergreen shrub, usually about 6′ tall, which grows extensively in the southern Allegheny Mountains. The flowers are profusely borne and frequently clothe the entire plant with color, since they appear before the new leaves are fully developed. The only point which can be mentioned against it is that its lavender-colored flowers are not all that might be wished for. However, the variety *album*, with white flowers, can be con-

sidered one of the best of all the rhododendrons for garden ornament. Also this species has been considerably used in hybridizing so that many garden hybrids are available, having the excellent foliage characteristics of *R. catawbiense,* and the better flower colors of other parents.

Catawbiense Hybrids (see page 253)   (hardy in Boston)

"Albert"—flowers pure white to pastel lilac (437/2), brown markings, 3″ dia.

"Album Grandiflorum"—flowers white with faint lavender tinge, 2⅜″ diameter.

"Arno"—flowers double, white inside petals and mallow-purple edge, purple markings, 3⅜″ diameter.

"Atrosanguineum"—flowers spiraea-red (025/1), purplish markings, 2⅜″ diameter.

"Charles Dickens"—flowers tyrian-purple (727/3), dark red markings, 2¼″ diameter.

"Everestianum"—flowers rosy lilac with frilled edges of petals

"F. L. Ames"—flowers fuchsia-purple (28/1–28/2), mustard-colored markings, 3¼″ diameter.

"Henrietta Sargent"—flowers persian-rose (628/1), brownish markings, 2⅜″.

"Kettledrum"—flowers magenta (27/1), yellow markings, 2⅝″ diameter.

"Lady Armstrong"—flowers fuchsine-pink (627/1), purple markings, 2½″ diameter.

"Mrs. C. S. Sargent"—flowers persian-rose (628/1), yellowish green markings, 3⅛″ diameter.

"President Lincoln"—flowers amaranth-rose (530/2), reddish orange markings, 2½″ diameter.

"Purpureum Elegans"—flowers bishop's violet (34/2), orange-brown markings, 3″ diameter.

"Purpureum Grandiflorum"—flowers imperial-purple (33/1), reddish orange markings, 2¼″ diameter.

"Roseum Elegans"—flowers fuchsia-purple (28/2), greenish markings, 2¾″ diameter.

Caucasian Hybrids (see page 254)

"Boule de Neige—flowers white, 2½″ diameter, greenish markings

"Goldsworth Yellow"—flowers apricot

"Nobleanum"—flowers scarlet

"Venustum"—flowers rose-red

Rhododendron decorum   18′   Zone 5   Sweetshell Rhododendron

*FLOWERS: white to pink
   TIME: early June
*FOLIAGE: evergreen, leaves 6–9″ long
HABITAT: western China
INTRODUCED: 1904

A rhododendron with fragrant waxy flowers, preferring light shade and some protection at the northern limits of hardiness. It is being grown in gardens on both Atlantic and Pacific coasts.

The Sweetshell Rhododendron (*R. decorum*).

Rhododendron discolor 15′ Zone 6 Mandarin Rhododendron

*FLOWERS: white to pale pink
TIME: June
*FOLIAGE: evergreen, leaves to 8″ long
HABITAT: central China
INTRODUCED: 1900

Another fragrant Chinese rhododendron which has proved popular in England, but has not been widely distributed in this country. It is closely akin to *R. fortunei*. One of its important features is its late bloom—as late as that of the native *R. maximum*.

Rhododendron fortunei 12′ Zone 6 Fortune Rhododendron

*FLOWERS: rosy lilac or blush, fragrant
TIME: late May
FOLIAGE: evergreen, light green, leaves to 8″ long
HABITAT: eastern China
INTRODUCED: 1859

This Chinese rhododendron has earned a permanent place in American horticulture. The individual flowers are as much as 3½″ or more in diameter. A few varieties are hardy as far north as Boston, but on Long Island and farther down the Eastern Seaboard and on the West Coast it is a decided asset in any rhododendron planting. The delicate colors, large size and fragrance of the flowers, make it an ideal subject for hybridization and many hybrids are available.

Fortune Rhododendron and some of its hybrids have individual flowers as much as 3½″ in diameter and have proved themselves valuable garden plants wherever they can be grown.

One, the "Duke of York," is growing perfectly at home in a protected spot at the Arnold Arboretum. It blooms just after *R. carolinianum* and just before the *R. catawbiense* hybrids, making it almost an essential if continuous rhododendron bloom is desired.

Fortunei Hybrids (see page 254)

"Duke of York"—flowers pastel lilac-pastel mauve (437/1–433/2) 3½″ diameter.
"Essex Scarlet"—flowers deep crimson
"Luscombei"—flowers rose-pink
"Ernest Gill"—flowers, rose-carmine
"Sunset"—flowers pale yellow, shaded pink
Many new seedlings originated by the late C. O. Dexter of Sandwich, Mass.

x Rhododendron gandavense   6–10′   Zone 4   Ghent Azalea

*FLOWERS: white—pink—red, single and double
    TIME: late May
HYBRID ORIGIN: *R. luteum x R. mortieri*
ORIGINATED: before 1890
    Many hybrids of mixed ancestry, some of which are hardy as far north as central Maine. A bright-colored ornamental group, some of the better varieties are:

"Altaclerense" one of many Ghent Hybrid Azaleas has flowers a rich orange-yellow.

Flowers Single

"Altaclerense"—orange-yellow

"Beaute Celeste"—scarlet

"Bijou des Amateurs"—dawn-pink (523)

"Charlemagne"—Chinese coral (614) to orange (12), prominent stamens—flowers 2″ diameter

"Coccinea Speciosa"—saturn red (13–13/1) filaments red, flowers 1⅝″ diameter

"Comte de Flandre"—carmine (21)

"Cymodece"—dawn-pink (523) with orange markings, flowers 2½″ dia.

"Daviesi"—white, blotched yellow

"Flamboyant"—orange

"Furst Camille von Rohan"—bud chrome-yellow; flowers white with yellow markings, flowers 2⅜″ diameter

"General Trauff"—rose-shaded orange

"Gloria Mundi"—fire-red (15/1) upper petal orpement-orange, flower 2″ diameter

"Heureuse Surprise"—white, shaded rose

"Irene Koster"—dawn-pink (523/1–523/3) with prominent yellow markings

"Nancy Waterer"—yellow

"Pallas"—jasper-red (18–18/2) with markings of Indian yellow on upper corolla, flower 1¾″ diameter

"Pucelle"—neyron-rose (623/3) with cadmium-orange markings, flowers 2"
   diameter
"Unique"—bronze

Flowers Double

"Bijou de Gentbrugge"—white, flushed pink
"Graf von Meran"—neyron-rose (623/3) and white in center
"Narcissiflora"—sulfur-yellow (1)
"Raphael de Smet"—white, flushed pink
"Souv. de Pres. Carnot"—cadmium-orange (8–8/2) and brick-red (016)
   flowers 1½" diameter

Rhododendron griffithianum Hybrids (see page 254)

"Beauty of Littleworth"—flowers white
"Coombe Royal"—delicate pink flowers
"Countess of Derby"—rose-pink flowers
"Gill's Crimson"—crimson flowers
"Isabella Mangles"—soft pink flowers
"Loderi"—white or shell-pink in several shades
"Queen o' the May"—white flowers

Rhododendron indicum   6'   Zone 6   Indian Azalea

*FLOWERS: red to scarlet, 2–3" diameter
   TIME: late June
FOLIAGE: evergreen, leaves to 1½" long
HABITAT: Japan
INTRODUCED: 1680
VARIETY: *balsaminaeflorum*—dwarf, flowers double, salmon-red, Balsam Azalea
   A bright red azalea from Japan and not to be confused with the so-called
Indian hybrid azaleas which actually have little of this species in them. This
species is hardier than the Indian greenhouse hybrids, and is grown out-of-doors.
It is about as hardy as *R. obtusum amoenum.*

Indian Azaleas (see page 251)

"Daphne Salmon"—flowers salmon-pink
"Fielders white"—flowers pure white
"Formosa"—flowers rose-purple
"Glory of Sunninghill"—flowers orange-scarlet
"Iveryana"—flowers white with faint rose stripes
"President Clay"—flowers orange-red
"Pride of Dorking"—flowers deep carmine
"Pride of Mobile"—flowers watermelon-pink
"Violacea Rubra"—flowers dark violet

Rhododendron japonicum   6'   Zone 5   Japanese Azalea

*FLOWERS: orange-red or salmon-red to brick-red, flowers 2–3" diameter, with
obnoxious odor
   TIME: late May
HABITAT: Japan

Of the Mollis Hybrid Azaleas, "Miss Louisa Hunnewell" is perhaps among the most popular, with rich orange-yellow flowers 3" in diameter.

INTRODUCED: 1861

An azalea that should not be in the foundation planting about the house if its obnoxious odor would be a drawback, since the odor is on a par with that of a skunk, although not so penetrating. However, it does have large flowers and is very hardy, being used considerably in breeding work because of these features. Otherwise its vigorous habit and profuse colorful flowers make it a prominent part of any garden when it is in bloom.

Rhododendron keiskei   8'   Zone 5   Keisk Rhododendron

*FLOWERS: mimosa yellow, 602/2, 1¾" diameter
    TIME: mid-May
*FOLIAGE: evergreen, leaves to 2¼" long
HABITAT: Japan
INTRODUCED: 1905

Interesting in flower because it is one of the very few evergreen rhododendrons with flowers of this delightfully pale yellow color. It might well be used in breeding work.

x Rhododendron kosterianum   5'   Zone 5   Mollis Hybrid Azaleas

*FLOWERS: large, yellow to red with many combinations
    TIME: late May
HYBRID ORIGIN: *R. molle* x *R. japonicum*
ORIGINATED: 1872

Mostly crosses between the Chinese *R. molle* (yellow) and the Japanese *R. japonicum* (red to yellow) but recently other mixed parentage has crept in. These hybrids are not as hardy as the Ghent hybrids because of the tender *R. molle* as one of the parents, and hence the varieties (except "Miss Louisa Hunnewell") are not much used. "Miss Louisa Hunnewell" if propagated asexually is an excellent hybrid. A few of the better varieties are:

"C. B. Van Nes"—flowers, fire-red
"Comte de Gomer"—flowers, soft red
"Comte de Papadopoli"—flowers rose, shaded orange
"Comtesse de Kerchove"—flowers pale pink or orange
"Consul Ceresole"—flowers porcelain-rose (620/1); 3½" diameter
"Hugo Koster"—flowers poppy-red (16/2) with orange markings; 2¾" diameter
"Miss Louisa Hunnewell"—flowers orange-yellow (7); 3" diameter
"Otto Lilienthal"—flowers ivory-white
"Phidias"—flowers double, light pink and yellow
"Snowdrift"—flowers white

x Rhododendron laetevirens   4'   Zone 4   Wilson Rhododendron

*FLOWERS: pink to purplish, 1" diameter
TIME: early June
*FOLIAGE: evergreen, light green, leaves to 3½" long
HYBRID ORIGIN: *R. carolinianum* x *R. ferrugineum*

A small-flowered, comparatively low-growing rhododendron that cannot compare favorably with the large-flowering types, but for a neat, small evergreen plant in the foundation planting, or in a partly shaded spot in the rock garden, it has merit.

Rhododendron lapponicum   1½'   Zone 2   Lapland Rhododendron

FLOWERS: purple, ½" diameter, bell-shaped
TIME: June
FOLIAGE: evergreen, leaves to ¾" long
HABITAT: mountains of North America, northern Europe, northern Asia

A prostrate shrub of very fine texture, well suited for a place in the rock garden or in the foreground of an ericaceous evergreen foundation planting.

Rhododendron macrophyllum   9'   Zone 6   California Rhododendron

*FLOWERS: pale rose to purplish
TIME: early June
FOLIAGE: evergreen, leaves to 6" long
HABITAT: Pacific Coast

This species is the western counterpart of the eastern *R. catawbiense*. Unfortunately it is not reliably hardy on the east coast north of Philadelphia but on the mountains and in the gardens along the Pacific Coast it is a common and much appreciated evergreen shrub. *R. macrophyllum* has been incorrectly termed *R. californicum*.

Rhododendron maximum   12–36′   Zone 3   Rosebay Rhododendron

FLOWERS: rose-colored to purple-pink, spotted olive-green to orange
    TIME: late June
*FOLIAGE: dark green, evergreen, leaves 5–10″ long
HABITAT: eastern North America
VARIETIES:
    album—flowers white
    purpureum—flowers deep pink to purple

This native species is perhaps the hardiest of all the evergreen rhododendrons, and certainly the tallest and most treelike of those hardy in the North. Its flowers are not as large as those of *R. catawbiense* but are free of the objectionable magenta color. They appear after the leaves of the current year's growth are well expanded. This new foliage hides the flower clusters to a considerable degree. The Rosebay Rhododendron then, is of value for its hardiness, for its tall habit of growth, for its long leaves, but when flowers alone are considered, there are many species and hybrids far more satisfactory. It requires semi-shade to do well and is frequently used in gardens in the northern United States merely as an evergreen background for more ornamental plantings.

Rhododendron maximum hybrids (see page 254)

    "Cunningham's White"—flowers white (*R. maximum x R. cinnamomeum*)
    "Album elegans"—flowers white, 2¾″ diameter
    "Anna L. Lamb"—mallow-purple flowers (630/2) 3½″ diameter
    "Wellesleyanum"—flowers white, tinged pink (*R. maximum x R. catawbiense*)

Rhododendron mucronatum   6′ rarely 9′   Zone 5   Snow Azalea

*FLOWERS: white, 2″ in diameter, fragrant
    TIME: early May
FOLIAGE: much branched, evergreen or half evergreen, but a poor grayish green color
HABITAT: Japan
INTRODUCED: 1819
VARIETIES:
    amethystinum—flowers pale lilac-purple spotted faintly pink
    narcissiflorum—flowers white, double, introduced about 1850
    plenum—flowers rose-purple, double, introduced 1819

The Snow Azalea is the hardiest white-flowered evergreen azalea, but only from Long Island south is it a serviceable and dependable plant. Its large white blossoms, and usually low habit of growth make it an excellent species to use in conjunction with the more brilliant Kurume types. The more or less grayish green foliage is not conducive to making the plant ornamental for its evergreen foliage alone. The varieties are useful for their bright-colored blossoms.

Rhododendron mucronulatum   6′   Zone 4   Korean Rhododendron

*FLOWERS: pale rosy purple
    TIME: mid-April
AUTUMN COLOR: yellow to bronzy crimson
HABITAT: north China, Manchuria, Korea, Japan
INTRODUCED: 1882

To many a gardener this appears to be an early flowering azalea, but actually it is one of the very few deciduous rhododendrons. The difference is merely academic for it is the first of all the rhododendrons and azaleas to bloom, commencing in New England during mid-April, but in Seattle often as early as the latter part of January. Because it blooms so early, the flowers may be killed by freezing weather, hence it might well be planted on a northern slope or some shaded spot where warm sun does not force the flowers to open prematurely. This earliness of blossom is enjoyed in some areas, but in others where late freezes are characteristic it might be inadvisable to plant this species. Local conditions in early spring or late winter, then, should be the deciding factor as to whether or not this species is used.

Rhododendron nudiflorum   6'   Zone 3   Pinxterbloom

*FLOWERS: light pink (phlox-pink 625/3), white before leaves, 1½" diameter
    TIME: late May
HABITAT: Massachusetts to North Carolina to Ohio

A native azalea—often called "Wild Honeysuckle" found over a large part of the eastern United States. A closely related species R. *roseum* has flowers that are more deeply colored.

Rhododendron obtusum   3'   Zone 6   Hiryu Azalea

*FLOWERS: orange-red to bright red, varying considerably
    TIME: mid-May
FOLIAGE: much branched, half evergreen to evergreen, leaves ½–1" long
AUTUMN COLOR: reddish
HABITAT: Japan
INTRODUCED: about 1844

This azalea, sometimes prostrate, is not a meritorious ornamental in its own right, but is of interest for its many and valuable ornamental varieties, of which the following are examples:

    amoenum—flowers double (hose in hose) rich magenta

        Introduced 1850, Zone 5, the flower color is very difficult to use in combination with others. The leaves are slightly less than an inch long.

    arnoldianum—flowers single, phlox-pink 625/1, Zone 4—A cross, *amoenum x kaempferi,* it is similar to *amoenum* except that it grows taller and is hardier. The flowers too are a better color, being a rich, rosy mauve to red. It originated as a chance seedling in the Arnold Arboretum in 1910 and now there are several named clons of this cross that have been distributed in the trade, chiefly dark red (crimson 22/1 to magenta 27/2) flowers 1½" diameter.

    "Hinodegiri"—flowers rose-madder 23/7, Zones 5–6. Not as hardy as *amoenum* but a much better crimson color, flower 1⅜" diameter. The foliage of both plants is superior to that of R. *mucronatum.* In fact, *amoenum* is used extensively as a clipped hedge for its small leaves and dense twiggy growth make it just right for this purpose.

    kaempferi—flowers single, porcelain-rose 620, 2⅜" diameter. Zone 5—Torch Azalea. The Torch Azalea is the common mountain azalea of Japan. Although it has been known for a very long time, it first appeared in the United States when Professor Sargent brought seeds to the Arnold Arboretum in 1892. Since

Ernest H. Wilson took this picture of Kurume azaleas in Japan in the town of Kurume (Kyushu) where this popular group of azaleas was originally developed. These have been pruned according to Japanese custom for display purposes.

that time it has grown splendidly and has proved to be the best bright red azalea for northern gardens. The Arnold Arboretum now has hundreds of these plants on its hillsides and, when in bloom, they make a better display than any other azalea. In places the woods look almost as if they were afire, the color is so vivid. Because the flowers may be injured by the hot sun, it is advisable to plant them in slightly shaded places, and they do well in heavy shade. Some of the plants are considerably over 5′ tall and may eventually attain a height of 10′ to 12′ with a correspondingly broad spread.

In New England the plants are partly deciduous, but farther south the leaves of *R. obtusum* varieties (except variety *kaempferi* which is wholly deciduous) are retained throughout the winter. The flowers of variety *kaempferi* range in color from salmon to a brick-red.

Kurume Azaleas—Zones 6–9 (see page 251)

The Japanese have developed and crossed the varieties of this species for centuries so that the general term "Kurume Azaleas" includes a large number of forms, which are greenhouse plants but many of which can be grown out of doors with some protection as far north as New York City. Possibly 50 named varieties are being grown in this country today. Some of the better varieties are:

"Apple Blossom"—flowers white, tinged pink

"Benigiri"—flowers deep red

"Christmas Cheer"—flowers brilliant red, double
"Coral Bells"—flowers shell-pink, shaded, double
"Daybreak"—flowers deep rose
"Fairy"—flowers almond-blossom pink
"Orange Beauty"—flowers orange to pink
"Peach Blossom"—flowers rose
"Pink Pearl"—flowers deep pink, double
"Prudence"—flowers white
"Salmon Beauty"—flowers salmon-pink, double
"Snowflake"—flowers white, double
"Sunbeam"—flowers salmon
"Vesuvius"—flowers brilliant salmon-red

Rhododendron occidentale   9'   Zone 6–7   Western Azalea

*FLOWERS: white or pinkish, yellow blotch, 1½–2" diameter
  TIME: late May
AUTUMN COLOR: scarlet and yellow
HABITAT: Oregon, California
  A handsome native of the Pacific Coast with showy flowers, popular in
Pacific Coast gardens. The species varies somewhat both in color and time of
bloom so that selections of the better forms are to be recommended.

Rhododendron prunifolium   8'   Zone 7

FLOWERS: crimson
  TIME: July
HABITAT: Georgia to Alabama
INTRODUCED: 1918
  One of the most conspicuous of the native azaleas when in flower.

Rhododendron racemosum   2–6'   Zone 5   Mayflower Rhododendron

*FLOWERS: numerous few-flowered clusters, rhodamine pink (587), flowers ¾"
diameter
  TIME: mid-May
*FOLIAGE: evergreen, leaves to 1½" long
HABITAT: western China
INTRODUCED: 1889
  A delightful early-flowering rhododendron with small numerous clusters of
flowers especially adapted for planting in the rockery or some similar spot where
a light winter cover can be given if necessary. A splendid shrub for massing,
probably even better when used this way than when used as an individual specimen.

Rhododendron roseum   9'   Zone 3   Roseshell Azalea

*FLOWERS: fragrant, corolla, bright pink (neyron-rose 623/1) 2" in diameter
  TIME: late May
FOLIAGE: dull bluish green

The Royal Azalea from Japan, one of the few azaleas with good autumn foliage coloration in the fall.

HABITAT: northeastern North America

A bright-colored native species with fragrant flowers, for many years considered a form of *R. nudiflorum*. Because of its color and fragrance (the flowers of *R. nudiflorum* are odorless) this species can be considered superior.

Rhododendron schlippenbachi 15' Zone 4 Royal Azalea

*FLOWERS: fragrant, rose pink (427/1 to 427/3), 3" in diameter
    TIME: mid-May
*AUTUMN COLOR: yellow, orange and crimson
HABITAT: Korea, Manchuria, Japan
INTRODUCED: 1893

A handsome azalea because of its good growth habits and general appearance. It has very large flowers and is fortunate in being in the group with colorful autumn foliage. These are two important reasons for including it in the garden.

Rhododendron smirnowi 6–18' Zone 4 Smirnow Rhododendron

*FLOWERS: many, corolla white to rosy red
    TIME: late May
*FOLIAGE: evergreen, leaves to 6" long
HABITAT: Caucasus

The Smirnow Rhododendron is not only beautiful in flower but resistant to the attacks of the lace bug because of the extremely woolly undersurface of the leaves. Hence it is well adapted to small gardens where spraying individual plants presents an unwanted chore.

INTRODUCED: 1886

Perfectly hardy as far north as Boston, this dense rhododendron makes a good ornamental not only for its large flowers but also because the undersurfaces of the leaves are covered with a conspicuous white, woolly tomentum that adds to its attractiveness. Because of this woolly undersurface, the plant is not infested with lace bug—an important maintenance item. Sometimes the flowers have corollas with a wavy margin which is another desirable characteristic. All in all this species, though little used yet in American gardens, can well be added to an ever lengthening list of worthy rhododendrons.

Rhododendron vaseyi   6–9'   Zone 4   Pinkshell Azalea

*FLOWERS: light rose
  TIME: mid-May
*AUTUMN COLOR: light red
HABITAT: North Carolina
VARIETY: *album*—flowers white

This native azalea is one of a very few with colorful autumn foliage in the fall, hence it has two seasons of interest in gardens. It does well in moist situations bordering ponds where its delicate pink flowers can be reflected in the water, or it will do well on drier soils. One of the best of the native azaleas.

Rhododendron viscosum   9′ rarely 15′   Zone 3   Swamp Azalea

*FLOWERS: corolla white or suffused with pink, very fragrant
    TIME: early July
AUTUMN COLOR: orange to bronze
HABITAT: Maine to South Carolina

The last of the azaleas to bloom, the Swamp Azalea is particularly at home in swampy situations, where its white fragrant flowers scent the air for some distance.

Rhododendron yedoense   5′   Zone 5   Yodogawa Azalea

*FLOWERS: spotted, cyclamen purple 30/2, 2″ diameter, double, 12 petals
    TIME: mid-May
FOLIAGE: dark green
AUTUMN COLOR: purplish
HABITAT: Korea and Japan
INTRODUCED: 1884
VARIETY: *poukhanense*—compact low shrub, but in shady places to 6′—flowers
        single, fragrant, petunia-purple 32/2, 1⅞″ diameter, with red markings.
        Korea, introduced 1905, Zone 4—flowering freely when quite small—
        blooms mid-May.

It is interesting to note that the double-flowered species was found first and given the specific name. Twenty years later the single-flowered form was discovered and a varietal name was designated for this. Both azaleas have reddish purple flowers that are very difficult to plant adjacent to red-flowering species since the colors clash. These plants can be used in conjunction with the pale, lemon-yellow colored *Cytisus praecox* which blooms at the same time, an excellent color combination.

Both the double-flowered species and its single-flowered variety are compact shrubs, dense and comparatively low. The species appears to be the less desirable as an ornamental because the flowers are not as numerous as are those on the variety. In massed plantings, these plants grow so closely together that they cover the soil completely.

Other Evergreen Rhododendron Species

There are actually hundreds of other rhododendrons that can be grown in the warmer parts of the United States (Zones 7–10) especially in the Pacific Northwest where the growing conditions are ideal and the summers are not too hot. At least 150 different species have already been brought into flower by an enthusiastic and energetic group of rhododendron growers in Oregon and Washington. It is not the object of this book to concentrate too much on any one group of plants, hence extensive notes on additional rhododendrons are out of place. However, for those who are interested and who have gardens in Zones 7–9 where the summer climate is neither too hot nor too dry, the following list of evergreen rhododendrons comprises a few which have been grown successfully and admired in those areas in addition to the many species and varieties already mentioned:

NAME	FLOWER COLOR	TIME OF BLOOM	HEIGHT
augustini	blue, lavender	April	18'
auriculatum	white	July, August	20'
calostrotum	rose	April	1'
campylocarpum	canary-yellow	April	8'
ciliatum	pale pink	March	3'
cinnabarinum	red	May	6'
chryseum	light yellow	April	2½'
decorum	white or shell-pink	April	18'
discolor	pink	June	15'
falconeri	creamy white to yellow	May	40'
fastigiatum	light purple	May	3'
forresti	crimson	April	1½'
griersonianum	brick-red	May	8'
heliolepsis	rose-purple	June	25'
hippophaeoides	lavender	April	3'
intricatum	lavender	April	1½'
lutescens	lemon-yellow	March	6'
moupinense	white, pink	February	3'
pemakoense	pink	March	1'
ponticum	purple	May, June	9'
radicans	purple	May	4"
rubiginosum	rose	April	30'
thomsoni	red	April	5'
williamsianum	pink	April	5'
yunnanense	pink	May	6'

Rhodotypos scandens   6'   Zone 5   Jetbead

FLOWERS: white, single, 2" diameter
    TIME: mid-May
*FRUIT: hard, shiny black berries
    EFFECTIVE: fall and winter
HABITAT: Japan and China
INTRODUCED: 1866

With white flowers of four petals and shiny black fruits remaining on the plant all winter, the Jetbead is often used in foreground plantings. It is comparatively low, faces the ground well and is one of the general-purpose shrubs which usually can be worked into any shrub border.

RHUS

The sumacs are native over a wide area of North America but do not compare favorably with other outstanding ornamental woody plants. They are chiefly valued for their fall interest, their bright red spikelike fruits and their brilliant (usually red) autumn color. They do remarkably well on dry soil, another important point in their favor. For this reason, and because they are very much a part of the roadside picture over great expanses of

America, they should not be discarded altogether. They should be used with discretion, and selected only when other plants have been considered but for some reason fail to suit the situation.

The sumac range in height from the tall-growing Staghorn Sumac (sometimes 30′) to the low-growing Fragrant Sumac (*Rhus aromatica*) seldom over 3′ high. This low species is well suited for massing along roads or walks, where its bright red fruits in small clusters appear in late summer. Its autumn foliage is a brilliant scarlet and, because of its procumbent habit of growth, can easily be cut and restrained.

It is sometimes noted that the sumacs do not fruit. This is because some plants have only pistillate flowers, others only staminate. There are plants with both kinds of flowers on the same plant and it is these that the nurseryman should propagate by asexual means. Frequently this is not done and the plants are grown from seed. Gardeners who buy such sumacs may be disappointed, for it is obvious that some of the plants propagated by seed will never bear any fruit.

The Smooth Sumac (*R. glabra*) is lower in growth than *R. typhina*. Both have cut-leaved forms that are sometimes considered ornamental, but *R. glabra laciniata* is not as hardy as either of the varieties of *R. typhina*. These cut-leaved forms are not usually massed together as are most sumacs but are used as individual specimens. It should be remembered that sumacs are short-lived plants, especially when grown with single trunks. Their wood is very weak and brittle, hence the larger the specimen, the more susceptible it is to damage from wind, snow and ice. Once a large branch is broken off, disease quickly sets in so that cut-leaved specimens, although very interesting for a time, quickly become permanently disfigured. Many plantsmen do not use them for this reason. Sometimes it is advisable to cut them nearly to the ground to keep them from growing too large and to keep the wood in vigorous condition.

The species is satisfactory in naturalized plantings, for they are best grown in groups. One exception might possibly be the Shiny Sumac (*R. copallina*), ornamental because of its lustrous dark green leaves. The fruits of this plant are not as striking as those of the others, but as a foliage specimen, where glossiness of leaves is an interesting feature, this species is the best in this genus. Its vivid, glossy-red fall color is probably the most striking autumn color of all the sumacs.

One other species worthy of note is the Chinese Sumac, *R. chinensis*, frequently planted under the name of *R. javanica*. This is the only sumac with really conspicuous flowers, small but in large, creamy white spikes almost a foot long, in early summer. Shrubs that flower at this time are scarce, the only reason for including this species.

It is common knowledge that several of the sumacs such as Poison Ivy and the Varnish Tree, are poisonous to the touch of many individuals, which is sufficient reason why they should not be planted.

Rhus aromatica   3'   **Zone 3**   **Fragrant Sumac**

FLOWERS: yellowish, small
    TIME: early May
FRUIT: red, small, berrylike
    EFFECTIVE: summer
*AUTUMN COLOR: yellow and scarlet
HABITAT: eastern United States

An excellent shrub which can be used in front of taller plants or on banks where its rapid growth (underground) and dense foliage quickly cover the soil. Its colorful early scarlet fruits and scarlet autumn coloring make it a valued ornamental. However, it might well be omitted from planting in dusty situations for its pubescent foliage retains the dust and makes it unsightly under certain conditions.

Rhus chinensis (javanica)   24'   **Zone 5**   **Chinese Sumac**

*FLOWERS: creamy white, small, pyramidal spikes, 8–10" long
    TIME: August
FRUIT: orange-red
    EFFECTIVE: fall
*AUTUMN COLOR: orange-red
HABITAT: China and Japan
INTRODUCED: 1784

Only of value for its large clusters of creamy white flowers in mid-summer at a time when few other woody plants are in flower, otherwise it might as well be omitted from further consideration.

Rhus copallina   30'   **Zone 4**   **Shining Sumac**

FLOWERS: greenish, small, in pyramidal spikes, 4–8" long
    TIME: early August
FRUIT: crimson (sexes separate)
    EFFECTIVE: fall and winter
*FOLIAGE: lustrous green
*AUTUMN COLOR: scarlet
HABITAT: eastern United States

One of the few sumacs which can be used as a single specimen if necessary, particularly on account of its lustrous deep green leaves and scarlet autumn color. It will do well on dry soil and on slopes, and might be used occasionally on the small property. One of the most ornamental sumacs. This and R. *chinensis* are the only sumacs with a winged mid-rib in the leaf, a simple item to remember in identifying them.

Rhus glabra   15–25'   **Zone 2**   **Smooth Sumac**

FLOWERS: greenish, small in pyramidal spikes, 4–10" long
    TIME: early July
*FRUIT: scarlet (sexes separate)
    EFFECTIVE: fall and winter
*AUTUMN COLOR: bright red
HABITAT: eastern United States

VARIETIES:

flavescens—yellow fruit, leaves turning yellow in the fall

laciniata—leaflets deeply divided

The Smooth Sumac makes an excellent plant for mass planting, hardy in the far north but not suitable as a screen or on small properties. There are some staminate flowering plants which will never fruit. If fruit is desired a special effort should be made to obtain plants asexually propagated from pistillate plants. The dried ripe fruit is occasionally employed as an astringent in gargles.

Rhus typhina   30'   Zone 3   Staghorn Sumac

FLOWERS: greenish, small in pyramidal spikes, 4–8" long

TIME: late June

*FRUIT: crimson, small (sexes separate)

EFFECTIVE: fall and winter

*AUTUMN COLOR: red

HABITAT: eastern United States

VARIETIES:

laciniata—leaflets deeply divided

dissecta—leaflets even more deeply cut than the above variety

It should be pointed out that there are some plants of this species (especially when grown from seed) that have staminate flowers only and hence will never bear fruits. The Staghorn Sumac, so named because its very fuzzy twigs are comparable to the young antlers of the deer, can be used in very dry soils and still be expected to do well. It is good for massing, makes a poor specimen and should not be given the space in a small garden. It does not make a good screen, but in a group or on poor dry soil, it can easily outshine almost every other shrub especially in the fall with its autumn color and all winter long with its colorful, pyramidal fruit clusters. When it is allowed to grow in clumps, the oldest and tallest plant should be in the center with progressively smaller plants all around the edges of the clump.

RIBES

Most of the plants in this genus, especially *Ribes nigrum*, serve as the alternate hosts for the destructive disease of five needled pines, the white pine blister rust. The most effective way of controlling the disease is to eliminate the *Ribes* from areas where the five needled pines are grown. There are at least 15 species of pines susceptible to this disease. Twenty-five of the states from Maine to California and from Washington to Georgia have been designated as "control areas" by the United States Department of Agriculture. Movement in these states or into them of any *Ribes* species is either forbidden or permitted only by severely stringent regulations. This creates such a confusing situation that many nurserymen, especially those with many out-of-state sales, simply do not want to be bothered with such complicated regulations and discard all their *Ribes* instead. As ornamentals, only a few of the *Ribes* are of value. Hence it may be well to exclude them from most gardens, especially in the following states: California, Connecticut, Delaware, Georgia, Idaho, Maine, Maryland, Massachusetts, Michigan,

Minnesota, Montana, New Hampshire, New Jersey, New York, North Carolina, Ohio, Oregon, Pennsylvania, Rhode Island, Tennessee, Vermont, Virginia, Washington, West Virginia, and Wisconsin.

Ribes alpinum   7½'   Zone 2   Alpine Currant

FLOWERS: greenish yellow, almost inconspicuous
    TIME: early May
FRUIT: scarlet berries (sexes separate)
    EFFECTIVE: late summer
*FOLIAGE: dark green, fine texture
HABITAT: Europe
INTRODUCED: 1588

An attractive foliage shrub, especially adaptable for hedge making. The
staminate form has been proved immune to the white pine blister rust, but U. S.
Department of Agriculture regulations list this with the susceptible species regardless. It makes a densely compact, upright low shrub, ideal as a hedge. Like
most other *Ribes* species its leaves appear very early in the season.

Ribes odoratum   6'   Zone 4   Clove Currant

*FLOWERS: petals reddish to yellow, fragrant
    TIME: early May
FRUIT: black berries (sexes separate)
    EFFECTIVE: late summer
AUTUMN COLOR: scarlet
HABITAT: east of Rocky Mountains, South Dakota to west Texas, east to Minnesota,
Arkansas

A popular old-fashioned favorite often seen in old gardens. Like the other
members of this genus, its leaves appear early in spring. Its aromatic yellow flowers simply cover the bush when they are open and its scarlet autumn color makes
it effective in the fall, especially if it is placed with a western exposure. However, it, too, is an alternate host for the white pine blister rust (see under *Ribes*).

Ribes sanguineum   12'   Zone 5   Winter Currant

*FLOWERS: red in small clusters
    TIME: mid-May
FRUIT: bluish black berries (sexes separate)
    EFFECTIVE: late summer
FOLIAGE: dark green
HABITAT: British Columbia to northern California

Native of the Pacific Coast this is a popular spring-flowering shrub which is
freely grown in many gardens there (see note under *Ribes*).

Robinia hispida   3'   Zone 5   Rose-Acacia

*FLOWERS: rose or pale purple, in clusters similar in size and shape to the flow-
ers of Wisteria
    TIME: early June
FRUITS: pods covered with conspicuous red hairs
    EFFECTIVE: late summer
HABITAT: Virginia and Kentucky to Georgia and Alabama

A popular native but because of its stoloniferous habit of growing it can become a vicious pest. This low shrub produces beautiful pendulous clusters of pink blossoms in the late spring. Its stout stems are covered with bright red bristles which add to its general color. However, it is one of the many shrubs of value only for the two-week period it is in bloom. For dry soils, and for planting on banks, for retaining the soils it has its merits, but it always needs plenty of space and no near-neighbors.

Robinia kelseyi	9'	Zone 5	Kelsey Locust

*FLOWERS: rose-colored in pendulous clusters
    TIME: late May
FRUIT: pods covered with red hairs
    EFFECTIVE: late summer
HABITAT: North Carolina

A handsome and graceful shrub, possibly more ornamental than *R. hispida* because the fruits are produced in large numbers. These are covered with bright red bristly hairs. The suckering species of *Robinia* are not troubled with borers nearly as much as are the tree species.

ROSA

Probably the most popular garden plant in the world is the rose and it may always have been through the centuries. Men have spent lifetimes with its hybridization; hundreds of volumes have been written about it and even today many business concerns throughout the length and breadth of the land are devoted solely to growing roses. Societies have been formed to study the rose and its use, entire periodicals are devoted to information about it. One of the most recent books on the subject contains the descriptions of 5284 varieties. Many rose species have contributed to the long list of hybrid teas, hybrid perpetuals, polyanthas and ramblers that we have today, and years of painstaking effort have been spent through the centuries in rose breeding, making the many fine varieties available today from modern commercial sources. Even now, nearly a hundred new rose varieties appear annually in this country alone.

Since rose culture is a science in itself, and since many reference works on the subject are easily available in every good library, the popular hybrid varieties will not be further discussed here. They form an important part of almost every garden, but to grow them properly one should carefully review this important literature.

There is a large group of roses which have not been as widely grown as they might, the native or wild roses of the world. It is these which I would like to discuss, since their culture takes less time, their requirements are not as demanding, and insect and disease problems do not appear to be as important as for more popular hybrids. There are species which could well be used in almost every garden and attention is here called to some of the more important for use in modern landscaping, and reasons why they should be grown.

The number of rose species has been a much debated point for many years. In 1892 Gandoger recognized 4266 species, while a few years before Bentham and Hooker recognized only 30—a rather striking difference of opinion! Professor Alfred Rehder suggests that there are probably between 150 to 200 species of roses in the temperate and subtropical regions of the northern hemisphere. On the basis of this estimate, it is of interest to note that over one-half of these are in the living collections at the Arnold Arboretum, and that one nursery has recently listed 93 species and botanical varieties in the form of two-year-old, field-grown plants.

In the first place, as these are the wild roses of the world, they are entitled to a place in any wild garden, in the woodlands or at the border of roadways and woods. Every wild garden typical of eastern North America should have at least one plant of the beautiful Virginia Rose which is so prominent along our eastern seacoast. Many species have been in cultivation for a long time. Centuries ago, before the advent of the "modern rose" it was these wild species which were grown and appreciated in gardens. The native Cabbage Rose of Europe, for instance, has been grown for over two thousand years. At one time it was used a great deal in Greek garlands, and later played a prominent part in the social festivities of the Romans. Certainly such a rose, rich in historical background, might well find a place in our modern garden if for nothing else than sentiment alone!

Many of the rose species are far more hardy than the commonly grown hybrids. Gardeners living in the northern United States and Canada should remember this for it means less care and less winter protection. Also, the wild species are less susceptible to insect pests and disease troubles; and this means less dusting, spraying and pruning, important factors in keeping any garden looking its best. It is the plants which require less care that should be more commonly grown, in order to reduce maintenance drudgery.

A formal rose garden is beautiful only when the roses are in bloom. Many of the rose species, however, are valuable in the landscape because they are attractive at more than one season of the year. A species like the Virginia Rose is of interest at every season of the year—in late spring and early summer when the light pink flowers appear, all through summer because of the shining dark green leaves, in the fall with its red fruits and beautiful orange autumn color, and in the winter because the red twigs and persistent fruits are bright-colored throughout the cold season. It is such plants—those that are of interest at more than one season—that should be more commonly grown in our gardens regardless of whether they are roses or dogwoods.

Many rose species are perfectly hardy shrubs, many can be grown in the shrub border or even in foundation plantings when desirable. The hybrid varieties, so popular in formal rose gardens, cannot be so used. The species add variety and interest when planted with any group of shrubs, for their flowers, fruits and foliage, and thus contribute considerably to the general landscape. There are many other reasons why rose species should be more commonly grown, but the points above made are sufficient to start a train of thought in the right direction.

It may be well in considering these roses to mention a few groups that are of special ornamental interest, for specific reasons. It is this diversity which makes them so valuable in our gardens. In the group of 61 species and varieties recommended, the following 23 are of merit for their double or semi-double flowers and are frequently desirable in preference to the single-flowered types.

Roses with Double or Semi-double Flowers

Rosa alba incarnata

R. arnoldiana   S

R. centifolia

R. centifolia muscosa

R. chinensis minima

R. damascena

R. damascena trigintipetala

R. damascena versicolor

R. eglanteria duplex

R. foetida persiana

R. gallica officinalis

R. harisoni   S

R. l'heritierana   S

R. multiflora platyphylla

R. odorata

R. odorata ochroleuca

R. odorata pseud-indica

R. roxburghi plena

R. rugosa albo-plena

R. rugosa plena

R. spinosissima alba plena

R. spinosissima lutea plena   S

R. xanthina   S

The colors of the flowers provide an interesting range and have most of the colors of the pampered hybrid teas, although it must be admitted that the delicate shadings in the latter are not found in the species. Frequently it seems desirable to have a rose of one special color, and so the recommended varieties are grouped according to the colors of their flowers which range from pure white, through the palest of yellows (R. primula), through the yellows and pinks to the deepest of reddest purples (R. gallica officinalis).

Rose Species or Varieties with White Flowers

Rosa alba incarnata

R. canina (also light pink)

R. coriifolia froebeli

R. damascena versicolor (striped pink)

R. helenae

R. multiflora

R. odorata gigantea

R. omeiensis

R. omeiensis pteracantha

R. rugosa alba

R. rugosa albo-plena

R. spinosissima alba plena

R. spinosissima altaica

R. virginiana alba

R. wichuraiana

Rose Species or Varieties with Yellow Flowers

Rosa chinensis mutabilis (changing to red)

R. foetida

R. foetida persiana

R. hugonis

R. odorata ochroleuca

R. odorata pseud-indica

R. primula

R. spinosissima

R. spinosissima lutea

R. spinosissima lutea plena

R. xanthina

Rose Species or Varieties with Pink Flowers

Rosa canina (also white)

R. carolina

R. centifolia

R. centifolia muscosa

R. eglanteria

R. eglanteria duplex

R. gallica

R. moschata nastarana

R. multiflora cathayensis

R. multiflora platyphylla

R. odorata

R. palustris

R. pendulina

R. roxburghi

R. roxburghi plena

R. rugosa rosea

R. setigera

R. setigera serena

R. spinosissima

R. virginiana

R. virginiana lamprophylla

R. webbiana

Rose Species or Varieties with Red Flowers

Rosa amblyotis

R. arnoldiana (deep crimson)

R. chinensis minima

R. damascena (blush to red)

R. damascena trigintipetala

R. foetida bicolor

R. gallica officinalis

R. l'heritierana

R. moyesi

R. rubrifolia

R. rugosa (also white)

R. rugosa plena

The fruits, too, are of interest in the fall and winter. Some species like *Rosa pendulina* have particularly effective red fruits. Some, like *R. spinosissima* have brown to black fruits that are not especially effective, and still others—especially some of the double-flowered—have very few fruits at all. See page 279 for other species in this category.

As far as the cultural needs of the rose species are concerned, they are few indeed. Naturally they do best in a good well-drained soil. Pruning can be confined to cutting out the older branches or a general thinning, when this seems to be in order. These roses should be treated as shrubs and not pruned unless there is some specific reason for so doing. They should be allowed to grow naturally. Of course, some, like *R. roxburghi* will make neater specimens than others like *R. alba*, and such points should be known and planned for in advance. All in all, however, they need little annual attention.

As far as disease and insect pests are concerned, their requirements are not as exacting as are those of the hybrid teas and perpetuals. New materials are continually coming on the market so that the somewhat persistent rose bugs and twig borers will in time, we hope, be killed by one application of spray.

The following species are certainly among the best of the wild roses of the world and are sufficiently diverse so that the gardener has an excellent group from which to select the few for his particular needs in his particular garden.

x **Rosa alba incarnata**   6'   Zone 4   Cottage Rose

*FLOWERS: white or blush, double, 2–3" diameter

    TIME: mid-June

FRUIT: orange to scarlet, ¾" diameter
EFFECTIVE: August to November
HYBRID ORIGIN: *R. corymbifera x R. gallica*
INTRODUCED: early colonial times
There are few species of roses with double white flowers, and this is one of the best. It blooms when most of the pink species are in flower and is really of outstanding merit for this reason.

Rosa amblyotis 5' Zone 2 Kamtchatka Rose
*FLOWERS: red, 2" diameter, single
TIME: early June
FRUIT: deep red
EFFECTIVE: late summer
HABITAT: Kamtchatka
INTRODUCED: 1917
One of the hardiest of the roses recommended chiefly for gardens in the Far North.

x Rosa arnoldiana 5' Zone 4 Arnold Rose
*FLOWERS: rose-red, semi-double
TIME: mid-June
HYBRID ORIGIN: *R. rugosa x R. borboniana,* before 1914

Rosa canina 9' Zone 3 Dog Rose
FLOWERS: single, dawn pink or white, 1½–2" diameter
TIME: mid-June
*FRUIT: scarlet, ¾" long
EFFECTIVE: fall
HABITAT: Europe
INTRODUCED: early colonial times
Much used as stock for grafting and included here merely for its historical value. A vigorous shrub, it has been widely grown especially in hedge rows, in Europe. In North America there are other roses more ornamental. During World War II, the fruits of this species were diligently sought as a source for one of the scarce vitamins.

Rosa carolina 3' Zone 4 Carolina Rose
*FLOWERS: Persian-rose, single 628/2
TIME: late June
*FRUIT: red
EFFECTIVE: very early fall
HABITAT: Maine, Wisconsin, Florida, Texas, Kansas
VARIETY: *alba*—flowers white
A beautiful rose, well suited for borders and thickets. It increases by underground stems, forming dense thickets similar to those of *R. virginiana* but the foliage is not as glossy and hence it is inferior to the Virginia Rose. However, since it is found over such a large part of the United States, this rose might be included among the best—certainly among the most useful.

Rosa centifolia   6'   Zone 5   Cabbage Rose

*FLOWERS: rhodamine pink, very double, 2½" diameter, very fragrant
     TIME: mid-June
HABITAT: east Caucasus
INTRODUCED: early colonial times
VARIETY: *centifolia muscosa*—rose with the under part (pedicel) of the flower excessively glandular or "mossy"—Moss Rose

The Cabbage Rose or "Rose of a Hundred Petals" has been known to the ancients for centuries. In fact it has been mentioned in literature as early as 270 B.C. and was one of the first wild roses introduced into cultivation. Many beautiful descendants have come down through the years from this rose and its old-fashioned popular variety the Moss Rose. It is noted for its fragrance, often called the true rose fragrance, and "attar of roses" is often made from the flowers. The Dutch painters, especially, have illustrated it a great deal. A few years ago this rose was difficult to find in any garden, but now it is creeping slowly back into popularity.

Rosa chinensis minima   10"   Zone 7   Fairy Rose

*FLOWERS: rose-red, single or double, 1" in diameter
     TIME: June
HABITAT: China
R. *chinensis* variety: *mutabilis*—sulphur-yellow changing to orange and then to red, a very interesting metamorphosis

The species was one of the parents of the so-called "baby ramblers" and of interest chiefly as novelties for their diminutive characteristics.

Rosa coriifolia froebeli   9'   Zone 4   Froebel Rose

*FLOWERS: creamy white, 2½" diameter, single
     TIME: mid-June
*FRUIT: red
     EFFECTIVE: early fall
HABITAT: Europe, western Asia
INTRODUCED: 1890

Vigorous habit and profusely-produced white flowers.

Rosa damascena   6'   Zone 4   Damask Rose

*FLOWERS: blush to red, double, very fragrant, 2¾–3½" diameter
     TIME: mid-June
FRUIT: red, pulpy
     EFFECTIVE: fall
HABITAT: Asia Minor
INTRODUCED: early colonial times
VARIETIES:
     versicolor—white-striped, blotched-pink, white, partially double—York and Lancaster Rose
     trigintipetala—semi-double red flowers—one of the most important roses from which "attar of roses" is extracted in European countries

The Damask Rose has been in cultivation since the sixteenth century and probably long before that. It is one of the forerunners of the modern hybrid perpetuals, and was probably grown in Gaul by the Romans and certainly was hybridized by early European plant breeders. The variety *versicolor* is the true York and Lancaster Rose. In 1455, Henry VI of the House of Lancaster was the ruler of all England. However, the Duke of York felt that he should be ruler instead, and as a consequence a long and bitter war was started, lasting until 1485. The members of the House of Lancaster and others loyal to it selected the semi-double dark red *Rosa gallica* or French Rose as their badge. Members of the House of York selected the double white *Rosa alba* as their badge. In 1485 Henry VII of the House of Lancaster married the heiress of the House of York in order to avert further bloodshed and a short time after this, so the story goes, a new rose appeared. This new rosebush had red flowers and pure white flowers but in addition some were both red and white. This became the York and Lancaster Rose, symbolic of the union of the House of Lancaster and the House of York. (The petals of this rose are not striped as they are sometimes in the flowers of *R. gallica versicolor*.) An interesting rose with an interesting history.

Rosa eglanteria   6′   Zone 4   Sweet Brier

FLOWERS: rose, pink, single
    TIME: mid-June
*FRUIT: orange to scarlet
    EFFECTIVE: fall
*FOLIAGE: sweet-scented
HABITAT: Europe
INTRODUCED: early colonial times
VARIETY: *duplex*—flowers double, pink

One of the common roses of Europe, especially seen in the hedge rows with *R. canina*. The Sweet Brier has sweet-scented foliage, the fragrance of which is easily noted after a rain. It can be grown as an informal hedge and clipped during the very early spring. In England, it is the only native rose sufficiently popular to be classed as a common garden plant. The young shoots were cut and prepared as candy for "sweetmeats" in the olden days when home-made wines and many sorts of conserves were prepared in every household.

Rosa foetida   9′   Zone 4   Austrian Brier

*FLOWERS: deep yellow, single, 2–3″ diameter with an unpleasant odor
    TIME: early June
FRUIT: red
    EFFECTIVE: fall
VARIETIES:
    bicolor—orient-red or coppery red, single, Austrian Copper Brier
    persiana—double, deep yellow, Persian Yellow

These roses, also, have been popular among gardeners since early colonial times. The single Austrian Brier and its double-flowering variety, Persian Yellow, bloom at the same time as the conspicuously colored Austrian Copper. Few roses are as vividly colored. The colorful blooms of the species and varieties complement each other when planted together, but the odor is unpleasant.

Rosa gallica   4'   Zone 5   French Rose

*FLOWERS: very fragrant, dark red or solferino-purple, large, single
   TIME: mid-June
FRUIT: brick-red
   EFFECTIVE: fall
HABITAT: central and southern Europe, west Asia
INTRODUCED: early colonial times
VARIETY: *officinalis*—flowers double, tyrian rose—Apothecary Rose or Double French
Rose

Another forerunner of the hybrid perpetuals, this rose has been a very popular one in the past, cultivated in Europe for centuries.

x Rosa harisoni   6'   Zone 4   Harison's Yellow Rose

*FLOWERS: double, mimosa-yellow, 2" diameter
   TIME: early June
FRUIT: nearly black, not ornamental
HYBRID ORIGIN: *R. foetida x R. spinosissima*
INTRODUCED: about 1830

A common favorite in American gardens; originated in this country. Its
wealth of double yellow blooms make it conspicuous for several weeks. Its fruits
are not ornamental. An old-fashioned favorite, always reliable.

Rosa helenae   15'   Zone 5   Helen Rose

*FLOWERS: small, white, single in clusters
   TIME: early June
FRUIT: dull orange
   EFFECTIVE: fall
HABITAT: central China
INTRODUCED: 1907

Discovered in China by E. H. Wilson and named after his wife, Helen. A
profuse flowering species, with flowers slightly larger than those of *R. multiflora*.
Needs plenty of room as it sometimes grows into a sprawling mass 18' in diameter.

Rosa hugonis   7'   Zone 5   Father Hugo Rose

*FLOWERS: canary-yellow, single, 2" diameter
   TIME: late May
FRUIT: dark scarlet to blackish red
HABITAT: central China
INTRODUCED: 1899

Free flowering and early to bloom, one of the best single yellow flowering
species and very popular among gardeners. It is taller-growing and more vigorous than the Scotch roses, and has deeper yellow flowers than does the Primrose
Rose.

Rosa laevigata   15'   Zone 7   Cherokee Rose

*FLOWERS: white, fragrant, 3" diameter
   TIME: May
HABITAT: China

INTRODUCED: before 1780
    An exotic, very fragrant rose which apparently came to this country over 150 years ago and has become widely naturalized from Georgia and Florida to Texas where it has been used extensively along fence rows.

x Rosa l'heritierana   12'   Zone 4   Boursault Rose

* FLOWERS: tyrian-purple 727/1, double or semi-double, 1½" diameter
    TIME: early June
FRUIT: small reddish
    EFFECTIVE: fall
HYBRID ORIGIN: *R. pendulina x R. chinensis* before 1820
    With almost thornless stems the flowers last a considerable time. It appears to do well in situations with a northerly exposure, places where other roses do not thrive.

Rosa moschata nastarana   6'   Zone 6   Persian Musk Rose

*FLOWERS: pinkish, single, 2" diameter
    TIME: June
FRUIT: small, reddish
    EFFECTIVE: fall

The white flowering Helen Rose is closely related to the Japanese Rose (*R. multiflora*) except that the flowers of the former are slightly larger.

HABITAT: Persia
INTRODUCED: 1879
    A geographical variety of the Musk Rose, this has more vigor, more flowers and a more upright habit of growth than does the species. Either the species or a variety is included in every "old-fashioned" collection.

Rosa moyesi   9'   Zone 5   Moyes Rose

*FLOWERS: blood-red, single, 2½" diameter
    TIME: mid-June
*FRUIT: deep orange-red, 2½" long
    EFFECTIVE: fall
HABITAT: western China
INTRODUCED: 1894
    Strikingly descriptive is the name "Heart of Gold" since it has the deepest red color of all the Chinese roses. The late Dr. Van Fleet liked this rose especially because of its deep red petals surrounding a golden center of stamens and he used it a great deal in his hybridization work.

Rosa multiflora   10'   Zone 5   Japanese Rose

*FLOWERS: usually white, single, small, 1" diameter, in many flowered pyramidal
    clusters
    TIME: mid-June
*FRUIT: many small red berries
    EFFECTIVE: fall and entire winter
HABITAT: Japan and Korea
INTRODUCED: 1868
VARIETIES:
    cathayensis—pale pink, single, Cathay Japanese Rose, China, 1907
    platyphylla—double, deep pink flowers, Seven Sisters Rose
        The reason for naming this the Seven Sisters Rose was the fact that the flowers in one cluster were frequently seven different colors or hues. Since 1817, when this was first introduced, it has been more or less popular spasmodically, but apparently does not make a sturdy bush and dies out rather easily.
    Perhaps the most vigorous of all the rose species, this splendid species is being used more and more as an ornamental. Although its flowers are small and white, they are produced in large quantities so that when the bush is in full bloom it is literally covered with blossoms. These are followed by myriads of small red berries which remain on the plant throughout the winter and afford food for the birds, so much so that this species is being widely planted for this reason alone.
    It also makes an excellent understock in grafting, especially a thornless strain which has recently become popular among nurserymen. There are nurseries which use it entirely as an understock for the grafting of hybrid tea and perpetual roses.
    One other important asset is its definite arching habit of growth. A mature plant may easily be 8' high and 12' across, a dense thicket of spiny growth. In fact, it is now being recommended by the United States Soil Conservation Service for hedge-row planting, where it not only affords an excellent medium for holding soil in place, but also is a perfect barrier and source of food for wild life.

Where plenty of space is available, this rose, requiring practically no care except an occasional pruning, might well be tried. It is one of the parents of the modern rambler.

Rosa odorata   15′   Zone 7   Tea Rose

*FLOWERS: pink, double, 2–3½″ diameter
TIME: June
FOLIAGE: evergreen or half evergreen
HABITAT: China
INTRODUCED: 1810
VARIETIES:
gigantea—tall vigorous shrub, creamy white, double flowers
ochroleuca—pale yellow double flowers
pseud-indica—flowers salmon-yellow, double, often called "Fortune's Double Yellow"

This species has been cultivated for centuries in the gardens of India and China. Several forms have been available in this country in the past, Frank H. Meyer, of the U. S. Department of Agriculture having brought one valuable strain from China. The species has been used a great deal in hybridizing work and is one of the parents of the hybrid tea roses. It is unfortunate that this beautiful species and its varieties are hardy only in the warmest parts of the United States.

Rosa omeiensis   12′   Zone 6   Omei Rose

FLOWERS: white, single, 1–1½″ diameter
TIME: early June
*FRUIT: red, pear-shaped, on yellow fruit stalks
EFFECTIVE: fall
*FOLIAGE: finely divided, fernlike
WINTER TWIGS: conspicuous, large red prickles
HABITAT: western China
INTRODUCED: 1901
VARIETY: *pteracantha*—with enlarged red prickles making the stems rather conspicuous in winter

A unique rose of particular interest for its colorful fruits, fernlike foliage and the colorful prickles of the variety, rather than for any special merit of its single white flowers.

Rosa palustris   6′   Zone 4   Swamp Rose

*FLOWERS: Persian-rose, single
TIME: June
*FRUIT: red
EFFECTIVE: fall
HABITAT: eastern United States

Native over a wide area, it is not superior to *R. virginiana* but is of value because it grows readily in wet or swampy places.

Rosa pendulina   3′   Zone 5   Alpine Rose

*FLOWERS: Persian-rose, single, 2″ in diameter
TIME: May–June

*FRUIT: bright red, pulpy, 1" long, ½" diameter, usually nodding
     EFFECTIVE: fall
HABITAT: mountains of southern and central Europe
INTRODUCED: 1789

An interesting rose because of its comparatively large, elongated, bright red fruits which remain effective on the plant well into late fall.

Rosa primula   8'   Zone 5   Primrose Rose

FLOWERS: mimosa-yellow or yellowish white, single, 1½" diameter
     TIME: late May
FRUIT: red, small
     EFFECTIVE: early fall
HABITAT: Turkestan to north China
INTRODUCED: 1910

Valued for its early flowers and aromatic young foliage, this is the first rose to bloom in the collection at the Arnold Arboretum. It has been confused with the smaller, less floriferous R. ecae, but is quite different with its more vigorous growth and larger flowers. Where a canker infests R. hugonis as it does in certain areas of the eastern United States, this is an excellent substitute.

Rosa roxburghi   7'   Zone 4   Roxburgh Rose

*FLOWERS: rhodamine-pink, single, 2½" diameter
     TIME: early June
*FRUIT: red, large, very prickly
     EFFECTIVE: fall
WINTER TWIGS: interesting exfoliating bark
HABITAT: China, Japan
INTRODUCED: 1828
VARIETY: plena—flowers double

This rose has been overlooked by the rank and file of commercial growers, yet it is one of the most interesting of all. It has large, bold compound leaves, large pink flowers, slightly white near the center, and round globose fruits covered with stout prickles. Added to these seasonal attractions is its very interesting peeling bark. Larger branches and stems are very similar in this respect to Kolkwitzia amabilis and because of this shredding bark, have interest all winter. A handsome vigorous species, it is one that should be grown considerably more than it is at present.

Rosa rubrifolia   6'   Zone 2   Redleaf Rose

FLOWERS: deep red, usually few, single, 1½" diameter
     TIME: early June
FRUIT: bright red, pulpy
     EFFECTIVE: fall
*FOLIAGE: bluish green, tinged with purplish red
AUTUMN COLOR: purplish red
WINTER TWIGS: purplish
HABITAT: mountains of central and southern Europe
INTRODUCED: 1814

Not yet common in American gardens, this Roxburgh Rose nevertheless has merit, both because of its large pink flowers and the interesting exfoliating bark of the older stems in the winter.

A very hardy rose, not especially important for its flowers or fruits but for its colorful foliage throughout the summer. It should be classed with *Elaeagnus angustifolia* as one of those plants which lend desirable color to an otherwise monotonously green shrub border.

Rosa rugosa   6′   Zone 2   Rugosa Rose

*FLOWERS: fuchsine-pink to white, single, 2½–3½″ in diameter
   TIME: early June
*FRUIT: brick-red, nearly 1″ in diameter
   EFFECTIVE: fall
FOLIAGE: rugose, dark green
*AUTUMN COLOR: orange
HABITAT: northern China, Korea, Japan
INTRODUCED: about 1845
VARIETIES:
   alba—flowers white, single
   albo-plena—flowers white, double
   plena—flowers double, fuchsia-purple
   rosea—flowers Persian-rose, single
   It is impossible to say too much in favor of this "Sea Tomato" of Japan, so called because in its native habitat it grows within reach of the salt water spray.

In fact it has become naturalized at several places along New England's sea coast where salt spray is continuously reaching it. Withstands clipping very well and is often used in formal clipped hedges. The many varieties and hybrids afford interesting combinations for flowers. Its extreme vigor and hardiness make it one of the most valued of all rose species for general planting. Not the least of its attributes are its gorgeous orange autumn color and its large, conspicuously red fruits. It hybridizes readily with other species and seems to be the least exacting of the rose species in cultivation. One of its hundreds of hybrids is "Max Graf," a trailing pink rose with single flowers which makes an excellent ground cover.

Rosa setigera 15′ Zone 4 Prairie Rose

*FLOWERS: rose, single, 2″ diameter
   TIME: early July
FRUIT: red
   EFFECTIVE: fall
AUTUMN COLOR: reddish
HABITAT: central North America
VARIETY: *serena*—thornless

For general landscaping purposes this species has merit where there is plenty of room for it to grow naturally in its wide-arching way. It is next to the last of the species roses to bloom. There is no room for it in the small garden where space is at a premium since it does not look well when kept confined by close pruning. It may grow shoots 12–15′ long in a single season. Its chief merits are its late blooming flowers, wide-arching habit of growth, and marked hardiness. It has been used considerably in hybridization work to produce a strain with late-blooming flowers.

Rosa spinosissima 3′ Zone 4 Scotch Rose

*FLOWERS: pink, white or yellow, single, 1–2″ diameter
   TIME: early June
FRUIT: black or dark brown, not ornamental
HABITAT: Europe, western Asia, North America
VARIETIES:
   alba plena—double white flowers
   altaica—pale yellow, almost white, more vigorous and less prickly than the species, flowers 3″ in diameter
   lutea—Persian-yellow rose more frequently seen in cultivation because it is easier to grow.—Yellow Scotch Rose
   lutea plena—flowers double, mimosa-yellow

More widely distributed over the temperate regions of the world than any other rose species and the only one known to be native in Iceland. It is low, dense and moundlike in habit and blooms profusely. The variation in flower color, size and doubleness is one of its several assets. A collection of ninety varieties of the Scotch Rose was assembled in England some time ago, showing how variable this group is. The Scotch Rose takes kindly to cultivation, an important fact that cannot be said of all rose species. The specific name is taken from the fact that the stems are covered with many small spines and bristles.

Rosa virginiana   6'   **Zone 3**   Virginia Rose

*FLOWERS: magenta to pink, single
    TIME: mid-June
*FRUIT: red berries, ½", late ripening
    EFFECTIVE: fall and winter
FOLIAGE: glossy
*AUTUMN COLOR: scarlet to orange
*WINTER TWIGS: red
HABITAT: Newfoundland, Virginia, Alabama and Missouri
VARIETIES:
    alba—flowers white
    lamprophylla—Glossy Virginia Rose—smaller than the species with very lustrous green leaves—3'

Widely distributed in eastern North America, this excellent native is of ornamental interest every season of the year, something which cannot be said of many roses. Its flowers in late spring, good foliage throughout the summer, brilliant autumn foliage and fruits, and colorful twigs all winter make it superior to many. It grows vigorously, often spreading by underground stems so that it should be restrained when planted in a small garden. It can be grown as an effective barrier. When it grows too rank, it is cut down to the ground with brush scythe or sickle bar, and quickly grows back into splendid form within two years. Most effective as an informal hedge when kept about 3 to 4' high.

Rosa webbiana   6'   **Zone 5**   Webb's Rose

*FLOWERS: venetian-pink, large, single
    TIME: mid-June
FRUIT: bright red
    EFFECTIVE: fall
FOLIAGE: very small leaves and leaflets
HABITAT: Himalayas to Afghanistan and Turkey
INTRODUCED: 1879

None too sturdy as a shrub, doing best with a southern exposure, this rose has very small leaves and leaflets. Its chief attractions are its young shoots, which are almost blue, and the young prickles, which are white as they appear.

Rosa wichuraiana   **Zone 5**   Memorial Rose

FLOWERS: single, white, 2" in diameter
    TIME: mid-July
FRUIT: reddish
FOLIAGE: semi-evergreen, lustrous
HABITAT: Japan, Korea, Formosa, eastern China
INTRODUCED: 1891

Adapted for covering banks and rocky slopes, it is the only species that is truly procumbent, and is one of the parents of the modern ramblers. First introduced into North America by the Arnold Arboretum, and was first used in this country to cover banks and slopes in Franklin Park, Boston. A valuable ground cover.

The Memorial Rose, one of the parents of the modern rambler roses and one of the best of all the roses as a ground cover.

Rosa xanthina   9′   Zone 5   Manchu Rose

*FLOWERS: sulfur yellow, semi-double, 1½–2″ diameter
    TIME: late May
HABITAT: northern China and Korea
INTRODUCED: 1906
    Very similar to *R. hugonis* except that the flowers are semi-double.

Rosmarinus officinalis   6′   Zone 6   Rosemary

FLOWERS: violet-blue, rarely white, in spikes
    TIME: winter and early spring
*FOLIAGE: evergreen, lustrous dark green, aromatic
HABITAT: southern Europe, Asia Minor
INTRODUCED: early colonial times
    A common herb or sub-shrub, valued for its aromatic fragrance, it has been used in gardens for centuries. At one time it was supposed to have a stimulating

Rosemary and English Ivy share the honors in making this garden pool attractive.

influence on the memory and was known as the "herb of memory." Honey made from rosemary blossoms is said to be unusually good. A fragrant oil is extracted from the plant. Rosemary grows well in sun and in soil slightly dry, but in moist soil it quickly becomes "leggy" and has to be severely restrained.

Rubus deliciosus   9'   Zone 4   Boulder Raspberry

*FLOWERS: mostly solitary, large, white, 1½" diameter
   TIME: late May
FRUIT: dark purple-raspberry
   EFFECTIVE: fall
HABITAT: Colorado
VARIETY: *plena*—flowers double. Rather difficult to locate in nurseries, but available, and a splendid garden plant in flower.
   A very graceful shrub with arching branches. This native of Colorado is one of the few *Rubus* species worthy of planting for its flowers.

Rubus odoratus   9'   Zone 3   Flowering Raspberry

FLOWERS: purple, fragrant, 2" diameter
   TIME: early July
FRUIT: red, flat raspberry
   EFFECTIVE: fall
HABITAT: Nova Scotia to Michigan, Tennessee and Georgia
   A shrub with bold foliage and arching branches with large 3–5 lobed leaves about 6" in diameter. The flowers appear continuously for several weeks and the

large maplelike leaves give this shrub an exotic appearance. It does best in moist soil where it will receive some shade during the day.

Ruscus aculeatus   1½–4′   Zone 7   Butcher's Broom

FRUIT: bright red berries, ½″ diameter
  EFFECTIVE: winter
*FOLIAGE: evergreen, leathery
HABITAT: south and western Europe
INTRODUCED: 1750
    A stiff low evergreen shrub with leathery, pointed leaves about 1½″ long. These branches are frequently cut, dried and dyed various colors and used in floral decorations. It can withstand hot sun, dry soil, and shade, making it a serviceable evergreen for certain situations. It needs an occasional thinning in the spring.

Sabal minor   3–4′   Zone 9   Dwarf Palmetto

    A stemless palm, with vigorous fan-shaped leaves, native of the extreme southeastern United States, adapted especially well to growing in swampy land. One of few palms native in this country outside strictly tropical regions.

Salix alba chermesina   75′   Zone 2   Redstem Willow

*WINTER TWIGS: orange to red
HABITAT: Europe and northern Africa
INTRODUCED: before 1850
    This is a variety of a standard tree, the White Willow, but if frequently cut and grown as a shrub, it has the most brilliant orange to red twigs of any woody plant in the North. If allowed to grow as a tree, the twig color is not nearly so pronounced.

Salix caprea   27′   Zone 4   Goat Willow

*FLOWERS: small composite heads or catkins about 1″ long
  TIME: March
HABITAT: Europe to northern Asia and northern Persia
INTRODUCED: early colonial times
    This species is the best of the "Pussy Willows" because it has the largest catkins. The sexes in willows are separate and the male of this species has those long, gray, fluffy catkins that eventually sprout many bright yellow stamens as they mature. The catkins of the female plant eventually have greenish colored pistils that are not nearly as pretty as those of the male. This willow is a vigorous shrub, of little interest the rest of the year, but the catkins come so early in the season that there may be room in the large garden for the shrub to serve just this one purpose. Larger catkins are frequently obtained by cutting the shrub to the ground every few years and thus forcing into vigorous growth. The native *Salix discolor*, of the United States, is also common in woods and swampy places over the eastern region but the catkins of this native are smaller than those of *S. caprea*.

Salix lucida 20' Zone 2 Shining Willow

FOLIAGE: lustrous, dark green
HABITAT: eastern North America
A tall-growing shrub with lustrous shining green leaves, very similar to those of the popular *S. pentandra,* or Laurel-leaved Willow. Only of value for its vigorous growth and shining green foliage.

Salix purpurea 9' Zone 4 Purple Osier

FLOWERS: very small, gray catkins
  TIME: March
*WINTER TWIGS: purple
HABITAT: Europe to north Africa to central Asia to Japan
INTRODUCED: long cultivated
Most willows are vigorous, often coarse, nondescript shrubs of little ornamental value. The Purple Osier is one of the better species, dense in habit, with fine leaves and purple twigs in winter. Of course it does well in swampy places. The twigs are frequently used in basket weaving, and the wood in making artist's charcoal. It does not rate as a valuable garden plant when compared with a hydrangea or a holly, but in certain moist situations, where a dense shrub requiring little care is needed, this species might be a possibility.

Salix repens 3' Zone 4 Creeping Willow

HABITAT: Europe and Asia
INTRODUCED: early colonial times
VARIETY: *rosmarinifolia*–leaves are linear, very narrow and large
Excellent low willows for poor, moist soil, or for display in an unused corner of the rock garden.

Salix tristis 1½' Zone 2 Dwarf Gray Willow

*FOLIAGE: leaves white underneath
HABITAT: Maine to Minnesota, south to Florida
A low willow for poor soil on a bank or in the rock garden. The general effect of the foliage is gray.

Salix uva-ursi prostrate shrub Zone 1 Bearberry Willow

HABITAT: Labrador to Alaska, south to New York
A low willow, used somewhat in rock gardens on the northwest Pacific Coast. Does best in high-altitude situations.

Salvia greggi 3' Zone 7 Autumn Sage

*FLOWERS: red to purplish red, 1" long, in 4" clusters
  TIME: fall
HABITAT: Texas and Mexico
A beautiful species with brilliant fall flowers. The variety *alba* has white flowers. Both are extremely drought resistant, an admirable trait.

SAMBUCUS

The elders are scarcely shrubs to be planted in the small garden. Their large, compound leaves are coarse in texture, they are vigorous in habit of growth, and mostly of interest for their white flowers or colored fruits— black, yellow, red or blue depending on the species and variety. They can be considered for larger plantings, for naturalizing, and their fruits are attractive to the birds. They seem to do well in a moist soil, some even in wet soil. When they become overgrown or unsightly they can be cut off near the ground and will quickly grow back again. Some, like *Sambucus canadensis* and *S. pubens*, which are found growing over nearly the entire length and half the breadth of this country, are natives. Because they are not necessarily first-class ornamentals, it seems advisable to recommend the native sorts in preference to introduced varieties. Consequently there are ten recommended varieties and twenty-eight suggested for rejection.

All have very small white flowers, borne in large clusters, flat in the case of *S. canadensis*, and rounded or even pyramidal in the case of *S. pubens*. For naturalizing, *S. canadensis* will prove satisfactory, but its variety *maxima* has much larger flower clusters, sometimes almost one foot in diameter, and should be used instead. The European counterpart of *S. canadensis* is *S. nigra* and some of its varieties are available from American sources. It does not have any characteristics sufficiently superior to those of *S. canadensis* to warrant planting both. It is probable that more varieties of *S. nigra* have been named merely because it has been cultivated in Europe for centuries and selection has continued for a far greater length of time. If flower alone is to be considered, *S. pubens* with much smaller flowers, blooms in mid-May with the Flowering Dogwood, while *S. canadensis* blooms in late June with the mock-oranges and *Rhododendron maximum*.

The individual fruits of these plants are less than one quarter of an inch in diameter but are borne in large numbers and are most conspicuous. In the case of the American Elder, the fruits are blue to black and appear in such large numbers that the weight of the fruit clusters bends the stem considerably. Jellies, various preserves and wine are made from the ripened fruits and, because of this interest, some strains have been selected for their larger and better fruits. One of these that has proved very popular is "Adams," a variety selected by the late William W. Adams, Union Springs, New York, for vigorous growth, productiveness and very large berries. The variety *maxima* also produces a large number of fruits late in the summer.

The fruits of the Scarlet Elder (*S. pubens*) are a brilliant red and appear in late June at about the same time the Canada Elder is in blossom, but it requires a cooler climate than does the Canada Elder. It should be noted that there is a red-fruited form of *S. canadensis* available.

Native in the northwestern United States is the Blue Elder, *S. coerulea*, with excellent soft gray-blue edible berries, to be recommended in that area. A variety of the Red Elder of Europe (*S. racemosa flavescens*) is also mentioned for it has yellow fruits, often tinged red.

It is seldom advisable to recommend a plant for its yellow foliage, but in the case of the elders an exception might be made. The foliage color of two varieties is so intense, and the vigor of the plants is so marked that they usually make healthy specimens and so are recommended in the following list because they have good yellow foliage throughout the growing season.

If a fine texture of foliage is desired, the three cut-leaved forms might be considered. It should be emphasized a second time that none of these elders should be considered as specimen plants on the small place. They are too vigorous and too coarse and far better plants are available. This morning I was looking at some of the plants in our nursery which are only three years old, grown from seed. Now they are vigorous specimens 8–10' tall, and so vigorous and deeply rooted that they will have to be pulled out with a tractor for disposal. In situations where their vigorous growth is desired, where their coarse character is not objectionable, and where plants may have to be treated roughly—even mowed off near the base occasionally— these elders might be considered. Most of them grow 10–12' tall (*S. coerulea* may even grow 30' or more in height) hence it is easily understood, that to grow satisfactorily and to look well, they need far more space than should be allowed them on the small grounds.

Sambucus canadensis varieties   12'   Zone 3   American Elder

*FLOWERS: white, small, in large flat clusters 6–8" in diameter
    TIME: late June
*FRUIT: blue to black small berries in large clusters
    EFFECTIVE: late summer
HABITAT: eastern United States
VARIETIES:
    acutiloba—leaflets very deeply divided
    "Adams"—selected for its numerous fruits, large clusters
    aurea—fruit cherry red, foliage yellow
    maxima—flower clusters 13" in diameter
    rubra—fruit scarlet
    These varieties can grow in very moist to almost wet soils, as well as fairly dry soils. A new, yellow-fruiting variety recently occurred in a seedling lot at the Arnold Arboretum and is being propagated.

Sambucus coerulea   45'   Zone 5   Blueberry Elder

*FLOWERS: yellowish white, small, in large flat clusters 7" in diameter
    TIME: late June
*FRUIT: blue-black but whitened by a heavy bloom
    EFFECTIVE: late summer
HABITAT: Pacific Coast of United States and Canada
    The fruit of this plant has a whitish blue appearance which is most attractive and makes this popular for planting on the Pacific Coast. It is very vigorous and, when cut back, may grow as much as 3–12' in one year.

Sambucus pubens   12'–24'   Zone 4   Scarlet Elder

*FLOWERS: yellowish white, in pyramidal clusters, 5" tall
    TIME: mid-May
*FRUIT: scarlet
    EFFECTIVE: early summer
HABITAT: eastern United States
VARIETY: *dissecta*—leaflets deeply cut
    This species and its variety are particularly prevalent in the moist mountainous regions of the eastern United States.

Sambucus racemosa varieties   12'   Zone 4   European Red Elder

*FLOWERS: yellowish white
    TIME: early May
*FRUIT: scarlet
    EFFECTIVE: summer
HABITAT: Europe and western Asia
INTRODUCED: 1596
VARIETIES:
    flavescens—fruit yellow with a red cheek
    plumoso-aurea—golden yellow leaves with deeply toothed leaflets
    Other varieties of this species are not recommended here since they are similar to the more common varieties of S. *canadensis*.

Santolina chamaecyparissus   1½'   Zone 7   Lavender-cotton

FLOWERS: bright yellow clusters
    TIME: summer
*FOLIAGE: evergreen, gray, woolly
HABITAT: southern Europe
INTRODUCED: cultivated 1596
    A bushy plant with procumbent stem but ascending branches chiefly of importance for its aromatic gray, woolly leaves. It is grown in poor sandy or gravelly soil and needs a stiff pruning annually, preferably after flowering, to prevent untidy over-vigorous growth.

Sarcococca ruscifolia   6'   Zone 7   Fragrant Sarcococca

FLOWERS: small white, fragrant
    TIME: fall
FRUIT: dark scarlet berries, ¼" diameter
    EFFECTIVE: fall
*FOLIAGE: dark green and lustrous, evergreen
HABITAT: central and western China
INTRODUCED: 1901
    A lustrous green-leaved evergreen, suitable for planting in either light or deep shade. Spreads by means of underground stems and so can be used as a tall ground cover especially when planted in small clumps a few feet apart. There is another species S. *saligna* which is probably lower in height under ordinary conditions, as is also S. *hookeriana humilis*, with black fruits.

Serenoa repens 3' Zone 8 Saw Palmetto

The hardiest of the palms, native even in North Carolina, widely distributed over large areas in the South, westward to Texas and Arkansas. It is mostly prostrate or with creeping branches and, when unmolested, grows into great masses over huge areas.

Severinia buxifolia 6' Zone 8 Chinese Box-orange

FLOWERS: small, white
    TIME: spring
FRUIT: round, black berry
    EFFECTIVE: fall
WINTER TWIGS: spiny
HABITAT: China and Formosa
An unusually spiny plant for use as hedges in the far South.

Shepherdia canadensis 7' Zone 2 Russet Buffalo-berry

*FRUIT: red berries in large clusters
    TIME: early summer
*FOLIAGE: gray-green to silver
HABITAT: central and northern North America
Not especially ornamental as the plant tends to grow open and straggly, the flowers are dioecious and hence plants of both sexes must be present to insure the production of the conspicuously colorful fruits. It should not be used in gardens with good soil where many much better shrubs can be grown. However, for very dry or alkaline situations, especially in the Mid-west and the prairie states, it can be grown in situations where many another shrub will fail. The fruit was made into jellies by the pioneers.

Siphonosmanthus delavayi 6' Zone 7

FLOWERS: short-stalked, white, fragrant
    TIME: March
FRUIT: bluish black berries
    TIME: summer
FOLIAGE: evergreen, glossy, ½–1" long
HABITAT: western China
INTRODUCED: 1890
A delightful little evergreen with small leaves, twiggy growth and wealth of waxy, fragrant flowers produced in the axils of the leaves in early spring. Prefers a situation in the full sun.

Skimmia japonica 4' Zone 7 Japanese Skimmia

*FLOWERS: yellowish white, sexes separate
    TIME: mid-May
*FRUIT: bright red berries
    EFFECTIVE: fall
*FOLIAGE: bright or yellowish evergreen, leaves to 5" long
HABITAT: Japan
INTRODUCED: 1838

This shade-loving evergreen is planted widely for its foliage, flowers and fruits. Sexes are separate, so that staminate flowers and pistillate flowers are on different plants. Strains or clons of the male plant are grown for their large clusters of fragrant white flowers, but the fruiting forms also have considerable ornamental value. These plants should not be planted in full sun, for they actually require shade.

| Skimmia reevesiana | 1½′ | Zone 7 | Reeves Skimmia |

*FLOWERS: perfect white flowers
  TIME: mid-May
*FRUIT: dull crimson-red
  EFFECTIVE: fall
*FOLIAGE: dark evergreen, leaves to 4″ long
HABITAT: China
INTRODUCED: 1849

This perhaps is the more desirable of the two *Skimmia* species, since the flowers are perfect and fruits are always borne. Also the plant is lower and more compact in habit.

| Sophora secundiflora | 3–8′ | Zone 7 | Mescal-bean |

*FLOWERS: violet-blue, fragrant, similar to the fragrance of violets, 1″ long
  TIME: February–April
FOLIAGE: evergreen, leaflets to 2½″ long
HABITAT: Texas, New Mexico

One of the meritorious native shrubs or trees. The starting of these plants proves discouraging because they may grow only 4–6″ during the first two years. However, since they are legumes, it may be that inoculating the soil where they are to be newly planted with some soil taken from where they are flourishing may prove helpful. Other legumes respond to such treatment. This species will withstand dry soil conditions.

| Sophora viciifolia | 7′ | Zone 5 | Vetch Sophora |

*FLOWERS: bluish violet to whitish, pealike
  TIME: early June
FOLIAGE: finely divided leaves
HABITAT: western China
INTRODUCED: 1897

A graceful, profusely-flowering shrub, the chief merit of which is its ability to grow and thrive in poor sandy soil on dry situations. Its gracefully arching habit and vetchlike foliage give it a decidedly light and feathery appearance in the garden.

SORBARIA

Highly ornamental in a mass planting and from a distance, the False Spireas are chiefly of interest during July and August when they are in bloom. They have little else to attract interest at other times of year, although they produce leaves very early in spring. With large compound leaves, and leaflets not unlike the leaves of spireas, the large, conspicuous creamy-white flower clusters, made up of very small spirealike flowers, are produced in terminal panicles. Some species like *Sorbaria sorbifolia* can be almost objectionable because of the vigorous habit of increasing rapidly by means of underground stolons. The two recommended species are not as vigorous in this respect. *Sorbaria aitchisoni* is the lower growing of the two, with brighter green foliage and red stems and leaf stalks. Dead flower clusters should be pruned off, and heavy renewal pruning should be given the plants every few years. Both species do well in poor soil, in full sun or partial shade, but they should not be used in the small garden, for they need plenty of room in which to grow and make spectacular summer displays in mass plantings.

Sorbaria aitchisoni   9'   Zone 6   Kashmir False Spirea
*FLOWERS: white, spirealike panicles, 10" long
   TIME: late July
HABITAT: Afghan, Kashmir
INTRODUCED: 1895

Sorbaria arborea   18'   Zone 5   Tree False Spirea
*FLOWERS: white, spirealike panicles, 12" long
   TIME: late July
HABITAT: central and western China
INTRODUCED: 1908
    A hardy species with slightly larger flower clusters than *Sorbaria aitchisoni*. The flower clusters are large and heavy, often bending the supporting branches so that they arch gracefully when in bloom.

Spartium junceum   10'   Zone 7   Spanish Broom
*FLOWERS: bright yellow, fragrant
   TIME: summer
*FOLIAGE: bluish green
HABITAT: Mediterranean Region and Canary Islands
INTRODUCED: 1548
    Not a true broom but closely related, it is an almost leafless shrub producing large masses of golden yellow flowers in summer. Considerable pruning is necessary to keep it neat in appearance. It is especially adapted for planting on hot dry banks and like the brooms it is hard to transplant and is best brought to the garden for the first time in pots.

SPIRAEA

    Approximately one hundred different species and varieties of spireas are growing in the Arnold Arboretum. Although many are native in this country, and many exotic types are widely distributed in the nurseries of the country, nevertheless they do not constitute a very important ornamental group as a whole. Only twenty-two are recommended, while the others are

Every gardener recognizes the white flowers and often arching habit of certain spireas.

not sufficiently important to be included because they are similar, or inferior, to those recommended.

In general, the spireas are planted for their white or red flowers borne mostly in flat clusters one to three inches in diameter, and some for their gracefully arching habit as well. Their fruits are dried seed pods. Only a few like *Spiraea prunifolia* are garnished with autumn color, and often this is variable, depending on certain environmental conditions. They range in height from the diminutive *S. decumbens,* only about a foot tall, to the Veitch Spirea which is the tallest, sometimes reaching 12′ in height. All are vigorous shrubs, growing with many slender branches coming from the base of the plant. They are not particular as to soil and situation, and because of this admirable trait, some have actually been overplanted. Vanhoutte's Spirea, with its splendid ornamental qualities and ability to grow almost anywhere, is widely planted so that it is now one of the commonest of shrubs.

Spireas will grow in sun or shade but the more sunshine they receive the better they will flower. They will grow in almost any kind of soil. They will respond better to a little pruning than almost any other group of plants. Some need far more attention than others but they can be divided definitely into two groups, *i.e.,* those that bloom on the previous year's wood (*S. thunbergi, S. arguta, S. prunifolia plena, S. nipponica, S. rotundifolia, S. vanhouttei, S. wilsoni*) and those that bloom on the current year's wood (the remainder of the recommended group). Those in the former group should be pruned just after flowering, those in the second group should be pruned early in spring before growth starts.

Some need far more attention than others as is frequently the case with S. *thunbergi* for the small twigs of this species frequently winterkill in the North and must be removed to keep the plant from becoming unsightly. The small S. *japonica* and S. *bumalda* varieties bloom far better and have much larger flower clusters, if they are thinned out early each spring, with only a few main branches left instead of many spindly ones which will have very small flower clusters. However, when necessary, all can be cut to within a few inches of the ground and be expected to recover quickly.

All spireas have fibrous roots and are easily moved, another reason for their popularity. With the right selection of species and varieties they bloom over a three-month period. They are serviceable as "fillers" in the shrub border and some of them are valued for their summer bloom coming at a time when few other woody plants are in flower.

Spiraea albiflora   1½′   Zone 4   Japanese White Spirea

*FLOWERS: white, in rounded to flat clusters
  TIME: July
HABITAT: Japan
INTRODUCED: 1868
    Dense, compact, low shrub with profuse late white flowers. It makes good color contrast when used with the red flowering S. *bumalda* and S. *japonica* varieties.

x **Spiraea arguta**   5–6′   Zone 4   Garland Spirea

*FLOWERS: pure white, flat clusters
  TIME: early May
HYBRID ORIGIN: S. *thunbergi x S. multiflora*
ORIGINATING: before 1884
    The most free-flowering and most showy of the early spireas, with flat flower clusters on arching branches, giving the impression of an early flowering S. *vanhouttei*—useful in the front of the shrub border as well as for a specimen.

x **Spiraea billiardi**   6′   Zone 4   Billiard Spirea

*FLOWERS: bright rose, pyramidal spikes
  TIME: late June
HYBRID ORIGIN: S. *douglasi x S. salicifolia*
ORIGINATED: before 1854
    Often desirable for planting in masses on banks, since it quickly increases by underground stems forming a dense mass of growth.

x **Spiraea brachybotrys**   8′   Zone 4

*FLOWERS: small bright pink in panicles, 1½–3″ long
  TIME: late June

HYBRID ORIGIN: *S. canescens x S. douglasi?*
ORIGINATED: before 1867
One of the best of the taller, summer-blooming spireas.

x Spiraea bumalda "Anthony Waterer"   2'   Zone 5

*FLOWERS: bright crimson, flat clusters often 6" in diameter
TIME: late June
HYBRID ORIGIN: *S. japonica x S. albiflora*
ORIGINATED: before 1890
Spiraea bumalda variety: *crispa*—of particular interest because of its peculiar, slightly twisted leaves. The flowers, in size and color, are practically identical with those of "Anthony Waterer."

"Anthony Waterer" is a most popular low spirea because it blooms intermittently for several weeks. The color of the flower is not as dark as that of *S. japonica atrosanguinea*. The young foliage is tinged pink when it first appears in the spring.

Spiraea canescens   6–10'   Zone 7   Hoary Spirea

*FLOWERS: white clusters, 2" in diameter
TIME: July
HABITAT: Himalayas
INTRODUCED: 1837
Sometimes this Hoary Spirea has its arching branches covered almost the entire length with 2" clusters of white flowers.

Spiraea cantoniensis   3'   Zone 6   Reeve's Spirea

*FLOWERS: pure white, roundish clusters 1–2" in diameter
TIME: late May
HABITAT: China and Japan
INTRODUCED: 1824
This seems to be one of the best, if not the best of the spireas, for the South. It manages to keep its foliage a greater part of the year in California and has wide-spread, graceful branches somewhat similar to those of the better known *S. vanhouttei.*

Spiraea decumbens   1'   Zone 5

FLOWERS: white, small clusters, not over 2" in diameter
TIME: June
HABITAT: southern Europe
INTRODUCED: 1830
Very low shrub, only suitable for rockeries.

Spiraea japonica atrosanguinea   4'   Zone 5   Mikado Spirea

*FLOWERS: deep crimson, flat clusters
TIME: mid-June
HABITAT: Japan
INTRODUCED: 1870
Spiraea japonica variety: *ovalifolia*—flowers white, otherwise practically identical with above variety.

The flowers of this variety are the deepest crimson of any of the spireas. Not as low and compact as "Anthony Waterer" but appears to be slightly more hardy. The flower clusters may be as much as 4–5″ in diameter.

x Spiraea margaritae   4′   Zone 4   Margarita Spirea

*FLOWERS: rosy pink, small, in flat clusters 3–6″ in diameter
   TIME: late June
HYBRID ORIGIN: *S. japonica x S. superba*
ORIGINATED: before 1890

One of the better spireas especially if pruned slightly early in spring in the same manner as *S. japonica*, i.e., the old stems cut out and the young stems cut back to 1′ above the ground, with considerable thinning at the same time. When this is done, the shrub will become a sheet of blossom, which can be still further augmented by cutting off dead flower clusters.

Spiraea nipponica rotundifolia   7′   Zone 4   Big Nippon Spirea

*FLOWERS: white, small flat clusters but numerous
   TIME: late May
FOLIAGE: almost bluish green
HABITAT: Japan
INTRODUCED: 1882

Vigorous handsome shrub with upright branches, this variety has larger leaves and flower clusters than the species. The foliage is dark green, almost bluish green, remaining on the plant long into the fall. Its general character is stiff, quite different from many of the gracefully arching spireas.

Spiraea prunifolia plena   9′   Zone 4   Bridalwreath Spirea

*FLOWERS: white, double
   TIME: mid-May
*AUTUMN COLOR: red to orange
HABITAT: Japan and central China
INTRODUCED: 1843

The double white flowers of this popular spirea are about the size of small buttons and it is one of the few spireas to turn a lustrous orange color in fall. Its leaves throughout the growing season are a lustrous green. It is superior to the species, for its flowers remain effective much longer and are considerably more showy. This variety was originally introduced by Von Siebold from Japan and E. H. Wilson found it growing wild in central China. It is still one of the most ornamental of this genus.

Spiraea salicifolia   4′   Zone 4   Willowleaf Spirea

FLOWERS: rose colored in pyramidal spikes
   TIME: early July
HABITAT: southeastern Europe to northeast Asia and Japan
INTRODUCED: 1586

This is rigidly upright in habit and spreads by suckers, hence good for naturalizing.

x **Spiraea superba**   3'   Zone 4   Striped Spirea

FLOWERS: light rose to pinkish, in terminal flat clusters
     TIME: late June
HYBRID ORIGIN: S. *albiflora* x S. *corymbosa*
INTRODUCED: 1873
     Because of its rather late flower and its height, this species has some merit.

Spiraea thunbergi   5'   Zone 4   Thunberg Spirea

*FLOWERS: small, pure white, in clusters of 2–5 flowers, before leaves appear
     TIME: early May
FOLIAGE: very fine texture
AUTUMN COLOR: occasionally yellow to orange
HABITAT: Japan, China
INTRODUCED: 1863
     A very popular spirea, this has been widely grown for many years. Its thin, feathery, graceful branchlets are covered with the small single white flowers before the leaves appear in spring. Under some conditions this, too, has foliage turning orange in fall. Flowers are small and abundant, but the plant needs much pruning for the small twigs tend to die out frequently.

Spiraea tomentosa   3'   Zone 4   Hardhack Spirea

*FLOWERS: deep rose to rose-purple, upright pyramidal spikes
     TIME: late June
HABITAT: eastern United States
VARIETY: *alba*—flowers white
     Good for naturalizing and planting in clumps in fields or open places as well as in damp places but does not make a particularly promising specimen plant.

x **Spiraea vanhouttei**   6'   Zone 4   Vanhoutte Spirea

*FLOWERS: pure white, flat clusters
     TIME: late May
AUTUMN COLOR: sometimes orange to red
HYBRID ORIGIN: S. *cantoniensis* x S. *trilobata*
ORIGINATED: before 1866
     It is only fair to say that in selecting good spirea species they all should be compared first with the general effectiveness of S. *vanhouttei*, for without a doubt, this is superior to many. Its profuse white flower clusters, gracefully arching habit, general dependability and vigorous growth have earned it a place in American gardens as being among the most valued of all. There are some species, which from a landscape viewpoint, are practically the same but I have not recommended these merely because Vanhoutte Spirea is widely distributed and easily available everywhere from nurseries.

Spiraea veitchi   12'   Zone 5   Veitch Spirea

FLOWERS: white, flat clusters over 2″ in diameter
     TIME: mid-June
HABITAT: central and western China

INTRODUCED: 1900

This is the tallest of the spireas and so can be useful at the rear of the shrub border where its height and slightly arching branches make a most effective background.

Spiraea wilsoni 7' Zone 5 Wilson Spirea

FLOWERS: pure white, clusters 2" in diameter
    TIME: early June
HABITAT: central and western China
INTRODUCED: 1900

The Wilson Spirea has creamy-white clusters of flowers on arching branches and in general looks somewhat like Vanhoutte Spirea. Branches, cut with their flowers open, will keep in water one full week without dropping the flowers.

Stachyrus praecox 12' Zone 6

FLOWERS: yellow in racemes 2–3" long
    TIME: March
FRUIT: greenish yellow berry with reddish cheek
    EFFECTIVE: summer
FOLIAGE: semi-evergreen
WINTER TWIGS: red
HABITAT: Japan
INTRODUCED: 1865

Because of very early flowers and small pendulous racemes in the axils of the leaves, this species should be used only in localities where late March freezes are uncommon. Peaty soil and leaf mold prove an excellent growing medium.

Stephanandra incisa 7' Zone 4 Cutleaf Stephanandra

FLOWERS: greenish white, loose, terminal panicles, 2" long
    TIME: mid-June
FOLIAGE: finely cut leaves
AUTUMN COLOR: reddish purple, to red
HABITAT: Japan, Korea
INTRODUCED: 1872

This is a graceful shrub in general appearance, with finely cut leaves, arching branches and slender stems. Not completely hardy in North, it tends to die back somewhat in severe winters, making pruning rather important. Its finely-divided leaves give it a fine texture not common in many woody shrubs and for this reason it can well be used in the foreground of the shrub border. The flower clusters are rather insignificant.

Stewartia malacodendron 18' Zone 7 Virginia Stewartia

*FLOWERS: white, 4" in diameter
*BARK: flaking bark on older branches
HABITAT: Virginia and Arkansas to Florida and Louisiana
    With very large summer flowers, and interesting bark.

Stewartia ovata grandiflora   15'   Zone 5   Showy Stewartia

*FLOWERS: large, white, 4" in diameter, purple stamens
    TIME: early July
AUTUMN COLOR: orange to scarlet
*BARK: flaking bark on older branches
HABITAT: Georgia

One of the prettiest of the stewartias because the large white flowers have a center of very beautiful purple stamens, an excellent color contrast. Added to this important feature of summer flowers is the fact that the foliage turns a splendid orange to scarlet in the autumn and the older bark on the large branches is flaky, so that there are interesting light and dark colored areas, similar to, but more colorful than, those of the sycamore.

Stewartia pseudo-camellia   30'   Zone 5   Japanese Stewartia

*FLOWERS: white, 2½" in diameter, cup-shaped
    TIME: early July
FOLIAGE: bright green
AUTUMN COLOR: purplish
*BARK: flaking bark on older branches
HABITAT: Japan
INTRODUCED: 1874

The flower is very similar to that of a single camellia, to which all stewartias are closely related, hence the specific name of this species. The flaking bark is more colorful than that of the other stewartias, being red and peeling off in large plates. It is difficult to discard any of these stewartias for they bloom during several weeks in summer at a time when few woody plants are in flower.

Styrax japonica   30'   Zone 5   Japanese Snowbell

*FLOWERS: white, about ¾" diameter, pendulous, bell-shaped
    TIME: early June
HABITAT: China, Japan
INTRODUCED: 1862

A wide-spreading shrub or tree, rather dense, with graceful small waxy-white, pendulous flowers in early June. An excellent specimen because of its curving horizontal branches and good dark green leaves. The interesting thing about the bloom is that the flowers appear after the leaves are fully developed, but the leaves are firmly held on the upper side of the branches and the pendulous flowers are clearly evident on the underside of all the small twigs and branches, so that their effect is not dimmed by the full foliage.

Styrax wilsoni   9'   Zone 7   Wilson Snowbell

*FLOWERS: white, about ¾" in diameter, pendulous, bell-shaped
    TIME: early June
HABITAT: western China
INTRODUCED: 1908

Even more branched than *Styrax japonica* this delightful shrub is well worth a trial in gardens of the warmer parts of the country, especially, because it bears its beautiful small, waxy-white flowers when it is very young, something which cannot be said of many of our woody plants.

Suaeda fruticosa   3'   Zone 6   Shrubby Goosefoot
FLOWERS: solitary, small, green
    TIME: July
FRUIT: lustrous black
    EFFECTIVE: fall
FOLIAGE: semi-evergreen
HABITAT: Alberta to southern California and New Mexico, also western and southern Europe, Asia, Africa
    Small shrub, only of value for planting in brackish situations or where it may be touched with salt water spray. It will grow under such conditions when many other plants will not.

Symphoricarpos albus laevigatus   6'   Zone 3   Snowberry
FLOWERS: very small in terminal spikes, pinkish
    TIME: mid-June
*FRUIT: white conspicuous berries, ⅜" in diameter
    EFFECTIVE: fall
HABITAT: Nova Scotia to Alberta, south to Minnesota and Virginia
    The Snowberry is one of the few woody shrubs with large white berries, very ornamental in the fall because they are on arching branches. Branches, when laden with fruit, bend over and touch the ground. In some areas the white fruits remain plump and white for weeks, while in others a disease attacks them and they quickly turn brown. In areas where the disease is prevalent, this plant might be omitted from the garden.

x Symphoricarpos chenaulti   3'   Zone 5   Chenault Coralberry
FLOWERS: small pink spikes
    TIME: mid-July
*FRUIT: small red berries in close terminal clusters, white on one side
    EFFECTIVE: fall
HYBRID ORIGIN: *S. microphyllus x S. orbiculatus*
ORIGINATED: before 1912
    The fruit of this handsome coralberry is slightly larger and more pink than that of the Indian Currant and differs in that it is white on the side hidden from the direct sunlight. It is excellent for using in the shrub border, and does well in any normally good, well drained soil.

Symphoricarpos orbiculatus 3–6' Zone 2 Indian Currant or Coralberry
FLOWERS: small, dense, yellowish white
    TIME: mid-July
*FRUIT: purplish red, corallike berries
    EFFECTIVE: fall
HABITAT: southeastern and south central United States
VARIETY: *leucoparus*—flowers pale greenish yellow, fruit white or whitish
    The Coralberry is native of a wide area in the United States. Its flowers are so small that they can almost be considered inconspicuous but the small red fruits are interesting, especially since they are produced all along the branches in small clusters. This shrub, usually only about 3' high, suckers readily and spreads easily which makes it an excellent plant for bank planting.

Symplocos paniculata   35′   **Zone 5**   Asiatic Sweetleaf

FLOWERS: white, fragrant, small clusters
     TIME: late May
*FRUIT: bright blue berry
     EFFECTIVE: October
HABITAT: Himalayas to China and Japan
INTRODUCED: 1875

A tall, wide-spreading, dense shrub, chiefly of merit for its bright pale blue berries about ¼″ in diameter but they do not remain on the plant more than a week after they have reached the peak of their color. The small, white, profuse flowers are fragrant, but these too, do not remain effective long. Because of these short periods of interest, there are better shrubs to be found for growing in the limited space of the small garden. On large estates or in parks, where space is available for unique plants, this might be a good selection.

SYRINGA

It must be disconcerting to the practical gardener to go through nursery catalogues in order to select a few lilacs for planting in his garden. At least 250 different named lilacs are offered by nurseries in this country now, and equally as many are being grown elsewhere. Truly a confusing number. Of course, the lilac is a popular flowering shrub, mostly valued for its fragrant flowers. Sometimes we see places where they have escaped cultivation or where they still grow as mute evidence of a former dwelling which has long since passed out of existence. They were not here before the white man came and undoubtedly were brought by the first settlers who came from Europe. Many species of lilacs have been introduced here from Asia and the most common of all, *Syringa vulgaris,* is a native of southern Europe.

In general, the lilacs are vigorous shrubs, although the Japanese tree lilac, *S. amurensis,* is a small tree that does very well when grown with a single trunk. They have their troubles like many other plants. They have no autumn color; only one—*S. oblata*—lays claim to autumn color, a dull red and not always dependable. Their fruits have no ornamental value whatsoever. Their vigorous habit makes them suited for screen plantings and even for use in hedges where their height is not a governing factor. They are easily grown, apparently do well in either acid or alkaline soil but respond to lime by better growth. Since so many gardeners admire lilacs it may be well to mention some of their troubles first, for no plant should be used without a full understanding of the difficulties to be encountered after the planting is done.

All lilacs are susceptible to lilac scale, a small insect very similar to the oyster shell scale. If not controlled, it will soon spread from plant to plant and eventually may increase so rapidly as to do serious injury to the planting. Spraying every year or so with a miscible oil while the plants are dormant is the simple means of keeping this pest under control, yet it must be done! Highway plantings devoted to long stretches of lilacs, even in New England, where the lilac is regarded in one state at least as the official state flower, have been known to die because it was not foreseen at planting time that plants should be sprayed to combat this pest.

The graft blight disease also causes serious trouble. In former years, lilacs were grafted on privet understock which grew rapidly and acted as an efficient "nurse" to the lilac scion. However, after the plant grew several years it was noted that a disease frequently attacked it at just about the graft union. A branch on the plant would suddenly die for no apparent reason, or in some cases the entire plant would quickly succumb. The disease may not strike a privet-grafted plant for years, but all of a sudden a withering or dying branch will be mute evidence of a possible quick death.

In recent years, propagating nurserymen have taken notice of this serious trouble, and are now growing "own root" lilacs. This is done either by growing them from cuttings according to new propagation methods; or of grafting them on privet, but planting the young grafts deep in the ground so as to force the scion itself to send out roots, and then cutting off the privet understock completely before the plants are sold. Any nurseryman who does not have "own root" lilacs need not be patronized (for his lilacs at least) since many reliable nurserymen are now growing good plants which will not be susceptible to the ravages of this disease.

The older branches of lilacs are frequently attacked by the lilac borer, a small boring grub which works into the base of the larger branches and may cause the death of some. The holes of the borer are usually noted by small amounts of sawdust at the openings. Branches infested with borers should be cut off below the borer holes and burned.

In the late summer, especially after wet rainy spells, the leaves of the lilacs may become white with mildew. This does little harm to the plant since the leaves are likely to drop off a few weeks later anyway, due to advent of cold weather. If the mildew is objectionable, it can be controlled slightly by dusting with powdered sulphur.

Pruning is very important in growing good lilacs, and particular attention should be given to renewal pruning every few years. As already stated, lilacs grow vigorously from the base. Many varieties, in fact the majority of the varieties of the common lilac, have the disconcerting habit of sending out new suckers from the base each year. On young plants these may be wanted, but the older a plant grows, the wider it frequently becomes until it soon grows out of bounds and its numerous suckers seriously encroach on other parts of the garden. This is bad for the plant itself because of the increased demand for nutrients made by the young suckers, frequently made at the expense of the flowers. Flowers become less numerous and smaller, sometimes the plant may even fail to bloom. Consequently, many of the suckers should be removed entirely and only a few allowed to remain and take the place of older branches which themselves may be removed for various reasons.

The famous lilac walk at the Arnold Arboretum, Boston, Massachusetts, where over 400 varieties bloom within a four week period.

Like the forsythias, privets, spireas and many other shrubs, the lilacs as a group can quickly recover from severe pruning. In fact most lilacs can be completely cut to within six inches of the ground in early spring, and be expected to make a good growth from the base during the current growing season. There has always been a question in my mind as to whether lilacs which were grown with a single stem would respond likewise. This spring we selected twelve old plants with single trunks about three to six inches in diameter, and cut them all off within a foot of the ground before the buds had begun to swell. By the end of June, all were again growing vigorously by sending out young shoots from the old stumps, which, prior to that "operation" had shown no obvious external growing points. Of course this is very drastic treatment especially if the plant is a valued one, but I merely mention it to show that these plants can be cut close to the ground and survive.

The better way to treat old plants is to take out a third of the old stems one year, another third the next and the remaining third the following year. In this manner, an old plant will be completely renewed over a three-year period, and still look fairly well during that time. A plant which has been cut to the ground does not add much in appearance to any garden, although there may reasonably be times when such drastic treatment is the better one to follow.

In order to have large blooms, it is advisable to keep the older wood restrained so that there is always a small amount of younger wood coming along; keep a majority of the young suckers at the base cut out, allowing only enough to grow to take the place of the older branches which will eventually be cut out; remove the dead flower clusters before they have time to form seeds. This last is particularly a good practice, since it not only aids in keeping the plants from becoming unsightly for the remainder of the year, but if the seeds are not allowed to form, more plant nourishment is available for the formation of flower buds for the coming year.

Many people are impatient about the length of time it takes young plants to bloom. Some, if not growing too vigorously, will bloom at a height of 4-5′, others may take longer. All lilac bushes should bloom, there are none that are "blind." It may be that the soil in which they are growing is too rich and they are putting all their efforts into vegetative growth. If this is the case, a slight root pruning might be helpful in promoting bloom. In other cases it may be that the soil is not just right. Digging a ditch around close to the base of the plant and mixing some superphosphate with the soil has shown definite effects. Pruning out some of the over-vigorous suckers has also been helpful. Patience and intelligent care are bound to result in good flowering.

By far the most popular and common among the lilacs are the varieties of *Syringa vulgaris,* many of which are popularly termed "French Hybrids." Many of these did originate in France, chiefly because of the untiring efforts of that famous French nurseryman, Victor Lemoine. However, many other splendid varieties have originated in this country as well as in Belgium and England. The greater number of them have single flowers, some have double. They can be divided into eight color groups. The varieties in the recommended list have been selected from a survey conducted by the Committee on Horticultural Varieties of the American Association of Botanical Gardens and Arboretums in 1942. Experts judged all the major collections in this country, rated the flowers, and these reports were correlated with other reports from nurserymen and private individuals. No other list, as far as I know, has been made up with such care and with the consideration of varietal performance in various parts of the country. Many lists have been made as a result of one individual's selections judged in one collection one year. The selections given here, however, are backed by the studied opinions of competent judges. Of course, they are not final, but the amateur, and the nurserymen as well, might do far worse than to make his selections from this carefully studied list.

Most of the varieties of S. *vulgaris* bloom within a two or three week period, starting just a trifle after the Flowering Dogwood, *Cornus florida,* starts to flower. Some of the lilac species, however, bloom later as well as earlier so that if one is interested in a sequence of lilac bloom it can be had for at least a six week period. It would start with S. *oblata dilatata* and then S. *hyacinthiflora* varieties, blooming the first of all lilacs, before the leaves

The Persian lilac (*Syringa persica*), valued because of its profuse flowers, was probably the first of the hybrid lilacs.

appear. The sequence continues with S. *vulgaris* and its many hybrids, then S. *villosa*, the Late Lilac; then the new Preston lilacs and finally, the last of all to bloom would be the Japanese Tree Lilac S. *amurensis japonica*. This last is truly a worthy specimen, with large creamy-white flower clusters and when grown with a single trunk it has cherrylike bark. In Boston it blooms the last of June.

Some of the lilac species are really valuable ornamentally. They are sufficiently varied as to habit, shape of flower, and method of growth to add considerable interest to any lilac collection. For instance, the Little Leaf Lilac (S. *microphylla*) has small flowers, and only grows 5–6′ tall but is nearly twice as wide. Added to this interesting habit is the fact that sometimes it blooms a second time—in the fall—and although it does not have as many flowers at this time, as in the spring, they are conspicuous nevertheless.

Both the Chinese and Persian lilacs and their varieties are valued for their multitudinous small flowers, making them excellent for cutting purposes. In fact, the Persian Lilac, if well grown, will have three-foot branches literally covered with flower clusters. Another plant, formerly believed to be its cut-leaved variety but now considered a species in its own right, S. *laciniata*, makes a specimen plant even when the flowers are not in bloom for its fine foliage and graceful habit are prominent throughout the entire growing season. The Persian Lilac and S. *laciniata* (cutleaf lilac) are the smallest of the lilacs.

The most fragrant of all the lilacs has been noted as the Hairy Lilac, S. *pubescens*. Some of the better late-flowering lilac hybrids have S. *reflexa* in their family tree. This lilac, called the Nodding Lilac, has not proved satisfactory in the Arnold Arboretum, but its red buds and pinkish flowers have given rise to some very beautiful hybrids. "Guinevere" and the S. *prestoniae* group are splendid examples. Only recently we have checked some forty-one late-flowering hybrids at the Arnold Arboretum and have come to the conclusion that based on flower, color and size, only a very few should be grown but these show considerable promise for prolonging the flowering season. The remainder are either inferior or practically identical with those selected.

The lilacs as a group, therefore, are vigorous and require only periodic attention. This attention they must have. Pruning and spraying at periodic intervals are absolutely essential to their general welfare, and if such attention cannot be given them, it is best not to plant them.

Syringa amurensis japonica   30′   Zone 4   Japanese Tree Lilac

*FLOWERS: creamy white in large pyramidal heads
    TIME: mid-June
BARK: trunk and older branches with cherrylike bark
HABITAT: Japan
INTRODUCED: 1876

Of special value because of the late bloom of the flowers. This Japanese Lilac is a tree, and can be grown with a single trunk. The shiny cherrylike bark is interesting in the winter, the large leaves and conspicuously vigorous habit is striking in spring and summer and the large creamy-white pyramidal flower clusters make it an outstanding plant, either as a specimen or in a group as screen or windbreak. The variety differs from the species in being more treelike in habit, taller, and slightly later to flower.

x Syringa chinensis   15′   Zone 5   Chinese Lilac

*FLOWERS: purple-lilac in small clusters
    TIME: late May
HYBRID ORIGIN: S. *laciniata* x S. *vulgaris*
ORIGINATED: 1777
VARIETIES:
    alba—white flowers
    saugeana—lilac-red flowers

The leaves of this species are midway in size between those of the Persian Lilac and the much larger leaves of the Common Lilac. Because of this, as well as the fact that it is midway in habit also, it is a valued addition to the lilac group affording a variation in size and foliage which is much needed. It is often spoken of as the first hybrid lilac, originating by chance in the Botanic garden at Rouen, France, in 1777.

x **Syringa henryi "Lutece"**   10'   Zone 2

*FLOWERS: pale violet-pink
    TIME: early June
HYBRID ORIGIN: *S. villosa x S. josikaea*
ORIGINATED: 1890
    This and *S. villosa* are very much alike except that this lilac has flowers that are more loose and a deeper pink color. Both bloom at the same time and can be displayed together advantageously.

x **Syringa josiflexa "Guinevere"**   9'   Zone 3

*FLOWERS: orchid-purple
HYBRID ORIGIN: *S. josikaea x S. reflexa*
ORIGINATED: 1920
    One of Miss Isabella Preston's (Ottawa, Canada) hybrids, this has flower clusters 9" long and nearly as broad. The clusters are rather loose, but the flower color does not fade in the full sun.

Syringa josikaea   12'   Zone 2   Hungarian Lilac

FLOWERS: lilac-violet
    TIME: early June
FOLIAGE: glossy
HABITAT: Hungary
INTRODUCED: 1830
    This species, slightly less handsome than *S. villosa,* is nevertheless included in the selected list because of its glossy green foliage and its ability to withstand clipping. It is frequently mistaken for *S. villosa* when not in flower, but the leaves are much more glossy.

Syringa laciniata   6'   Zone 5   Cutleaf Lilac

*FLOWERS: pale lilac, distributed all along the branches
*FOLIAGE: leaves deeply lobed
HABITAT: Turkestan and China
INTRODUCED: 1614
    Formerly called *S. persica laciniata* this is an interesting example of a plant which has been misnamed by the botanists for years. William H. Judd, Propagator at the Arnold Arboretum for many years, pointed out that this plant reproduces readily from seed (whereas *S. persica* is almost completely sterile), thus forcing the botanists to raise this former "variety" to specific rank and reduce *S. persica* to a hybrid. Regardless of this, the Cutleaf Lilac is an unusually delicate and beautiful plant often having shoots 3' long, literally covered with pale lilac-colored flowers, making an excellent garden specimen.

Syringa microphylla   6'   Zone 5   Littleleaf Lilac

FLOWERS: pale lilac
    TIME: late May
HABITAT: north China
INTRODUCED: 1910

No other lilac has the broad habit of this plant, almost twice as broad as it is high. The leaves are only about one fourth the size of those of the common lilac. Occasionally the plant bears a few flowers in the fall—not many, but enough to make it interesting some years. The flower panicles are not over 2¾" long, but the landscape value of the plant is chiefly because of its habit, unique among the lilacs.

Syringa oblata dilatata   12'   Zone 3   Korean Early Lilac

*FLOWERS: pinkish
    TIME: early May
AUTUMN COLOR: reddish, often a rich wine-red
HABITAT: Korea
INTRODUCED: 1917

The earliest to bloom of all the lilacs, this species is also the only one with autumn color. The autumn color is not as good as that of some of the viburnums but is noticeable and all other lilacs lack it. The flowers appear a week to ten days before those of the Common Lilac and come just before the leaves are open. As a consequence, the flowers are not nearly as prominent as they would be with a dark green foliage background. However, the species and this hardy variety have some merit.

x Syringa oblata dilatata x S. vulgaris

VARIETIES:
    "Assessippi"—pinkish mauve
    "Pocahontas"—reddish purple
HYBRID ORIGIN: by F. L. Skinner, Manitoba, Canada
INTRODUCED: 1935

These excellent hybrids bloom before most of the S. *vulgaris* varieties; they are very fragrant and bloom freely with rather large open trusses.

Syringa oblata giraldi x S. vulgaris

    "Catinat"—originated 1922—single—pinkish
    "Lamartine"—originated 1911—single—pinkish
    "Louvois"—originated 1921—single—violet
    "Necker"—originated 1920—single—pinkish
    "Turgot"—originated 1920—single—pinkish
    "Viliars"—originated in 1920—single—lilac

All are early-flowering hybrids, blooming before the leaves are developed and at least 7–10 days before the varieties of the common lilac.

x Syringa persica   6'   Zone 5   Persian Lilac

*FLOWERS: pale lilac
    TIME: late May
FOLIAGE: small leaves
HYBRID ORIGIN: S. *afghanica* x S. *laciniata*
ORIGINATED: about 1753

In habit, this is the smallest of the lilacs. When properly grown, the branches are often covered with the small flower clusters. It is almost completely sterile

LEFT: *Syringa prestoniae* "Isabella," one of the best of the Preston lilacs.

RIGHT: The Nodding Lilac, S. *reflexa* is one of the parents of the Preston hybrids. Although the flower buds are red, the flowers gradually fade white. It has not performed as well as most of the other lilacs as a specimen and so is mentioned here chiefly for breeding purposes.

and probably has not been found wild in any country. On the other hand the cut-leaved form, previously called S. *persica laciniata* has been found wild in several places and was probably one of the parents of S. *chinensis*.

x Syringa prestoniae varieties   9'   Zone 2   Preston Lilac

*FLOWERS: pink to deep pink

    TIME: early to mid-June

HYBRID ORIGIN: S. *villosa* x S. *reflexa*

ORIGINATED: before 1925

VARIETIES:

    "Isabella"—largest pyramidal flower panicles, pink

    "Audrey"—dense cluster, 7" × 6", phlox-purple

    "Handel"—tight clusters 5" × 3", buds amaranth-rose, and flowers fade white

    "Donald Wyman"—deepest pink to almost reddish flowers with buds and
        flowers same color

    Some time before 1925, Miss Isabella Preston, Horticulturist of the Canadian Experimental Station, Ottawa, Canada, made the initial cross resulting in a large number of seedlings, many of which were named by the Station later. This was unfortunate for among these seedling-clons there was a great similarity. The cross has been made since by other plant breeders. The variety "Donald Wyman" is one made by Mr. F. L. Skinner of Dropmore, Manitoba, Canada. All are very hardy lilacs and bloom about two weeks after the varieties of S. *vulgaris*

The Late Lilac (S. *villosa*) a very hardy and vigorous species. This too is one of the parents of the Preston hybrids.

have finished. They are sturdy, dense and upright in habit, with leaves as large as those of S. *villosa*. They bear large pyramidal spikes of flowers, those of the variety "Isabella" being the largest. The size of the flower clusters, the general shape and the intensity of color varies somewhat but those varieties in the recommended list are the best of these variations. A splendid group of late-blooming lilacs, not particularly fragrant but making outstanding specimens, they are also excellent when used as windbreaks or in flowering hedges.

Syringa sweginzowi	9'	Zone 5	Chengtu Lilac

*FLOWERS: reddish lilac
   TIME: early June
HABITAT: northwest China
INTRODUCED: 1894

Syringa villosa	9'	Zone 2	Late Lilac

*FLOWERS: rosy lilac to white
   TIME: early June
HABITAT: north China
INTRODUCED: 1882

One of the hardiest of all the lilacs. It is especially valued for its dense, upright habit, as well as for its late flowers which appear a week after the flowers of S. *vulgaris* have passed. It is not so fragrant, but certainly makes a worthy garden specimen, and a very dense screen.

Syringa vulgaris   20′   **Zone 3**   Common Lilac

*FLOWERS: lilac, fragrant
   TIME: mid-May
HABITAT: southeastern Europe
INTRODUCED: 1563
VARIETY: *alba*—flowers white

No lilac is native of the United States or Canada but this Common Lilac has escaped cultivation in many places and certainly appears "native" in many sections. It is this species which has given rise to many of the so-called "French" hybrids that are among the popular lilacs of today. It is this dense, vigorous, upright growing lilac which is commonly grown everywhere, suckering easily from the base, sometimes far more than it should. Such suckers should be thinned, and only a few allowed to grow to replace some of the older branches.

Recommended Varieties

White

SINGLE
   "Vestale"
   "Mont Blanc"
   "Jan Van Tol"
   "Marie Finon"

DOUBLE
   "Edith Cavell"
   "Ellen Willmott"

Violet

SINGLE
   "De Miribel"
   "Cavour"

DOUBLE
   "Marechal Lannes"
   "Violetta"

Blue and Bluish

SINGLE
   "President Lincoln"
   "Decaisne"
   "Maurice Barres"

DOUBLE
   "Olivier de Serres"
   "Emile Gentil"
   "Duc de Massa"

Lilac

SINGLE
   "Marengo"
   "Jacques Callot"

DOUBLE
   "President Fallieres"
   "Henri Martin"
   "Victor Lemoine"
   "Leon Gambetta"

Pink and Pinkish

SINGLE
   "Lucie Baltet"
   "Macrostachya"

DOUBLE
   "Mme. Antoine Buchner"
   "Katherine Havemeyer"
   "Montaigne"

Magenta

SINGLE
   "Marechal Foch"
   "Mme. F. Morel"
   "Capitaine Baltet"

DOUBLE
   "Paul Thirion"
   "Paul Deschanel"
   "Mrs. Edward Harding"

Purple (or deep Purple)

SINGLE
   "Monge"
   "Mrs. W. E. Marshall"
   "Ludwig Spaeth"

Tamarix odessana   6′   **Zone 4**   Odessa Tamarix

*FLOWERS: pink, small, fluffy in general appearance
   TIME: mid-July

[?]FOLIAGE: minute leaves, texture feathery
HABITAT: Caspian region
INTRODUCED: about 1885

The lowest of this genus, blooming on the current year's growth. Because of its small size this is the best for small gardens and the easiest species to keep pruned. The minute pink flowers and extremely small, almost scalelike leaves, give all *Tamarix* species a light, aery texture not found in most other shrubs. Because it blooms on the current year's growth it should be pruned when dormant in the early spring.

Tamarix parviflora   15′   Zone 4   Small-flowered Tamarix

*FLOWERS: pink, small, fluffy in general appearance
    TIME: late May
*FOLIAGE: leaves minute, texture feathery
HABITAT: southeastern Europe

This is the only one of the recommended species blooming on the previous year's growth, hence it should be pruned immediately after flowering. Its texture, both of flowers and foliage, is identical with that of *T. odessana* and is only recommended because it blooms earlier. Most *Tamarix* species do well in fairly dry soil and this does well in seashore plantings.

Tamarix pentandra   15′   Zone 2   Five Stamen Tamarix

*FLOWERS: pink, small, fluffy in general appearance
    TIME: mid-July
*FOLIAGE: leaves minute, texture feathery
HABITAT: southeastern Europe to central Asia
INTRODUCED: 1883

The hardiest species of *Tamarix*, this should be heavily pruned in order to keep it within a reasonable height, otherwise it tends to grow very bare and open at the base. It has the same flower and foliage texture as *T. odessana* and is also good for seashore planting.

TAXUS

The yews are the darkest green of all evergreen shrubs and, without question, the most striking. They flourish in many kinds of soils and withstand clipping and pruning, thus making perfect hedges and screens as well as excellent specimens. Their bright red fleshy fruits are conspicuous during the fall. It is fortunate that they are represented by a large number of varieties ranging in size and shape so that they can be used for a large number of garden purposes.

The yew has been known and valued for centuries, records having shown that pieces of wood of the English Yew, *Taxus baccata*, have been found under glacial deposits in England.

Two principal species provide the ornamental varieties for American gardens, namely, *T. cuspidata*, the Japanese Yew, and *T. baccata*, the so-called English Yew. With trunk circumferences of at least 30′ there are yews in England which must be a thousand years old. Robin Hood and his Merry

Boxwood withstands shearing as well as any evergreen.

Men used stout cudgels made from yew, as were their long bows and cross bows. Even before this, spears were made from this sturdy wood, for a spear is known to have been dug from underneath a peat-deposit bog in England and is estimated to have been over 3000 years old.

These excellent evergreens are rather slow in growth when compared with deciduous shrubs, with wood that is hard and close grained. The yews resemble each other so much that a few botanists have suggested in the past that there is only one species, *T. baccata,* and that all other yews are merely geographical varieties of this.

Poisonous properties of the yews have been recorded. Caesar writes that Cativolcus, King of Eburones, poisoned himself by drinking the juice from the yew. The toxic material is probably an alkaloid named taxine, a heart depressant, present in the leaves, but not to such a great extent in the twigs and bark. Although many cases of cattle poisoning have been reported where cattle eat the foliage, there are instances where the branches have been lopped off in the pasture with no known ill effects. Illness and death among western cattle have frequently been attributed to their eating large quantities of the foliage and twigs of *T. brevifolia.* While the seed or stone in the fruit is poisonous, the fleshy pulp of the fruit, the only part of the plant that might be eaten by humans, is not poisonous.

Many a yew has failed to produce the decorative, colorful fruits and therefore caused disappointment. This is because the sexes are separate, the staminate flowers on one plant, the pistillate flowers on another. Both are necessary to insure fruiting. One staminate plant is sufficient for every six or eight pistillate or fruiting plants. If a specimen-fruiting plant is desired, it can be placed in the spot with the staminate plant nearby in an inconspicuous or partly hidden location. If a group of fruiting plants is desired, the staminate plant may be hidden in the center of the group and kept fairly inconspicuous by clipping. (For differences in flower buds of the two sexes see page 29.)

There are approximately 40 species and varieties of yews being grown in the United States, although not all are available from nurseries. Of the seven species grown, the Chinese Yew, *T. chinensis,* and the Pacific Yew, *T. brevifolia,* are little seen in cultivation and are not here recommended.

The English Yew is the least hardy. Although certain varieties—with some winter protection—can be safely grown as far north as Boston, yet *T. baccata* is not dependably hardy north of New York. Since it has been carefully grown for hundreds of years, it is only natural to expect that a number of forms have originated and have been propagated. The Japanese species has been grown extensively outside of Japan for less than half a century and consequently comparatively few varieties of it are to be found in commercial nurseries in this country up to this time.

In the Old World, the English Yew is widely distributed from England to North Africa and western Asia. It grows as a tree, from 30 to 60' high, with needles usually two-ranked and blunt at the end. Over thirty varieties have been named but some are difficult to obtain in this country and several are closely similar. The yews are all comparatively slow growing, but particularly well adapted for hedges and topiary work. In England, topiary work has been a hobby with gardeners for centuries and many splendid examples of painstaking pruning are to be seen about the countryside there.

In all probability, the most famous variety of the English Yew is *T. baccata stricta,* popularly called the Irish Yew. Two pistillate trees were found on a farm in Ireland about 1780, differing from the ordinary English Yew in having several leaders all densely upright in habit of growth. Even the needles on the twigs were arranged differently from the English Yew, distributed around all sides of the twig rather than being two-ranked in a flat spray. It is from cuttings of these two trees that the Irish Yew has been propagated. It is highly valued for its upright habit of growth and is excellent for formal planting.

Another popular variety is the Westfelton Yew, *T. baccata dovastoni,* a tree with erect trunk and horizontal branches, with branchlets pendulous. This plant makes a splendid specimen. It was first raised in Shrewsbury, England, in 1777. It has long been a popular form and it may be of interest to know that there is a form with yellow foliage.

Not all varieties of the English Yew are trees. For instance, the variety *adpressa* is a wide-spreading low shrub with needles only half as long as those of the species. Fortunately this variety is a fruiting form. The Spreading English Yew, *T. baccata repandens,* is a low, almost prostrate form, grown considerably in northern United States where it is apparently more hardy than any other variety of English Yew. If clipped and restrained, it may grow three feet or so in height, with the young branchlets decidedly pendulous. If allowed to grow unrestrained, it becomes very prostrate in habit and literally creeps along the ground.

The Japanese Yew, *T. cuspidata,* was first introduced into this country in 1861 by Dr. George R. Hall, a doctor who practiced medicine in the foreign settlement of Shanghai for a number of years. Later he became interested in collecting plants in both China and Japan, and in sending them back to the United States. This plant has shown its good qualities time and time again and now is being grown by the majority of American nurseries. It has proved itself hardy under trying winter conditions; although not fool-proof, it can be grown where many other evergreens cannot. The nomenclature of the varieties of this plant is still greatly confused.

In Bailey's "Cyclopedia" published in 1917, and in numerous other articles written before and since that time, it has been pointed out that *T. cuspidata* is a tree. Hence, the variety erroneously listed in many nursery catalogues as *T. cuspidata capitata* actually is *T. cuspidata.* However, this misunderstanding of names has probably been augmented by the fact that there is a variety of *T. cuspidata* which has spreading upright branches, forming a low center, and in cross section looks broadly V-shaped. Practically every nursery has it and practically every nursery calls this *T. cuspidata.* To alleviate confusion, this form has been named *T. cuspidata expansa.* It is readily known that when seed of *T. cuspidata* is sown, many interesting seedlings will appear, varying considerably in shape and height, and a certain proportion of them will have this desirable spreading upright shape.

Fortunately these dignified evergreens are comparatively free of serious pests. Occasionally an old plant may be attacked by the strawberry root weevil and the needles will begin to drop. This may frequently be controlled by the use of poison baits for the beetles, and pyrethrum sprays on the ground for the grubs that do the damage. D.D.T. is also proving practicable in the control of this pest.

For specimens, for hedges, for backgrounds, for any one of many uses, the yews are excellently well suited; and because of their large number and variety of shapes and sizes, it is not exaggeration to say that there is a yew for every garden where evergreens can be grown.

Taxus baccata   60'   Zone 6   English Yew

*FRUIT: fleshy, single-seeded, red berry
    EFFECTIVE: fall
*FOLIAGE: evergreen, lustrous, dark green, needlelike
HABITAT: Europe, northern Africa, western Asia
INTRODUCED: early colonial times

VARIETIES:

adpressa—Shortleaf English Yew—dense, broad, conical bush

dovastoni—Westfelton Yew—upright in habit with horizontal branches and dark green foliage

elegantissima—Elegant English Yew—vigorous wide-spreading bush with main branches mostly horizontal with young foliage striped yellow

erecta—Broom Yew—upright in habit but much wider in growth than Irish Yew

repandens—Spreading English Yew—the hardiest (Zone 4) of all

stricta—Irish Yew—rigidly columnar and upright in habit, one of the most picturesque of all varieties

Over 30 varieties of the English Yew have been listed and the above are perhaps the most prominent.

Taxus canadensis   3–6′   Zone 2   Canada Yew

FRUIT: red, fleshy berries
  EFFECTIVE: fall
FOLIAGE: evergreen, needlelike, yellow green
HABITAT: Newfoundland to Virginia, Iowa and Manitoba
VARIETY: *stricta*—branches stiffly upright, discovered by Richard Wyman in a block of *T. canadensis*, 1929, at Framingham, Mass.

This yew, native in North America, is the hardiest of the yews but certainly not the handsomest. It withstands shade much better than the other species but does not fruit as well nor is its foliage as dark a green as that of other species. Plants of this species are frequently monoecious.

Taxus cuspidata   50′   Zone 4   Japanese Yew

*FRUIT: red, fleshy berries
  EFFECTIVE: fall
*FOLIAGE: evergreen, needlelike, dark
HABITAT: Japan and Korea
INTRODUCED: 1855

One of the best narrow-leaved evergreens for ornamental purposes. Many varieties are being grown in this country. The following are some of the best:

aurescens—young shoots tinged yellow a greater part of the growing season. The plant is a dwarf with 20-year-old plants in the Arnold Arboretum only 1′ high and 3′ in diameter.

densa—a low shrub, twice as broad as high with very dark green foliage. The first plants of this variety came to the old Parson's Nursery at Flushing, Long Island, from Japan, many years ago. It is smaller than the variety *nana*, 40-year-old specimens being only 4′ high and 8′ in diameter. It is one of the most handsome of the dwarf evergreens.

expansa—a name given to a large proportion of *T. cuspidata* seedlings with a vase-shaped habit. The species is a tree with a central leader, but many of the vase-shaped plants sold in American nurseries today as *T. cuspidata* are actually *T. cuspidata expansa*. It has an open center, no central leaders, with foliage much more loose and open than that of the varieties *densa* and *nana*. It can be easily distinguished from the variety *thayerae* by its more upright branches (45–60

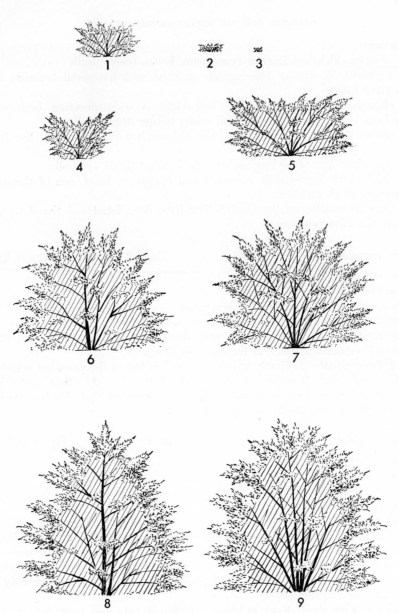

Forms and approximate sizes of *Taxus cuspidata* varieties as they are growing in the Arnold Arboretum.

		HEIGHT	SPREAD
1.	*Taxus cuspidata densa*	4′	8′
2.	*T. cuspidata aurescens*	1′	3′
3.	*T. cuspidata minima*	8″	8″
4.	*T. cuspidata expansa*	5′	8′
5.	*T. cuspidata thayerae*	8′	16′
6. 7.	*T. cuspidata nana*	15′	20′
8. 9.	*T. cuspidata*	20–25′	15–20′

The Dwarf Japanese Yew (*Taxus cuspidata nana*) is ideally adapted to this situation, where its slow growth and dark green foliage make this terrace planting attractive throughout the entire year.

degree angle from base of plant) and its open center, not flat-topped as in *thayerae*. Also it is only half again as wide as tall, where *thayerae* is twice as wide as tall. Both make excellent plants for use on the home grounds.

"Hiti"—an unusually narrow, upright clon, originating in the Hite Nursery, Pomfret Center, Conn.

nana—this variety has been called var. *brevifolia* incorrectly, for this is the specific name given to the Western Yew, native on the Pacific Coast. Some of the plants in the Arnold Arboretum are now approximately 40 years old and are about 10′ high and 20′ in diameter. It is recognized by its shrublike habit of growth, its spreading branches covered with short branchlets, and also its leaves, which are shorter and slightly more dull than those of the species. This is commonly available in the trade and makes an excellent specimen.

thayerae—named by E. H. Wilson in 1930, these plants are said to be seedlings grown from one plant in the Thayer Estate at South Lancaster, Massachusetts. In 1916 and 1917 a number of seedlings were grown by William Anderson, Superintendent of the Thayer Estate. These, according to Mr. Anderson, were grown from seed of one plant, a form of *T. cuspidata* intermediate between the species and *T. cuspidata nana*. A selection of these seedlings was made in 1924 and sent to the Arnold Arboretum, later being given the varietal name *thayerae* by E. H. Wilson. When these plants were received, October 1, 1924, they were 2–3′ high and 3′ in diameter. Now these plants are approximately 8′ tall and 16′ in diameter. Although there is some variation among them, all have

uniformly wide-spreading branches which are almost horizontal, coming out at
the base of the plant at about a 30 degree angle and the lower branches arching and frequently touching the ground. The centers of the plants are filled with
foliage and not hollow, the top is flat, and the general form is somewhat rec-
tangular, twice as wide as high. This variety is not a clon, since the original
plants were selected as a group. However, since *T. cuspidata* seedlings vary so
greatly, it would be advisable to propagate this variety (and others also) asexually, rather than to grow large numbers of seedlings and make varietal selections
from forms too young to properly assess.

x Taxus media   40′   Zone 4

*FRUIT: fleshy, one-seeded red berry
    TIME: fall
*FOLIAGE: evergreen, needlelike
HYBRID: *T. cuspidata x T. baccata*
INTRODUCED: about 1900

About 1900, a new species of yew originated as a result of a cross between
the English and Japanese Yews. Mr. T. D. Hatfield, Superintendent of the famous
Hunnewell Estate in Wellesley, Mass., had grown a number of seedlings which
were given the specific name of *T. media*. This hybrid is broadly pyramidal, frequently has a central leader and grows into tree form. The hardy qualities of the
Japanese Yew and the ornamental qualities of the English Yew are merged in
this plant to give an excellent ornamental evergreen. One of the seedlings, resulting from this cross, developed into a plant considerably more dense than the
species, and has been named after its originator, *hatfieldi*.
VARIETIES:

    browni—fine, dense, conical form
    hatfieldi—Hatfield Yew, a pyramidal shrub with upright branches, dense in
habit and very popular.
    hicksi—Hicks Yew—originating at Hick's Nurseries, Westbury, Long Island,
columnar in habit and excellent for formal accent in the garden. It is similar to
the Irish Yew but considerably hardier.
    kelseyi—Berrybush Yew, semi-dwarf, fruits freely, at only 4–5 years old,
named after F. W. Kelsey, New York, about 1915.
    Taxus media is known chiefly for the first two forms. Both are very popular
and are fruiting types provided of course they are propagated asexually from the
original plants. However, many other forms of *T. media* have arisen. One in
particular has the general shape of Hicks Yew but is staminate, hence it does
not have the very desirable colorful fruits. The propagation of such plants should
be confined to a minimum.

Teucrium chamaedrys   10″   Zone 5   Chamaedrys Germander

FLOWERS: purple or rose in small spikes
    TIME: summer
HABITAT: central and southern Europe and western Asia
INTRODUCED: 1750

Dense, sub-shrub, it is used in the rockery, in foreground of evergeen plantings or as a low, bordering hedge in the perennial or rose garden. A very neat
plant.

Thuja occidentalis   60'   Zone 2   American Arbor-vitae

*FOLIAGE: evergreen, scalelike
HABITAT: eastern North America

This species is a native tree but there are many slow-growing forms that can be considered shrubs, commonly used in foundation plantings. They are of interest for their form and evergreen foliage and seem to do best in gardens where the climate is not too dry. In nature, these plants are always found in moist woods, often near water, and so should have a moist rich soil in which to grow. The varieties with yellow foliage turn an undesirable dirty yellow green in winter and so should be avoided. All varieties can be sheared and in certain situations make excellent hedges, especially in areas where the summer climate is cool and moist. Some of the better varieties are:

bodmeri—large, dense, grows mostly in clumps.
ericoides—dwarf, bushy form with needle-shaped leaves, brownish in winter.
globosa—dwarf, globular form, bright green foliage.
hoveyi—not as definitely globose as *globosa* but round and rather irregular in shape.
"Little Gem"—a very low, dense, compact form, often only a foot tall but several feet in diameter. Sometimes this is termed *T. occidentalis pumila*.
robusta—often termed "wareana" or "sibirica"; hardy, tall but dense form, with bluish green foliage.
umbraculifera—rigidly upright, with a flat top, the specimen in the Arnold Arboretum is 8' tall and 10' in diameter at the base.

Thuja orientalis   50'   Zone 6   Oriental Arbor-vitae

*FOLIAGE: evergreen, lustrous, scalelike
HABITAT: northern China and Korea
INTRODUCED: before 1737
VARIETIES:

bakeri—foliage light green, seems to withstand hot, dry locations.
bonita—cone-shaped, leaves tipped yellow, in use on Pacific Coast.
decussata—dwarf, bushy
flageliformis—branches drooping and threadlike, in use on Pacific Coast.
globosa—dwarf, globose habit.
meldensis—narrow, pyramidal form, irregular in habit.
sieboldi—low and rounded in habit, somewhat like an old-fashioned beehive in shape.
stricta—dense, pyramidal habit
texana-glauca—pyramidal, blue green foliage, being used on Pacific Coast.

Thymus serpyllum   Ground cover   Zone 4   Mother-of-Thyme

FLOWERS: rosy purple, small, terminal heads
    TIME: late May
*FOLIAGE: evergreen, leaves small, aromatic, to ½" long
HABITAT: Europe, western Asia, northern Africa
INTRODUCED: early colonial times

Low almost herbaceous plant, highly variable with many varieties listed and suitable only as a rock garden plant or between stepping stones where it can creep slowly over rocks and will not be crowded out by weeds or other plants.

The Sargent Weeping Hemlock, a variety of the native *Tsuga canadensis*, makes a fine specimen. This particular plant is over 50 years old, but younger (and smaller) specimens make interesting focal points in the rock garden.

Thymus vulgaris   Ground cover   Zone 5   Common Thyme

FLOWERS: lilac to purplish, small spikes
   TIME: late May
*FOLIAGE: evergreen, leaves small, aromatic, leaves to ½″ long
HABITAT: southern Europe
INTRODUCED: early colonial times

A popular low plant for the rock garden or to border walks or between stepping stones in places where weeds and other plants will not encroach on it. Widely used and valued for its aromatic flowers and foliage.

Tripetaleia paniculata   6′   Zone 5

*FLOWERS: small, white, in terminal panicles 6″ long
   TIME: August
HABITAT: Japan
INTRODUCED: 1892

An interesting, rather rare shrub, closely related to the rare American *Elliotia* and of interest chiefly for its delicate panicles of white terminal flowers in late summer. Unusual and not too difficult to cultivate, hence of interest.

Tsuga canadensis   90′   Zone 4   Common Hemlock

*FOLIAGE: lustrous dark evergreen, needlelike
HABITAT: Nova Scotia to Minnesota, and Illinois, south on mountains to north Georgia and north Alabama

VARIETY: *pendula*—low form with pendulous branches forming a dense hemispherical bush, broader than high. Sargent Weeping Hemlock

Normally a tree, this species is only included here because it can be kept 3–4′ high by judicial pruning and if this is done it makes one of the best hedges it is possible to grow. The advantages of using either the Canada or the Carolina hemlock in the hedge are that these plants can be pruned in a stiffly rigid shape if desired, or the hedge can be clipped in a general mounded form and the long graceful shoots allowed to grow gracefully for a year or even two, when they must be pruned back hard in the early spring or the plant soon grows out of shape. Thus the planting serves the dual purpose of formal hedge one year and informal hedge the next.

Also the shrubby pendulous form, known as the Sargent Weeping Hemlock is a particularly graceful plant, for use as a specimen in the rock garden or beside the pool, where its wide-spreading, pendulous branches quickly give it the appearance of being two or three times as broad as it is high.

VACCINIUM

Blueberries, in landscaping the home grounds, are of importance chiefly as foliage plants, especially in the fall when their autumn foliage turns a brilliant scarlet. One of the species is evergreen and, though not hardy in the northeastern states, is widely used in other parts of the country where it does well, especially on the Pacific Coast. In general, the blueberries require acid soil, and usually poor soil as well. Some of the blueberry-growing areas in Maine, Massachusetts, New York and Wisconsin, where the Highbush Blueberry (*Vaccinium corymbosum*) is cultivated for its fruits, are on poor, worn out, sandy soil which is considered best for its growth.

Fortunately, the blueberries are not susceptible to serious diseases or insect pests, and certainly in the garden these can be overlooked entirely. They are frequently found native in moist and even wet areas but notwithstanding will do well in normal soil. Two of the species, V. *angustifolium* and V. *pallidum,* are known to grow well in dry soil. The latter is called the Dryland Blueberry, and is used primarily for this attribute. It is not particularly ornamental, but will afford growth in dry, sandy, acid soil, where other plants may find it extremely difficult to grow. The Pennsylvania Blueberry, V. *angustifolium laevifolium,* is native over nearly half the country, does not grow much over a foot high, and is excellent for planting as an undercover in the woods or even as a ground cover in acid-soil plantings. As a special ornament or single specimen it has no merit whatsoever. Because of its habit of growth, low and stoloniferous, it can be cut off near the surface of the ground with a scythe and be expected to quickly grow back again.

The real ground cover is the diminutive Mountain Cowberry or Mountain Cranberry. It forms dense mats less than six inches tall and withstands the coldest weather in the North. It does not survive the hot dry weather of the southern summers, hence when used, plenty of moisture and cool shade should be available during the summer months. The true Cranberry,

V. oxycoccus, is not recommended because of its sometimes difficult culture, and this Mountain Cranberry is only recommended for special situations in the northern part of the country.

The Box Blueberry, *V. ovatum,* is one of the important shrubs of the Northwest, where it is native along the Pacific Coast. It is an evergreen shrub, growing as high as 12', with dark, glossy green leaves an inch or two in length. Young shoots are a brilliant copper-bronze when they first emerge. Its foliage is in great demand the country over by florists who use it as filler in bouquets, wreaths, etc., and considerable care should be taken in its conservation now, or it will not be long before it disappears from all but the most inaccessible parts of the Pacific Coast area. A grand foliage shrub for use in Zone 7, especially where the atmosphere is moist.

The most important and widely usable blueberry for landscape use is the Highbush Blueberry, *V. corymbosum,* grown over a greater part of the country in gardens, fast becoming of interest commercially as a source of fruits, and native over nearly half the United States. It is a deciduous shrub, reaching 12' in height, but in gardens can easily be kept considerably lower by proper pruning. The foliage turns a bright scarlet in the fall, sometimes even orange, which adds considerably to its brilliance. It will grow in either shade or full sun, making a much more compact plant in the sun. The fruit is an edible blue-black berry, and the so-called "cultivated blueberries" of commerce are from one of the many selected clons of this plant.

Over a period of years certain plants were found producing bigger and sometimes better fruits than others. These have been selected and propagated. It has been only within the past fifteen or twenty years that means of rapid asexual propagation of these plants has been found, so that now they are becoming available to an ever-widening market. If fruit is not desired, blueberries can be let alone with only occasional "renewal" pruning. Usually, however, when one has a few plants of this species in the shrub border, it is a matter of personal pride to force them to produce large fruits. This takes the right variety in the first place, and the right kind of timely pruning in the second place. As far as varieties are concerned over twenty-eight have been selected at one time or another.

Two-year-old plants, 10–12" high, are best to buy—for the beginner at least. It will take several years of growing to bring these into bearing, but since they may prove serviceable for fifty years or more (if desired) a few years of training at the beginning is worthwhile. Peat moss is an excellent medium to mix with the soil when they are first planted, and to use as a mulch later. It should be remembered however that in a foundation planting next a stucco house, the splashing of water from the foundation may make the soil alkaline eventually, and this condition must be corrected if it does occur.

If it is necessary to prune for fruit production, a few points should be kept in mind. *V. corymbosum* tends to fruit heavily, and if all flower buds are allowed to bear, the fruits will be small, regardless of the variety. Hence some thinning is necessary to produce the larger fruits. The fruit buds are on twigs formed the previous year, hence pruning can be done in early spring before the plant starts to grow. It is the vigorous shoots growing from the base of the plant, or the strong-growing lateral branches that produce the best fruits, not the weaker short twigs. Some of these might be removed, especially older branches which are covered with shorter twigs. Also, low-spreading branches on the ground might be cut off since fruits borne on these frequently get very dirty.

Varieties differ in habits of growth and pruning needs. For instance, "Rubel" does not need much of its terminal-shoot growth cut, while "Cabot" does, since it is a more vigorous-growing variety. With a little practice, the fruit buds, being more plump, can be distinguished from leaf buds.

With six species of this genus in the recommended list, and twenty-seven species and varieties suggested as rejections, it would appear that this group is not very important in landscape planting. This, in general, is true. Other plants will grow in acid soil and have brilliant fall coloring. The fruits of *Vaccinium* species are not ornamental, and many gardeners do not want to be bothered with them, for they do bring the birds, in many cases objectionable birds. In some places where the backyard gardener is trying to grow a few blueberries for their fruits, everything goes well until a day or two before he decides to pick them, when a flock of birds will come out of nowhere and his carefully tended fruits will be stripped in no time. In order to protect them from his feathered competitors, he will have to go to elaborate means of using netting, scarecrows and other devices. In fact, I saw one garden tended by an elderly gentleman who apparently had lost his crops during prior fruiting seasons. This particular time he had a series of tin cans and pans hung up in an ingenious way so that the slightest breeze would create quite a din ostensibly to scare the birds away. I never did get back to ask him about his crop that season!

Vaccinium angustifolium laevifolium   8″   Zone 2   Lowbush Blueberry

FLOWERS: white, small, waxy
   TIME: late May
FRUIT: bluish black berries
   EFFECTIVE: late summer
AUTUMN COLOR: scarlet
HABITAT: eastern North America

This lowbush blueberry, grown over a wide area of the acid-soil lands and abandoned pasture lands in the eastern United States, is used chiefly as a woody ground cover. In many sections these areas are burned and fertilized regularly, primarily to increase the fruit production of these plants.

Vaccinium arboreum   27′   Farkleberry

FLOWERS: white, small, waxy
   TIME: summer

FRUIT: blue berries
   EFFECTIVE: early fall
FOLIAGE: evergreen, leaves to 2″ long
HABITAT: southeastern United States
   Grown as an evergreen in the South where its lustrous green leaves and
diminutive waxy, white flowers promote its value as a garden ornament.

Vaccinium corymbosum   12′   Zone 3   Highbush Blueberry

FLOWERS: white or pinkish
   TIME: late May
FRUIT: blue-black berries
*AUTUMN COLOR: scarlet
WINTER TWIGS: red
HABITAT: eastern United States
   The Highbush Blueberry is the most ornamental of the deciduous blueberries. It is native over a wide area and when the soil is right it can be grown
into an excellent specimen with vigorous branches, good foliage and upright
red twigs all winter long. It is from this species that so many clons have been
selected from the wild for commercial blueberry growing. From an ornamental
viewpoint any plant of this species has merit in the fall because of its scarlet
autumn color and in the winter for its red twigs.

Some of the varieties noted for large fruits might be

"Atlantic"—originated 1940, late bearing
"Burlington"—originated 1940, late bearing
"Cabot"—originated 1930, early bearing
"Concord"—originated 1935, bearing in mid-season
"Dixi"—originated 1942, bearing in mid-season
"Jersey"—originated 1935, late bearing
"June"—originated 1935, early bearing
"Pemberton"—originated 1940, late bearing
"Pioneer"—originated ? bearing in mid-season
"Raucocas"—originated 1935, early bearing
"Rubel"—originated 1912, late bearing
"Stanley"—originated 1935, bearing in mid-season
"Wareham"—originated ? late bearing
"Weymouth"—originated 1942, early bearing

Vaccinium ovatum   10′   Zone 7   Box Blueberry

FLOWERS: white or pink, waxy, small
   TIME: late April
FRUIT: black berries
   EFFECTIVE: summer
*FOLIAGE: evergreen, lustrous, leaves to 1¼″ long
HABITAT: Pacific Coast of United States and Canada
   Chiefly valued for its evergreen leaves, the branches being cut by the car-
load for the florist industry. A good shrub for planting on the Pacific Coast but
none too hardy in the East.

The Box Blueberry (*Vaccinium ovatum*), an evergreen native of the Pacific Coast, is used by florists throughout the entire country and in this form—cut greens—is more or less familiar to everyone. It does make a fine garden plant where it is hardy.

Vaccinium pallidum   3'   Zone 3   Dryland Blueberry

FLOWERS: white
    TIME: late May
FRUIT: blue berries
*AUTUMN COLOR: scarlet
HABITAT: eastern United States
    A good blueberry for planting in dry soil.

Vaccinium vitis-idaea minus   Ground cover   Zone 2   Mountain Cranberry

FLOWERS: pink to red
    TIME: late May

FRUIT: dark red berries
FOLIAGE: evergreen, leaves to ¾" long
HABITAT: northern United States and Canada

A small-leaved, evergreen ground cover, 4–8" high and very hardy, doing best in moist soil situations. Its fruits are used for jellies and preserves.

VIBURNUM

The beauty and interest in many a shrub planting is greatly enhanced by including a few viburnums. These are most serviceable shrubs, many of them having decided ornamental value every season of the year. Several are valued for their flowers, in the spring; others are valued for their beautiful glossy, green foliage throughout the summer; still others are valued for their vivid autumn coloration, and many for their bright-colored fruits in late summer and fall. In fact, the fruits on some plants remain a greater part of the winter. Thus, the viburnums add interest in the garden during every season of the year, and since some are common in nurseries and many others can be located with a little effort, it is advisable to examine this interesting group carefully and see exactly what each species and variety has to contribute to the landscape picture.

The collection of viburnums at the Arnold Arboretum contains over seventy species and varieties, most of which are commercially available. Supplementing the seventy species and varieties already being grown in New England are others less hardy, which will grow farther south where climate is milder. In a large group of plants like this, there are bound to be wide ornamental possibilities available.

It may be of interest to note a few things which all of the viburnums have in common. In the first place, they all have opposite simple leaves, either deciduous or evergreen. The flowers are usually very small, borne in flat, rounded or pyramidal clusters but always terminal. They are white to pink, usually being a creamy white to a pure white. Some species may have two types of flowers: the small, comparatively inconspicuous, fertile flowers, and the larger, more conspicuous, sterile flowers, similar to those of certain hydrangeas. The fruit is a fleshy, one-seeded drupe and may be red, yellow, blue or black in color and anywhere from ⅜ to ¾" in diameter. It is these attractive fruits, borne in clusters, for which this genus is particularly noted ornamentally. The viburnums comprise a good, sturdy group of shrubs, easily grown and easily maintained. They are subject to few pests. Eastern and central Asia have contributed many of the best to be found in the garden of today, yet we should not overlook the handsome natives of North America which are always dependable, frequently under adverse growing conditions.

Viburnums for Flower

The first viburnum to bloom is *Viburnum fragrans*. Ordinarily, one or two flowers in each cluster start to open in March, the remaining flowers

The Linden Viburnum (*V. dilatatum*) is always covered with flowers late every spring, followed by brilliant red fruits in the fall. Like many another viburnum it is attractive as a single specimen or in massed plantings.

finally opening in April or whenever the weather is sufficiently mild. Since this species blooms so early in the season, the flowers are frequently killed by late frosts, and sometimes the flower buds themselves are partly frozen so that the inflorescences have a blasted appearance when open. Consequently, *V. fragrans* is of much greater value farther south where milder winters do not injure the flower buds. The blooming season progresses with *V. sieboldi* flowering in late April and then more and more viburnums coming into flower until *V. acerifolium* and *V. pubescens* open in mid-June and end the flowering sequence.

For fragrance, in the North, the new hybrid *V. burkwoodi* leads the list, closely followed by *V. carlesi* and *V. fragrans*. In the South, *V. odoratissimum* is strikingly fragrant in flower.

The snowballs are, of course, the most conspicuous of all in flower, and these are grown primarily for their large, sterile flower clusters. The flower cluster of every viburnum is made up of a large number of small flowers which in themselves are not conspicuous, but which in mass give the appearance of the Wild Carrot or Queen Anne's Lace. Some of the flower heads are merely flat, others are more pyramidal, and still others—especially those with the conspicuous, sterile flowers—are round. The snowballs come in this last group and are three in number. The European Snowball, *V. opulus*

Some viburnums like the Doublefile Viburnum (left) have flat flower clusters with small fertile flowers in the center of the cluster and larger sterile flowers around its perimeter. Other species have flower clusters with all fertile flowers, like those of the Nannyberry (right).

roseum, was probably the first one introduced into the United States, possibly coming to this country from Europe during colonial times. Although it is the hardiest of the three, it is the least desirable for it is the one most susceptible to severe infestations of plant lice. They attack the plant in large numbers and the result is a twisting and contorting of the flowers, leaves and stems, making an undesirable appearance. By far the better of the two hardy in the North is the Japanese Snowball, *V. tomentosum sterile,* which was introduced into England about 1844 and reached this country shortly after. This is not nearly as susceptible to infestations of plant lice. Although it was killed to the ground as far south as Philadelphia during the severe winter of 1933–34, in normal winters it is hardy in New England. Besides having large flower clusters, it has horizontal branches which give the plant a unique layered appearance, especially in the winter when branching habits are more evident.

The Chinese Snowball, *V. macrocephalum sterile,* comes from China and is not hardy in the North, but from Washington, D. C., southward, it is the best, for it has the largest flower heads. These are 3–6″ in diameter, and those of *V. tomentosum sterile* being 2½–3″ and those of *V. opulus roseum* being 2–2½″. Hence, where hardy, the Chinese form is the best of the snowballs.

Some viburnums, although not snowballs, have flat flower clusters and a few sterile flowers on the outer edge of each cluster, which gives a large and more pronounced appearance to the flower clusters. Such species includes *V. opulus, V. sargenti, V. trilobum, V. tomentosum,* and *V. macrocephalum.* The flower heads of the first two are about 3″ in diameter; of the next two species, 2½–4″; and of the last species, 3–5″.

As far as the color of viburnum flowers is concerned, most are white or creamy white. A few species, like *V. fragrans, V. carlesi, V. suspensum* and one or two others, have pink flower buds and the flowers themselves may sometimes be pink, often fading white.

Viburnums for Fruit

The majority of the viburnums (exceptions are the double-flowered varieties and a few others) are prized for their bright-colored fruits either at maturity or at some time during the ripening process. They add color in the garden from early summer, when V. *tomentosum* is in fruit, until late winter. At the same time, they provide excellent bird food. Some of the fruits are simply black, like those of V. *acerifolium*. These are not particularly conspicuous but, nevertheless, prove very attractive to birds. The fruits of others, like those of V. *sieboldi*, are eventually black but just before maturity are a brilliant red. Since they remain in an immature state for some time, they prove decidedly ornamental—in fact, so much so that usually the fruits of this plant are all eaten by the birds before they turn black. Even after the fruits have fallen, the bright red-colored fruit-stalks remain a long time, lending considerable color to the plant until late in fall. Enough cannot be said of this excellent species for landscape use; for, with its fine dark green foliage, its tall, often treelike habit, and its good flowers and fruits, it can always be considered at the top of the list for any purpose.

The fruits of most viburnums are anywhere from ⅜-⅝" in diameter or in length, being fleshy and containing one seed. The brilliant red fruits of the native V. *trilobum* or its European counterpart the commonly planted V. *opulus* are bright red at maturity and remain on the plants a long time. Such red-fruiting viburnums as these and V. *dilatatum*, and V. *sargenti* are excellent for ornamental use because, when well covered with their bright red fruits, they are conspicuous for quite a distance.

The yellow-fruited viburnums are quite rare. Yet, they should not be, since they are readily propagated from cuttings and are as easily grown as the red-fruiting forms. There are three: V. *opulus xanthocarpum*, V. *sargenti flavum* and V. *dilatatum xanthocarpum*. In all respects other than the color of their fruits, these plants resemble their respective species. V. *opulus xanthocarpum* is an Old World plant and has been in commerce for many years, while the yellow-fruiting form of V. *sargenti* has been growing for nearly 40 years in the Arnold Arboretum, where it was named in 1904. *Viburnum dilatatum xanthocarpum* was described 20 years ago and has been growing in the Arboretum ever since, having originated as a chance seedling. These three shrubs are valued because they add variety to the red-, blue- and black-fruiting viburnums. They should not be recommended for use in place of the others, but in conjunction with the others. Since there are few shrubs with bright yellow fruits, these vigorous bushes should be propagated and grown in far greater numbers than they are at present. There are always places where unusually beautiful plants, such as these, can be used to show off to best advantage. One yellow-fruiting V. *sargenti flavum* in front of two plants of V. *sargenti* would afford an excellent color combination in the fall which would be well worth the effort.

And finally, there are some viburnums, the fruits of which go through a series of interesting color changes. For instance, the fruits of V. *cassinoides* and V. *lentago* go through a series of colors from green to pink and red to dark blue. Often several of these colors are evident on the same cluster and even on the same berry. It goes without saying that such plants are ornamentally valuable in the fall.

Since V. *fragrans* is one of the first viburnums to flower, it is also one of the first to bear colored fruits, these appearing during early summer. These are immediately followed by the black fruits of V. *carlesi* and the red fruits of V. *tomentosum* and later on in the summer, the red fruits of V. *sieboldi*. Immediately following this, the fruits of the majority of the viburnums start to mature and change color. The fruit of some (like V. *sieboldi, cassinoides* and *setigerum*) will soon fall off after fully maturing or else be eaten by the birds, while fruit of others (like V. *opulus* and V. *lentago*) will remain on the plants far into the winter.

Foliage and Autumn Coloration

Most of the plants in this genus are dense shrubs, forming a mass of green foliage. An exception would be V. *alnifolium*, which is a loose, open-growing plant at best, preferring the moist, shaded conditions of the mountains rather than the garden. Other exceptions are plants like V. *prunifolium*, V. *rufidulum*, V. *lentago*, and V. *sieboldi*, which can almost be classified as small trees since they are the largest growing of the group and frequently have a well-defined trunk. All in all, the foliage of the viburnums is a good dark green. Certain plants are particularly valued for their foliage. In the North, such would be the case with V. *sieboldi*, the rugged, somewhat wrinkled leaves of which are excellent. A little farther south, the handsome, wrinkled leaves of V. *rhytidophyllum*, the lustrous dark green leaves of V. *rufidulum*, and the evergreen leaves of V. *davidi, V. henryi, V. odoratissimum, V. suspensum* and V. *tinus*, make these plants good ornamentals throughout the entire year. Some varieties of certain species have yellow-colored leaves (or variegated) but the use of such plants should always be carefully restricted.

The autumn color of the foliage of the viburnums varies on the red side. Some, like V. *prunifolium*, can be expected to turn a fiery scarlet when weather conditions are at an optimum. On the other hand, some like V. *dilatatum* turn a russet red; some a purple red, like V. *lentago*. V. *dentatum* turns a beautiful glossy red, while V. *acerifolium* is not particularly outstanding since its foliage turns a purplish color in the fall. Although not all are outstanding in the fall, many are and can easily be considered among the best of shrubs for fall display.

Viburnum acerifolium   6'   Zone 3   Mapleleaf Viburnum

FLOWERS: yellowish to white, small in flat clusters
  TIME: mid-June

FRUIT: black berries
  EFFECTIVE: fall
AUTUMN COLOR: purplish
HABITAT: northeastern United States
  The only redeeming feature of this plant is its ability to withstand shade in situations where other viburnums will not do well.

Viburnum alnifolium   12′   Zone 3   Hobblebush

FLOWERS: white in large flat clusters
  TIME: early May
FRUIT: red to black berries
AUTUMN COLOR: reddish
HABITAT: northeastern United States
VARIETY: *alnifolium praecox*—flowers about three weeks earlier than species
  This species also is serviceable only in moist, wooded areas. Here it thrives but in open gardens other viburnums should be used in preference.

x Viburnum burkwoodi   6′   Zone 5   Burkwood Viburnum

*FLOWERS: pinkish to white, fragrant
FRUIT: red to black berries
AUTUMN COLOR: claret
HYBRID ORIGIN: *V. carlesi x V. utile*
ORIGINATED: 1924
  This is proving a popular substitute for *V. carlesi* and I think justly so. It is just as hardy, is more vigorous in habit, and is easily propagated by cuttings, therefore free of the disease which so frequently kills grafted plants of *V. carlesi*. Until thoroughly tried over a wide area it should not be recommended unreservedly as a substitute for the other species.

Viburnum carlesi   5′   Zone 4   Fragrant Viburnum

*FLOWERS: pink to white in small clusters, fragrant
  TIME: mid-May
FRUIT: black berries
AUTUMN COLOR: reddish to wine red
HABITAT: Korea
INTRODUCED: 1902
  Many people admire this viburnum a great deal because the flower buds are pink, and when open, the white flowers are deliciously fragrant. I think it has been over-rated because it often is susceptible to a graft disease for which there is no cure, it is hard to propagate, and its fruits appear in early summer when they are quickly devoured by hungry birds who have difficulty locating edible berries so early in the season.

Viburnum cassinoides   6′   Zone 3   Withe-rod

FLOWERS: creamy white, in flat clusters
  TIME: early June
*FRUIT: green to red to black berries
  EFFECTIVE: fall

*AUTUMN COLOR: red
HABITAT: northeastern United States

A very hardy, serviceable viburnum, this species can be depended upon for a wonderful display of fruits in fall and a splendid vivid red autumn color. The fruits are not very large in diameter but go through a wonderfully beautiful transfiguration from green to yellowish to red to black, sometimes with all colors clearly present in one bunch of berries. It does well in either normal or moist soil and, although it might not be considered a good specimen alone, it lends itself very well to massing or planting in wooded areas. It will do almost equally well in full sun or partial shade.

| Viburnum davidi | 3′ | Zone 7 | David Viburnum |

FLOWERS: white in clusters
    TIME: June
*FRUIT: light blue berries
    EFFECTIVE: September–October
*FOLIAGE: evergreen, dark leathery, leaves to 5½″ long
HABITAT: western China
INTRODUCED: 1904

The leaves of this species are deeply creased or pleated with veins—making it a very handsome, low evergreen.

| Viburnum dentatum | 15′ | Zone 2 | Arrow-wood |

FLOWERS: creamy white, flat clusters
    TIME: early June
FRUIT: blue berries
    EFFECTIVE: fall
*AUTUMN COLOR: glossy red
HABITAT: eastern United States

A vigorous shrub with many shoots coming from the base, this is not a viburnum for specimen use but it grows well in almost any soil in almost any situation. It can be used as a "filler" in any shrub border or massed for general foliage effects, for it grows rapidly.

| Viburnum dilatatum | 9′ | Zone 5 | Linden Viburnum |

*FLOWERS: creamy white, flat clusters
    TIME: early June
*FRUIT: bright red berries
    EFFECTIVE: fall
*AUTUMN COLOR: russet-red
HABITAT: eastern Asia
INTRODUCED: before 1845
VARIETY: xanthocarpum—yellow fruit

One of the best of the viburnums for its very colorful bright red fruits. Dense and compact in habit, it is usually covered with red fruits every fall, the fruit clusters being sometimes as much as 5″ in diameter. The yellow-fruiting variety is just as clean a shrub with regularly formed foliage and both are very dense, well adapted for either specimen planting or for massing in general.

Arrow-wood (*Viburnum dentatum*)

Viburnum fragrans   9'   Zone 5   Fragrant Viburnum

*FLOWERS: buds pink, flowers white, fragrant
    TIME: early April
FRUIT: red to black berries
    (not effective)
AUTUMN COLOR: reddish
HABITAT: northern China
INTRODUCED: 1910

This plant is only of value for its very early flowers, the earliest of all the viburnums to bloom, appearing long before the leaves. The buds are red and the flowers gradually mature white and are fragrant. There is a real white-flowering form now being grown, variety *album*. In the North, there are many winters when many of the flower buds are killed by low temperatures so it is only from New York, south, that this plant can be used with safety. The fruit is not conspicuous very long, changing from red to black very quickly.

Viburnum henryi   9'   Zone 7   Henry Viburnum

FLOWERS: white, in pyramidal clusters
    TIME: spring
FRUIT: red to black berries
    EFFECTIVE: fall
*FOLIAGE: evergreen, leaves to 5″ long
HABITAT: central China
INTRODUCED: 1901

Handsome in fruit, especially because its flower and fruit panicles are slightly pyramidal in shape.

Viburnum japonicum   6′   Zone 7   Japanese Viburnum

FLOWERS: white and fragrant
    TIME: spring
FRUIT: red berries
    EFFECTIVE: fall
*FOLIAGE: evergreen, lustrous, leaves to 6″ long
HABITAT: Japan
INTRODUCED: 1859
    A lustrous-leaved, sturdy evergreen, for growing in the South.

Viburnum lantana   15′   Zone 3   Wayfaring Tree

FLOWERS: white in flat clusters
    TIME: mid-May
FRUIT: red to black berries
    EFFECTIVE: fall
*AUTUMN COLOR: red
HABITAT: Europe, western Asia
INTRODUCED: early colonial times
    A stout upright shrub, this is one of the few viburnums which will grow well
in dry soil. Although the fruit is black at maturity, it turns from green to red in
a slowly interesting way. During the winter the fruit is not beautiful, looking
more or less like small dried raisins, but it is a source of bird food.

Viburnum lentago   30′   Zone 2   Nannyberry

*FLOWERS: white in flat clusters
    TIME: late May
*FRUIT: black berries
    EFFECTIVE: fall and winter
*AUTUMN COLOR: purplish red
HABITAT: eastern United States
    Another native, vigorous viburnum, which makes a dense mass, and if al-
lowed, the branches of old plants will arch over and rest on the ground, often
taking root. It is useful as a background and screen and is very effective on the
edges of woodlands. The fruit is also a valued winter food of the birds. Shiny
green leaves with a splendid fall color add to its usefulness.

Viburnum macrocephalum sterile   12′   Zone 6   Chinese Snowball

*FLOWERS: white, snowball-like
    TIME: late May
FOLIAGE: semi-evergreen in South
HABITAT: garden form from China
INTRODUCED: 1844
    The largest (and the least hardy) of the snowballs, growing very well from
Philadelphia, southward. The large flower clusters are sometimes 6–8″ in di-
ameter and are dependable for a splendid display, providing the plant has a
rich soil and is growing in a spot not exposed to severe winter weather.

Viburnum nudum   15'   Zone 6   Smooth Withe-rod

*FLOWERS: creamy white in clusters
    TIME: late June
*FRUIT: blue-black berries
    EFFECTIVE: September–October
FOLIAGE: lustrous shiny leaves
*AUTUMN COLOR: red
HABITAT: eastern United States

Very similar to the more northern V. *cassinoides*, this species is only recommended because it may be more adaptable in the South than is its northern relative.

Viburnum odoratissimum   10'   Zone 9   Sweet Viburnum

*FLOWERS: small, white, fragrant, in pyramidal clusters 3–6" high
    TIME: May
FRUIT: red to black berries
    EFFECTIVE: fall
FOLIAGE: evergreen, leaves 6" long, glossy
HABITAT: India, Japan

An excellent viburnum for southern gardens, with foliage as handsome, or more so, than that of rhododendrons. In deep, moist soils it may grow into a small pyramidal tree, 20' tall.

Viburnum opulus   12'   Zone 3   European Cranberry-bush

*FLOWERS: white, in flat clusters
    TIME: late May
*FRUIT: red berries
    EFFECTIVE: fall and winter
*AUTUMN COLOR: red
HABITAT: Europe, northern Africa, northern Asia
INTRODUCED: probably in colonial times
VARIETIES:

    nanum—dwarf, apparently non-fruiting form, seldom over 2' tall
    xanthocarpum—with golden yellow fruit

Because of a margin of sterile flowers around the cluster, the European Cranberry-bush is much more prominent in flower than most viburnums except possibly the snowballs. It is similar to the native V. *trilobum* but its fruits are too tart for making preserves. The leaves are lobed somewhat like those of the red maple and its dense, vigorous growth make it suitable for planting in any shrub border. The dwarf form has been used in rock gardens or in low hedges, while the sterile flowering form or European Snowball as it is called, is most susceptible to the disfiguring attacks of plant lice which cause the twigs and leaves to curl and frequently cause a material stunting of the growth and effectiveness of the plant. In northern gardens the Japanese Snowball, V. *tomentosum sterile*, should be used; and of course in the South the Chinese Snowball is best

The European Snowball (LEFT) is often infested with lice which mar leaves, twigs and flowers. In the example above only the leaves have been contorted. The Japanese Snowball on the right (*V. tomentosum sterile*) is the one recommended for planting in the North, even though it is slightly less hardy.

Viburnum prunifolium   15′   Zone 3   Black Haw

*FLOWERS: white in flat clusters
   TIME: mid-May
*FRUIT: blue-black berries
   EFFECTIVE: fall
*AUTUMN COLOR: shining red
HABITAT: eastern United States

Often this plant has been recommended as a substitute (in form) for some of the hawthorns. Sometimes it is grown as a small tree with a single trunk. The fruits have been used for preserves since colonial times and in certain areas strains have been selected particularly because the fruits are large and palatable. Sometimes these fruits are ½″ long, about the largest on any viburnum, and are produced in great profusion. An excellent plant as a specimen or for massing.

Viburnum rhytidophyllum roseum   9′   Zone 5   Pink Leathery Viburnum

FLOWERS: light pink in flat clusters
   TIME: June
*FRUIT: red to black berries
   EFFECTIVE: fall
*FOLIAGE: handsome, wrinkled leaves
HABITAT: central and western China
INTRODUCED: 1900

This variety of the Leathery Viburnum is perhaps more ornamental than the species merely because the otherwise uninteresting flower buds are pink. The foliage is distinctly outstanding, a lustrous dark green and very wrinkled, with leaves as much as 6" long. In warmer areas of the South it is definitely an evergreen. Most conspicuous are the brilliant half-ripe red fruits. It should have rich, well-drained soil in order to grow well, and seems to be at its best in slightly shaded situations.

Viburnum rufidulum   30'   Zone 5   Southern Black Haw

*FLOWERS: creamy white, in flat clusters
    TIME: late May
*FRUIT: dark blue berries
    EFFECTIVE: fall
FOLIAGE: lustrous green leaves
*AUTUMN COLOR: red
HABITAT: southeastern United States
    The southern counterpart of V. *prunifolium*.

Viburnum sargenti flavum   12'   Zone 4   Yellow Sargent Cranberry-bush

*FLOWERS: white in flat clusters
    TIME: late May
*FRUIT: golden yellow berries
    EFFECTIVE: fall
AUTUMN COLOR: red
HABITAT: northeast Asia
INTRODUCED: 1904
    The yellow-fruiting Sargent Cranberry-bush is similar to *Viburnum opulus xanthocarpum* except that it may be slightly more colorful and more vigorous. This too has a ring of larger sterile flowers around the outside of the flower cluster. Because there are only three good yellow-fruiting viburnums, it was thought advisable to include all three in the recommended list. Usually such plants are propagated asexually, in this case it is easily done by cuttings. However, three years ago I had a batch of seedlings sown from seed of V. *sargenti flavum* and the first year—when the seedlings were only 6" high, I noticed a remarkable difference in the color of the leaf petioles between certain plants. Some plants had leaf petioles all yellowish to yellow green, while the leaf petioles of other plants were markedly reddish. In the fall of that first season, and every fall since, the red petioled plants turned a red autumn color and years later had red fruits, while the yellowish petioled plants had a yellowish green autumn color and eventually had yellow fruits. Hence the color of the fruit eventually borne by plants can be foretold years in advance of bearing, merely by the color of the leaf petioles. Needless to say this is a very useful observation.

Viburnum setigerum aurantiacum   12'   Zone 5
                                        Orange Fruited Tea Viburnum

*FLOWERS: white in flat clusters
    TIME: early July
*FRUIT: orange berries
    EFFECTIVE: fall

The Siebold Viburnum, possibly the most ornamental of all deciduous viburnums because of excellent foliage, flowers, fruits, autumn color and habit of growth.

HABITAT: central and western China
INTRODUCED: 1907

Outstanding among the viburnums because it is the only one with glorious orange-colored fruits. The leaves have been used for making a tea by the Chinese monks in areas where it is native. Not as dense a specimen as some other species but is extraordinary in fruit.

Viburnum sieboldi   30'   Zone 4   Siebold Viburnum

*FLOWERS: creamy white in flat clusters
    TIME: late May
*FRUIT: red to black berries on red fruit-stalks
    EFFECTIVE: summer
*FOLIAGE: rugose, dark green lustrous foliage
    AUTUMN COLOR: red
HABITAT: Japan
INTRODUCED: 1880

If I were to choose only one viburnum for my garden, I think it would be this because of the splendid long (6") leaves, its very desirable branching habit which results in rounded masses of foliage interspersed with open areas where lights and shadows add much interest, and also because of its colorful fruits. Although these are black at maturity, they remain unripe and bright red for several weeks in summer, and even after they turn black and fall off or are eaten

by birds, their red fruit-stalks remain another three or four weeks to give color
to the plant at a time when the fruits of most other shrubs are not sufficiently
ripened to be colorful. As a specimen plant it is the best of the viburnums for
the northern United States at least.

Viburnum suspensum   6'   Zone 9   Sandankwa Viburnum

FLOWERS: white, tinted rose, fragrant
   TIME: June
FRUIT: red berries
   EFFECTIVE: fall
*FOLIAGE: evergreen, leathery, 2–5" long, glossy
HABITAT: southern Japan
   Another evergreen viburnum for the deep South.

Viburnum tinus   10–20'   Zones 7–8   Laurestinus

*FLOWERS: white to pinkish
   TIME: winter to spring
FRUIT: metallic-blue berries, eventually black
   EFFECTIVE: late summer
*FOLIAGE: evergreen, very dark glossy green leaves 1½–4" long
HABITAT: Mediterranean region
INTRODUCED: colonial times
   Considered an indispensable shrub in many southern gardens. Gardeners
who are not familiar with its idiosyncrasies should be cautioned against giving
it too much water, especially during the summer for if too much soft vigorous
growth occurs it tends to winter-kill and become unsightly throughout the winter.
Distinguished from other evergreen viburnums by its luxuriant masses of entire
leaves. It forms an excellent hedge which can remain unclipped for years and
still keep its good form. The variety *lucidum*, with larger leaves, is apparently
not as susceptible to attacks from thrips and red spider as is the species.

Viburnum tomentosum mariesi 9' Zone 4 Maries Doublefile Viburnum

*FLOWERS: creamy white, in flat clusters
   TIME: late May
*FRUIT: bright red berries
   EFFECTIVE: fall
AUTUMN COLOR: dull red
WINTER TWIGS: branching horizontal
V. *tomentosum* variety: *sterile*—sterile flowers, Japanese Snowball
   The Maries variety of the Doublefile Viburnum is recommended in preference to the species V. *tomentosum*, merely because the flower clusters are larger
and hence both they and the fruit are more conspicuous. The Japanese Snowball
has sterile flowers and is the best of the three snowballs for use in the North even
though it is not quite as hardy as its European relative, for it is not nearly as
susceptible to the disfiguring attacks of plant lice. All forms of V. *tomentosum*
have a delightful horizontal branching habit which, in the case of Maries variety,
is augmented by the fact that the flat flower and fruit clusters are all nicely borne

Maries Doublefile Viburnum, like all other varieties of the species V. *to-mentosum*, has a horizontal branching habit which adds materially to its effectiveness at all seasons.

on the upper side of the branches. An excellent specimen, it is worthy of placing in any garden, and may need some slight protection in gardens north of New York. It may easily grow as broad as tall.

Viburnum trilobum   12′   Zone 2   American Cranberry-bush

*FLOWERS: white, in flat clusters
    TIME: late May
*FRUIT: scarlet, edible berries
    EFFECTIVE: fall and winter
*AUTUMN COLOR: red
HABITAT: southern Canada and northeastern United States

Similar to the European Cranberry-bush, this species is more hardy and its fruits can be used for preserves. In fact several strains such as "Andrews," "Hahs," and "Wentworth" have been selected specifically for this purpose. If edible fruits and additional hardiness are not factors in selection, the European Cranberry-bush is the plant to use because it is more easily available from commercial sources.

Vinca major   Ground cover or trailing vine   Zone 7   Big Periwinkle

*FLOWERS: bright blue
    TIME: mid-May
FOLIAGE: dark lustrous green

HABITAT: southern Europe, western Asia
INTRODUCED: 1789

Adapted to only the warmer parts of the country, this trailing vine makes an excellent ground cover. Its variegated-leaved varieties, *elegantissima* and *variegata*, are widely grown as ornamental greenhouse pot plants.

Vinca minor   Ground cover   Zone 4   Periwinkle or Myrtle

*FLOWERS: lilac-blue, single
   TIME: late April
*FOLIAGE: evergreen, dark lustrous
HABITAT: Europe and western Asia, often escapes cultivation
INTRODUCED: cultivated since ancient times
VARIETIES:
   alba—white flowers
   atropurpurea—purple flowers
   "Bowles Variety"—flowers light blue, plant a strong grower
   multiplex—flowers purple, double

An excellent evergreen ground cover doing equally well in sun or shade, with persistent roots that assist it in becoming established in all but the poorest soils. It is commonly said of certain shaded situations that if Periwinkle or Pachysandra will not grow, nothing will. The plants are easily multiplied by division and a planting of several varieties is often advisable. "Bowles Variety" is a strong grower, tending to grow more in clumps than as procumbent vines. The species is excellent for planting on banks to hold the soil, and a few bulbs planted amongst the vines adds to the general effectiveness of the planting in early spring.

Vitex agnus-castus   9'   Zones 6–7   Chaste-tree

FLOWERS: lilac or pale violet, small, fragrant
   TIME: mid-August
FOLIAGE: gray, aromatic
HABITAT: southern Europe and western Asia
INTRODUCED: 1750
VARIETIES:
   alba—white flowers
   rosea—pink flowers

The Chaste-tree has gray aromatic foliage of somewhat coarser texture than *Vitex negundo incisa,* but the flowers are more prominent and bloom from July to September. The plant should be treated like *Buddleia davidi* for it dies back nearly to the ground in the northern part of its hardiness zone. If gray foliage or late summer bloom is not necessarily desirable in the garden, better and hardier shrubs might be selected, for these Chaste-trees are rather exotic looking and rather difficult to blend with other shrubs.

Vitex negundo incisa   15'   Zone 5   Cut-leaved Chaste-tree

FLOWERS: lilac or lavender, loose clusters of small flowers
   TIME: mid-August
FOLIAGE: gray, fine texture, aromatic
HABITAT: northern China, Korea
INTRODUCED: 1750

A vigorous, open shrub, with finely cut leaves of better texture than those of *Vitex agnus-castus* although the flowers are not as prominent. This species, also, should be given the same type of pruning treatment in the North as *Buddleia davidi* since it tends to die back nearly to the ground in cold places. Its loose open habit, fine gray foliage and late summer flowers (blooming in July and August) are its chief characteristics of value. Where these are not needed, better shrubs can easily be selected.

WEIGELA

This genus contains several species and many varieties and hybrids of more or less merit. They are of value chiefly for their bright-colored flowers and a few of the forms have colored or variegated foliage. They are vigorous growers, having many branches appearing at the base of the plant. The leaves are opposite and about 4 inches long. The flowers are funnellike, about an inch long and in some varieties nearly as broad, usually borne 3 to 5 in a cluster on short lateral branches. The plants have little if any autumn color, and the fruit is a dry capsule of no ornamental value. In the North these plants suffer considerable winter injury some years, and there seems to be some general die-back of branches annually. In other words, in my experience these shrubs have not been "clean" but always seem to require some annual pruning. While they are in flower they are meritorious —if their flower buds have not been injured by winter cold. In general, they have been overemphasized in garden planting, for there are only a few areas in the country where they seem to do well all the time.

They require little attention from the standpoint of spraying for insect and disease pests. For that reason they are to be commended. Also, the variegated form of *Weigela florida* is about the most interesting of any of the variegated forms of woody plants which can be grown in the northeastern United States. These weigelas all hybridize freely. The flower colors have been compared with those of the English Horticultural Colour chart and are usually not one solid color but a mixture, the predominant color being the one mentioned in the following notes. They are borne along the vigorous-growing branches and are quite colorful, some varieties blooming in mid-May and others following, the flowers remaining on some well into mid-June and even later. Those forms with French varietal names probably originated in the great French nursery of Victor Lemoine. It is unfortunate that so many have been named in the past, for there are many that are similar. In selecting only 17 species and varieties and suggesting the rejection of 44, it should be pointed out that these 17 have proved themselves to be the best under conditions prevalent in the Arnold Arboretum, but that under another set of conditions some of the other varieties might prove superior.

x **Weigela** "Bouquet Rose"   12'   **Zone 5**

*FLOWERS: phlox-pink, trumpet-shaped
    TIME: mid-May

x Weigela "Bristol Ruby" 5' Zone 4

*FLOWERS: Tyrian-Rose, 1" diameter, trumpet-shaped
    TIME: mid-May
HYBRID ORIGIN: *W. florida* x "Eva Rathke"
ORIGINATED by Alex Cummings, Bristol, Conn., 1941

"Bristol Ruby" is apparently growing into a much better weigela than the popular old-fashioned favorite "Eva Rathke," one of its parents. Of importance in the North is that it is hardier; the flowers are slightly larger and last longer and it is one of the darkest red of all weigelas. A new variety, "Vaniceki," is proving even more hardy than "Bristol Ruby," slightly lighter in color, and with slightly larger flowers.

x Weigela "Conquerant" 12' Zone 5

*FLOWERS: magenta, trumpet-shaped
    TIME: mid-May
HYBRID ORIGIN: *W. praecox* x?
ORIGINATED: 1905
    Blooms profusely.

x Weigela "Dame Blanche" 12' Zone 5

*FLOWERS: almost pure white, trumpet-shaped
    TIME: late May
HYBRID ORIGIN: *W. hortensis* x *W. coraeensis*
ORIGINATED: 1905

x Weigela "Esperance" 10' Zone 5

*FLOWERS: light pink, trumpet-shaped
    TIME: early June
    One of the last of the weigelas to bloom.

Weigela florida alba 9' Zone 5

*FLOWERS: white, sometimes pinkish, trumpet-shaped
    TIME: early June
HABITAT: Korea, northern China
INTRODUCED: 1845
W. florida varieties:
    variegata—leaves with a yellow border, flowers deep red
    "Venusta"—rhodamine-pink—hardiest of all weigelas, Zone 4—blooms mid-May
    "foliis purpuriis"—purplish foliage

x Weigela "Gracieux" 12' Zone 5

*FLOWERS: white and magenta, trumpet-shaped
    TIME: mid-May

x Weigela "Richesse" 9' Zone 5

*FLOWERS: pale pink, trumpet-shaped
    TIME: mid-May

x **Weigela "Gratissima"**　　　12'　　　Zone 5

*FLOWERS: rose Bengal, trumpet-shaped
　　TIME: early June
HYBRID ORIGIN: W. hortensis x W. florida
INTRODUCED: 1888

Weigela japonica sinica　　　18'　　　Zone 6　　　Chinese Weigela

*FLOWERS: white and red, trumpet-shaped
　　TIME: late May
HABITAT: central China
INTRODUCED: 1908
　　This plant has the peculiarity of bearing white and red flowers as well as yellowish and red flowers.

x **Weigela "Lavallei"**　　　12'　　　Zone 5

*FLOWERS: rose-opal, trumpet-shaped
　　TIME: late May
HYBRID ORIGIN: W. floribunda x W. coraeensis
ORIGINATED: 1884

Weigela maximowiczi　　　4'　　　Zone 5　　　Maximowicz Weigela

*FLOWERS: napels-yellow, trumpet-shaped
　　TIME: mid-May
HABITAT: Japan
INTRODUCED: 1915
　　Valued chiefly for its yellow flowers.

Weigela praecox　　　6'　　　Zone 5　　　Early Weigela

*FLOWERS: fuchsia-purple, trumpet-shaped
　　TIME: early May
HABITAT: Korea
INTRODUCED: 1894
　　The earliest of all weigelas to bloom.

x **Weigela "Seduction"**　　　12'　　　Zone 5

*FLOWERS: magenta-rose, trumpet-shaped
　　TIME: mid-May
HYBRID ORIGIN: about 1914

Xanthoceras sorbifolium　　　20'　　　Zone 5　　　Shinyleaf Yellowhorn

FLOWERS: small, white, in racemes, 10" long
　　TIME: late May
FRUIT: green burrs, similar to horsechestnuts
　　EFFECTIVE: fall
FOLIAGE: lustrous, dark green
HABITAT: northern China

Yellow-root (in the foreground) grows rapidly by underground stolons and makes a fairly dense ground cover requiring practically no maintenance.

INTRODUCED: 1866

This little known shrub has shiny pinnately-compound leaves with small racemes of white flowers somewhat similar to small wisteria clusters, appearing in late May. A rather unusual specimen, good as large shrub or small tree, but difficult to transplant.

Xanthorhiza simplicissima   2′   Zone 4   Yellow-root

FLOWERS: small, brownish purple, almost inconspicuous
   TIME: early May
HABITAT: New York to Kentucky and Florida

An excellent, tall, ground cover or border shrub, increasing rapidly by underground stolons and making a dense mass of foliage throughout the spring and summer. It is neat, for the plants reach a uniform height of about 24″. It is only of value for its foliage, since the flowers and fruits are none too conspicuous. Bark and root are yellow.

Yucca filamentosa   3′   Zone 4   Adams Needle

FLOWERS: creamy white, pendulous, 2–3″ in diameter, in spikes 1–3′ tall
   TIME: mid-July
FOLIAGE: evergreen, leaves stiffly upright
HABITAT: southeastern United States

Many yuccas are native of southern United States and Mexico. They thrive in hot dry situations. Their rigid, pointed leaves, and large spikes of creamy white

Dusty Zenobia is valued for its excellent grayish foliage throughout the spring, summer and fall.

to yellowish flowers make them conspicuous—almost too conspicuous wherever used. This species, one of the hardiest, can represent the entire group with its many hybrids indicative of the landscape over large areas of the southern United States and Mexico.

Zamia integrifolia   1½'   Zone 9   Coontie

A cycad or near relative to the palms, this is an evergreen, native in the West Indies, with beautiful fernlike dark green leaves. It will grow both in sun and shade, in poor or wet soil. Chiefly used in Florida and along Gulf of Mexico.

Zenobia pulverulenta   6'   Zone 5   Dusty Zenobia

FLOWERS: slender, nodding pedicels, white, bell-shaped, ½" in diameter
   TIME: mid-June
FOLIAGE: gray to gray-green
AUTUMN COLOR: red
HABITAT: North Carolina to Florida

Closely related to the blueberries, this plant does well in sandy, acid soil and is used chiefly for its gray foliage to form a point of interest among the normally green-leaved shrubs. An excellent addition to the ericaceous border, rockery or acid-soil woodland planting.

VINES

VINES prove an essential part of almost every garden. They are used for ornament as well as for the utilitarian purposes of screening walls or objectionable views from the garden proper. There are many vines available from commercial sources, each one of which has its own peculiar merits. Before selecting a group of vines or even a single vine for use in the garden, review carefully the exact reasons for using it, then select the one which will best fulfil that particular purpose.

Generally speaking, vines can be segregated into three general groups depending on how they climb. Some, like the Boston Ivy, climb by attaching small, rootlike holdfasts to the wall as a means of support. Sometimes these are modified tendrils with small circular discs at the tips. Others, like Clematis and Grape, climb by winding tendrils or leaflike appendages, which act as tendrils, around the object on which they are growing. The third group, like Bittersweet and Wisteria, climb by twining. It is obvious that one must know in advance how each vine climbs so that a proper means of support can be provided for those which are eventually selected.

Most vines will quickly revert to a tangled mass of foliage if allowed to grow over the ground without some means of support. Such growth may be desirable in some instances for a ground cover, but usually, in the small garden, these plants should be neat in appearance and to keep them this way takes very little time. The area to be covered should be studied carefully to determine what type of vine should be used, *i.e.*, clinging or twining, and to ascertain whether a comparatively slow-growing, neat-appearing vine will prove satisfactory, or whether a vigorous-growing sort should be used, which may need more attention. Vines like the English Ivy may elongate only 4–8 feet in a season, whereas the Kudzu Vine may elongate 50 feet or more in a single season, once the plant has become well established.

Pergolas, trellises, fences and other such supports may need one or more vines depending on the area to be covered and how dense the resulting foliage is desired to be. If a long trellis or tall fence is to be clothed in green foliage, rapid-growing vines should be selected and planted about every five feet. If, on the other hand, a pleasing, more or less open effect is to be obtained on a pergola, where a complete coverage of foliage is not

Japanese wisteria (*Wisteria floribunda*), actually a vine but grown at the Kew Gardens in England in tree form by pruning.

necessarily the chief requisite, then one vine, preferably of the slower-growing type may be all that is needed to twine its way at will among the supports. Certain types of Clematis vines often prove admirable when grown in this way.

Several of the more commonly used vines tend to grow vertically as fast as possible and then to branch out with a mass of foliage near the top. This type of growth should not be allowed while the plants are young, for it easily makes a plant unsightly and unwieldy, often necessitating its being cut to the ground and regrown. If such vines are trained horizontally at first, even if it is necessary to wind them around supports or tie them to the proper supports so that the area which they are expected to cover is first reached horizontally, then vertical growth can be more easily controlled by allowing lateral shoots to grow at the proper places.

In training vines, it is of interest to note that all twining vines do not twine in the same direction. There is not a haphazard method of twining. The plants of each species invariably twine in one direction, and it is just as easy to wind young vines around their supports in the right direction as it is in the wrong direction. Interesting notes can be made of this phenomenon, and the following is a short list to indicate what can be expected from a few twiners:

Twining vines may climb by twining from left to right (*Celastrus scandens* on the left) or they may climb by twining from right to left as does *Lonicera japonica halliana* on the right.

VINES THAT TWINE BY CLIMBING FROM LEFT TO RIGHT

Actinitia arguta

A. kolomikta

A. melanandra

A. polygama

A. purpurea

Akebia pentaphylla

A. quinata

A. trifoliata

Aristolochia durior

A. kaempferi

A. mandshuriensis

Celastrus flagellaris

C. hypoleuca

C. loeseneri

C. orbiculatus

C. scandens

Menispermum canadense

M. dauricum

Periploca graeca

P. sepium

Wisteria frutescens

W. macrostachya

W. sinensis

VINES THAT TWINE BY CLIMBING FROM RIGHT TO LEFT

Berchemia racemosa

Dioscorea villosa

Lonicera henryi

L. japonica halliana

L. sempervirens

Schisandra chinensis

Wisteria floribunda

W. formosa

Sometimes after a study of all available vines, it is found that none of the clinging type is desired; that, from the ornamental viewpoint, a twiner is more appropriate. Twining vines can be satisfactorily grown on any type of wall, stone or wood, merely by the use of copper wires properly attached. Copper is suggested because it weathers quickly and soon becomes inconspicuous. Twining vines grown in such a manner can be easily removed from the building, when it is to be painted or repointed, by the simple expedient of taking down the wire and laying the entire vine on the ground during the period. This can be done at any time, even when the vine is in full leaf and actively growing. Hence twining vines can prove useful on flat surfaces provided they are handled properly.

Twining vines such as Bittersweet, Fiveleaf Akebia and the Fleece Vine can be used to twine about rainspouts and disguise them, even on shingled houses, if the owner plans beforehand to prune them roughly every few years. Such vines grow rapidly and will quickly completely cover a rainspout on a three-story building. However, the vine must be severely restrained by heavy pruning, to prevent it from growing more than is necessary to perform the comparatively simple task of covering the rainspout. If this is not done, the vine can grow out of bounds very quickly and become a nuisance if not a menace. When repairs are to be made to the rainspout or the house, such vigorous-growing vines can be cut off at or near the ground level without seriously affecting their chances of again growing up to the top of the house, especially if the cutting back is done in the early spring and not in the very late summer. Wisteria would not lend itself to such treatment since it is usually grown for its flowers, and it takes several years to produce vines capable of flowering. Bittersweet, on the other hand, can be so treated and fruit two years after being cut down, especially if some of the older stems can be saved at least a few feet above the ground.

Some Recommended Twining Vines

Actinidia species	*Muehlenbeckia complexa*
Akebia quinata	*Polygonum auberti*
Aristolochia durior	*Pueraria thunbergiana*
Celastrus species	*Schisandra propinqua*
Kadsura japonica	*Smilax* species
Lonicera species	*Trachelospermum* species
Mandevilla suaveolens	*Tripterygium regeli*
Menispermum canadense	*Wisteria* species

CLINGING VINES

Clinging vines should not be planted on wooden houses for the obvious reason that their small rootlike holdfasts may penetrate and damage the wood, and also that they would have to be removed and torn away from the building every time painting or repair work is done. Then too, many cling so tightly to the wall surface that they undoubtedly tend to keep that surface more moist and so aid in its disintegration. On stone surfaces they are ideal. Several vines suited for this purpose are in the following lists. Occasionally they are planted to grow over stone walls or rock piles, or even to climb up tree trunks.

The Climbing Hydrangea, *Hydrangea petiolaris,* is ideal for this purpose, since it tends to grow directly up the trunk of a tree, or in a very slow spiral around it, so that it does not constrict translocation in the trunk. Twining vines like Bittersweet and Wisteria should never be used on trees since they twine so rapidly that they quickly restrict translocation in the tree trunk and seriously injure the tree if they do not kill it outright. The Climbing Hydrangea (and some similar types) can be judiciously used on tall open trunks like those of the elms, with a striking display of ornamental interest. This is particularly true if the vine is trained somewhat, pruned a trifle here and there so that its straight upward growth is assured.

One of the finest specimens of the Climbing Hydrangea I have ever seen was planted on a tree trunk in front of the house long occupied by Ernest H. Wilson. The tree, an American Elm, was gracefully beautiful in its own right, as many elms are, but with the vine growing up its trunk to the lower branches it was of unusual interest to all who passed under it. Many gardeners like the unadorned beauty of such tree trunks, but for those who might like to add an additional spot of interest, the Climbing Hydrangea might be a possibility. In the South, the English Ivy (*Hedera helix*) has proved similarly interesting and in places where Euonymus scale is not an ever present menace, some of the Euonymus group can be used likewise.

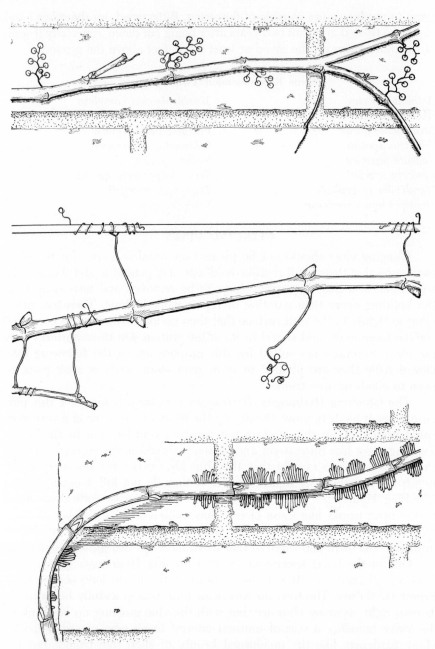

The three methods used by certain vines to cling to supports are clearly illustrated here. At the top is the Boston ivy (*Parthenocisus tricuspidata*) clinging by means of small tendrils at the ends of which are small adhesive discs. In the center is the grape with its tendrils, always quick to wrap themselves about anything with which they come in contact. At the bottom is the climbing hydrangea (*Hydrangea petiolaris*) with small rootlike hold-fasts, firmly attaching the vine to either brick or wood.

Clinging by Rootlets, Rootlike Holdfasts or Tendrils with Discs

Campsis species
Doxantha unguis-cati
Euonymus fortunei varieties
Ficus pumila
Hedera species
Hydrangea petiolaris

Parthenocissus tricuspidata and varieties
P. quinquefolia saint-pauli
Phaedranthus buccinatorius
Pileostegia viburnoides

Clinging by Means of Tendrils

Ampelopsis species
Bignonia capreolata
Boussingaultia baselloides
Cissus incisa
Clematis species (tendrils in the form of modified leaf stalks)
Cobaea scandens
Distictis lactiflora

Doxantha unguis-cati
Parthenocissus henryana
P. heptaphylla
P. quinquefolia
P. quinquefolia engelmanni
Passiflora species
Phaedranthus buccinatorius
Vitis species

RAPID–GROWING VINES

Rapid-growing vines are frequently desired to play a temporary or a permanent part in the garden plan which can be fulfilled by no other type of plant material. Rapid-growing vines are not always the most ornamental, but their number is rather large and many good varieties will be found in the following list, which are easily obtainable in the various areas of the United States where they are grown. These were all included in a list recommended by the Arnold Arboretum, after a careful study of vines growing in all parts of the country, as among the best of the vines for camouflage purposes in this country during World War II.

Easily Available Rapid-Growing Vines

	APPROX. ELONGATION IN ONE YEAR [*]
Actinidia arguta	15–20′
A. chinensis	25′
Akebia quinata	3–15′
Ampelopsis aconitifolia	12–15′
A. arborea	12–15′
A. brevipedunculata	15–20′
Aristolochia durior	4–6′
Bignonia capreolata	15–20′
Boussingaultia baselloides	4–6′
Campsis grandiflora	5–10′
C. radicans	10′

[*] These are actual measurements in most cases, but it is obvious that the amount of elongation in any one year depends on many factors and may vary considerably. Soil, situation, amount of rainfall and age of plant all govern the amount of growth. The figures, then, are only comparative and are used here to show which vines are the most vigorous.

Easily Available Rapid-Growing Vines (Continued)

	APPROX. ELONGATION IN ONE YEAR
Celastrus orbiculata	14'
C. scandens	10'
Cissus incisa	5–10'
Clematis montana	6–10'
C. paniculata	15'
C. texensis	6–10'
C. virginiana	20'
C. vitalba	18–20'
C. viticella	18–20'
Cobaea scandens	6–10'
Distictis lactiflora	25'
Doxantha unguis-cati	20'
Ficus pumila	7'
Hedera helix	4–8'
Lonicera etrusca superba	10'
L. japonica halliana	18–20'
L. sempervirens	10–15'
Mandevilla suaveolens	4–6'
Menispermum canadense	6–10'
Muehlenbeckia complexa	5–10'
Parthenocissus heptaphylla	6–10'
P. quinquefolia	6–10'
P. tricuspidata	6–10'
Passiflora species	6–15'
Phaedranthus buccinatorius	5–12'
Polygonum auberti	10–15'
Pueraria thunbergiana	30–50'
Trachelospermum jasminoides	5'
Vitis amurensis	30'
V. californica	30'
V. coignetiae	40'
V. labrusca	20'
Wisteria floribunda	5–7'
W. sinensis	5–7'

VINES FOR DIFFERENT PURPOSES

The following lists of vines are suggested for different purposes. These are not infallible by any means. A vine growing in the North may be completely deciduous, but in the far South it may be almost completely evergreen. Such is the case with Hall's Honeysuckle and some of the Clematis species. It is also true that certain vines can be made to grow on banks, in dry soils, or as ground covers, by a little careful training and fertilization, whereas normally they would not be expected to do well under such conditions. The true gardener will want to experiment on his own with other species and varieties and may be rewarded with success if he goes about making his selections intelligently.

Vines for Flowers

Bignonia capreolata
Boussingaultia baselloides
Campsis species
Clematis species
Cobaea scandens
Distictis lactiflora
Hydrangea petiolaris
Lonicera species
Lycium halimifolium
Mandevilla suaveolens

Passiflora caerulea
Phaedranthus buccinatorius
Pileostegia viburnoides
Plumbago capensis
Polygonum auberti
Rosa (ramblers)
R. wichuraiana
Trachelospermum species
Tripterygium regeli
Wisteria species

Vines for Colorful Fruits

Ampelopsis aconitifolia
A. brevipendunculata
Celastrus species
Clematis—most species
Euonymus fortunei vegeta
E. obovata

Kadsura japonica
Lycium halimifolium
Parthenocissus species
Schisandra propinqua
Smilax species

Vines Withstanding Shade

Actinidia species
Akebia quinata
Aristolochia durior
Clematis species
Euonymus species
Hedera species
Hydrangea petiolaris

Lonicera species
Menispermum canadense
Parthenocissus species
Pileostegia viburnoides
Smilax species
Trachelospermum species
Vitis species

Vines for Banks

Akebia species
Celastrus flagellaris
Clematis paniculata
C. vitalba
C. viticella
Euonymus fortunei vegeta
Hedera helix
Lonicera japonica halliana

Lycium halimifolium
Menispermum canadense
Parthenocissus quinquefolia
Pueraria thunbergiana
Rosa—ramblers
R. wichuraiana
Smilax rotundifolia
Vitis species

Vines for Use as Ground Covers

Akebia quinata
Ampelopsis arborea
Celastrus species
Euonymus obovata
Hedera helix
Lonicera henryi
L. japonica halliana

Menispermum canadense
Muehlenbeckia complexa
Parthenocissus henryana
P. quinquefolia
Pueraria thunbergiana
Rosa wichuraiana

Vines Withstanding Dry Soil Conditions

Ampelopsis arborea

Boussingaultia baselloides

Campsis radicans

Cissus incisa

Clematis texensis

Ficus pumila

Lonicera sempervirens

Parthenocissus heptaphylla

P. quinquefolia

P. tricuspidata

Polygonum auberti

Pueraria thunbergiana

Vines Withstanding Moist to Wet Soil Conditions

Boussingaultia baselloides

Campsis radicans

Cissus incisa

Clematis virginiana

Menispermum canadense

Smilax rotundifolia

Trachelospermum species

Open Growing Vines

(Not suitable for screening purposes)

Ampelopsis aconitifolia

A. brevipendunculata

Clematis—large flowering hybrids and
  their parents

Lonicera caprifolium

L. etrusca

L. etrusca superba

L. flava

L. heckrotti

L. sempervirens

L. tellmanniana

L. tragophylla

Mandevilla suaveolens

Parthenocissus quinquefolia

Vines for the Great Plains Area

Aristolochia durior

Celastrus orbiculata

C. scandens

Clematis paniculata

C. virginiana

Lonicera sempervirens

Parthenocissus quinquefolia

Vitis amurensis

V. labrusca

Vines That Are Evergreen or Semi-Evergreen in the South

	E—EVERGREEN
	S—SEMI-EVERGREEN
Ampelopsis arborea	S
Bignonia capreolata	S–E
Boussingaultia baselloides	E
Cissus incisa	S
Clematis armandi	S–E
C. texensis	S–E
C. paniculata	S–E
Cobaea scandens	E
Distictis lactiflora	E
Doxantha unguis-cati	E
Euonymus fortunei species	E
Ficus pumila	E
Hedera helix	E

	E—EVERGREEN S—SEMI-EVERGREEN
Kadsura japonica	E
Lonicera etrusca	S—E
L. henryi	S—E
L. hildebrandiana	E
L. japonica halliana	S—E
L. sempervirens	S—E
Muehlenbeckia complexa	E
Passiflora caerulea	E
Phaedranthus buccinatorius	E
Pileostegia viburnoides	E
Schisandra propinqua	E
Smilax megalantha	E
Trachelospermum asiaticum	E
T. jasminoides	E

Vines That Are Evergreen or Semi-Evergreen in the North

	E—EVERGREEN S—SEMI-EVERGREEN
Akebia quinata	S
Clematis paniculata	S
Euonymus fortunei and varieties	E
Hedera helix and varieties	E
Lonicera japonica halliana	S
L. henryi	S

RECOMMENDED VINES

Actinidia arguta　　Twining vine　　30′　　Zone 4　　Bower Actinidia

HABITAT: Japan, Korea, Manchuria
INTRODUCED: 1874

A high-climbing, vigorous twining vine, valued chiefly for its dense foliage, making it one of the better vines for screening purposes. The glossy-green leaf blades appear at the end of red petioles, a colorful combination. The sexes are separate, but neither flowers nor fruits are ornamental. Preserves have been made from the fleshy fruits which are about 1″ in diameter. It develops into a rank growing plant in good soil.

Actinidia chinensis　　Twining vine　　25′　　Zone 7　　Chinese Actinidia

FLOWERS: creamy white changing to buff-yellow, fragrant
　　TIME: mid-June
HABITAT: China
INTRODUCED: 1900

A handsome, vigorous twining vine of tropical appearance with its young growth covered with prominent red hairs producing a rich velvety effect. The

flowers and fruits are not especially ornamental. The vine should be so trained
that the quick growing young shoots are easily seen for it is these that are the
most colorful. The edible fruit has a flavor similar to gooseberries, but in all actinidias it should be remembered that the sexes are separate and both must be
present to insure fruiting. The flowers appear on wood made the previous year
so in pruning in the early spring, if flowers are desired, plenty of the previous
year's wood should be left. This is the handsomest and most vigorous of the
actinidias. It will cover a space 30′ × 30′.

Actinidia polygama   Twining vine   15′   Zone 4   Silver-vine

FLOWERS: white, fragrant
   TIME: late June
FOLIAGE: staminate plant silvery
HABITAT: Japan and China
INTRODUCED: 1861

    This species is very attractive to cats and they will even climb through
greenhouse ventilators to get to it. If they can reach it they will claw and tear it to
shreds. The foliage is partly variegated, especially that of the staminate plants,
the upper part of the leaves being silvery white to yellowish. This is not a very
strong climber.

Akebia quinata   Twining vine   30–40′   Zone 4   Fiveleaf Akebia

FLOWERS: purple, small, ½–1″ diameter, in clusters
   TIME: mid-May
*FOLIAGE: semi-evergreen
HABITAT: central China, Korea, Japan
INTRODUCED: 1845

    A dainty, vigorously growing twiner, the Fiveleaf Akebia makes one of the
best foliage vines. It grows so rapidly that it sometimes becomes a pest by escap-
ing and spreading over considerable ground where it can easily kill plants as
does the native Bittersweet. Trained around a wire or waterspout on the house
it is easily one of the neatest and best of foliage vines and can be easily controlled. If cut to the ground it quickly grows back. The large purple, fleshy fruit
pods are not always produced for apparently insects and wind do not facilitate
pollinization in most areas. Hand pollination, by rubbing the staminate flowers
over the pistillate flowers at the proper time usually results in fruit formation.
The peculiar staminate flowers and the larger pistillate flowers are frequently
produced in the same cluster.

Ampelopsis aconitifolia   Vine   Zone 4   Monks Hood Vine

FRUIT: berries orange or yellow when fully ripe, sometimes bluish before ma-
turity, in clusters
   EFFECTIVE: fall
HABITAT: northern China
INTRODUCED: 1868

    A luxuriant vine, not a good screen, but with foliage of interest because of
the delicately shaped leaves.

Ampelopsis arborea   Vine   Zone 7   Pepper-vine

FOLIAGE: dark green, semi-evergreen
HABITAT: southeastern United States

A vine which is widely grown throughout the southeastern United States for various ornamental purposes. It climbs by means of attaching its tendrils to supports. The leaves are doubly compound and it suckers readily.

Ampelopsis brevipedunculata   Vine   Zone 4   Porcelain Ampelopsis

*FRUIT: berries changing from pale lilac to yellow and finally to bright blue, rarely whitish, in clusters
EFFECTIVE: fall
HABITAT: northeastern Asia
INTRODUCED: 1870

The Porcelain Ampelopsis is a vigorous climber (tendrils) with deeply lobed leaves, its chief asset being the very colorful fruits in the fall. These are berries about ¼" in diameter borne in medium-sized clusters, colored green, yellow, whitish and porcelain blue all in the same cluster at the same time. It does not make as dense a foliage screen as some of the other foliage vines, but its colorful fruit in the fall is not equalled in beauty by that of any other woody vine.

Ampelopsis humulifolia   Vine   Zone 5   Hop Ampelopsis

FRUIT: berries usually few, pale yellow, bluish cheek or entirely pale yellow or pale blue
EFFECTIVE: fall
*FOLIAGE: lustrous bright green
HABITAT: northern China
INTRODUCED: 1868

A climbing, shrubby vine (climbing by tendrils) with handsome foliage resembling that of a true grape, with leaves lustrous above and white beneath. Only of value for its foliage since the fruits are not borne profusely.

Ampelopsis megalophylla   Vine   30'   Zone 6

HABITAT: western China
INTRODUCED: 1894

Chiefly valued for its large compound leaves, 10–25" long, climbing by means of attaching its tendrils to supports.

Aristolochia durior   Twining vine   30'   Zone 4   Dutchman's Pipe

*FOLIAGE: dark green
HABITAT: central United States

Dutchman's Pipe is a vigorous twining vine with large leaves sometimes as much as 12" long, that has been a popular vine since colonial times. The common name is applied because of the peculiar flowers shaped somewhat like a small, curved Meerschaum pipe. They are fairly inconspicuous, not being produced in large numbers and are hidden almost entirely by the leaves. There is no special autumn color. For covering porch trellises or for screening purposes this large leaved vine is most satisfactory. Plenty of room should be given it for expansion since it quickly crowds out less vigorous vines planted near by.

Bignonia capreolata   Vine to 60′   Zone 6   Cross-vine

*FLOWERS: orange-red, 1½–2″ long
   TIME: late May
FOLIAGE: evergreen
AUTUMN COLOR: reddish green
HABITAT: southern United States

   A very popular vine throughout the South, this vigorous vine climbs by means of tendrils. The beautiful and profuse orange-red flowers are its crowning glory. The name "Cross-vine" comes from the fact that a cross is clearly seen when the wood is sectioned transversely. It is excellent for screen planting.

Boussingaultia baselloides   Vine   Zone 9   Madeira Vine

*FLOWERS: white, fragrant in racemes, 1′ long
   TIME: late summer
FOLIAGE: evergreen, leaves 3″ long, lustrous
HABITAT: tropical America

   A vigorous vine, climbing by the use of tendrils, it can grow 20′ or more in a single season and will quickly go out of control in moist ground.

Campsis grandiflora   Clinging vine   20′   Zone 7   Chinese Trumpet Vine

*FLOWERS: funnel-shaped, scarlet, 3″ diameter
   TIME: August
HABITAT: China
INTRODUCED: 1800

   Because of its larger flowers, this is the showiest *Campsis* species climbing by means of rootlike holdfasts but needing considerable assistance. Like other members of this genus, the foliage is of coarse texture.

Campsis radicans   Clinging vine   30′   Zone 4   Trumpet Vine

*FLOWERS: orange to scarlet, trumpet-shaped flowers, 2″ diameter
   TIME: mid-July
HABITAT: Pennsylvania to Missouri, Florida and Texas

   A shrubby vine, clinging to stone or woodwork by means of small rootlike holdfasts but often needs additional support to hold it in place since it becomes very heavy. Its brilliant flowers in mid-summer are its chief attraction. The larger flowered hybrid *C. tagliabuana* variety "Madame Galen" with corolla 2½″ in diameter is more showy in the North where *C. grandiflora* cannot be grown. Both vines can climb to 30′ or more.

x Campsis tagliabuana "Madame Galen"   Clinging vine   25′   Zone 4

*FLOWERS: orange and scarlet, funnel-shaped, 2½″ in diameter
   TIME: July
HYBRID ORIGIN: *C. grandiflora x C. radicans*
ORIGINATED: before 1858

   Almost as showy as the Chinese Trumpet-vine, with flowers larger than those of *C. radicans*. It can be used in place of *C. radicans*, where available, if the more conspicuous flowers seem desirable. Like the other two species in this genus it climbs by means of small rootlike holdfasts but frequently becomes so heavy that a strong wind or ice storm may force a large portion of the vine away from a building unless it is held in place with wire.

Celastrus flagellaris Twining vine 24′ Zone 4 Korean Bittersweet

FLOWERS: inconspicuous
  TIME: June
FRUIT: yellow and red berries, sexes separate
  EFFECTIVE: fall
AUTUMN COLOR: yellow
HABITAT: northeastern Asia
INTRODUCED: 1905

The importance of this twining vine comes from the fact that the stipules are small, hooked spines, hence it is one of the few thorny vines available. It makes a good vine for bank planting, especially as a barrier in parks or lawn areas where taller spiny shrubs would be out of place. The fruits are smaller than those of *C. orbiculata* and *C. scandens* and less profusely borne. All *Celastrus* species have staminate flowers on one plant and pistillate or fruiting flowers on another plant and both types must be comparatively near each other to insure fruiting. For further notes on fruiting see *C. scandens*.

Celastrus orbiculata Twining vine 36′ Zone 4 Oriental Bittersweet

FLOWERS: inconspicuous
  TIME: June
*FRUIT: yellow and red berries, sexes separate
  EFFECTIVE: fall and winter
AUTUMN COLOR: yellow
HABITAT: China and Japan
INTRODUCED: 1860

An excellent twining vine, differing from *C. scandens* chiefly in that the leaves are more rounded, and the fruits are in small lateral clusters, not in large terminal clusters as are those of *C. scandens*. For notes on fruiting—all *Celastrus* species have staminate flowers on one plant and pistillate flowers on another—see remarks under *C. scandens*.

Celastrus scandens Twining vine 20′ Zone 2 American Bittersweet

FLOWERS: inconspicuous, sexes separate
  TIME: June
*FRUIT: yellow and red berries
  EFFECTIVE: fall and winter
*AUTUMN COLOR: yellow
HABITAT: eastern North America

One of the most ornamental of our hardy northern vines, climbing by twining. It is vigorous in habit and can kill shrubs or small trees to which it becomes attached merely by tightly girdling stems and branches. The staminate and pistillate flowers are usually on different plants so that both types should be fairly close together to insure good fruiting of the pistillate form.

Many nurserymen are now growing plants asexually propagated so that the sexes are kept separate, and thus fruiting plants can be bought even though they have neither flowers nor fruits at time of purchase. A small staminate plant could be placed in the same hole at fruiting time and pruned to a minimum, or branches from a staminate plant could be tied in the pistillate plant at flowering time. Although there are plants that are polygamodioecious (with both male and female flowers) none of these have flowered well as far as I have seen.

The American Bittersweet has fruits in terminal clusters, first appearing yellow in early fall and later, when the yellow capsules crack open, the bright red berries inside are displayed. An excellent vine, easily grown, but which should have some intelligent maintenance in order to produce fruits.

Cissus incisa   Vine   30′   Zone 8   Ivy Treebine or Marine Ivy

HABITAT: southern and south central United States

Climbing by means of tendrils.

CLEMATIS

Much has been written about the beautiful clematis but still they do not appear in many gardens. The reasons are probably that they require a limestone or alkaline soil, and are susceptible to diseases, which, in some areas, may not be understood or may be very difficult to control. The clematis are treated here as a group, many of them are worthy additions to any garden, and some of the large-flowered hybrids are the delight of many gardeners who so enthusiastically care for them. The conspicuously colored parts of the flowers are not true petals but sepals, not an important point but one worth knowing if one wishes to be correct in speaking of the floral parts.

A nursery catalogue featuring clematis can easily entice one into buying several of the yellow, pink, red, blue, purple and white flowered varieties with flowers sometimes as much as 10 inches in diameter. From such a pictorial display one might consider clematis culture simple. On the contrary, not everyone will succeed with clematis, but for those who are willing to try, a few of the more important cultural notes are given here which may prove helpful.

There are at least 40–50 species of clematis hardy in the northern United States, many of them grown splendidly by the late Colonel J. E. Spingarn of Amenia, New York, who probably did more than any other single person to popularize them in this country. One of the most beautiful species is a native of Texas called *Clematis texensis* but hardy as far north as Bar Harbor, Maine. A five-year-old plant can be covered with thousands of scarlet to rose-pink urn-shaped flowers about an inch long. The exotic *C. paniculata* is noted for its early fall flowers that are deliciously fragrant. Of course the many large-flowered hybrids are the delight of the clematis connoisseur and in fact all who see their pictures in the catalogues, especially if they are unfamiliar with the trials and tribulations necessary to bring them into proper bloom.

Clematis have opposite leaves and climb by twisting their leaf stalks about the means of support, using them as tendrils. Some of the species such

LEFT: The dainty, red flowering Texas Clematis.
RIGHT: The plumy seeds of many clematis add much to their effectiveness in the fall.
These are the fruits of *Clematis paniculata.*

as *C. paniculata, C. vitalba* and *C. texensis* are vigorous growers, making a dense mat of foliage in a short time and so are useful for screening purposes. *C. lanuginosa,* for instance, one of the parents of the largest hybrid group, only grows about six feet high whereas *C. paniculata* may grow thirty feet or even more. Some of the others, especially the large-flowered hybrid types, are loose and open in habit of growth and do not reach such great lengths or make such dense masses of foliage.

Culture

Clematis are best transplanted in the spring, but many of the large-flowered hybrids can be planted at other times since they are grown in pots and so are easily transportable. A light loamy soil with some lime added is of the best texture. Plenty of moisture and a cool soil seem to be of prime importance for good growth. Another requisite, though sometimes not deemed necessary, is some shade, especially for the less-vigorous growing forms. Sometimes a mulch of peat moss or even spent hops, to which lime has been added, proves helpful in keeping the ground cool about the roots.

There is considerable discussion concerning the attention the stems should be given at the surface of the soil. Colonel Spingarn used a zinc collar about the base of the vines, others have used sand in an inverted flower pot or merely plain coal ashes, methods used to prevent the inroads of a stem rot that proves destructive under certain conditions. Once this

Many clematis hybrids have conspicuously large "flowers" which are actually clusters of smaller flowers surrounded by conspicuous flower sepals. Some of the "flowers" may be as much as 10 inches in diameter.

disease is noted and stems commence to die, a competent plant pathologist should be consulted at once regarding the best current means for controlling it. At present "Fermate" is being used as a spray at bi-weekly intervals starting in June. Other materials will undoubtedly be found that are just as good or better.

The more vigorous-growing species need little pruning. Cold winters frequently kill above-ground parts of some hybrids so that pruning live tissue is sometimes unnecessary. One should know whether plants bloom on the previous year's wood or bloom on wood made during the current year of growth to be able to prune the plants properly. For instance, "Belle of Woking," "Duchess of Edinburgh," "Sir Garnet Wolseley" and other hybrids of *C. patens* and *C. florida,* all bloom on the previous year's wood, hence they should be pruned only after they flower. These all bloom early in the season, about mid-spring. On the other hand a long list of hybrids of *C. lanuginosa* and *C. patens, C. jackmani* and *C. texensis,* such as "Crimson King," "Lord Neville," "Nelly Moser," "Ramona" and many others—all bloom on the growth made during the current year, and so can be pruned in early spring to within a few feet of the ground. They bloom from early summer to fall. Since this problem of pruning is of the utmost importance in clematis culture, some of the clematis have been divided into the following specific groups:

Clematis Blooming on Previous Year's Wood

C. alpina	*C. macropetala*
"Belle of Woking"	"Miss Bateman"
"Duchess of Edinburgh"	*C. montana*
"Edouard Desfosse"	*C. ochroleuca*
C. florida	*C. patens*
"Lasurstern"	"Sir Garnet Wolseley"
"La Lorraine"	

Clematis Blooming on Current Year's Wood

"Ascotiensis"	"Marie Boisselot"
"Comtesse de Bouchaud"	"Nelly Moser"
"Crimson King"	*C. orientalis*
"Duchess of Albany"	"Otto Froebel"
"Elsa Spaeth"	*C. paniculata*
"Gypsy Queen"	"Perle d'Azur"
C. jackmani	"Prins Hendrik"
C. jouiniana	"Ramona"
"Lady Caroline Neville"	*C. tangutica*
C. lanuginosa	*C. texensis*
"Lord Neville"	"Ville de Lyon"
"Madame Edouard André"	*C. viticella*
"Mme Van Houtte"	*C. vitalba*
"Mrs. Cholmondeley"	*C. viorna*

Only a few clematis can be used for screen plantings since most are not sufficiently dense or vigorous. But grown over pergolas or upright supports about the garden or allowed to ramble over a pile of rocks or on a fence, or even to wander through some open growing shrubbery in a partially shaded nook of the garden—these are the proper ways they should be grown. They can also be used in pots or tubs for house or conservatory decoration. They make admirable cut flowers, lasting as long as ten days when placed in water. It is impossible to mention all of the good varieties, or to make a selection of "the best" of this diverse group, since new hybrids are constantly appearing. However, the following is a list of some of the more useful species and some of the better known of the many hybrids now being grown in this country.

Clematis alpina   Vine   6′   Zone 5   Alpine Clematis

*FLOWERS: violet-blue, single, about 3″ in diameter
    TIME: early May
FRUIT: plumy seed heads
    EFFECTIVE: summer
HABITAT: southern and central Europe to northeastern Asia
INTRODUCED: 1753
    One of the first of this genus to flower.

Clematis armandi   Vine   15′   Zone 7   Armand Clematis

*FLOWERS: white, 1–1¼″ in diameter, in showy panicles
    TIME: spring
FOLIAGE: evergreen
HABITAT: central and southern China
INTRODUCED: 1907
    One of the few clematis which should be pruned after it is through flowering because it blooms on wood made the previous year. This makes an excellent garden plant in the Pacific Northwest and quickly reaches a spread of 50′ and even 100′ there.

Clematis florida   Vine   12′   Zone 7   Cream Clematis

*FLOWERS: creamy white, purple stamens, solitary, 2½–3″ in diameter
    TIME: late June
FRUIT: plumy seed heads
    EFFECTIVE: fall
FOLIAGE: deciduous or half evergreen
HABITAT: central China
INTRODUCED: 1776
    Blooming slightly before the *C. lanuginosa* hybrids, *C. florida* and its hybrids are valued chiefly for this feature.
    Some hybrids with this species as one of the parents are:
    "Belle of Woking"—double silvery gray, introduced 1885
    "Duchess of Edinburgh"—double white, introduced 1877

x Clematis jackmani   Vine   12′   Zone 5   Jackman Clematis

*FLOWERS: violet-purple, 5–7″ diameter
    TIME: mid-July
FRUIT: plumy seed heads
    EFFECTIVE: fall
HYBRID ORIGIN: *C. lanuginosa x C. viticella*
ORIGINATED: about 1860
    The first so-called "large-flowered hybrid" was *C. jackmani* exhibited in England for the first time in 1863. It is still at the top of the list in popularity because its large violet-purple flowers are of a color not shown in any other vine. It can be heavily pruned in early spring since it flowers on shoots made the current year.
    Some of the better hybrids with this species as one of the parents:
    "Comtesse de Bouchaud," flowers satiny rose, introduced before 1915

"Gypsy Queen," dark velvety purple, introduced 1877
"Madame Edouard André," flowers velvety purplish red, introduced 1892
"Mrs. Cholmondeley," flowers light blue, introduced about 1875

x Clematis jouiniana   Vine   12'   Zone 4   Jouin Clematis

*FLOWERS: white to purplish, 1" in diameter
  TIME: early August
FRUIT: plumy seed heads
  EFFECTIVE: fall
HYBRID ORIGIN: *C. heracleifolia x C. vitalba*
ORIGINATED: before 1900

Clematis lanuginosa   Vine   6'   Zone 5   Ningpo Clematis

*FLOWERS: white to pale lilac, 6–8 sepals, 5–10" in diameter
  TIME: summer
FRUIT: plumy seed heads
  EFFECTIVE: fall
HABITAT: China
INTRODUCED: 1850

Mentioned in this list since it is one of the parents of an ever-increasing list of large-flowered hybrids. Many of its hybrids surpass it in beauty and color.

Some of the better hybrids of this species are:

"Crimson King" flowers bright red		introduced 1916
"Elsa Spaeth"	bright blue	1891
"Lady Caroline Neville"	mauve	1866
"Lord Neville"	dark plum	about 1870
"Nelly Moser"	pale mauve with red bar	1897
"Prins Hendrik"	azure blue	before 1912
"Ramona"	blue	1874
"W. E. Gladstone"	lilac	1881
"Perle d'Azur"	light blue	about 1875

x Clematis lawsoniana henryi   Vine   6'   Henry Clematis

*FLOWERS: white, 6" diameter
  TIME: summer
HYBRID ORIGIN: *C. lanuginosa x C. viticella*

Clematis macropetala   Vine   10'   Zone 5   Big-petal Clematis

*FLOWERS: azure-blue, large, 2½–4" diameter, with many sepals
  TIME: spring
HABITAT: northern China and Siberia
INTRODUCED: 1910

An unusually distinguished plant in flower with the center of each flower filled with a number of petallike segments, decreasing in size towards the center of the flower and paler in tint than the four large sepals on the outside. Each flower is produced on a slender stock 3" long that gives it a unique nodding appearance.

LEFT: *Clematis montana rubens* with flowers rosy red to pink.
RIGHT: The very popular Sweet Autumn Clematis (*C. paniculata*).

Clematis montana rubens   Vine   24′   Zone 5   Pink Anemone Clematis

*FLOWERS: rosy red to pinkish, 2–2½″ diameter
    TIME: May
FRUIT: plumy seed heads
    EFFECTIVE: summer
HABITAT: central and western China
INTRODUCED: 1900

One of the most beautiful of the early oriental clematis species and a favorite of E. H. Wilson's who gets the credit for introducing this ornamental from China. Since it blooms so early it should be noted that the flower buds occur on the previous year's wood. The flowers are similar in shape to those of the Japanese Anemone and the new young foliage is a pleasing bronzy crimson color.

Clematis paniculata   Vine   30′   Zone 5   Sweet Autumn Clematis

*FLOWERS: white, very fragrant, profuse
    TIME: late August
*FRUIT: plumy seed heads
    EFFECTIVE: fall
FOLIAGE: semi-evergreen, lustrous
HABITAT: Japan
INTRODUCED: 1864

One of the best ornamentals in the clematis group because the vine itself has great vigor, making a mass of dense lustrous leaves, because the flowers are profusely borne and very fragrant, and because the fluffy, silvery seed heads make a display after the flowers have gone. It is seldom attacked by insect or disease pest and can be recommended as one of the easiest clematis to grow, as well as one which has proved very popular.

Clematis patens   Vine   12′   Zone 7   Lilac Clematis

*FLOWERS: white to violet-blue, 5–7″ diameter with 6–8 sepals
   TIME: late May
FRUIT: plumy seed heads
   EFFECTIVE: summer
HABITAT: China
INTRODUCED: 1836
   This species and *C. florida* are two of the larger flowering species blooming on wood formed the previous year. Together with *C. lanuginosa* and *C. jackmani* it is one of the important species in breeding the large-flowered ornamental types. Some of the hybrids with this as one of the parents are:

      "Sir Garnet Wolseley" flowers bronzy blue   introduced 1880
      "Lasurstern"   deep purplish blue   1906
      "Edouard Desfosse"   violet   1877

Clematis tangutica   Vine   9′   Zone 5   Golden Clematis

*FLOWERS: bright yellow, solitary, 3–4″ in diameter
   TIME: June
FRUIT: plumy seed heads
   EFFECTIVE: early fall
HABITAT: northwestern China
INTRODUCED: 1890
   One of the best, if not the best, of the yellow-flowered clematis species. A very conspicuous vine in flower, superior in every way to *C. orientalis*, another yellow-flowered species.

Clematis texensis   Vine   6′   Zone 4   Scarlet Clematis

*FLOWERS: bright scarlet, bell-shaped, profuse
   TIME: July
FRUIT: plumy seed heads
   EFFECTIVE: fall
HABITAT: Texas
   This excellent native should appear in gardens far more than it does. If grown in a sheltered spot it starts to bloom in early summer and continues until frost even in New York and New England. Its bright scarlet, bell-shaped flowers are profusely borne and make it the most ornamental of the species native in North America. It frequently dies down to the ground each winter, but sprouts quickly from the base the following spring and blooms on the current year's growth.
   One of the hybrids of this species is "Duchess of Albany" with red flowers, introduced in 1897.

Clematis virginiana   Vine   18′   Zone 4   Virgin's Bower

*FLOWERS: white, small
   TIME: late August

*FRUIT: plumy seed heads
   EFFECTIVE: fall
AUTUMN COLOR: purple
HABITAT: eastern North America

A native that is not one of the best of its group for ornament, nevertheless it is common along the roadsides and has a place in the wild garden or in wooded planting. Its more conspicuous flowering relatives should be used in the small garden where space is at a premium.

Clematis vitalba　　　Vine　　　30′　　　Zone 4　　　Travelers' Joy

*FLOWERS: white, slightly fragrant, nearly 1″ in diameter
   TIME: late August
*FRUIT: plumy large seed heads
   EFFECTIVE: fall
HABITAT: Europe and northern Africa
INTRODUCED: before 1820

One of the vigorous-growing species, it does have small flowers so that its rapidity of growth, its late summer bloom and its very fluffy seed heads in the fall are its important features rather than the size of the individual flowers. The common name comes from the fact that the flowers are slightly fragrant, and the odor proves quite refreshing to the traveler on a hot summer's day. An excellent vine for growing over fence or garden pergola where dense foliage is wanted.

Clematis viticella hybrids　　　　　12′　　　　　Zone 4

"Ascotiensis"	flowers azure-blue	introduced 1880
"Ville de Lyon"	reddish purple	1900
"Kermesiana"	intense bright red	1883

Additional miscellaneous hybrids of possible merit—there are many but these few were recommended by the late J. E. Spingarn, who grew them all:

"La Lorraine," pink and lavender flowers, on previous year's wood
"Madame Van Houtte," white flowers, on the current year's wood
"Marie Boisselot," white flowers, on the current year's wood
"Otto Froebel," gray-flushed pink flowers, on current year's wood
"Miss Bateman," white flowers on previous year's wood
"The Bride," white flowers on previous year's wood

Cobaea scandens　　　Vine　　　40′　　　Zone 9　　　Cup and Saucer Vine

*FLOWERS: pendulous lavender to purple, bell-shaped, 2″ diameter on graceful foot-long stems
   TIME: spring and summer for at least 6 months
HABITAT: Mexico

A delightful flowering vine, climbing by means of tenacious tendrils and useful especially for its extremely long flowering period. A good ornamental for southern gardens.

Distictis lactiflora　　　Vine　　　　　Zone 9

FLOWERS: purple to white, shaped like morning glory, 2″ long and 2″ in diameter
   TIME: summer and fall

Euonymus fortunei varieties showing the differences in the leaves.
LEFT TO RIGHT: Varieties *radicans, minima* and *vegeta* (one of two fruiting
varieties)

HABITAT: Mexico

This is a comparatively recent introduction into southern California but should prove popular since it is reported to have grown from seed to 20′ in one year. Another ornamental vine of long flowering season with trumpet-shaped flowers, climbing by means of tendrils.

Doxantha unguis-cati　　　Clinging vine　　　Zone 8　　　Cat-claw Vine

*FLOWERS: yellow, 3″ long and 2½″ in diameter
　TIME: early spring
FOLIAGE: evergreen, leaflets 2″ long
HABITAT: West Indies to Argentina

This climber has few enemies but its chief fault lies in that it tends to get sparse of foliage and branches near the base. This of course can be remedied by

The Evergreen Bittersweet (*Euonymus fortunei vegeta*) can be trained, if clipped occasionally, to grow on and cover a split sapling fence; or it can be allowed to ramble up tree trunks.

proper pruning. Although it has tendrils, these are tenacious and equipped with claws (from which it gets its name) and it can cling to hot wall surfaces of stone or wood surprisingly well.

Euonymus fortunei   Clinging vine to sub-shrub   Zone 5   Wintercreeper

*FOLIAGE: evergreen, leaves ½–2″ long
HABITAT: China
INTRODUCED: 1907

This species and its several varieties are the hardiest of the evergreen vines. They cling to walls, rocks and trunks by means of small rootlike holdfasts. Some of the varieties climb and cling better than others but all varieties are very important ornamentally. The species and all but two of the varieties (*carrierei* and *vegeta*) rarely bear fruit for they all apparently are juvenile forms. However, if a planting of *E. fortunei* once becomes well established, it is not long before several "sports" appear and some of the other varieties will quickly arise. *E. fortunei carrierei* is one of the first to become evident and it does flower and fruit. The best form for fruits is *E. fortunei vegeta*, often called the Evergreen Bittersweet, for it bears orange fruits in the utmost profusion. All forms make good ground covers for they creep rapidly and root readily all along the branches. Some of the more important varieties are:

carrierei—very shiny leaves sometimes 2″ long. It is a semi-shrub, fruits well and clings to walls and stones well. This variety is called the glossy winter-creeper.

colorata—this makes an excellent ground cover with leaves an inch long turning a purplish red in the fall and remaining that color all winter long.

gracilis—leaves with white, yellow or even pink margin.

minima—minute leaves less than ½" long. The variety *kewensis* has even smaller leaves. They are admirable where a small space is to be covered but they do grow slowly and where large areas are to be planted one of the larger leaved more vigorous varieties should be used.

radicans—trailing or climbing, with leaves about 1" long, this has been one of the most serviceable of all the forms.

"Silver Queen"—similar to *E. fortunei gracilis* except that the margin of the leaves are completely white. This plant certainly is conspicuous wherever it is grown in quantity.

vegeta—perhaps the most ornamental of all, this variety has rounded leaves 1–1½" diameter, thick and leathery. A semi-shrub, sometimes called the Evergreen Bittersweet, it grows as a shrub about 4' high and was first introduced into this country in 1876 by the Arnold Arboretum. An excellent variety, quick rooting and easy to propagate, this form might well be in every garden not only because of its evergreen foliage but because of the wealth of colorful fruits it bears in the fall.

Euonymus obovata   Ground cover   Zone 3   Running Euonymus

FRUIT: scarlet berries
   EFFECTIVE: fall
AUTUMN COLOR: red
HABITAT: eastern United States
INTRODUCED: 1820

Used strictly as a ground cover this deciduous Running Euonymus grows more vigorously than the evergreen types and so can be expected to cover a larger area in a shorter time. The brilliant red autumn color also adds to its attractiveness in the fall.

Ficus pumila   Clinging vine   Zone 9   Creeping Fig

*FOLIAGE: evergreen, leaves 1–4" long
HABITAT: China, Japan, Australia

An excellent vine for covering walls, the young stems make a dense network, often grafting themselves together where they cross and attaching themselves to walls by small rootlets. The leaves are small, heart-shaped and held closely to the stems so that a mature vine displays a solid wall of green. As it matures, the leaves become larger, erect branches grow out from the younger stems and inedible puffy figs are produced. It should be pruned before it reaches this stage to keep the young growth vigorous.

Hedera canariensis   Clinging vine   Zone 7   Algerian Ivy

FRUIT: black berries
   EFFECTIVE: fall
*FOLIAGE: dark green, thick and leathery
HABITAT: Canary Islands and northern Africa

INTRODUCED: 1833

A rapid-growing evergreen vine, used outdoors only in the South. Its outstanding variety "Canary Cream" is used because the leaves have a margin of cream or ivory color and some of the leaves have no color at all.

Hedera helix   Clinging vine   90′   Zone 5   English Ivy

FRUIT: black berries
   EFFECTIVE: fall
*FOLIAGE: evergreen, leaves 3–5 lobed to 4″ long
HABITAT: Europe
INTRODUCED: early colonial times
VARIETIES:
   "Albany"—erect and shrubby in habit
   aureo-variegata—leaves variegated yellow
   baltica—merely a hardier form of the species, hardy with some protection in Boston
   cavendishi—leaf margin variegated white to ivory
   conglomerata—small leaves, usually not over 1½″ long, two-ranked on stiff upright stems
   digita—leaves five to seven lobed
   minima—small lobed leaves, very unstable in habit
   "Pittsburgh"—lateral shoots appear in most of the leaf axils

Dr. George H. M. Lawrence of the Bailey Hortorium, Cornell University, has made a special study of this species and finally recognized only 38 varieties. Certainly there are many available in the trade but the nomenclature is very much mixed. *Hedera helix* is more widely distributed in western Europe than any other species. It has escaped cultivation and become naturalized in several places in the United States and in Europe as well. It is the most variable species of the genus, especially in its juvenile forms. There are so many clons, probably because the plant itself has been cultivated for centuries and variants are usually propagated and continued. These plants are all easy to cultivate, make admirable ground covers where hardy, and are grown over wire fences in southern California, simulating excellent hedges. They are widely used for clinging to walls and tree trunks by means of their small rootlike holdfasts. One of the best evergreen vines for the South as well as the North.

Hydrangea petiolaris   Clinging vine   75′   Zone 4   Climbing Hydrangea

*FLOWERS: flowers white, in large flat clusters, 6–10″ in diameter
   TIME: mid-June
HABITAT: Japan, China
INTRODUCED: 1865

This is a true vine, clinging to supports by means of small rootlike holdfasts. The lateral branches may extend as much as 3′ from the main stem, and when grown on the side of a brick building it is really interesting. The large, flat flower clusters have sterile flowers along the perimeter of the cluster. The reddish shredding bark on older stems is of interest in the winter time. The plant can be used to splendid advantage on old walls or rock piles. It is frequently mixed up in the trade with *Schizophragma hydrangeoides* but the two can be

This Climbing Hydrangea was planted by E. H. Wilson in front of his home. As is apparent from the picture, the vine does not detract from the graceful appearance of the elm on which it grows nor does it do the tree any harm.

easily told apart because the leaves of the hydrangea are lustrous above and the leaf margin is regularly serrate while the leaves of *Schizophragma* are not lustrous and they are markedly coarsely dentate.

Jasminum mesnyi   Vine   10′ to sub-shrub   Zone 8   Primrose Jasmine

*FLOWERS: yellow, single, 1½″ diameter
   TIME: spring and summer
FOLIAGE: semi-evergreen
HABITAT: China
INTRODUCED: 1900

   The most strikingly beautiful of the jasmines grown in this country unfortunately is one of the least hardy. Its large yellow flowers and soft green foliage are more ornamental than those of *J. nudiflorum*. E. H. Wilson collected it in China for the Veitch Nursery Company of England, but even there it suffers severe frost damage. In southern Italy it is reported to do well.

Jasminum nudiflorum   Vine   15′ to sub-shrub   Zone 5   Winter Jasmine

*FLOWERS: bright yellow, solitary, ¾–1″ in diameter
    TIME: early April
WINTER TWIGS: green
HABITAT: China
INTRODUCED: 1844

The hardiest of the jasmines, this is being grown as far north as Boston when given some winter protection or grown against warm walls of buildings. This plant is one to be used at the top of walls or banks where the graceful branches can droop to best advantage. In the South it blooms in the winter and its solitary yellow flowers can be forced into bloom indoors when twigs are cut any time during winter. It seems to prefer a warm, dry, sunny location in order to produce the maximum number of flowers but will quickly become untidy unless pruned occasionally.

Jasminum officinale   Vine 30′ to sub-shrub   Zone 7   Common White Jasmine

*FLOWERS: white, fragrant
    TIME: summer
FOLIAGE: semi-evergreen
WINTER TWIGS: green
HABITAT: Persia to Kashmir and China
INTRODUCED: cultivated since ancient times

A semi-climbing shrub, it is well known and widely used in the South. The fragrant flowers are borne intermittently all summer and it is used for covering arbors and trellises in sun or light shade. A popular plant requiring little attention, it has been grown and appreciated in this country and in Europe for a long time.

Kadsura japonica   Twining vine   12′   Zone 7   Scarlet Kadsura

FLOWERS: yellowish white, ¾″ diameter
    TIME: June–September
FRUIT: scarlet berries in clusters, 1″ in diameter
    EFFECTIVE: fall
*FOLIAGE: evergreen, leaves to 4″ long
    AUTUMN COLOR: reddish green
HABITAT: Japan, Korea
INTRODUCED: 1846

Lonicera caprifolium   Twining shrub   Zone 5   Sweet Honeysuckle

*FLOWERS: white or yellowish white, trumpet-shaped, 2″ long, in whorls, fragrant
    TIME: early June
FRUIT: orange-red berries
    EFFECTIVE: late summer
HABITAT: Europe and western Asia
INTRODUCED: before 1850

Lonicera etrusca   Twining vine   50′   Zone 7   Etruscan Honeysuckle

*FLOWERS: yellowish white, tinged purple, trumpet-shaped, fragrant, 2″ long
   TIME: late June
FOLIAGE: evergreen or semi-evergreen; leaves 3″ long
HABITAT: Mediterranean region
INTRODUCED: 1750
VARIETY
   superba   Cream Honeysuckle
*FLOWERS: several whorls, slightly larger than species

Lonicera flava   Twining vine   Zone 5   Yellow Honeysuckle

*FLOWERS: orange-yellow, trumpet-shaped in whorls, fragrant
   TIME: early June
HABITAT: southeastern and southern United States
   Only slightly twining, this is considered to be the handsomest of the native honeysuckle vines. The flowers are produced in terminal whorls, one to three whorls on a stalk.

Lonicera heckrotti   Vinelike   Zone 5   Everblooming Honeysuckle

*FLOWERS: purple outside, yellow inside corolla, in spikes, trumpet-shaped, 2″ long
   TIME: summer
HABITAT: origin unknown
INTRODUCED: before 1895
   A popular vinelike shrub, valued for its bright flowers, appearing throughout the summer from June until frost. The buds are actually carmine and as they open the deep yellow inside of the corolla lends a beautiful second color to the bloom.

Lonicera henryi   Twining vine   Zone 4   Henry Honeysuckle

FLOWERS: yellowish red to purplish red
   TIME: late June
FRUIT: black berries
   EFFECTIVE: September–October
*FOLIAGE: half-evergreen
HABITAT: western China
INTRODUCED: 1908
   Similar in many respects to *L. japonica halliana* except that it is slightly more hardy. It makes a fine tangle over rocks or on the ground as a ground cover.

Lonicera hildebrandiana   Twining vine   80′   Zone 9   Giant Honeysuckle

*FLOWERS: creamy white, in pairs 3½–6″ long, fragrant, with diameter of 2–3″
   TIME: summer
FRUITS: berries 1″ long
   EFFECTIVE: fall

FOLIAGE EVERGREEN: leaves 3–6″ long
HABITAT: Burma, Siam, China
INTRODUCED: 1888

Almost a monstrosity, yet if well grown this vigorous evergreen vine will have the largest flowers, fruits and leaves of any *Lonicera* species. For this reason it certainly should be mentioned and possibly tried in gardens in the extreme South.

Lonicera japonica halliana   Twining vine   Zone 4   Halls Honeysuckle

*FLOWERS: white, trumpet-shaped, turning yellow with age, fragrant
TIME: early June
FRUIT: black berries
EFFECTIVE: fall
*FOLIAGE: semi-evergreen to evergreen
AUTUMN COLOR: bronze
HABITAT: eastern Asia, naturalized in United States
INTRODUCED: before 1860

A vigorous exotic vine which has taken kindly to American conditions and has become widely naturalized. In fact it has actually become a pest in certain parts of southern Pennsylvania, Maryland and Virginia where it grows rampantly beside the roads and along the railroad rights of way. When confined to growing on a trellis, its dense habit (it clings by twining), its good foliage and deliciously fragrant flowers, its bronze autumn color and ability to grow in almost any soil, make it one of the most popular of vines. It will grow well in either sun or shade and is frequently used as a ground cover especially on steep banks because it grows quickly and easily roots wherever its stems touch moist soil. Several varieties are available from commercial sources, with flowers tinged red to purple on the outside. One especially, *L. japonica aureo-reticulata,* has leaves that are veined or netted with yellow, thus making it a rather conspicuous landscape specimen, but it is a shy bloomer and does not grow as fast as the species. The Chinese name for this plant means "gold and silver flower," singularly appropriate.

Lonicera sempervirens   Twining vine   50′   Zone 3   Trumpet Honeysuckle

*FLOWERS: orange to scarlet, trumpet-shaped, 2″ long
TIME: mid-June to August
FRUIT: red berries
EFFECTIVE: fall
HABITAT: eastern United States

A handsome vine with orange to scarlet trumpet-shaped flowers appearing for several months in the summer. Occasionally it is infested with plant lice. It is one of the hardier honeysuckle vines and so can be recommended especially for northern gardens where some of the larger flowered species are not hardy. The leaves at the end of the branches are joined together at their bases and the flowers are scentless.

x Lonicera tellmanniana   Twining vine   Zone 5   Tellmann Honeysuckle

*FLOWERS: deep yellow, trumpet-shaped in 2 whorls
TIME: June throughout the summer

HYBRID ORIGIN: *L. tragophylla x L. sempervirens*
ORIGINATED: before 1927

This is one of the most satisfactory results of *Lonicera* hybridization in which the best of the Chinese species and almost the best of the American species are united. The slender flowers are in terminal heads—usually about two whorls of about 6–12 blossoms, 2″ long. The flowers are yellow but the buds are flushed pink to red—a delightful color combination. It is a vigorous grower and well worthy of a trial wherever it proves hardy. The roots of this plant should be kept cool.

Lonicera tragophylla   Twining vine   50′   Zone 5   Chinese Woodbine

*FLOWERS: bright yellow in terminal clusters 2½–3½″ long
   TIME: mid-June and throughout the summer
FRUIT: red berries
   EFFECTIVE: fall
HABITAT: western China
INTRODUCED: 1900

One of the larger flowered and more showy of the northern growing honeysuckles. It does best when grown in a shady spot and apparently prefers a limestone soil in order to do best.

Lycium halimifolium   5′   Zone 4   Common Matrimony-vine

FLOWERS: small, lilac-purple
   TIME: late June
FRUIT: scarlet to orange-red berries
   EFFECTIVE: fall
HABITAT: southeastern Europe to western Asia
INTRODUCED: early colonial times

One of the poor soil shrubs, this plant is valued for its dense growth, its prickly branches and its bright red fruits in the fall. Strictly speaking it is not a vine, but a rambling shrub. Its branches bend over and touch the ground, often growing prostrate on the surface of the soil. It is very easy to grow and in many places has escaped cultivation forming dense thickets. It is not considered a "clean" shrub, and can spread rapidly and become a nuisance where the soil is to its liking. For poor soil and especially on banks, it fulfils its best purpose. It should be added, however, that the Chinese species, *L. chinense*, has larger leaves, fruits and flowers and makes a better ornamental, but because the European species is now so widely distributed in this country and has become naturalized, the differences between the two are probably not sufficiently great to recommend a change to *L. chinense*.

Mandevilla suaveolens   Twining vine   15–20′   Zone 9   Chilean Jasmine

FLOWERS: white to pinkish, fragrant, 2″ in diameter
   TIME: June to August
HABITAT: Argentina

Not a dense vine, but one which grows loosely and openly, with narrow heart-shaped leaves and funnellike flowers affording a picturesque subject for winding around a pillar.

Menispermum canadense Twining vine 12′ Zone 4 Common Moonseed

FRUITS: black berries, ⅛″ diameter
    TIME: fall
HABITAT: eastern United States
    A dense vine which usually is killed to the ground in the winter, but quickly grows back the following spring. It is not very tall, but increases rapidly by underground stems and can easily become a pernicious pest in the garden for this reason. Usually used only for its ivylike foliage or as a rampant ground cover.

Muehlenbeckia complexa   Twining vine   Zone 5   Wire Vine

HABITAT: New Zealand
INTRODUCED: 1842
    A twining vine with small leaves less than an inch long which can quickly cover rocks and fences. One of its chief merits is that it can withstand serious saline conditions at the seashore, an obvious advantage for any foliage plant of this nature.

Parthenocissus henryana   Vine   Zone 8   Silver Vein Creeper

*FOLIAGE: variegated white, purplish on undersurface
HABITAT: central China
INTRODUCED: 1895
    This vine should be grown in the shade where its striking foliage develops more color. The leaves have a white stripe along the mid-veins especially when young, and are claret-purple on the undersurface. It is not too desirable as a clinging type of vine.

Parthenocissus heptaphylla   Vine   Zone 8   Sevenleaf Creeper

HABITAT: Texas
    Another rapid-growing vine, climbing by means of tendrils, with seven leaflets, 2½″ long.

Parthenocissus quinquefolia   Vine   Zone 3   Virginia Creeper

FRUIT: bluish black, slightly bloomy berries
    EFFECTIVE: fall
AUTUMN COLOR: brilliant red
HABITAT: eastern United States
VARIETIES:
    engelmanni—leaflets smaller than the species, making a more refined specimen
    saint-pauli—leaflets smaller, clings better to stone work than either of above
    A high-climbing vine—climbing chiefly by means of tendrils, and native over a greater part of the eastern United States. Often called "Woodbine" it is frequently used in gardens but is a little too loose and open for many situations. Where stone walls or trellises are to be covered it can do remarkably well. Either of the smaller-leaved varieties might also be used for they are much more refined in appearance. All turn a vivid scarlet in the fall and are about the first of the woody plants to show fall color. Because of its wide distribution and its general usefulness, it should not be omitted from any list of vines.

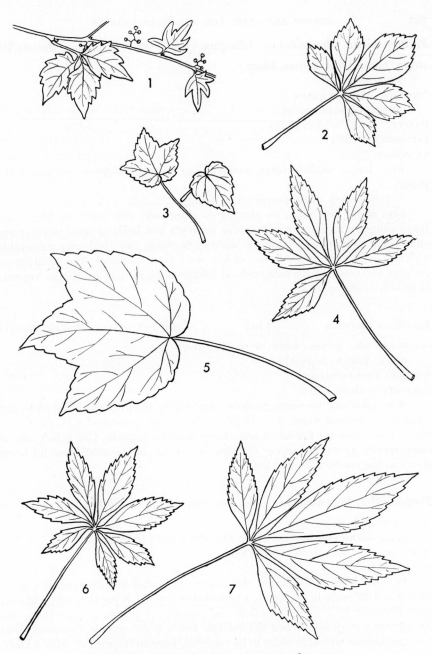

Leaf outlines of *Parthenocissus* species and varieties

1. *Parthenocissus tricuspidata lowi*
2. *P. quinquefolia Saint-Pauli*
3. *P. tricuspidata veitchi*
4. *P. quinquefolia engelmanni*
5. *P. tricuspidata*
6. *P. heptaphylla*
7. *P. quinquefolia*

Parthenocissus tricuspidata   Clinging vine   60'   Zone 4   Boston Ivy

FRUIT: bluish black berries, bloomy
  EFFECTIVE: fall
*FOLIAGE: lustrous leaves
  AUTUMN COLOR: scarlet
HABITAT: Japan, central China
INTRODUCED: 1862
VARIETIES:
  lowi—leaves smallest, often broader than long, apple-green, purplish when young
  veitchi—leaves small, purple when young
  One of the best vines for clinging to stonework. This native of China and Japan clings by means of small rootlike holdfasts and holds to stone work or any other solid support, tenaciously. It withstands trying city conditions remarkably well and quickly grows to the top of five story stone buildings. The small-leaved varieties are excellent for more refined foliage displays, but are not as vigorous in growth as the species.

Passiflora caerulea   Vine   Zone 7–8   Passion Flower

*FLOWERS: blue to pure white, 4" in diameter
  TIME: June to September
FOLIAGE: semi-evergreen
HABITAT: southern Brazil
  A popular vine for warm gardens, climbing by tendrils, and believed by the Spaniards, who first found it in Brazil, to have been associated with the Crucifixion. The leaves are five-lobed and almost immune to pests. This is only one of many species grown in warmer climates, but is one of the most beautiful being grown in the southern United States.

Phaedranthus buccinatorius   Clinging vine   Zone 9   Blood Trumpet Vine

*FLOWERS: red, trumpetlike
  TIME: entire year in some areas, May–November in others
*FOLIAGE: evergreen, leaflets to 3" long
HABITAT: Mexico
  In Santa Barbara, California, this vine was reported to have covered a space 50' tall and 45' wide in two years, a remarkable growth! A popular, very vigorous vine, climbing by means of tendrils and rootlets, it proves an excellent plant for screening purposes. When the tendrils touch a flat surface, tenacious discs ¼–½" are formed which, in order to be removed, have to be pried off with a knife.

Pileostegia viburnoides   Clinging vine   45'   Zone 7

*FLOWERS: white, hydrangealike
  TIME: late August to October
*FOLIAGE: evergreen, leaves 5–6" long, dark green and glossy
HABITAT: southern China
INTRODUCED: 1908

The Silver Fleece Vine (*Polygonum auberti*) is always a mass of white flowers in late summer.

Closely resembling the Climbing Hydrangea in its method of attaching itself to walls, it has foliage something like the English Laurel. One of the best evergreen climbers, seemingly doing best in full shade with freely borne flowers in late summer.

Plumbago capensis   Climbing shrub   Zone 9   Cape Plumbago

*FLOWERS: pale blue, 1″ diameter
    TIME: all summer
FOLIAGE: light green
HABITAT: South Africa

A shrubby climber, not a true vine, common in warm countries, and valued for its summer flowers. In some parts of California it flowers continually and should be allowed to clamber at will in its graceful fashion, rather than be restrained artificially. It needs full sun but requires little water.

Polygonum auberti   Vine   Zone 4   Silver Fleece Vine

*FLOWERS: white or greenish white to pinkish in dense panicles
    TIME: August
FOLIAGE: light green
HABITAT: western China
INTRODUCED: 1899

A handsome, vigorous, twining vine that may grow as much as 20–30′ in a single season. The foliage is dense and bright green, and the small greenish white flower clusters appear in large numbers late in summer when few woody plants are in bloom. The fruits are not very effective. Its vigor and conspicuous late bloom are its chief assets in the garden.

Pueraria thunbergiana   Vine   75′   Zone 6   Kudzu Vine

FLOWERS: violet-purple, beanlike, mostly hidden by foliage
     TIME: July
HABITAT: China, Japan
INTRODUCED: cultivated 1885

The fastest growing of all woody vines outside the warmer parts of the country, this Kudzu Vine may produce shoots 60′ long in a single season. It climbs by twining but does it in a lazy sort of way, the shoots winding around the supports only a few times where other vines like Bittersweet or Fleece Vine would twine around many times. Its beanlike leaves are coarse, and its tremendously rapid growth tends to make it more or less open, unless pruning or proper training is undertaken to keep all areas covered by the vine properly filled with shoots. It may kill to the ground annually as far north as New York but in many sections in Zone 6, it comes back rapidly each summer to produce much foliage. Its flowers and fruits are not ornamentally effective for they are mostly hidden by the large leaves. For covering a large area in a short time it should be the first vine considered, within its hardiness range.

x Rosa (rambler roses)   8–20′   Zone 5   Rambler Roses

*FLOWERS: single and double in large clusters, white, pink and red
     TIME: June
HYBRID ORIGIN: *R. multiflora x R. wichuraiana* and other species

The inclusive term "Rambler Rose" embraces a number of hybrids of *R. multiflora*, *R. wichuraiana*, *R. setigera* and others, as well as climbing sports of hybrid teas and perpetuals. They do not twine nor attach themselves to supports, hence are not true vines. They always need to be tied up to the means of support. Some grow only 8–10′ high, others 20–25′ depending on their heredity and general growing conditions. Old canes should be cut out immediately after flowering to allow the more vigorous younger canes plenty of room. These are the ones which will bloom the next year. In the North, rambler roses frequently must be laid on the ground and covered to protect them from winter cold. All considered, rambler roses need a great deal of care (pruning, spraying, fertilizing, mulching and protection from winter cold) when compared with true vines, yet thousands of gardeners all over the country feel well repaid for this extra trouble when the plants burst into gorgeous bloom. They are commonly used on arbors, trellises, fences, stone walls and buildings. On Nantucket Island they are sufficiently hardy to grow completely over the roofs of small cottages, making a never-to-be-forgotten sight when in full bloom.

There are hundreds of rambler roses available, of all kinds. Some have very long blooming periods, others bloom only once. The following list comprises only a few important varieties to show the variations in this group of plants:

NAME	DATE OF INTRODUCTION	FLOWERS	COLOR	HEIGHT
"Blaze"	1932	semi-double	scarlet	15'–
"Dr. Huey"	1914	semi-double	maroon	15'–
"Dr. W. Van Fleet"	1910	double	pink	15–20'
"Doubloons"	1934	double	yellow	15–20'
"Excelsa"	1909	double	red	12–18'
"Flash"	1938	double	orange-scarlet	6–8'
"Golden Glow"	1937	double	yellow	20'
"Hiawatha"	1904	single	crimson	15–20'
"Mme. Gregoire Staechelin"	1929	double	pink	13–14'
"Mermaid"	1918	double	yellow	6–9'
"New Dawn"	1930	double	pink	15'
"Paul's Scarlet"	1916	semi-double	scarlet	20'
"Silver Moon"	1910	semi-double	white	20'

Schisandra propinqua   Twining vine   Zone 8   Himalayan Magnolia-vine

*FLOWERS: orange, ¾" in diameter, sexes separate
   TIME: summer
*FRUIT: red berries only on pistillate plants
   EFFECTIVE: fall
FOLIAGE: evergreen
HABITAT: Himalayas
INTRODUCED: 1828

Another of the evergreen vines worthy of trial for southern gardens. However, the sexes are separate and both staminate and pistillate plants must be in the near vicinity to insure the fruiting of the pistillate plants.

Smilax megalantha   Twining vine   18'   Zone 7   Coral Greenbrier

FRUIT: coral-red, in umbels 2" in diameter
   EFFECTIVE: October
*FOLIAGE: evergreen, leaves 9" long and 6" wide
HABITAT: China
INTRODUCED: 1907

A handsome climbing vine with excellent lustrous foliage, scattered spines and brilliant coral-red fruits. It must be remembered that in *Smilax* the sexes are separate so that both male and female plants must be present in order to insure fruiting. Even without the fruit, the handsome foliage of this vigorous vine makes it worth while in the garden.

Smilax rotundifolia   Twining vine   30'   Zone 4   Common Greenbrier or Horse Brier

FRUIT: black berries
   EFFECTIVE: fall
HABITAT: eastern North America

The Common Greenbrier, with prickly twining stems, often very vigorous and definitely tenacious. The foliage is a good green and the plant is used to make a dense thicket or tangle—often impenetrable—where that seems desirable. This is one of the most vigorous of this group.

Trachelospermum asiaticum   Twining vine   15′   Zone 7–8   Yellow Star
                                                                                    Jasmine
*FLOWERS: yellowish white, fragrant
    TIME: April–July
*FOLIAGE: evergreen, leaves to 3″ long
HABITAT: Japan, Korea
INTRODUCED: 1880
    Somewhat similar to *T. jasminoides* except for the color of the flowers and the fact that it is slightly more hardy. Also the young growth is a ruddy bronze.

Trachelospermum jasminoides   Twining vine   Zone 9   Star Jasmine
*FLOWERS: white, fragrant, in small clusters, 1″ in diameter
    TIME: April–July
*FOLIAGE: evergreen, dark green, leaves to 3″ long
HABITAT: China
    A popular, evergreen, twining vine for gardens in the far South. The white fragrant flowers have twisted petals somewhat the shape of a pin wheel. It should be planted in the moist cool shade. The extreme fragrance of the blossoms is one of its best attributes. It is rapid in growth and makes a thick screen.

Tripterygium regeli   Shrub or vine   8′   Zone 4   Tripterygium
*FLOWERS: small, white in large pyramidal clusters, 8–10′ long
    TIME: summer
HABITAT: Manchuria, Korea, and Japan
INTRODUCED: 1905
    A scrambling shrubby vine which can be trained to grow either as a shrub or as a vine. As the latter, it needs some means of support. Its chief ornamental value is its large creamy white, pyramidal clusters of small flowers in early summer. A coarse textured vine, but unique as vines go, because of these flowers.

VITIS

The grapes are coarse vines, clinging by means of tendrils. There are many of them, a selection of several hundred being offered in American nurseries today chiefly for their fruits. From the ornamental viewpoint, grapes are used chiefly as rapid-growing screens, although some are used for the dual purpose of ornament and fruit production. Grapes are especially infested with Japanese beetles, and in the areas where these insects are prevalent, it might be well to omit growing these vines for this reason. Viewed from close range, grape vines with their large leaves are very coarse, and unless rapidity of growth is an important factor, other vines with finer leaves might be used.

    Grape vines viewed at a distance, however, make a dense mat of green foliage and there are frequently situations where these rapid-growers can be used advantageously. There are a few with autumn-colored foliage, but in many instances, especially on smaller properties, if grapes are to be grown for some ornamental purpose, good fruit-producing varieties might just as well be selected. As far as pruning is concerned, it is but a simple operation when these vines are used for screening purposes, since they must merely be restrained to the permanent area they are supposed to cover. It is not necessary to cut the previous year's wood back to a few buds each spring as is done for the production of fruits. The few recommended here have some particular ornamental characteristics, but are not the only species which can be used in general screening operations.

Vitis amurensis   Vine   Zone 4   Amur Grape

FRUIT: black grapes
    EFFECTIVE: fall
FOLIAGE: coarse
    AUTUMN COLOR: crimson to purplish
HABITAT: Manchuria, Amur region
INTRODUCED: about 1854

A vigorous grape, more hardy than the Glory Vine but not quite so rapid in growth.

Vitis californica   Vine   Zone 7   California Grape

FRUIT: glaucous-white, rather dry, but pleasant-tasting grapes
    EFFECTIVE: fall
FOLIAGE: coarse
    AUTUMN COLOR: red
HABITAT: Oregon to California

Native on the Pacific Coast, with little to recommend it in preference to cultivated varieties except that its foliage turns color in the fall.

Vitis coignetiae   Vine   Zone 5   Glory Vine

FOLIAGE: coarse
    AUTUMN COLOR: red
HABITAT: Japan
INTRODUCED: 1875

A handsome vine with leaves 10" in diameter—a vigorous grower, sometimes its shoots increase their length by as much as 50' in a single season. For a rapid growing screen it is ideal, covering a thousand square feet of trellis in a few years, probably the most rapid growing of the grapes.

Vitis labrusca   Vine   Zone 5   Fox Grape

FRUIT: purple-black, sometimes red-brown or amber-green
    EFFECTIVE: fall
FOLIAGE: dark green above
HABITAT: New England to Georgia, Tennessee and South Indiana

A rampant grower and one of the parents of most of the American grapes now in cultivation. Widely distributed throughout the eastern United States.

Vitis riparia   High-climbing vine   Zone 2   Riverbank Grape

FRUIT: purple-black, densely bloomy grapes
  EFFECTIVE: fall
FOLIAGE: lustrous, bright green beneath
HABITAT: Nova Scotia and New Brunswick to Manitoba, Kansas, Colorado, Missouri and Texas

A very hardy species native over a large area of the United States. Its staminate flowers are fragrant but not sufficiently prominent to be effective ornamentally.

WISTERIAS

The wisterias are vigorous twining vines that can grow to great lengths, if given proper soil. Under normal conditions, all wisterias should bloom, some varieties blooming much earlier in the life of the plant than others. However, circumstances have been such that some vines have failed to bloom for extremely long periods. Of course if the garden is in the northern United States there is always the possibility that the flower buds have been killed by severe cold. If this is not the case and the vine still does not bloom then other steps should be taken.

The vegetative growth should be retarded, either by a continual cutting back of the elongating shoots in the late spring or early summer, or by root pruning. If these fail then a ditch around the plant might be dug 1½′ deep and several feet from its base depending on its size. Superphosphate could be mixed with the soil as it is thrown back to fill this ditch, several pounds for each inch in diameter of the trunk. This combined root pruning and application of superphosphate has helped both wisterias and flowering dogwoods, in producing blooms. It might best be done in the very early spring, since the flower buds for the following year are formed in the very early summer.

Wisterias sometimes are grown as standards but these are awkward and hard to use especially in the small, informal garden. Suckers should not be allowed to sprout from the base of any wisteria, if possible, since the best colored varieties are usually grafted and such suckers might well yield flowers of less desirable understock.

Wisteria floribunda   Twining vine   24′   Zone 4   Japanese Wisteria

*FLOWERS: violet to violet-blue, in pendulous racemes 12–36″ long
  TIME: late May
HABITAT: Japan
INTRODUCED: 1830

A vigorous vine, not as common in American gardens as is the Chinese species. The flower clusters in some well-grown varieties may be 2½′ long or even longer. E. H. Wilson measured the flower racemes of one variety in Japan that was 5′4″ long. The flowers in these long racemes do not open simultaneously. They open progressively, first the flowers at the upper end and then gradually

"Macrobotrys," a variety of the Japanese Wisteria. Ernest H. Wilson took this picture in Japan where this variety has been grown for centuries. Some of the flower clusters on this plant measured 52″ in length.

towards the bottom of the cluster so that when the last blossoms are fully open, the blossoms at the top of the cluster have faded. This is a variable species with many varieties being offered in the trade. Varieties should be selected carefully for known color forms and bought from nurseries which propagate them asexually, since plants grown from seed may take decades to bloom. The following are some of the best available; all are growing in a collection of nearly 40 wisteria varieties in the Arnold Arboretum at Boston:

Flowers—white:

alba or "Longissima Alba," racemes 15″ long, slightly fragrant

Flowers—purple with buds having a reddish purple tint:

"Naga Noda"—racemes 18″ long, very fragrant
"Macrobotrys"—racemes up to 36″ long in well-grown specimens, the longest of all and very fragrant

Flowers—purple with a bluish tint:

"Geisha"—dense clusters at least 12″ long, slightly fragrant
"Sierra Madre"—long clusters (18″ or more), fragrant, with individual flowers the largest of any of the wisterias; originally found in a California garden, a splendid specimen

Flowers pink:

> *rosea*—only variety with the true pink flowers, racemes at least 12" long and extremely fragrant; one of the best varieties of this species

Flowers mostly white, but inner part of the flower purple:

> "Kuchi Beni"—racemes 14" long and very fragrant; not recommended in place of the white-flowered varieties, but is a very interesting color form

Wisteria macrostachya   Twining vine   24'   Zone 5   Kentucky Wisteria

*FLOWERS: lilac-purple in pendulous racemes up to 10" long
   TIME: early June
HABITAT: Missouri to Tennessee and Texas

Only of ornamental interest because it blooms after all other species and varieties are about past. The flowers are satisfactory but if time of bloom is not an essential feature this variety might well be omitted.

Wisteria sinensis   Twining vine   25'   Zone 5   Chinese Wisteria

*FLOWERS: blue-violet, slightly fragrant, dense pendulous racemes 7–12" long
   TIME: late May
HABITAT: China
INTRODUCED: 1816
VARIETIES:

> *plena*—flowers double but plant not a profuse bloomer
> *alba*—flowers white; the variety "Jako" in the trade is probably a selected form of *alba* and is extremely fragrant; both are excellent varieties

The flowers of this species and its varieties open simultaneously along the rather short racemes in contrast to those of W. *floribunda* which do not. Slightly more tender and less fragrant than the Japanese Wisteria it is nevertheless an old-fashioned favorite in this country. The flower clusters are dense and compact and usually freely produced so that a vine in full flower makes a very beautiful specimen. This species usually has from 7–13 leaflets, while the Japanese Wisteria has 13–19.

BAMBOOS

BAMBOOS are of interest in the garden chiefly as novelties, for in North America we are fortunately blessed with plant materials which are far superior in ornamental values. However, there are some gardens, especially in the South and on the Pacific Coast, where a massive bamboo with its gracefully swaying stems and leaves, appears to be just the right plant for just the right place. Bamboos are even available for those having gardens in the North, although the tall-growing species are limited to the warmer parts of the country.

These massive grasses can be grown in gardens where the temperatures rarely go below zero. Many are grown at the Bureau of Plant Industry Station at Glenn Dale, Maryland, and some are sufficiently hardy to grow as far north as Boston. Even when temperatures go to − 15° F. there are some species which may be killed to the ground level, but which will quickly send up new shoots in the spring. These plants are really not necessary in the garden where so many other woody plants of greater ornamental value are available. But, from the novelty viewpoint, some gardeners may wish to include them in the garden plan.

All bamboos are members of the great grass family, varying in height from 6 inches to about 120 feet, although the larger species are purely tropical and the tallest species hardy in the temperate zone reach about 70–80 feet. The culms, or stems, may vary from 1/16 of an inch in diameter to massive stalks one foot in diameter and live for several years. Some very large species can be seen at the Barbour Lathrop Plant Introduction Garden of the U. S. Department of Agriculture at Savannah, Georgia, where many of the species and varieties hardy in that latitude are being tested for growth and general suitability for various economic purposes in this country.

Those who know something of the needs of certain peoples living in the tropics, know that bamboos in some form or other are among the most valuable plants available to these people, yielding wood for almost every utilitarian need, including water piping, rudimentary tool making, bridge building, housing, and furniture making; the leaves are used in roof thatching and the young stalks are even used for food. The knowledge of these diverse economic uses of the plant in the tropics probably enhances the interest of those living in the Temperate Zone and consequently many gardeners have a desire to bring a bit of the tropics into their garden planting.

Not many bamboos prove completely winter hardy in the North, for a cold winter may kill the culms, leaves and branches of even the hardiest species. Hence they are not "evergreen" except in very mild winters. This is not necessarily serious, especially if the roots have been well protected, for the plants may quickly sprout new culms the following spring. In the South, many of the species are strictly evergreen, although they do have the disconcerting and untidy habit of dropping their older leaves in the summer. It is impossible to state the exact temperatures at which the leaves of bamboos will be killed, since amount of sunshine, wind and even soil moisture are all variable factors which must be taken into consideration. Sometimes the cold has been just enough to kill the leaves, but not enough to kill the culms and branches, so that when spring comes such culms will send out new leaves directly. The killing of the leaves in winter, then, is not too serious. Because of winter cold, in the North, at least, bamboos cannot be grown commercially for their wood, since several years are required for the culms to fully mature.

Bamboos normally grow in clumps, often massive clumps, while their more hardy relatives growing in the North are running bamboos, that is, the rhizomes run horizontally either on the surface of the soil or just below it. Such species have jointed rhizomes, with nodes and internodes, and it is from lateral buds on some of these nodes that the culms grow, often forming dense thickets. The true roots develop in a whorl from each node of the rhizome. It is very important that every gardener contemplating the planting of these running bamboos realizes they have this habit of growth, for it is obvious that such plants can quickly become pernicious weeds. Such is very definitely the case with most of these hardy species. Once they have become well established in a garden where they have not been restrained, they may quickly over-run much valuable garden space and be very difficult to eradicate completely.

This important fact should be recognized in planting them, and the best method is to sink concrete or sheet-iron walls about four feet deep in the ground surrounding the area where they are to be grown. Even then care must be taken that they do not grow under or over such barriers. All bamboos need good moist soil in which to grow, and do well if given a mulch about their roots over the winter. With these few cultural hints, they are easily grown, and the number from which it is possible to select is dependent chiefly on winter climate.

New shoots are produced during warm weather in early spring, and it usually takes 5–8 weeks for them to grow to their full height. In the larger sorts grown in the South, this means that a culm will grow as much as 70 feet in eight weeks, almost ten feet a week! In fact, this growth can actually be seen at certain stages if a specially marked board is placed directly back of the culm being studied. Flowering is variable among the bamboos. Sometimes a plant will die after it has produced a large number of flowers and fruits. Fortunately, however, the seed production is not profuse and even

Tree bamboos (background) are grown only in the tropics and in the warmer parts of the Temperate Zone. These are growing in Harvard's Atkins Garden and Research Laboratory, Soledad, Cuba.

though a few flowers or seeds are produced (at very irregular intervals) the plant may not die.

At least two bamboos are native in the southern states but these are not ornamental. The following twelve bamboos are among those selected by Mr. Robert A. Young of the Bureau of Plant Industry of the U. S. Department of Agriculture, after a careful study of many types being grown both at the trial gardens of the Bureau of Plant Industry, Glenn Dale, Maryland, and Savannah, Georgia. They are among the hardiest and most ornamental, although it should be repeated that with milder winter climates many other species and varieties can be grown successfully.

The hardier bamboos are mostly native of China and Japan. Generic lines among these bamboos have not been too clearly drawn and for this reason botanists have been transferring species from one genus to another intermittently and they probably will continue to do so as more is learned about the plants in question. The following names are those accepted at present:

Arundinaria graminea   3½–16′   Zone 6

Also termed *Pleioblastus gramineus*, with leaves distinctly grasslike, 4–10″ long and ¼–½″ wide, a native of Japan. In the North, this is one of the lower-growing plants, spreading by underground rhizomes.

Arundinaria simoni   8′   Zone 7   Simon Bamboo

Another bamboo with one excellent point in its favor—it does not have a strong tendency to run and so grows in a fairly dense clump. The leaves are 3–12″ long and ⅓–1¼″ wide. Not a spectacular species when compared with some of the others.

Phyllostachys aurea   30′   Zone 8

One of the earlier species of this genus introduced into the United States, it does not creep too rapidly and so can be forced to grow in clumps, with some attention, for a few years at least. The leaves are about 5″ long with 2–3 on a twig. At the base of nearly half the culms, the nodes are shortened together, making such stems desirable as interesting fishing poles or walking sticks. The specific name does not refer to the leaves which are normally green.

Phyllostachys bambusoides   70′   Zone 7–8   Timber Bamboo

The real timber bamboo, one of the tallest species growing in this country. Plants in this genus are characteristically open in habit of growth, with very fine feathery foliage, with leaves usually not much over 6″ long. *P. henryi* is supposed to be one of the better edible bamboos. The young sprouts are cut shortly after they appear above the ground in somewhat the same way that asparagus is used.

Pseudosasa japonica   7–16′   Zone 6   Metake or Arrow Bamboo

This species is still widely grown as *Arundinaria japonica*. It is probably the first oriental bamboo introduced into this country, shortly after 1850, probably the most widely grown species in present ornamental plantings. Its leaves remain evergreen with temperatures as low as 7° F., and it spreads but slowly by underground rhizomes, one of the reasons why it has proved popular. In warm climates the culms may grow 16′ tall and individual leaves are 5–12″ long with 4–11 leaves bunched together near the tip of the culm. This is unquestionably still one of the better ornamental kinds.

It is of interest to note that failure to locate adequate sources of the young shoots of this plant in this country was one of the factors contributing to the deaths of the first Giant Pandas brought to the New York Zoological Gardens in 1937. Later the species and a few other bamboos were located in sufficient quantities (1942) to feed other Giant Pandas introduced from China and these eventually survived.

Sasa chrysantha   5′   Zone 6

With slightly larger leaves than *A. graminea,* it also grows slightly taller, spreading by underground rhizomes.

Sasa palmata   5–8′   Zone 5–6

Also termed *Sasa senanensis,* this is a striking bamboo, having proved hardy in the Arnold Arboretum for years, even though it is killed to the ground in some winters. It has also been established at places in the vicinity of New York City. In the Arnold Arboretum the culms grow about 5′ tall, with the leaves 15″ long and as much as 3½″ wide, one of the largest-leaved of the bamboos hardy

Sasa palmata, one of the hardier bamboos adapted to northern plantings.

in the North. It has a neat, attractive appearance, spreads by means of under-ground rhizomes and is not injured appreciably by temperatures as low as 5° F.

Sasa pumila   2'   Zone 6   Ground Bamboo

This is a low, grasslike native of Japan, often termed *Pleioblastus pumilus,* which is a vigorous grower and must be kept under the strictest control or it will soon take over the garden. In fact it might best be grown only in moist waste land, where some plant is needed to cover the land and at the same time com-pete with weed growth. The leaves tend to dry and curl up in sunny, dry, situa-tions in summer, hence it might best be used in partial shade.

Sasa variegata   3'   Zone 5–6

A truly handsome Japanese species which has been growing in the Arnold Arboretum for many years. The leaves are striped with white, or creamy white, 5–10 on each culm and about 2–6" long. There are winters in the Arboretum when the foliage is unmolested by winter cold, but this cannot be depended upon. It is of interest to note that the pleasingly variegated foliage keeps its good color throughout most years, but this is another bamboo which spreads by under-ground rhizomes.

Sasa veitchi   1½–3½'   Zone 6

A broad-leaved, dwarf, running bamboo native of Japan and has been used as a dense mat of foliage on the ground only 18" high. The leaves are 2–7" long and ⅝–1½″ wide, and may turn brownish to white on the margins in the fall, striking in some situations but not in others.

Semiarundinaria fastuosa   15–25′   Zone 5   Narihira Cane

The stateliest and probably the most handsome of the hardy bamboos. It spreads but slowly by underground rhizomes and is named after a legendary Beau Brummel of Japan. It withstands temperatures as low as zero with little injury.

Shibataea kumasaca   3–6′   Zone 6

Another low Japanese running bamboo with leaves 1½–3″ long which suffer more or less winter injury at temperatures below 10° F.

THE NAMING OF HORTICULTURAL VARIETIES

MANY an intelligent plantsman is up against a blank wall when it comes to providing a name for some new plant he thinks he has found. Shall the name be in Latin or in English? Shall it be a botanical variety, a horticultural variety, or a "form"? If it is a hybrid, just what is the correct procedure in order to give it a proper name that will be accepted by horticulturists and botanists alike? There is an ever-increasing tie between the botanist and the practical plantsman, as far as the scientific names of plants are concerned, for both groups have agreed that it is best to follow the International Rules of Botanical Nomenclature, as approved by the International Botanical Congress, Cambridge, England, 1930.

Even though everyone agrees to the International Rules, the naming of new plants is difficult, and in the following discussion it is hoped that the correct procedure for naming new varieties is clearly set forth.

Variety

First it is necessary to understand the concept of a botanical variety. The correct definition might be:—A variety is a subdivision of a species composed of individuals differing from other representatives of the species in certain minor characters which are often of geographical significance, and which are usually perpetuated through succeeding generations by seed.

Form

A form is a subdivision of a species or variety, usually differing in only one character and often appearing sporadically throughout the range of the species; it is usually perpetuated vegetatively but may be perpetuated by seed, in which case only a certain percentage, as a rule, will be identical with the original form and the remainder will revert to the species or variety.

In some cases no clear line between a variety and a form can be drawn. Also, the two terms have been and are used interchangeably, so that differentiation is often exceedingly difficult. Both the variety and the form as above described should be given a Latin name, and the original, published description should include a short Latin description. The form or the variety may occur again in nature, and if it conforms to the original description, it would be given the same name no matter where or when it occurs.

Clon

On the other hand, there is a large group of plants which fail to come true from seed. Individuals in this group may be outstanding and are perpetuated solely by asexual propagation of one kind or another. Such plants may be considered forms or they may be considered clons (often spelled clones). A clon is a group of plants composed of individuals reproduced vegetatively from a single plant. Hence, though a form may also be propagated vegetatively (a clon must be), the form may appear again anywhere at anytime and should be given the same name as its predecessor, whereas the clon constitutes a group of plants propagated from a single specimen, and if all the members of this group should happen to die, no plant in the same genus should ever be given the same name again regardless of where or when it occurs.

If the plant is considered a form, it is given a Latin name, and any time in the future that a plant is found conforming to the original description, it takes the same Latin name. In other words, a form name is one given to a group of individuals which may have originated over widely separated areas. A clon name is one given to a single individual and its vegetatively propagated progeny.

If considered a clon, the plant is given a vernacular name—a noun or an adjective used as a noun, in any language as "Transcendent," "Snow White," "Dolgo," or "Wabiskaw." Any plant with such a name must be propagated asexually in a direct line from the one original plant.

Selecting the New Name

It is evident from the above descriptions or terms that giving Latin names (species, varieties, forms) to plants should be done by individuals who are trained taxonomists. In the past many plantsmen have tried to give Latin names to so-called "new" individuals, but because they did not know the entire group thoroughly nor the literature on the subject, such names, in many instances, have proved worthless and unfortunately continue to clutter up many a nursery catalogue.

Consequently, the amateur should give a horticultural varietal name in English; unless he is certain he has a new species, variety or form, in which case he should get confirmation of his Latin name and Latin description from a trained taxonomist who is in a position to know the literature pertaining to the plant group in question.

If a certain plant is given a varietal name in English, it will always designate that particular clon even though some taxonomist at some future date may, in working over several similar clons, mention their similarity and give a Latin name (variety or form) to the group. This is possible and permissible, but the clon name still remains in use for that particular plant regardless.

Horticultural varietal names in English (*i.e.*, clon names) would be best for most new varieties of *Philadelphus* appearing that may be worthy of naming. Such names should be simple and to the point whenever possible. "Cole's Glorious" is a very good one. "Mr. C. S. Sargent" or "Prof. C. S. Sargent" are not. The name might better be "Professor Sargent" or "Charles S. Sargent." The same brevity is needed with the prefix "Mrs." or "Miss." It is far better to give the full name, as "Henrietta White" rather than "Mrs. White" or "Mrs. A. R. White," or "Mrs. Alfred R. White." Taking the last two instances as examples, such names are easily confused in making labels and it is never long before such varieties become changed to "Mr. Alfred R. White" and finally to "Alfred R. White."

Rules for Selecting New Horticultural Variety Names

The International Horticultural Conference in London (1930) adopted several resolutions dealing with the naming of horticultural varieties. These have also appeared as an Appendix in the International Botanical Rules published in 1935. It behooves everyone who is interested in the naming of new horticultural varieties to study these resolutions and follow them in selecting new names for all plants.

1. Names of horticultural varieties must not be translated when transferred from other languages, but must be preserved in the language in which they were originally described. Where desirable a translation may be placed in brackets after the varietal name.

2. So far as possible, names of horticultural varieties should consist of a single word; the use of not more than three words is permitted as a maximum.

3. A varietal name in use for one variety of a kind of plant should not be used for another variety of that kind, even though it may be attached to a different species. Thus the use of the name *Syringa prestoniae* "Isabella" should preclude the use of "Isabella" as a varietal name for any other species of *Syringa*, such as *Syringa vulgaris* "Isabella." Similarly there should be but one *Rhododendron* "F. L. Ames," one *Clematis* "Belle of Woking," and so on.

4. Varietal names likely to be confused with one another should be avoided. For instance, the use of the name "Alexander" should preclude the use of "Alexandra," "Alexandria," and "Alexandrina" as varietal names for the same kind of plant.

5. Where personal names are used to designate varieties, the prefix Mr., Mrs., Miss, and their equivalents should be avoided.

6. Excessively long words and words difficult to pronounce should be avoided.

7. The articles "a" and "the" and their equivalents should be avoided in all languages when they do not form an integral part of the substantive. For instance, "Colonel," not "The Colonel"; "Giant," not "The Giant"; "Bride," not "The Bride."

8. All the names of horticultural hybrids are formed as provided in the International Rules of Botanical Nomenclature. If a Latin name has been

given to a hybrid form of uncertain origin which cannot be referred to a Latin binomial, it must be treated like a vernacular (fancy) name; *e.g.,* *Rhododendron* "Atrosanguineum," *Rhododendron* "Purpureum Grandiflorum."

Publishing the Name

To be valid under the International Rules of Botanical Nomenclature, the Latin or scientific names of species, varieties, and forms must be "validly published" in a work accessible to botanists and the public in general, and a short description in Latin must accompany the original description.

In publishing the names of horticultural varieties (clons), the Latin description is not required, but the description in English (or any other language written in Roman characters) should appear in a recognized horticultural or botanical periodical, monograph or other dated scientific publication. The mention of a clon in a catalogue or in the report of an exhibition without a description is not considered valid publication even though a figure is given.

Naming Hybrids

From a botanical point of view, a cross may be designated by a formula consisting of the names of two plants joining to make the cross, *i.e., Syringa reflexa x S. villosa.* Whenever it seems "useful or necessary" a name may be given to this cross, *i.e., Syringa prestoniae,* in this case the name being given because the plant has considerable ornamental value, is grown a great deal, and the single name is more usable than the formula; it will include all the crosses, however different between the two species, but the individual crosses, treated as clons, retain their horticultural names under it.

It is correct (and always best for the amateur) to use the formula in speaking of a new cross, rather than to run into the difficulties of selecting a new Latin name.

It is of the utmost importance to realize that hybrids are made up of clons which vary considerably in many characters. For instance, *Syringa prestoniae* is a hybrid (*Syringa reflexa x S. villosa*), the flower sizes varying considerably. In fact, some plants resulting from this cross are practically worthless ornamentally. So, when one merely buys x S. *prestoniae,* one may obtain anything within the limits of this cross, some decidedly inferior and some very good ornamentally. But x S. *prestoniae* "Isabella" is a clon with definite characteristics, and one is able to know in advance just what characteristics this particular clon will have. Consequently, horticultural varietal names should be given to the offspring of all crosses, providing the plants are worthy of naming.

Examples

1. A dogwood is found which has yellow fruits but in every other respect is identical with *Cornus florida.* Is it a variety, form or clon? Upon

careful investigation it is found that yellow-fruited dogwoods have appeared at widely separated places in the eastern United States. Hence it is not a clon for it cannot have been vegetatively propagated from a single specimen. It is not a variety for it differs from the species in only one character. Hence it is a form, and is given the name *Cornus florida xanthocarpa*.

2. A new crabapple has been found with unusually large double flowers. Nothing exactly like it has been described before, though some of its foliage characters are similar to those of *Malus halliana*, and others similar to those of *M. baccata*. Investigation shows that a cross between these two species has been named x *M. hartwigi*, but on looking up the description of this cross, the new plant does not seem exactly to fit. Since it obviously is a hybrid, it is also a clon, and the name "Katherine" is given it. At present it will be known merely as *Malus* "Katherine." If at some future time fruits are available, it may be that this will definitely belong to the hybrid species x *M. hartwigi*, and then it will be known as *M. hartwigi* "Katherine," or still may be called *M.* "Katherine." In any event, it will always keep the name "Katherine" regardless of what hybrid species it is associated with, and all its offspring must be asexually propagated in a direct line from the one original plant now growing in Durand-Eastman Park in Rochester, New York. (It is always well to use quotation marks around all clonal names to differentiate them unmistakably from all other names.)

Conclusion

In naming new horticultural varieties it is essential to:

1. Understand the differences between a species, variety, form and clon as here defined.

2. Understand the rules for naming horticultural varieties as here set forth.

3. Select the name.

　　a. If a species, variety or form, obtain confirmation from a trained taxonomist regarding the name itself and the Latin description which must accompany its first publication, and which must conform to the International Rules of Botanical Nomenclature.

　　b. If a clon or horticultural varietal name, be certain that it conforms to the rules set down here.

4. Publish the name and description.

　　a. If a Latin name, publish (with Latin description) in some botanical periodical available to botanists and the general public as well.

　　b. If a horticultural name, publish (without Latin description) in some acceptable horticultural or botanical publication easily available to all.

SECONDARY PLANT LIST

THE following shrubs and vines are among the host of plants growing in this country which should not be tried until others have first been grown. They should not be considered "discards" by any manner of means, since it may well be that with further trials, or in certain areas and under certain growing conditions, some of them may still become among "the best." As one landscape architect judiciously put it "there is a place for every plant." For the small garden, or for the gardener with limited space, energy and funds, the plants in this secondary list might well be omitted, at least temporarily, until those in the recommended list have been given every opportunity for success. (See pages 1–4)

There have been several reasons for placing these plants in a secondary list. Many plantsmen will not agree with the following listings nor the reasons for placing certain plants in a secondary list. The time for the research necessary in making this list will have been worthwhile if it merely impresses gardeners with the fact that some plants are more useful in our gardens than others, and time and space should not be given to plants with inferior qualities. The gardener will undoubtedly want to make his own list, and he can well start by critically examining this one.

Numbers after the plants represent the reasons for placing them in this group. They are as follows:

1. The plant is not superior to the varieties given in the recommended list. Many plants are practically identical, from a landscape viewpoint, differing merely in more pubescence on the leaf, a slightly different type of leaf margin, fruit which may be only slightly different in shape, size or pubescence—many factors, but in the garden such plants look alike and serve identical purposes. Such minor differences do not seem sufficient to clutter up our nurseries and gardens with plants of many different names.
2. The plant has inferior flowers to those in the recommended list.
3. The plant has inferior fruits to those in the recommended lists.
4. The plant has poor foliage. Included are many variegated-leaved plants and those with so-called "golden" leaves, but actually many of these prove very difficult to grow and may look well for only a very short period. The "golden"-leaved evergreens are outstanding examples (most of them at least) of plants which look disreputable throughout the winter months. It would seem that such plants should

be avoided or used only after serious consideration has been given to better plants.

5. The plant has inferior colored twigs. Some plants are grown specifically for this characteristic in winter, and the best varieties have been selected in the recommended list.
6. The plant has a poor habit of growth.
7. The plant is unusually troubled with an insect or disease pest.
8. The plant cannot be located in the nurseries and arboretums of this country. So many times we run across interesting varieties described in botanical texts, but impossible to locate in nurseries. Upon investigation it is shown that many such interesting varieties are only represented by herbarium specimens, in some cases only the original ones from which they were first named. No such plants have been included in the recommended list.
9. The plant, or one of its parts, is poisonous.
10. Evergreens with poor winter foliage. If an evergreen does not appear at its best in the winter, it should be given up in preference to one that does.
11. A parasitic shrub—only a very few are so recorded.

Abelia biflora 1, 3
  engleriana 1, 2, 3
  graebneriana 1, 3
  grandiflora sherwoodi 1, 3
  serrata 1, 3
  spathulata 1, 3
  triflora 1, 3
  umbellata 1, 3
  uniflora 1, 3
  zanderi 1, 3
Abies fraseri prostrata 2, 3, 6
Acanthopanax divaricatus 2, 3, 4, 6
  giraldi 2, 3, 4, 6
  giraldi inermis 2, 3, 4, 6
  henryi 2, 3, 4, 6
  lasiogyne 2, 3, 4, 6
  leucorrhizus 2, 3, 4, 6
  leucorrhizus fulvescens 2, 3, 4, 6
  leucorrhizus scaberulus 2, 3, 4, 6
  senticosus 2, 3, 4, 6
  senticosus inermis 2, 3, 4, 6
  sessiliflorus 2, 3, 4, 6
  sessiliflorus parviceps 2, 3, 4, 6
  setchuenensis 2, 3, 4, 6
  sieboldianus variegatus 2, 3, 4, 6
  simoni 2, 3, 4, 6
  ternatus 2, 3, 4, 6

Acer campestre albo-variegatum 2, 3, 4
  c. hebecarpum 1, 2, 3
  leiocarpum 1, 2, 3
  postelense 2, 3, 4
  schwerini 2, 3, 4
  tauricum 1, 2, 3
  ginnala semenovi 1, 2, 3
  japonicum and most varieties 1, 2, 3
  palmatum aureum 4, 6
  atro-dissectum 4, 6
  "Aoba-no-fuye" 4, 6
  "Aocha-nishiki" 4, 6
  "Akikaje-nishiki" 4, 6
  atrodissectum variegatum 4, 6
  "Hatsu-yuki" 4, 6
  hessei 1, 2, 3
  involutum 4, 6
  laciniatum 1, 2, 3
  lutescens 4, 6
  "Nishiki-gasane" 4, 6
  "Okushimo" 4, 6
  "Osakazuki" 4, 6
  pictum album 4, 6
  pictum aureum 4, 6
  reticulatum 4, 6
  roseo-marginatum 4, 6
  rubrum 4, 6

Acer (*Continued*)
  palmatum (*Continued*)
    scolopendifolium 4, 6
    sessilifolium 4, 6
    "Shishi-gashira" 4, 6
    "Tsuru-nishiki" 4, 6
    "Urime-nishiki" 4, 6
    versicolor 4, 6
    "Wabihito" 4, 6
  sieboldianum 1, 2, 3
  tataricum 1, 2, 3
Actinidia callosa 1
  kolomikta 2, 3, 4, 8
  purpurea 2, 3, 4
Aesculus discolor 1, 2, 3
  pavia 1, 2, 3
Akebia pentaphylla 1
  trifoliata 1
Amelanchier alnifolia 1, 2, 7
  amabilis 1, 2, 7
  bartramiana 1, 2, 7
  florida 1, 2, 7
  grandiflora rubescens 1
  humilis 1, 2, 7
  oblongifolia 1, 2, 7
  ovalis 1, 2, 7
  prunifolia 1, 2, 7
  sanguinea 1, 2, 7
  spicata 1, 2, 7
  stolonifera 1, 2, 7
Amorpha fruticosa 1, 2, 3, 4
  glabra 1, 4
  nana 1, 4
Ampelopsis bodinieri 1
  brevipedunculata elegans 1, 4
    citrulloides 1
  cordata 1
  delavayana 1
  tricuspidata purpurea 4
Andrachne species 2, 3, 4, 6
Andromeda glaucophylla 1, 3
Aralia chinensis 1, 2
  spinosa 1, 2
Aristolochia heterophylla 1, 4
  kaempferi 1
  manshuriensis 1
  moupinensis 1
  tomentosa 1, 4

Aucuba chinensis 4
Bauhinia densiflora 6
Berberis aetnensis 7
  aggregata 7
    pratti 7
  amurensis 7
  angulosa 7
  aristata 7
    coriaria 7
  asiatica 7
  atrocarpa 7
  bergmanniae 7
  brachypoda 7
  bretschneideri 7
  canadensis 7
  chenaulti 7
  chinensis 7
  chitria 7
  crataegina 7
  cretica 7
  declinata 7
    oxyphylla 7
  diaphana 7
  dictyoneura 7
  dictyophylla 7
  dielsiana 7
  durobrivensis 7
  edgeworthiana 7
  emarginata 7
    britzensis 7
  fendleri 7
  francisci-ferdinandi 7
  globosa 7
  henryana 7
  heteropoda 7
  hookeri 7
    virides 7
  hybrida serrata 7
  ilicifolia 7
  koehneana 7
  laxiflora 7
    langeana 7
  lecomtei 7
  leichlini 7
  lucida 7
  lycium 7
  macracantha 7
  meehani 7
  mitifolia 7

morrisonensis 7
nitis 7
notabilis 7
oblonga 7
orthobotrys 7
ottawensis 7
parvifolia 7
poireti 7
  latifolia 7
  weichangensis 7
polyantha 7
provincialis 7
pruinosa 7
rubrostilla 7
sanguinea 7
sargentiana 7
soulieana 7
spaethi 7
thibetica 7
thunbergi maximowiczi 1
turcomanica integerrima 7
umbellata 7
vanfleeti 7
vernae 7
viridis 7
vulgaris 7
  alba 7
  atropurpurea 7
  enuclea 7
  lutea 7
  macrocarpa 7
  nigra 7
  sheyalle 7
  sulcata 7
  violacea 7
wilsonae stapfiana 7
  subcaulialata 7
xanthoxylon 7
Berchemia racemosa 1, 6
Betula chinensis 1, 2, 3
  fontinalis 1, 2, 3, 4
  glandulifera 1, 2, 3
  humilis 1, 2, 3
  nana 1, 2, 3
  potanini 1, 2, 3
  pumila 1, 2, 3, 4
  wilsoni 1, 2, 3, 4
Buckleya distichophylla 11

Buddleia albiflora 2, 3
  asiatica 2, 3
  fallowiana 1, 3
  forresti 2, 3
  intermedia 1, 2, 3
  japonica 1, 2, 3
  myriantha 2, 3
  nivea 2, 3
  stenostachya 1, 2, 3
Buxus balearica 1, 2, 3
  microphylla sinica 1, 2, 3
  sempervirens glauca 1, 2, 3
    marginata 1, 2, 3, 4
    pyramidata 1, 2, 3
    rotundifolia 1, 2, 3
    wallichiana 1, 2, 3, 8
Callicarpa americana 1, 2
  a. lactea 1, 3
  dichotoma 1, 3
  japonica angustata 1, 2
    leucocarpa 1, 3
Calycanthus fertilis 1
  f. ferax 1
    nanus 6
  floridus ovatus 1
  mohri 1
  occidentalis 1, 2, 6
Caragana aurantiaca 1, 3
  boisi 1, 3
  brevifolia 1, 3
  brevispina 1, 3
  chamlagu 1, 3
  decorticans 1, 3
  densa 1, 3
  gerardiana 1, 3
  jubata 1, 3
  spinosa 1, 3
  tragacanthoides 1, 3
Caryopteris incana 1, 4
  mongholica 1, 2
Castanea alnifolia 1, 2, 7
  crenaia 1, 2, 7
  pumila 1, 2, 7
  seguini 1, 2, 7
Cephalanthus occidentalis angustifolius 1, 3
  o. pubescens 1, 3
Cephalotaxus drupacea 1, 2
  fortunei 1, 2

dunbari 1
foemina 1
glabrata 1
hemsleyi 1
horseyi 1
mas alba 3
   aurea 4, 8
   nana 8
   sphaerocarpa 1
   variegata 1, 4, 8
monbeigi 1
obliqua 1
poliophylla 1, 3
pubescens 1
pumila 1, 3
rugosa 1, 3
sanguinea 5
   atrosanguinea 8
   variegata 4, 5
sessilis 1
slavini 1, 5
stolonifera coloradensis 3, 5
Camellia cuspidata 3, 8
saluenensis 1, 3
sinensis 2, 3
Coronilla emeroides, 1, 2, 3, 4
emerus 1, 2, 3, 4
juncea 1, 2, 3, 4
Corylopsis platypetala 1, 3
wilsoni 1, 3
Cotoneaster acutifolia 1
adpressa 1
ambigua 1
amoena 1, 3
apiculata 1
bullata 1, 3
dielsiana 1
glabrata glaucophylla 1
horizontalis variegata 4
hupehensis 1
ignava 1
integerima 1
melanocarpa 1, 3
moupinensis 1, 3
multiflora 1
nitens 1, 3
racemiflora 1, 3
   desfontaini 1, 3
   microcarpa 1, 3

nummularia 1, 3
royleana 1, 3
veitchi 1, 3
rosea 1
rotundifolia 1
salicifolic 1
   rugosa 1, 4
tenuipes 1, 3
uniflora 1, 2
zabeli 1
Cydonia oblonga 1, 2, 6, 7
Cytisus ardoini 1, 3
austriacus 1, 3
   heuffeli 1, 3
   virescens 1, 3
ciliatus 1, 3
   grisebachi 1, 3
decumbens 1, 3
elongatus 1, 3
emeriflorus 1, 3
hirsutus 1, 3
   hirsutissimus 1, 3
leiocarpus 1, 3
multiflorus durus 8
   incarnatus 1, 3
nigricans elongatus 1, 2, 3
praecox luteus 1, 3
purpureus albus 1, 3
   atropurpureus 1, 3
ratisbonensis 1, 3
   biflorus 1, 3
scoparius plenus 1, 3
   sulphureus 1, 3
sessilifolius 1, 3
   leucanthus 1, 2, 3
supinus 1, 2, 3
Deutzia candelabrum erecta, 2, 3
c. fastuosa 1, 2, 3
carnea 1, 3
   densiflora 1, 3
   lactea 1, 3
   stellata 1, 3
chuni 1, 3
discolor 1, 3
   major 1, 3
glabrata 2, 3
glomeruliflora 2, 3
hypoglauca 2, 3
hypoleuca 1, 3

suspensa atrocaulis 2, 3
   decipiens 2, 3
   pubescens 2, 3
   variegata 3, 5
   viridissima 1, 2, 4
Fortunearia sinensis 1, 2, 3
Gaylussacia baccata 1
  dumosa 1
  frondosa 1
Genista anglica 1, 3
  germanica 1, 6
  nyssana 1, 3
  ovata 1, 3
  sagittalis 1, 3
  tinctoria anxantica 1, 3
   hirsuta 1, 3
   humilior 1, 3
Grewia biloba 1, 3
Hamamelis japonica and
  varieties 1, 2
Hedera canariensis striata 4
  colchica 1, 8
  nepalensis 8
  rhombea 1
Hedysarum multijugum 1
Helwingia japonica 1, 2, 3
Hibiscus syriacus 1, 3
   "Albus Plenus" 1, 3
   "Banner" 1, 3
   "Bicolor" 1, 3
   "Boule de Feu" 1, 3
   "Coerulea Plena" 1, 3
   "Comte de Haimont" 1, 3
   "Crested Beauty" 1, 3
   "Double Rouge" 1, 3
   "Duc de Bretagne" 1, 3
   "Elegantissimus" 1, 3
   "Glenwood's Favorite" 1, 3
   "Grandiflorus Superbus" 1, 3
   "Lady Stanley" 1, 3
   "Pompon Rouge" 1, 3
   "Puniceus" 1, 3
   "Purity" 1, 3
   "Purpureus Plenus" 1, 3
   "Ranunculaeflora" 1, 3
   "R. W. Downer" 1, 3
   "Roseus" 1, 3
    "Plenus" 1, 3

   "Rubra Plena" 1, 3
   "Sir Charles de Breton" 1, 3
   "Snow Storm" 1, 3
   "Speciosus" 1, 3
    "Plenus" 1, 3
   "Totus Albus" 1, 3
   "Van Houtte" 1, 3
   "Variegatus" 1, 3
   "Violaceous" 1, 3
    "Plenus" 1, 3
   "W. R. Smith" 1, 3
Hydrangea anomala 1, 2, 3
  arborescens 1, 2, 3
   australis 1, 3
   oblonga 1, 3
   sterilis 1, 2
  bretschneideri 1, 2, 3
   glabrescens 1, 2, 3
  cinerea 1, 2, 3
   sterilis 1, 2
  paniculata 1, 2, 3
  radiata 1, 2, 3
  serrata 1, 2, 3
  xanthoneura 1, 2, 3, 6
   setchuenensis 1, 2, 6
Hypericum androsaemum 1, 3
  dawsonianum 1, 2, 3
  densiflorum 1, 2
  inodorum 1, 2, 3
  lobocarpum 1, 2, 3
  nudiflorum 1, 3
  patulum 1, 2, 3
  splendens 1, 3
Iberis sempervirens garrexiana 1, 2, 3
Ilex crenata latifolia 1, 2, 3
  c. luteo-variegata 2, 3, 4
  dubia 1, 2
  fargesi 1, 2
  franchetiana 1, 2
  geniculata 1, 2
  integra 1, 2
  montana 2, 3
  pernyi veitchi 1, 2
  rugosa 1, 2
  serrata 1, 2
  verticillata cyclophylla 1, 2
   padifolia 1, 2
   tenuifolia 1, 2

Indigofera incarnata 1, 2, 3
 i. alba 1, 2, 3
Itea virginica 1, 3
Jamesia americana 1, 3
Jasminum beesianum 2, 6
 stephanense 1, 2
Juniperus chinensis alba 4
 c. aurea 10
  aureo-globosa 4
  japonica 10
   "aureo-variegata" 10
   "pfitzeriana aurea" 10
  smithi 10
  communis aurea 4
  "aurea spica" 10
  horizontalis alpina 1
   glomerata 1
   variegata 4
  phoenicea 1
  sabina variegata 4
  squamata 4
   wilsoni 1
  virginiana reptans 1
Kalmia cuneata 6
 polifolia 1, 3
Kerria japonica picta 3, 4
Leitneria floridana 2, 3, 6
Lespedeza buergeri 1, 2, 3
 cuneata 2, 3
 maximowiczi 1, 3
Leucothoe axillaris 1, 3
 grayana 1, 3
 recurva 1, 3
Ligustrum acuminatum 1
 a. macrocarpum 1
 acutissimum 1
 chenaulti 1
 compactum 1
 delavayanum 1, 6
 ibota 1, 3, 4, 6
 indicum 1
 insulare 1
 massalongianum 1
 sinense multiflorum 1
 strongylophyllum 1
 vulgare argenteo-variegatum 4, 7
  aureo-variegatum 4, 7
  aureum 4, 7
  buxifolium 7

chlorocarpum 3
glaucum 1, 7
leucocarpum 3, 7
xanthocarpum 3
Lindera obtusiloba 1
 praecox 1
Lonicera affinis pubescens 1
 alpigena 2
 alseuosmoides 1, 2
 altmanni 1, 2
  hirtipes 2
  pilosiuscula 2
 americana 1
 amoena 1
  alba 1
  rosea 1
 angustifolia 1
 arizonica 1
 bracteolaris 2
 browni 1
 canadensis 1
 chrysantha 2
  latifolia 2
  longipes 2
  regeliana 2
  villosa 2
 ciliosa 1, 2
 coerulea 2
  altaica 2, 3
  angustifolia 2, 3
  dependens 2, 3
  edulis 2, 3
  glabrescens 2, 3
  graciliflora 2, 3
  praecox 2, 3
  salicifolia 2, 3
  viridifolia 2, 3
 conjugialis 1
 demissa 1
 discolor 1
 ferdinandi 2
  induta 2
  leycesterioides 2
 gracilipes albiflora 1
 heteroloba 1, 3
 hispida 1
  bracteata 1
 hispidula vacillans 1
 iberica 1, 2

implexa 1
involucrata 1
  humilis 1
  serotina 1
koehneana 1
korolkowi aurora 1
  zabeli 1
maacki erubescens 1
maximowiczi 2
  sachalinensis 2
microphylla 2
minutiflora 1
muendeniensis 1
muscaviensis 1
nervosa 3
nigra 3
notha 2
  alba 2
  carnea 2
  carneo-rosea 2
oblongifolia 1
obovata 3
orientalis 2, 3
  caucasica 2, 3
  longifolia 2, 3
periclymenum 7
praeflorens 2
prolifera 1
purpusi 1
quinquelocularis translucens 1
ruprechtiana 2
  calvescens 2
  xanthocarpa 2
similis delavayi 3
standishi 1
subdentata 2
subsessilis 1
tatarica fenzli 2
  latifolia 4
  leroyana 1, 2
  pallens 2
tatarinovi 1
  leptantha 1
tenuipes 2
trichosantha 1
  acutiuscula 1
utahensis 1
vilmorini 1
webbiana 2

xylosteoides 2
xylosteum 2
  glabrescens 2
  lutea 2
  mollis 2
yunnanensis 1
Lycium chinense 1, 6
  pallidum 1
Lyonia ligustrina 1, 3
  ovalifolia 1, 8
Mahoberberis neuberti 1, 4
Mahonia nervosa 1
  pinnata 1
  wagneri 1
Menispermum dauricum 1
Menziesia ferruginea 1, 2, 3
  pentandra 1, 2, 3
  pilosa 1, 2, 3
Morus australis 1, 2, 3
Myrica gale 1, 2, 3
Neillia affinis 1
Nemopanthus mucronatus 2, 3, 4
Osmanthus americanus 1, 10
  ilicifolius variegatus 4, 10
    aureo-marginatus 4, 10
Osmarea burkwoodi 1
Pachistima myrsinites 1
Pachysandra axillaris 1, 2
Periploca graeca 1, 9
  sepium 1, 9
Philadelphus "Amalthee" 1, 3
  "Banniere" 1, 3
  burkwoodi 1, 3
  californicus 1, 3
  caucasicus 2, 3, 4
  coronarius aureus 4
    pumilus 2, 3, 6
    salicifolius 3, 4
  coronarius speciossisimus 1, 3
  "Coupe d'Argent" 1, 3
  delavayi 1, 2, 3
  "Dresden" 2, 3
  "Edsoni" 2, 3
  "Enchantment" 1, 3
  falconeri 1, 3
  "Favorite" 1, 3
  "Fleur de Neige" 1, 3
  floridus faxoni 1, 3
  "Gerbe de Neige" 1, 3

Ptelea trifoliata 1, 2, 3
Purshia tridentata 1, 3
Pyracantha angustifolia 1, 7
  crenulata 3, 7
  c. kansuensis 3, 7
Quercus ilicifolia 1, 2, 3, 6
Rhamnus alaternus 1, 2, 3
  alnifolia 1, 2, 3
  caroliniana 1, 2
  cathartica 1, 2, 4
  tinctoria 1, 2
Rhus aromatica illinoensis 1, 2
  a. serotina 1, 2
  chinensis roxburghi 1, 2
  delavayi 1, 2
    quinquejuga 1, 2
  diversiloba 2, 9
  glabra cismontana 1, 2
  hybrida 1, 2
  michauxi 1, 2
  orientalis 2, 9
  radicans 2, 9
    rydbergi 2, 9
  toxicodendron 2, 9
  trilobata 1, 2
  verniciflua 2, 9
  vernix 2, 9
Ribes—most species 1, 2, 7
Robinia boyntoni 1, 3, 6
  elliotti 1, 3, 6
  fertilis 1, 3, 6
  hartwigi 1, 3, 6
  slavini 1, 3, 6
Rosa acicularis 2
  a. engelmanni 1
    bourgeauiana 2
    nipponensis 2
  agrestis 1
  arkansana 2
  arvensis 1
  beggeriana 2
  bella 1
  blanda 1
  canina exilis 1
  carolina glandulosa 1
    villosa 1
  caudata 2
  centifolia cristata 1
    parvifolia 1

cerasocarpa 1
chinensis viridiflora 1, 6
cinnamomea 1
  plena 1
clinophylla 8
coriifolia 2
corymbifera 2
davidi 1
  elongata 1
davurica 1
duponti 1
ecae 6
fedtschenkoana 2
giraldi 2
glutinosa 2
hawrana 2
henryi 1
hibernica 2
horrida 2
involuta 2
kochiana 1
koreana 2
laxa 1
macouni 1
malyi 1
marginata 1
mariae-graebnerae 1
maximowicziana 1
micrantha 2
moschata 1
moyesi fargesi 1
  rosea 1
multiflora calva 1
multibracteata 1, 2
nitida 2
nutkana 1
  hispida 1
pendulina oxyodon 1
  pyrenaica 1
pomifera 2, 6
reversa 1
richardi 1
roxburghi normalis 1
  hirtula 1
rugosa kamtchatica 2, 3, 4
sempervirens 1, 2, 8
sericea 1
setigera inermis 1
  tomentosa 1, 2

Rosa *(Continued)*
  spaldingi 1
  spinosissima hispida 1
    luteola 1
    pimpinellifolia 1
  spinulifolia 1
  suffulta 1
    alba 1
  tomentosa 1
  ultramontana 1
  waitziana macrantha 6
  watsoniana 8
  willmottiae 1
  woodsi 1
    fendleri 1
  xanthina spontanea 1, 2
Rubus—most species 1, 2, 6
Salix amygdalina 1, 2, 3
  amygdaloides 1, 2, 3
  aurita 1, 2, 3
  brachycarpa 1, 2, 3
  candida 1, 2, 3
  cinerea 1, 2, 3
  discolor 2, 3
  glaucophylloides 1, 2, 3
  herbacea 1, 2, 3
  humilis 1, 2, 3
  longifolia 1, 2, 3
  medemi 1, 2, 3
  moupinensis 1, 2, 3
  myrsinifolia 1, 2, 3
  petiolaris 1, 2, 3
  petrophila 1, 2, 3
  phylicifolia 1, 2, 3
  vestita 8
  viminalis 1, 2, 3
Sambucus canadensis 1, 3
  c. chlorocarpa 3
    submollis 1
  coerulea neo-mexicana 1
    velutina 1
  fontenaysi 1
  leiosperma 1
  melanocarpa 1
    fuerstenbergi 3
  microbotrys 1
  nigra 1
    alba 1, 3
    albo-variegata 1, 4

    aurea 1
    aureo-variegata 1
    heterophylla 1
    laciniata 1
    pendula 6
    plena 3
    rotundifolia 1
    viridis 1, 3
  racemosa 1
    laciniata 1
    ornata 1
    purpurea 1
    tenuifolia 1
  sieboldiana 1
Schisandra chinensis 1
Schizophragma hydrangeoides 1, 4
  integrifolium 1, 4
Securinega suffruticosa 4
Shepherdia argentea 1, 4
Sibiraea laevigata 4
Smilax—most species 1, 2, 6
Solanum dulcamara 9
Sorbaria arborea glabrata 1, 3
  a. subtomentosa 1, 3
  assurgens 1, 2, 3
  sorbifolia 1, 2, 6
Sorbaronia species 1
Spiraea alba 1, 3
  alpina 1, 2, 3
  arcuata 1, 3
  bella 1, 2, 3
  betulifolia 1, 3
  blanda 1, 3
  blumei 1, 3
  brumalis 1, 3
  bullata 1, 3
  bumalda 1, 3
    froebeli 1, 3
  cana 1, 3
  cana x *thunbergi* 2, 3
  canescens glaucophylla 1, 3
  canescens myrtifolia 1, 3
  cantoniensis lanceata 2, 3
  chamaedryfolia 1, 3
    stenophylla 1, 3
    transiens 1, 3
    ulmifolia 1, 3
  cinerea 1, 3
  corymbosa 2, 3

douglasi i, 3
fontenaysi alba 2, 3
foxi 1, 2, 3
fritschiana 2, 3
gemmata 2, 3
gieseleriana 2, 3
henryi 1, 3
hypericifolia 2, 3
   acuta 1, 3
inflexa 2, 3
japonica 2, 3
   fortunei 2, 3
   macrophylla 2, 3
   rosea 1, 3
   ruberrima 1, 3
latifolia 2, 3
longigemmis 1, 3
media 2, 3
   glabrescens 2, 3
   mollis 2, 3
   sericea 2, 3
microthyrsa 2, 3
mollifolia 1, 2, 3
multiflora 1, 2, 3
nipponica 1, 2, 3
notha 1, 3
nudiflora 2, 3
oxyodon 1, 3
pachystachys 1, 2, 3
pikoviensis 1, 2, 3
prunifolia 1, 2, 3
   simpliciflora 1, 2, 3
pubescens 1, 2, 3
pyramidata 2, 3
revirescens 1, 3
rubra 1, 3
sansouciana 1, 3
sargentiana 1, 3
schinabecki 2, 3
syringaeflora 2, 3
trichocarpa 1, 2, 3
trilobata 1, 2, 3
uratensis 1, 3
virginiana 1, 3
watsoniana 1, 3
zabeliana 1, 3
Staphylea bumalda 2, 3, 4, 6
   colchica 2, 3, 4, 6

   pinnata 2, 3, 4, 6
   trifolia 2, 3, 4, 6
Stephanandra tanakae 2, 4, 6
Stewartia ovata 1, 2, 3
Stranvaesia davidiana 7
Styrax americana 1, 2
Symphoricarpos albus 3
   occidentalis 1, 2, 3
   oreophilus 1, 2, 3
   rotundifolius 1, 2, 3
Syringa amurensis 1, 3
   diversifolia 2, 3
   vulgaris x *oblata dilitata* 1, 3
      "Evangeline" 1, 3
      "Excel" 1, 3
      "Minnehaha" 1, 3
   vulgaris x *oblata giraldi* 1, 3
      "Berryer" 1, 3
      "Claude Bernard" 1, 3
      "Fenelon" 1, 3
      "Grace" 1, 3
      "Muriel" 1, 3
      "Norah" 1, 3
      "Scotia" 1, 3
   josiflexa "Enid" 1, 3
      "Lynette" 1, 3
   josikaea eximea 1, 2, 3
      "H. Zabel" 1, 3
   julianae 2, 3
   komarowi 2, 3
   meyeri 2, 3
   pekinensis 2, 3
   pinetorum 2, 3
   pinnatifolia 2, 3
   potanini 2, 3
   prestoniae "Ariel" 1, 3
      "Beatrice" 1, 3
      "Caliban" 1, 3
      "Cassandra" 1, 3
      "Celia" 1, 3
      "Charmian" 1, 3
      "Cleopatra" 1, 3
      "Diana" 1, 3
      "Dorcas" 1, 3
      "Elinor" 1, 3
      "Francisca" 1, 3
      "Hecla" 1, 3
      "Hermia" 1, 3
      "Hermione" 1, 3

Syringa (*Continued*)

prestoniae (*Continued*)

    "Horace" 1, 3

    "Lavinia" 1, 3

    "Lychorida" 1, 3

    "Nerissa" 1, 3

    "Nocturne" 1, 3

    "Oberon" 1, 3

    "Octavia" 1, 3

    "Ophelia" 1, 3

    "Patience" 1, 3

    "Paulina" 1, 3

    "Portia" 1, 3

    "Puck" 1, 3

    "Regan" 1, 3

    "Silvia" 1, 3

    "Timandra" 1, 3

    "Titania" 1, 3

    "Ursula" 1, 3

    "W. T. Macoun" 1, 3

reflexa 1, 2, 3

sweginzowi superba 1, 3

tomentella 1, 2, 3

velutina 2, 3

vulgaris "Abel Carriere" 1, 3

    "A. B. Lamberton" 1, 3

    "Adelaide Dunbar" 1, 3

    "Admiral Farragut" 1, 3

    "Alba Grandiflora" 1, 3

    "Alba Virginalis" 1, 3

    "Albert the Good" 1, 3

    "Alexander Hamilton" 1, 3

    "Alice" 1, 3

    "Alice Case" 1, 3

    "Alice Eastwood" 1, 3

    "Aline Mocqueris" 1, 3

    "Allison Gray" 1, 3

    "Alma" 1, 3

    "Alphonse Lavallee" 1, 3

    "Ambassadeur" 1, 3

    "A. M. Brand" 1, 3

    "Ambrose Verschaffelt" 1, 3

    "Amethyst" 1, 3

    "Ami Schott" 1, 3

    "Amoena" 1, 3

    "Anna" 1, 3

    "Anne Shiach" 1, 3

    "Archeveque" 1, 3

    "Archiduchesse Charlotte" 1, 3

"Arthur William Paul" 1, 3

"Ashes of Roses" 1, 3

"Astra" 1, 3

"Aucubaefolia" 1, 3

"Aurea" 1, 3

"Avon" 1, 3

"Azurea Plena" 1, 3

"Banquise" 1, 3

"Belle De Nancy" 1, 3

"Beranger" 1, 3

"Betty Louise" 1, 3

"Bicolor" 1, 3

"Bleuatre" 1, 3

"Blue Hyacinth" 1, 3

"Boule Azuree" 1, 3

"Boussingault" 1, 3

"Calvin C. Laney" 1, 3

"Candeur" 1, 3

"Capitaine Perrault" 1, 3

"Carley" 1, 3

"Carmen" 1, 3

"Carmine" 1, 3

"Carolyn Mae" 1, 3

"Catinat" 1, 3

"C. B. Van Nes" 1, 3

"Celestial Blue" 1, 3

"Champlain" 1, 3

"Charlemagne" 1, 3

"Charles Baltet" 1, 3

"Charles Joly" 1, 3

"Charles Sargent" 1, 3

"Charles X" 1, 3

"Charlotte Morgan" 1, 3

"Charm" 1, 3

"Christophe Colomb" 1, 3

"City of Chehalis" 1, 3

"City of Gresham" 1, 3

"City of Kalama" 1, 3

"City of Kelso" 1, 3

"City of Longview" 1, 3

"City of Olympia" 1, 3

"City of Vancouver" 1, 3

"City of Woodland" 1, 3

"Clara" 1, 3

"Clara Cochet" 1, 3

"Clarence D. Van Zandt" 1, 3

"Claude De Lorrain" 1, 3

"Coerulea Superba" 1, 3

"Colbert" 1, 3

"Colmariensis" 1, 3
"Col. Wm. R. Plum" 1, 3
"Comte Adrien De Montebello" 1, 3
"Comte De Kerchove" 1, 3
"Comte Horace De Choiseul" 1, 3
"Comtesse Horace De Choiseul" 1, 3
"Condorcet" 1, 3
"Cora McCormack" 1, 3
"Corinne" 1, 3
"Crampel" 1, 3
"Crepuscule" 1, 3
"Croix de Brahy" 1, 3
"Dame Blanche" 1, 3
"Danton" 1, 3
"Dawn" 1, 3
"De Jussieu" 1, 3
"De Louvain" 1, 3
"De Saussure" 1, 3
"Delphinium" 1, 3
"Desfontaines" 1, 3
"Diderot" 1, 3
"Dillia" 1, 3
"Diplomate" 1, 3
"Downfield" 1, 3
"Doyen Keteleer" 1, 3
"Dr. Charles Jacobs" 1, 3
"Dr. Lindley" 1, 3
"Dr. Maillot" 1, 3
"Dr. Masters" 1, 3
"Dr. Nobbe" 1, 3
"Dr. Noble" 1, 3
"Dr. Troyanowsky" 1, 3
"Dr. Von Regal" 1, 3
"Dresden China" 1, 3
"Duchesse De Brabant" 1, 3
"Duchesse D'Orleans" 1, 3
"Dusk" 1, 3
"Eden" 1, 3
"Edmond About" 1, 3
"Edmond Bossier" 1, 3
"Edouard Andre" 1, 3
"Edward A. Schmidt" 1, 3
"Ekenholme" 1, 3
"Elihu Root" 1, 3
"Elizabeth Mills" 1, 3
"Emil Liebig" 1, 3

"Emile Lemoine" 1, 3
"Ethel duPont" 1, 3
"Etna" 1, 3
"Etoile De Mai" 1, 3
"Firmament" 1, 3
"Fluffy Ruffles" 1, 3
"Francisque Morel" 1, 3
"Frank Klager" 1, 3
"Frau Bertha Dammann" 1, 3
"Frau Wilhelm Pfitzer" 1, 3
"Fred C. Wilke" 1, 3
"Fred L. Klager" 1, 3
"Fred Payne" 1, 3
"Fritz" 1, 3
"Fuerst Bulow" 1, 3
"Fuerst Lichtenstein" 1, 3
"Gaudichaud" 1, 3
"Geant Des Batailles" 1, 3
"Geheimrat Heyder" 1, 3
"Geheimrat Singelmann" 1, 3
"General Drouot" 1, 3
"General Elwell S. Otis" 1, 3
"General Grant" 1, 3
"General (John) Pershing" 1, 3
"General Pershing" (of Lemoine) 1, 3
"General Kitchener" 1, 3
"General Sheridan" 1, 3
"General Sherman" 1, 3
"George W. Aldridge" 1, 3
"George Bellair" 1, 3
"George Claude" 1, 3
"Gigantea" 1, 3
"Gilbert" 1, 3
"Gismonda" 1, 3
"Gladwyne" 1, 3
"Gloire De Lorraine" 1, 3
"Gloire De La Rochelle" 1, 3
"Gloire De Moulins" 1, 3
"Glory" 1, 3
"Glory of Mt. Hope" 1, 3
"Godron" 1, 3
"Goliath" 1, 3
"Grace Orthwaite" 1, 3
"Grand Duc Constantin" 1, 3
"Heather" 1, 3
"Heavenly Blue" 1, 3
"Henri Robert" 1, 3
"Henry Clay" 1, 3

Syringa (*Continued*)

   vulgaris (*Continued*)

      "Henry Wadsworth Longfellow" 1, 3

      "Henry Ward Beecher" 1, 3

      "Herman Eilers" 1, 3

      "Hippolyte Maringer" 1, 3

      "Hiram H. Edgerton" 1, 3

      "Holly Ann" 1, 3

      "Hugo De Vries" 1, 3

      "Hugo Koster" 1, 3

      "Irvina" 1, 3

      "J. De Messemaeker" 1, 3

      "James Booth" 1, 3

      "James Stuart" 1, 3

      "Jane Day" 1, 3

      "Jean Bart" 1, 3

      "Jean Mace" 1, 3

      "Jeanne D'Arc" 1, 3

      "Joan Dunbar" 1, 3

      "Joyce" 1, 3

      "Jules Ferry" 1, 3

      "Jules Simon" 1, 3

      "Julien Gerardin" 1, 3

      "Justi" 1, 3

      "Kate Harlin" 1, 3

      "Kate Sessions" 1, 3

      "Katherine" 1, 3

      "Konigin Luise" 1, 3

      "Lady Lindsay" 1, 3

      "Lamarck" 1, 3

      "La Mauve" 1, 3

      "Languis" 1, 3

      "Laplace" 1, 3

      "La Tour D'Auvergne" 1, 3

      "Laura Cox" 1, 3

      "Laura L. Barnes" 1, 3

      "Lavaliensis" 1, 3

      "Lavender Pearl" 1, 3

      "Lavoisier" 1, 3

      "Le Goulois" 1, 3

      "Lemoinei" 1, 3

      "Le Notre" 1, 3

      "Leon Mathieu" 1, 3

      "Leon Portier" 1, 3

      "Leon Simon" 1, 3

      "Leonie Lambert" 1, 3

      "Leopold II" 1, 3

      "Le Printemps" 1, 3

      "Liberti" 1, 3

      "Lila Rosa" 1, 3

      "Lillian Lee" 1, 3

      "Linne" 1, 3

      "L'Oncle Tom" 1, 3

      "Louis Henry" 1, 3

      "Louis Van Houtte" 1, 3

      "Louise" 1, 3

      "Louise Marie" 1, 3

      "Lucienne Bruchet" 1, 3

      "Ma Bennet" 1, 3

      "Madeleine Lemaire" 1, 3

      "Magellan" 1, 3

      "Marc Micheli" 1, 3

      "Marceau" 1, 3

      "Marechal De Bassompierre" 1, 3

      "Marguerite" 1, 3

      "Marie Legraye" 1, 3

      "Marleyensis" 1, 3

      "Marleyensis Pallida" 1, 3

      "Martha" 1, 3

      "Massena" 1, 3

      "Mathieu De Dombasle" 1, 3

      "Maurice De Vilmorin" 1, 3

      "Maxime Cornu" 1, 3

      "Maximowicz" 1, 3

      "Michel Buchner" 1, 3

      "Milton" 1, 3

      "Mireille" 1, 3

      "Miriam Cooley" 1, 3

      "Mlle. Fernande Viger" 1, 3

      "Mlle. Melide Laurent" 1, 3

      "Mme. Abel Chatenay" 1, 3

      "Mme. Amelie Duprat" 1, 3

      "Mme. Auguste Gouchault" 1, 3

      "Mme. Briot" 1, 3

      "Mme. Casimir Perier" 1, 3

      "Mme. Catherine Bruchet" 1, 3

      "Mme. De Miller" 1, 3

      "Mme. Fallieres" 1, 3

      "Mme. Felix" 1, 3

      "Mme. Florent Stepman" 1, 3

      "Mme. Henri Guillaud" 1, 3

      "Mme. Jules Finger" 1, 3

      "Mme. Kreuter" 1, 3

      "Mme. Lemoine" 1, 3

      "Mme. Leon Simon" 1, 3

      "Mme. Moser" 1, 3

      "Monique Lemoine" 1, 3

"Montesquieu" 1, 3
"Montgolfier" 1, 3
"Monument" 1, 3
"Monument Carnot" 1, 3
"Moonglow" 1, 3
"Moonlight" 1, 3
"Moritz Eichler" 1, 3
"Mrs. A. Belmont" 1, 3
"Mrs. B. S. Williams" 1, 3
"Mrs. Calvin Coolidge" 1, 3
"Mrs. Flanders" 1, 3
"Mrs. John W. Davis" 1, 3
"Mrs. Trapman" 1, 3
"Mrs. Watson Webb" 1, 3
"Murillo" 1, 3
"My Favorite" 1, 3
"Nancy Frick" 1, 3
"Naomi" 1, 3
"Naudin" 1, 3
"Negro" 1, 3
"Night" 1, 3
"Nigricans" 1, 3
"Noisetiana Alba" 1, 3
"Obelisque" 1, 3
"Old Rose" 1, 3
"Othello" 1, 3
"Paradise" 1, 3
"Pasteur" 1, 3
"Patrick Henry" 1, 3
"Paul Hariot" 1, 3
"Pearl" 1, 3
"Peau De Chamois" 1, 3
"Perle Von Stuttgart" 1, 3
"Perle Von Teltow" 1, 3
"Philemon" 1, 3
"Pierre Joigneaux" 1, 3
"Planchon" 1, 3
"President Carnot" 1, 3
"President Chauvet" 1, 3
"President Harding" 1, 3
"President John Adams" 1, 3
"President Lambeau" 1, 3
"President Lebrun" 1, 3
"President Loubet" 1, 3
"President Massart" 1, 3
"President Monroe" 1, 3
"President Poincare" 1, 3
"President Roosevelt" 1, 3
"President Viger" 1, 3

"Prince De Beauvau" 1, 3
"Prince Imperial" 1, 3
"Prince Notger" 1, 3
"Prince of Wales" 1, 3
"Princess Alexandra" 1, 3
"Princess Marie" 1, 3
"Princess Pink" 1, 3
"Princess Camille De Rohan" 1, 3
"Princess Clementine" 1, 3
"Priscilla" 1, 3
"Prodige" 1, 3
"Prof. E. H. Wilson" 1, 3
"Prof. E. Stoekhardt" 1, 3
"Prof. Sargent" 1, 3
"Pulverulenta Tricolor" 1, 3
"Pyramidal" 1, 3
"Pyramidalis Alba" 1, 3
"Quadricolor" 1, 3
"Queen Anne" 1, 3
"Rabelais" 1, 3
"Reaumur" 1, 3
"Reine Elisabeth" 1, 3
"Reine Marguerite" 1, 3
"René Jarry Desloges" 1, 3
"Renoncule" 1, 3
"Rochambeau" 1, 3
"Roi Albert" 1, 3
"Roland Mills" 1, 3
"Ronsard" 1, 3
"Rosace" 1, 3
"Roseau Grandiflora" 1, 3
"Rubella Plena" 1, 3
"Rubra Insignis" 1, 3
"Ruby" 1, 3
"R. W. Mills" 1, 3
"Sarah Sands" 1, 3
"Saturnale" 1, 3
"Sauerbrey" 1, 3
"Savanarole" 1, 3
"Schermerhorn" 1, 3
"Schneelavine" 1, 3
"Scipion Cochet" 1, 3
"Senateur Volland" 1, 3
"Silver King" 1, 3
"Sonia Colfax" 1, 3
"Souv. De Alice Harding" 1, 3
"Souv. De Billiard" 1, 3
"Souv. de Henri Simon" 1, 3
"Souv. De Louis Thibaut" 1, 3

oxycoccus 1
  intermedium 1
parvifolium 1
praestans 1
torreyanum 1
uliginosum 1
virgatum 1
  tenellum 1
vitis-idaea 1
  majus 1
Viburnums acerifolium glabrescens
    2, 3, 4
a. ovatum 2, 3, 4
betulifolium 1, 2, 6
bitchiuense 1, 2, 6
bracteatum 1, 6
buddleifolium 1, 2, 6
burejaeticum 1, 2, 3
cotinifolium 1, 3
cylindricum 2, 3
ellipticum 1, 6
erosum 1, 3
  taqueti 1, 3
furcatum 1, 6
hupehense 1, 6
jacki 1, 3
lantana discolor 1, 3
  rugosum 1, 3
  variegatum 1, 3
lentago sphaerocarpum 1
lobophyllum 1
macrocephalum keteleeri 2, 3
molle 3
  leiophyllum 3
mongolicum 2, 3
nudum angustifolium 1
odoratissimum variegatum 4
opulus roseum 7
  variegatum 4
orientale 1
ovatifolium 1
pauciflorum 4, 6
pubescens 1, 2, 3
  canbyi 1, 2, 3
  deami 1, 2, 3
  indianense 1, 2, 3
  longifolium 1, 2
rafinesquianum 1, 6
  affine 2, 6

rhytidocarpum 1, 6
rhytidophylloides 1, 6
rhytidophyllum 1
sargenti 1
  calvescens 1
scabrellum 1
schensianum 3, 6
setigerum 1, 3, 6
sieboldi reticulatum 1
sympodiale 1
tomentosum 1, 3
  lanceatum 1, 3
  parvifolium 1, 3
  rotundifolium 1, 3
urceolatum 1, 3
veitchi 1, 6
vetteri 1, 6
wrighti 1
  hessei 1
Vitex negundo 1, 3
Vitis aestivalis 1, 4
baileyana 1, 4
champini 1, 4
cinerea 1, 4
doaniana 1, 4
lincecumi 1, 4
monticola 1, 4
palmata 1, 4
piasezki 1, 4
rotundifolia 1, 4
thunbergi 1
wilsonae 1, 4
Weigela "Abel Carriere" 1, 3
  "Andre Thouin" 1, 3
  "Avalanche" 1, 3
  "Avant-Garde" 1, 3
  "Camelon" 1, 3
  "Candida" 1, 3
  "Congo" 1, 3
  "Conquete" 1, 3
  "Doubenton" 1, 3
  "Desbois" 1, 3
  "Dr. Baillon" 1, 3
  "Emile Galle" 1, 3
  "Eva Rathke" 1, 3
  "Feerie" 1, 3
  "Fleur de Mai" 1, 3
  "Floreal" 1, 3

Weigela (*Continued*)
  floribunda 2, 3
    grandiflora 2, 3
    versicolor 2, 3
  florida 1, 3
  "Groenwegeni" 1, 3
  "Gustave Mallet" 1, 3
  "Hendersoni" 1, 3
  hortensis 2, 3
    nivea 2, 3
  "Ideal" 1, 3
  "Intermedia" 1, 3
  "Isoline" 1, 3
  japonica 1, 3
  "Le Printemps" 1, 3
  "Majesteaux" 1, 3
  "Marc Tellier" 1, 3
  "Mme. Lemoine" 1, 3
  "Montesquieu" 1, 3
  "Pavillon Blanc" 1, 3
  "Pres. Ducharte" 1, 3
  "Simondsi" 1, 3
  "Stelzneri" 1, 3
  "Striata" 1, 3

  "Styriaca" 1, 3
  "Vanhouttei" 1, 3
  "Venosa" 1, 3
  "Verschaffelt" 1, 3
  "Vestale" 1, 3

Wisteria floribunda carnea 2
  f. "Kyushaku" 2
    "Mrs. McCullagh" 6
    "Murashi-noda" 1
    "Royal Purple" 1
    "Russelliana" 1
    "Shiro-noda" 2
    "Ushijima" 2
    variegata 4
  frutescens 1, 2
    nivea 1, 2
  japonica 1, 2
  venusta 2
    plena 1
    violacea 2

Zanthoxylum americanum 1, 2, 3
  schinifolium 1, 2
  simulans 1, 2

Zenobia pulverulenta nuda 4

INDEX

Only those plants in the General List of Recommended Plants are included in this index. All scientific names are included and most of the common names. Horticultural variety names are not included for they would make this index too cumbersome. They can be easily found by turning to the genus and species in the text, pages 92–406. If a plant is not listed here it may be found in the Secondary Plant List, pages 412–432.

433

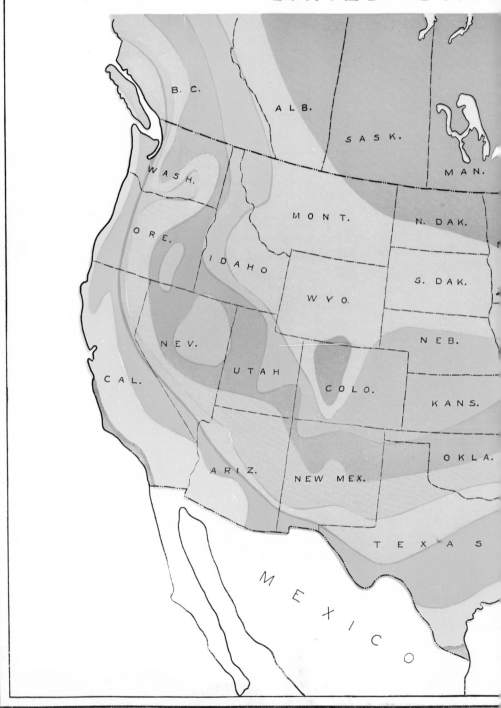